Mastering Windows Server 2016

A comprehensive and practical guide to Windows Server 2016

Jordan Krause

BIRMINGHAM - MUMBAI

Mastering Windows Server 2016

Copyright © 2016 Packt Publishing

All rights reserved. No part of this book may be reproduced, stored in a retrieval system, or transmitted in any form or by any means, without the prior written permission of the publisher, except in the case of brief quotations embedded in critical articles or reviews.

Every effort has been made in the preparation of this book to ensure the accuracy of the information presented. However, the information contained in this book is sold without warranty, either express or implied. Neither the author, nor Packt Publishing, and its dealers and distributors will be held liable for any damages caused or alleged to be caused directly or indirectly by this book.

Packt Publishing has endeavored to provide trademark information about all of the companies and products mentioned in this book by the appropriate use of capitals. However, Packt Publishing cannot guarantee the accuracy of this information.

First published: October 2016

Production reference: 1191016

Published by Packt Publishing Ltd.
Livery Place
35 Livery Street
Birmingham B3 2PB, UK.

ISBN 978-1-78588-890-8

www.packtpub.com

Credits

Author
Jordan Krause

Reviewer
Anderson Patricio

Commissioning Editor
Kartikey Pandey

Acquisition Editor
Meeta Rajani

Technical Editor
Pankaj Kadam

Copy Editor
Laxmi Subramanian

Proofreader
Safis Editing

Indexer
Rekha Nair

Production Coordinator
Shraddha Falebhai

Cover Work
Shraddha Falebhai

About the Author

Jordan Krause is a Microsoft MVP in the Cloud and Datacenter Management - Enterprise Security group. He has the unique opportunity to work daily with Microsoft networking technologies as a senior engineer at IVO Networks. Jordan specializes in Microsoft DirectAccess, and has authored one of the only books available worldwide on this subject. Additional writings include books on Windows Server 2012 R2 and the new Windows Server 2016. He spends the majority of each workday planning, designing, and implementing DirectAccess and VPN solutions for companies around the world.

Committed to continuous learning, Jordan holds Microsoft certifications as an MCP, MCTS, MCSA, and MCITP Enterprise Administrator. He regularly writes tech notes and articles reflecting his experiences with the Microsoft networking technologies, which can be found at http://www.ivonetworks.com/news.

Jordan also strives to spend time helping the DirectAccess community, mostly by way of the Microsoft TechNet forums. Always open to direct contact, he encourages anyone needing assistance to head over to the forums and find him personally. Jordan lives and works in the ever-changing climate that is Michigan.

About the Reviewer

Anderson Patricio is a Canadian Microsoft MVP, and is an IT consultant based in Toronto. His areas of expertise are Microsoft Exchange, Skype for Business, Azure, System Center, and Active Directory.

Anderson is an active member of the Exchange Community and he contributes to forums, blogs, articles, and videos. In English, he contributes regularly at ITPROCentral.com, MSexchange.org, and TechGenix.com. In Portuguese, his website, http://www.AndersonPatricio.org, contains thousands of Microsoft Tutorials to help the local community, alongside his speaking engagements at TechED in South America and MVA Academy training courses. You can follow him on Twitter at http://www.twitter.com/apatricio.

He has reviewed several books, such as *Windows PowerShell in Action*, Bruce Payette and *PowerShell in Practice*, Richard Siddaway by Manning Publications, and *Microsoft Exchange 2010 PowerShell Cookbook*, Mike Pfeiffer by Packt Publishing.

www.PacktPub.com

eBooks, discount offers, and more

Did you know that Packt offers eBook versions of every book published, with PDF and ePub files available? You can upgrade to the eBook version at www.PacktPub.com and as a print book customer, you are entitled to a discount on the eBook copy. Get in touch with us at customercare@packtpub.com for more details.

At www.PacktPub.com, you can also read a collection of free technical articles, sign up for a range of free newsletters and receive exclusive discounts and offers on Packt books and eBooks.

https://www.packtpub.com/mapt

Get the most in-demand software skills with Mapt. Mapt gives you full access to all Packt books and video courses, as well as industry-leading tools to help you plan your personal development and advance your career.

Why subscribe?

- Fully searchable across every book published by Packt
- Copy and paste, print, and bookmark content
- On demand and accessible via a web browser

Instant updates on new Packt books

Get notified! Find out when new books are published by following @PacktEnterprise on Twitter or the *Packt Enterprise* Facebook page.

Table of Contents

Preface	**xi**
Chapter 1: Getting Started with Windows Server 2016	**1**
What is the purpose of Windows Server?	**2**
It's getting "cloudy" out there	**3**
Private cloud	4
An overview of new features	**5**
The Windows 10 experience	5
Software-Defined Networking	5
PowerShell 5.0	5
Built-in malware protection	6
Soft restart	6
Nano Server	6
Web Application Proxy	7
Shielded virtual machines	7
Navigating the interface	**7**
The new Start menu	8
The hidden Admin menu	9
Using the Search function	10
Pin programs to the taskbar	12
The power of right-click	13
Using the new Settings screen	**16**
Two ways to do the same thing	20
Creating a new user through the Control Panel	20
Creating a new user through the Settings menu	21
Task Manager	**22**
Task View	**26**
Summary	**28**

[i]

Table of Contents

Chapter 2: Installing and Managing Windows Server 2016 — 29
Installing Windows Server 2016 — 29
- Burning that ISO — 30
- Installing from USB — 31
- Running the installer — 31

Installing roles and features — 35
- Installing a role using the wizard — 36
- Installing a feature using PowerShell — 41

Centralized management and monitoring — 44
- Server Manager — 44
- Remote Server Administration Tools — 49
- Azure Server Management Tools — 50
- Does this mean RDP is dead? — 51
  - Remote Desktop Connection Manager — 51

Sysprep enables quick server rollouts — 52
- Installing Windows Server 2016 onto a new server — 54
- Configuring customizations and updates onto your new server — 54
- Running sysprep to prepare and shut down your master server — 55
- Creating your master image of the drive — 57
- Building new servers using copies of the master image — 58

Summary — 59

Chapter 3: Core Infrastructure Services — 61
What is a domain controller? — 62
Using AD DS to organize your network — 63
- Active Directory Users and Computers — 64
  - User accounts — 65
  - Security Groups — 66
  - Prestaging computer accounts — 67
- Active Directory Domains and Trusts — 69
- Active Directory Sites and Services — 70
- Active Directory Administrative Center — 71
  - Dynamic Access Control — 73
- Read-only domain controllers — 73

The power of Group Policy — 74
- The Default Domain Policy — 75
- Create and link a new GPO — 77
- Filtering GPOs to particular devices — 80

DNS overview — 81
- Different kinds of DNS records — 83
  - Host record (A or AAAA) — 84
  - Alias record – CNAME — 85

Mail Exchanger record	87
Name Server record	88
Ipconfig /flushdns	88
DHCP versus static addressing	**89**
The DHCP scope	90
DHCP reservations	91
Back up and restore	**94**
Schedule regular backups	94
Restoring from Windows	97
Restoring from the disc	98
MMC and MSC shortcuts	**102**
Summary	**105**
Chapter 4: Certificates in Windows Server 2016	**107**
Common certificate types	**108**
User certificates	108
Computer certificates	109
SSL certificates	109
Single-name certificates	111
Subject Alternative Name certificates	112
Wildcard certificates	112
Planning your PKI	**113**
Enterprise versus standalone	113
Root versus subordinate	114
Can I install the CA role onto a domain controller?	115
Creating a new certificate template	**115**
Issuing your new certificates	**119**
Publishing the template	120
Requesting a cert from MMC	122
Requesting a cert from the Web interface	126
Creating an autoenrollment policy	**129**
Obtaining a public authority SSL certificate	**134**
Creating a Certificate Signing Request (CSR)	135
Submitting the certificate request	137
Downloading and installing your certificate	138
Exporting and importing certificates	**140**
Exporting from MMC	140
Exporting from IIS	141
Importing onto a second server	142
Summary	**142**

Table of Contents

Chapter 5: Networking with Windows Server 2016 — 143
Intro to IPv6 — 144
Networking toolbox — 149
Ping — 149
Tracert — 151
Pathping — 152
Test-Connection — 153
Telnet — 155
Packet tracing with Wireshark or Netmon — 159
TCPView — 159
Building a routing table — 160
Multihomed servers — 161
Only one default gateway — 161
Building a route — 163
Adding a route with Command Prompt — 163
Deleting a route — 165
Adding a route with PowerShell — 166
Software-Defined Networking — 167
Hyper-V Network Virtualization — 168
Private clouds — 168
Hybrid clouds — 170
How does it work? — 170
Summary — 173

Chapter 6: Enabling Your Mobile Workforce — 175
DirectAccess – automatic VPN! — 176
The truth about DirectAccess and IPv6 — 176
Prerequisites for DirectAccess — 178
Domain joined — 178
Supported client operating systems — 179
DirectAccess servers get one or two NICs? — 179
Single NIC mode — 179
Edge mode with two NICs — 180
More than two NICs? — 180
To NAT or not to NAT? — 181
6to4 — 181
Teredo — 182
IP-HTTPS — 182
Installing on the true edge – on the Internet — 182
Installing behind a NAT — 183
Network Location Server — 184
Certificates used with DirectAccess — 185
SSL certificate on the NLS web server — 186
SSL certificate on the DirectAccess server — 186

Table of Contents

Machine certificates on the DA server and all DA clients	187
Do not use the Getting Started Wizard!	188
Remote Access Management Console	**190**
Configuration	191
Dashboard	192
Operations Status	193
Remote Client Status	194
Reporting	194
Tasks	195
DirectAccess versus VPN	**196**
Domain-joined versus non-domain-joined	196
Auto versus manual launch	197
Software versus built-in	197
Password and login issues with VPN	198
Web Application Proxy	**199**
Requirements for WAP	**200**
Server 2016 improvements to WAP	**201**
Preauthentication for HTTP Basic	201
HTTP to HTTPS redirection	201
Client IP addresses forwarded to applications	202
Publishing Remote Desktop Gateway	202
Improved administrative console	203
Summary	**204**
Chapter 7: Hardening and Security	**205**
Windows Defender	**206**
Installing Windows Defender	206
Exploring the user interface	207
Disabling Windows Defender	208
Windows Firewall – no laughing matter	**208**
Two Windows Firewall administrative consoles	209
Windows Firewall settings	210
Windows Firewall with Advanced Security	210
Three different firewall profiles	212
Building a new Inbound Rule	213
How to build a rule for ICMP?	216
Managing WFAS with Group Policy	218
Encryption technologies	**222**
BitLocker and the Virtual TPM	222
Shielded VMs	223
Encrypting File System	224
IPsec	224

Configuring IPsec	225
Advanced Threat Analytics	**229**
Lightweight Gateway	**231**
General security best practices	**231**
Get rid of perpetual administrators	231
Use distinct accounts for administrative access	232
Use a different computer to accomplish administrative tasks	233
Never browse the Internet from servers	233
Role-Based Access Controls	234
Just Enough Administration	234
Device Guard	235
Credential Guard	236
Summary	**236**
Chapter 8: Tiny Servers	**237**
Why Server Core?	**238**
No more switching back and forth	239
Interfacing with Server Core	**240**
PowerShell	242
Cmdlets to manage IP addresses	243
Setting the server hostname	245
Joining your domain	246
Server Manager	248
Remote Server Administration Tools	249
Accidentally closing Command Prompt	251
Roles available in Server Core	**253**
Nano Server versus Server Core	**254**
Sizing and maintenance numbers	254
Accessibility	255
Capability	256
Installation	256
Setting up your first Nano Server	**257**
Preparing the VHD file	257
Creating a virtual machine	260
Nano Server Image Builder	**260**
Administering Nano Server	**261**
Nano Server Recovery Console	261
Remote PowerShell	263
Windows Remote Management	265
Other management tools	265
Summary	**266**

Chapter 9: Redundancy in Windows Server 2016 — 267
Network Load Balancing — 268
Not the same as round-robin DNS — 269
What roles can use NLB? — 269
Virtual and dedicated IP addresses — 270
NLB modes — 271
Unicast — 271
Multicast — 272
Multicast IGMP — 273
Configuring a load balanced website — 273
Enabling NLB — 274
Enabling MAC address spoofing on VMs — 274
Configuring NLB — 275
Configuring IIS and DNS — 280
Test it out — 282
Flushing the ARP cache — 283
Failover clustering — 284
Clustering Hyper-V hosts — 285
Scale-Out File Server — 286
Clustering tiers — 286
Application layer clustering — 287
Host layer clustering — 287
A combination of both — 287
How does failover work? — 288
Setting up a failover cluster — 288
Building the servers — 289
Installing the feature — 290
Running the Failover Cluster Manager — 290
Running cluster validation — 291
Running the Create Cluster wizard — 294
Clustering improvements in Windows Server 2016 — 295
Multi-Site clustering — 295
Cross-domain or workgroup clustering — 296
Cluster Operating System Rolling Upgrade — 296
Virtual Machine Resiliency — 297
Storage Replica — 298
Stretch Cluster — 298
Cluster to Cluster — 298
Server to Server — 298
Storage Spaces Direct — 299
Summary — 300

Chapter 10: Learning PowerShell 5.0 — 301
Why move to PowerShell? — 302
- Cmdlets — 302
- PowerShell is the backbone — 304
- Scripting — 305
- Server Core and Nano Server — 305

Working within PowerShell — 305
- Launching PowerShell — 306
- Default Execution Policy — 307
  - Restricted — 308
  - AllSigned — 308
  - RemoteSigned — 308
  - Unrestricted — 308
  - Bypass — 308
- Using the Tab key — 309
- Useful cmdlets for daily tasks — 310
- Using Get-Help — 313
- Formatting the output — 314
  - Format-Table — 314
  - Format-List — 316

PowerShell Integrated Scripting Environment — 317
- PS1 file — 317
- Integrated Scripting Environment — 319

Remotely managing a server — 322
- Preparing the remote server — 323
  - WinRM service — 323
  - Enable-PSRemoting — 324
  - Allowing machines from other domains or workgroups — 325
- Connecting to the remote server — 326
  - Using –ComputerName — 326
  - Using Enter-PSSession — 327
- Testing it with Server Core and Nano Server — 330

Desired State Configuration — 330
Summary — 332

Chapter 11: Application Containers and Docker — 333
Understanding application containers — 334
- Sharing resources — 334
- Isolation — 335
- Scalability — 336

The differences between hypervisors and containers — 337
Windows Server Containers versus Hyper-V Containers — 338
- Windows Server Containers — 339
- Hyper-V Containers — 340

Starting a container with PowerShell	**341**
Preparing your container host server	341
Starting a Windows Server Container	344
What is Docker?	**347**
Docker on Windows Server 2016	348
Docker Hub	349
Docker Trusted Registry	**350**
Summary	**351**
Chapter 12: Virtualizing Your Datacenter with Hyper-V	**353**
Designing and implementing your Hyper-V Server	**354**
Installing the Hyper-V role	355
Using virtual switches	**358**
External virtual switch	360
Internal virtual switch	361
Private virtual switch	361
Creating a new virtual switch	**362**
Implementing a new virtual server	**363**
Starting and connecting to the VM	367
Installing the operating system	368
Managing a virtual server	**370**
Hyper-V Manager	370
Settings menus	372
Checkpoints	375
Hyper-V Console, RDP, and PowerShell	376
Shielded VMs	**377**
Encrypting the VHDs	379
Hyper-V Server 2016	**380**
Summary	**383**
Index	**385**

Preface

We are in the year 2016. In fact, we are almost towards the end of it! How amazing to look back and reflect on all of the big changes that have happened in technology over the past 15 years. In some ways, it seems that Y2K has just happened and everyone has been scrambling to make sure their DOS-based and green screen applications are prepared to handle four-digit date ranges. It seems unthinkable to us now that these systems could have been created in a way that was so short-sighted. Did we not think the world would make it to the year 2000? Today, we build technology with such a different perspective and focus. Everything is centralized, redundant, global, and cloud driven. Users expect 100% uptime, from wherever they are, on whatever device that happens to be sitting in front of them. The world has truly changed.

And as the world has changed, so has the world of technology infrastructure. This year, we are introduced to Microsoft's Windows Server 2016. Yes, we have officially rolled past the half-way marker of this decade and are quickly on our way to 2020, which has always sounded so futuristic. We are living in and beyond Doc and Marty's future, we are actually testing hoverboards, and even some of the wardrobe predictions given to us through cinema no longer seem so far-fetched.

From a user's perspective, a consumer of data, backend computing requirements are almost becoming irrelevant. Things such as maintenance windows, scheduled downtime, system upgrades, slowness due to a weak infrastructure – these items have to become invisible to the workforce. We are building our networks in ways that allow knowledgeworkers and developers to do their jobs without consideration for what is supporting their job functions. What do we use to support that level of reliability and resiliency? Our datacenters haven't disappeared. Just because we use the words "cloud" and "private cloud" so often doesn't make it magic. What makes all of this centralized, "spin up what you need" mentality happen is still physical servers running in physical datacenters.

Preface

What drives the processing power of these datacenters for most companies in the world? Windows Server. In fact, I recently attended a Microsoft conference that had many talks and sessions about Azure, Microsoft's cloud resource center. Azure is enormous, offering us all kinds of technologies and leading the edge as far as cloud computing and security technologies. I was surprised in these talks to hear Windows Server 2016 being referenced time and time again. Why were Azure presenters talking about Server 2016? Because Windows Server 2016—the same Server 2016 that you will be installing into your datacenters—is what underpins all of Azure. It is truly ready to service even the heaviest workloads, in the newest cloud-centric ways. Over the last handful of years, we have all become familiar with Software-Defined Computing, using virtualization technology to turn our server workloads into a software layer. Now we are hearing more and more about expanding on this idea with new technologies such as Software-Defined Networking and Software-Defined Storage, enhancing our ability to virtualize and share resources at a grand scale.

In order to make our workloads more flexible and cloud-ready, Microsoft has taken some major steps in shrinking the server platforms themselves and creating brand new ways of interfacing with those servers. We are talking about things like Server Core, Nano Server, Containers, Hyper-V Containers, and the Server Management Tools. Windows Server 2016 brings us many new capabilities, and along with those capabilities come many new acronyms and terminology.

Let's take some time together to explore the inner workings of the newest version of this server operating system, which will drive and support so many of our business infrastructures over the coming years. Windows Servers have dominated our datacenter's rackspaces for more than two decades, will this newest iteration in the form of Windows Server 2016 continue that trend?

What this book covers

Chapter 1, *Getting Started with Windows Server 2016*, gives us an introduction to the new operating system and an overhead view of the new technologies and capabilities that it can provide. We will also spend a little bit of time exploring the new interface for those who may not be comfortable with it yet.

Chapter 2, *Installing and Managing Windows Server 2016*, dives right into the very first thing we will have to do when working with Server 2016, install it! From there, we will start to expand upon Microsoft's centralized management mentality, exploring the ways that we can now manage and interact with our servers without ever having to log into them.

Chapter 3, Core Infrastructure Services, gives us a solid baseline on the technologies that make up the infrastructure of any Microsoft-centric network. We will discuss the "big three" — AD, DNS, and DHCP — and also address some Server Backup capabilities as well as a cheat-sheet list of MMC and MSC shortcuts to make your day job easier.

Chapter 4, Certificates in Windows Server 2016, jumps into one of the pieces of Windows Server that has existed for many years and yet the majority of server administrators that I meet are unfamiliar with. Let's take a closer look at certificates as they become more and more commonly required for the new technologies that we roll out. By the end of this chapter, you should be able to spin up your own PKI and start issuing certificates for free!

Chapter 5, Networking with Windows Server 2016, begins with an introduction to that big scary IPv6, and continues from there into building a toolbox of items that are built into Windows Server 2016 and can be used in your daily networking tasks. We will also discuss Software-Defined Networking.

Chapter 6, Enabling Your Mobile Workforce, takes a look at the three remote access technologies that are built into Windows Server 2016. Follow along as we explore the capabilities provided by VPN, DirectAccess, and the Web Application Proxy.

Chapter 7, Hardening and Security, gives some insight into security and encryption functions that are built into Windows Server 2016. Security is the top focus of CIOs everywhere this year, let's explore what protection mechanisms are available to us out of the box.

Chapter 8, Tiny Servers, throws us into the shrinking world of headless servers. We will take a look at both Server Core, which has existed for years unbeknownst to many IT personnel, and also at Nano Server, which is brand new for Server 2016.

Chapter 9, Redundancy in Windows Server 2016, takes a look at two different platforms in Server 2016 that provide powerful data and computing redundancy. Follow along as we discuss Network Load Balancing as well as Failover Clustering.

Chapter 10, Learning PowerShell 5.0, gets us into the new, blue command-line interface so that we can become comfortable using it, and also learn why it is so much more powerful than command prompt. PowerShell is quickly becoming an indispensable tool for administering servers, especially if you are interested in Nano Server.

Chapter 11, Application Containers and Docker, brings the terms open source and Linux into a Microsoft book! Let's figure out together why Microsoft thinks this new containers thing is going to be such a big deal, and try out some of the new tools that we will have to learn in order to start using these containers to enhance our DevOps story.

Preface

Chapter 12, Virtualizing Your Datacenter with Hyper-V, covers a no-brainer topic to learn when working in a Microsoft network. Organizations have been moving their servers over to virtual machines in mass quantities over the past few years. Let's use this chapter to make sure you understand how that hypervisor works and gives you the resources needed to build and manage one if and when you have the need.

What you need for this book

Each technology that we discuss within the pages of this book is included in or relates directly to Windows Server 2016. If you can get your hands on a piece of server hardware and the Server 2016 installer files, you will be equipped to follow along and try these things out for yourself. We will talk about and reference some enterprise-class technologies that require stiffer infrastructure requirements, and so you may have to put the actual testing of those items on hold until you are working in a more comprehensive test lab or environment, but the concepts are all still included in this book.

We will also discuss some items that are not included in Server 2016 itself, but are used to extend the capabilities and features of it. Some of these items are provided to us by Azure, such as the Server Management Tools, and some are provided by third parties, such as in the case of using Docker to interact with your containers. Ultimately, you do not need to use these tools in order to manage your new Windows Server 2016 environment, but they do enable some pretty cool things that I think you will want to look into.

Who this book is for

Anyone interested in Windows Server 2016 or in learning more in general about a Microsoft-centric datacenter will benefit from this book. An important deciding factor when choosing which content was appropriate for such a volume was making sure that anyone who had a baseline in working with computers could pick this up and start making use of it within their own networks. If you are already proficient in the Microsoft infrastructure technologies and have worked with prior versions of Windows Server, there are some focused topics on the parts and pieces that are brand new only in Server 2016. On the other hand, if you are currently in a desktop support role or if you are coming fresh into the IT workforce, care was taken in the pages of this book to ensure that you will receive a rounded understanding not only of what is brand new in Server 2016, but what core capabilities it includes that are carry-over from the previous versions of the operating system, but are still critical knowledge to have when working in a Microsoft-driven datacenter.

Conventions

In this book, you will find a number of text styles that distinguish between different kinds of information. Here are some examples of these styles and an explanation of their meaning.

Code words in text, database table names, folder names, filenames, file extensions, pathnames, dummy URLs, user input, and Twitter handles are shown as follows: "Now instead of using a simple dir, give this command a try: Dir | Format-List."

A block of code is set as follows:

```
Get-WmiObject -Class Win32_OperatingSystem -ComputerName localhost
 | Select-Object -Property @{n="Last Boot Time";
e={[Management.ManagementDateTimeConverter]::
ToDateTime($_.LastBootUpTime)}}
```

Any command-line input or output is written as follows:

```
route add -p 192.168.1.0 mask 255.255.255.0 192.168.0.254 if 12
```

New terms and **important words** are shown in bold. Words that you see on the screen, for example, in menus or dialog boxes, appear in the text like this: "Next you simply press the **Submit** button."

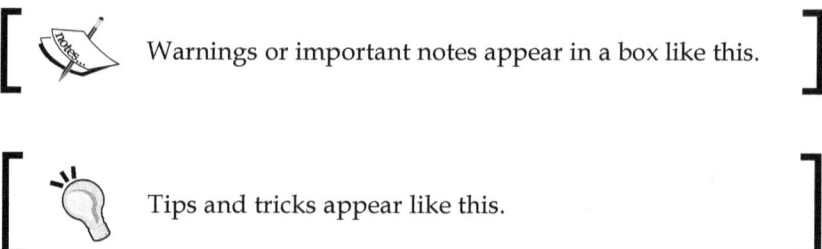

> Warnings or important notes appear in a box like this.

> Tips and tricks appear like this.

Reader feedback

Feedback from our readers is always welcome. Let us know what you think about this book—what you liked or disliked. Reader feedback is important for us as it helps us develop titles that you will really get the most out of.

To send us general feedback, simply e-mail feedback@packtpub.com, and mention the book's title in the subject of your message.

If there is a topic that you have expertise in and you are interested in either writing or contributing to a book, see our author guide at www.packtpub.com/authors.

Customer support

Now that you are the proud owner of a Packt book, we have a number of things to help you to get the most from your purchase.

Errata

Although we have taken every care to ensure the accuracy of our content, mistakes do happen. If you find a mistake in one of our books—maybe a mistake in the text or the code—we would be grateful if you could report this to us. By doing so, you can save other readers from frustration and help us improve subsequent versions of this book. If you find any errata, please report them by visiting http://www.packtpub.com/submit-errata, selecting your book, clicking on the **Errata Submission Form** link, and entering the details of your errata. Once your errata are verified, your submission will be accepted and the errata will be uploaded to our website or added to any list of existing errata under the Errata section of that title.

To view the previously submitted errata, go to https://www.packtpub.com/books/content/support and enter the name of the book in the search field. The required information will appear under the **Errata** section.

Piracy

Piracy of copyrighted material on the Internet is an ongoing problem across all media. At Packt, we take the protection of our copyright and licenses very seriously. If you come across any illegal copies of our works in any form on the Internet, please provide us with the location address or website name immediately so that we can pursue a remedy.

Please contact us at copyright@packtpub.com with a link to the suspected pirated material.

We appreciate your help in protecting our authors and our ability to bring you valuable content.

Questions

If you have a problem with any aspect of this book, you can contact us at questions@packtpub.com, and we will do our best to address the problem.

1
Getting Started with Windows Server 2016

A number of years ago, Microsoft adjusted its operating system release ideology so that the latest Windows Server operating system is always being structured very similarly to the latest Windows client operating system. This has been the trend for some time now, with Server 2008 R2 closely reflecting Windows 7, Server 2012 feeling a lot like Windows 8, and many of the same usability features that came with the Windows 8.1 update are also included with Server 2012 R2. Given this, it makes sense that the new Windows Server 2016 will look and feel much like a Windows 10 experience because that just released last year. Many folks who I work with and have talked to have not yet test driven Windows 10 in their own networks, and are not overly familiar with the interface, so it is important to establish a baseline for usability and familiarity in the operating system itself before diving deeper into the technologies running under the hood. Let's spend a few minutes exploring the new graphical interface and options that are available for finding your way around this latest release of Windows Server.

- What is the purpose of a Windows Server?
- It's getting "cloudy" out there
- An overview of new features
- Navigating the interface
- Using the new Settings screen
- Task Manager
- Task View

What is the purpose of Windows Server?

Silly question? I don't think so. A good question to ponder, especially now that the definition for servers and server workloads is changing on a regular basis. The answer to this question for Windows clients is simpler. A Windows client machine is a requestor, consumer, and contributor of data.

From where is this data being pushed and pulled? What enables the mechanisms and applications running on the client operating systems to interface with this data? What secures these users and their data? This is the purpose of servers in general. They are housing, protecting, and serving up the data to be consumed by clients. Everything revolves around data in business today. Our e-mail, documents, databases, customer lists, everything that we need to do business well, is data. Data that is critical to us. Servers are what we use to build the fabric upon which we trust our data to reside.

We traditionally think about servers in a client-server interface mentality. A user opens a program on their client computer, this program reaches out to a server in order to retrieve something, and the server responds as needed. This idea can be correctly applied to just about every transaction you may have with a server. When your domain-joined computer needs to authenticate you as a user, it reaches out to Active Directory on the server to validate your credentials and get an authentication token. When you need to contact a resource by name, your computer asks a DNS server how to get there. If you need to open a file, you ask the file server to send it your way. Servers are designed to be the brains of our operation, and often by doing so transparently. Especially, in recent years, large strides have been taken to ensure resources are always available and accessible in ways that don't require training or large effort on the part of our employees.

In most organizations, many different servers are needed in order to provide your workforce with the capabilities they require. Each service inside Windows Server is provided as, or as part of, a **Role**. When you talk about needing new servers or configuring a new server for any particular task, what you are really referring to is the individual role or roles that are going to be configured on that server in order to get the work done. A server without any roles installed is useless, though depending on the chassis can make an excellent paperweight.

If you think of roles as the meat and potatoes of a server, then the next bit we will discuss is sort of like adding salt and pepper. Beyond the overhead roles you will install and configure on your servers, Windows also contains many **Features** that can be installed, which sometimes stand alone, but more often complement specific roles in the operating system. Features may be something that complements and adds functionality to the base operating system such as Telnet Client, or a feature may be added to a server in order to enhance an existing role, such as adding the Network Load Balancing feature to an already-equipped remote access server. The combination of roles and features inside Windows Server is what equips that piece of metal to do work.

This book will, quite obviously, focus on a Microsoft-centric infrastructure. In these environments, the Windows Server operating system is king, and is prevalent across all facets of technology. There are alternatives to Windows Server, and different products which can provide some of the same functions to an organization, but it is quite rare to find a business environment anywhere that is running without some semblance of a Microsoft infrastructure. Windows Server contains an incredible amount of technology, all wrapped up in one small installation disk. With Windows Server 2016, Microsoft has gotten us thinking out of the box for what it means to be a server in the first place, and comes with some exciting new capabilities that we will spend some time covering in these pages. Things like PowerShell and Nano Server are changing the way that we manage and size our computing environments; these are exciting times to be or to become a server administrator!

It's getting "cloudy" out there

There's this new term out there, you may have heard of it—Cloud. While the word cloud has certainly turned into a buzzword that is often misused and spoken of inappropriately, the idea of cloud infrastructure is an incredibly powerful one. A cloud fabric is one that revolves around virtual resources—virtual machines, virtual disks, and even virtual networks. Being plugged into the cloud typically enables things like the ability to spin up new servers on a whim, or even the ability for particular services themselves to increase or decrease their needed resources automatically, based on utilization. Think of a simple e-commerce website where a consumer can go to order goods. Perhaps 75% of the year they can operate this website on a single web server with limited resources, resulting in a fairly low cost of service. But the other 25% of the year, maybe around the holiday seasons, utilization ramps way up, requiring much more computing power.

Prior to cloud mentality, this would mean that the company would need to have their environment sized to fit the maximum requirements all the time, in case it was ever needed. They would be paying for more servers and much more computing power than was needed for the majority of the year. With a cloud fabric, giving the website the ability to increase or decrease the number of servers it has at its disposal as needed, the total cost of such a website or service can be drastically decreased. This is the major driving factor of cloud in business today.

Private cloud

While most people working in the IT sector these days have a pretty good understanding of what it means to be part of a cloud service, and many are indeed doing so today, a term which is being pushed into enterprises everywhere and is still many times misunderstood is **private cloud**. At first, I took this to be a silly marketing ploy, a gross misuse of the term cloud to try and appeal to those hooked by buzzwords. Boy was I wrong. In the early days of private clouds, the technology wasn't quite ready to stand up to what was being advertised. Today, however, that story has changed. It is now entirely possible to take the same fabric that is running up in the true, public cloud, and install that fabric right inside your datacenter. This enables you to provide your company with cloud benefits such as the ability to spin resources up and down, and to run everything virtualized, and to implement all of the neat tips and tricks of cloud environments, with all of the serving power and data storage remaining locally owned and secured by you. Trusting cloud storage companies to keep data safe and secure is absolutely one of the biggest blockers to implementation on the true public cloud, but by installing your own private cloud, you get the best of both worlds. Stretchable compute environments with the security of knowing you still control and own all of your own data.

This is not a book about clouds, public or private. I mention this to give a baseline for some of the items we will discuss in later chapters, and also to get your mouth watering a little bit to dig in and do a little reading yourself on cloud technology. You will see the Windows Server 2016 interface in many new ways with the cloud, and will notice that so many of the underlying systems available in Server 2016 are similar if not the same as those becoming available inside **Microsoft Azure**, which is Microsoft's cloud services platform. In these pages, we will not focus on the capabilities of Azure, but rather a more traditional sense of Windows Server that would be utilized on-premise. With the big push toward cloud technologies, it's easy to get caught with blinders on and think that everything and everyone is quickly running to the cloud for all of their technology needs, but it simply isn't true. Most companies will have the need for many on-premise servers for many years to come; in fact many may never put full trust in the cloud and will forever maintain their own datacenters. These datacenters will have local servers that will require server administrators to manage them. That is where you come in.

An overview of new features

The newest version of the Windows Server operating system is always an evolution of its predecessor. There are certainly pieces of technology contained inside which are brand new, but there are even more places where existing technologies have been updated to include new features and functionality. Let's spend a few minutes to give an overhead view of some of the new capabilities that exist in Windows Server 2016.

The Windows 10 experience

Lately, a new release to any Microsoft operating system has meant learning a new user interface, and Server 2016 is no exception. If you have been using and have become familiar with navigating around Windows 10, you should find yourself fairly comfortable with driving the new server operating system as well. We will actually cover quite a bit on this topic in just a minute, right inside this first chapter as we learn some tips and tricks for moving around smoothly and efficiently within the new interface.

Software-Defined Networking

An idea that started to take shape in Server 2012 was **Software-Defined Networking (SDN)**, though at that time the only realistic functionality was provided by the specific component of Hyper-V Network Virtualization. Similar to the idea of virtualizing the server hardware platforms into virtual machines, we now have the capability to virtualize our network layer, which provides various benefits, especially for large organizations and cloud service providers. We will explore updates and features within SDN later in this book.

PowerShell 5.0

PowerShell is the new Command Prompt. More than that, PowerShell is arguably the most powerful configuration tool for every aspect within Windows Server. Most functions in Windows have a graphical interface from which you can make changes and adjust settings, and these GUIs have PowerShell counterparts, which allow you to perform the same actions from a command line. In fact, some features in Windows cannot even be performed without PowerShell; it is becoming that integral. We have a chapter coming up later, which will discuss new functionality and ideas in this latest version of PowerShell.

Built-in malware protection

Microsoft has been including its own malware protection in the client operating systems since Windows 8, but never before on a server platform. Times have changed. Windows Defender has been improved, and it now runs by default in Windows Server 2016! Take a closer look at this feature in *Chapter 7, Hardening and Security*.

Soft restart

There's a new reboot sheriff in town. In an effort to speed up reboots, there is an optional reboot setting now called **soft restart**. This is a feature to be installed within the Windows Server 2016 operating system, and once installed, it provides the capability to initiate a soft restart. So what is a soft restart? It is a restart without hardware initialization. In other words, it restarts the operating system without restarting the whole machine. It is important to note that this feature needs to be specifically installed, and it is invoked when restarting by adding a special switch to either the shutdown command, or the Restart-Computer cmdlet. Here are examples of each:

- Using the shutdown command:

    ```
    shutdown /r /soft /t 0
    /r = restart | /soft = soft restart | /t 0 = zero seconds until reboot initiates
    ```

- Using the Restart-Computer cmdlet:

    ```
    Restart-Computer -Soft
    ```

Nano Server

You've probably heard of Server Core, but I doubt many of those reading this book have deployed it. Unfortunately, the powerful security story behind Server Core is going largely unused, but Microsoft expects this to change completely with the release of Nano Server in Windows Server 2016. Nano Server has a greatly decreased security footprint, and incredibly small hardware requirements. In the next few years, it is expected that many companies will swing a lot of their workloads from traditional servers over to Nano Servers. Make sure to check out *Chapter 8, Tiny Servers*.

Web Application Proxy

Web Application Proxy (WAP) is a role that was introduced in Windows Server 2012 R2 and provides us with the ability to reverse proxy web applications. In other words, we can take internal web resources like Outlook Web Access or SharePoint sites, and publish them securely out to our remote users on the Internet. WAP in Server 2012 R2 came with very limited functionality, and that combined with some pretty steep installation requirements means that almost nobody is using it in production. We are talking about it here in our chapter on remote access because a number of new functions have been provided with the Server 2016 version, and we hope that many more folks will start deploying this new remote access technology.

Shielded virtual machines

So many companies are running a majority of their servers as virtual machines today. One of the big problems with this is that there are some inherent security loopholes that exist in the virtualization host platforms of today. One of those holes is backdoor access to the hard disk files of your virtual machines. It is quite easy for anyone with administrative rights on the virtual host to be able to see, modify, or break any virtual machine that is running within that host. And these modifications can be made in almost untraceable ways. Take a look inside *Chapter 12*, *Virtualizing Your Datacenter with Hyper-V*, to learn how the new capability to create **shielded virtual machines** closes up this security hole by implementing full disk encryption on those VHD files.

Navigating the interface

Unfortunately, Microsoft turned a lot of people off with the introduction of Windows 8 and Server 2012, not because functionality or reliability was lacking, but because the interface was so vastly different than it had been before. It was almost like running two separate operating systems at the same time. You had the normal desktop experience, in which all of us spent 99.9% of our time, but then there were also those few moments where you found yourself needing to visit the full page Start menu. More likely you stumbled into it without wanting to. However you ended up there, inside that fullscreen tablet interface, for the remaining 0.01% of your Server 2012 experience you were left confused, disturbed, and wishing you were back in the traditional desktop. I am, of course, speaking purely from experience here. There may be variance in your personal percentages of time spent, but based on the conversations I have been involved with, I am not alone in these views. And I haven't even mentioned the magical self-appearing Charms bar. Some bad memories are better left in the recesses of the brain.

Getting Started with Windows Server 2016

The major update of Windows 8.1 and Server 2012 R2 came as a welcome relief to these symptoms. There was an actual Start button in the corner again, and you could choose to boot primarily into the normal desktop mode. However, should you ever have the need to click on that Start button, you found yourself right back in the full page Start screen, which I still find almost all server admins trying their best to avoid at all costs.

Well, it turns out that Microsoft has been listening because the interface in Windows 10 and Windows Server 2016 seems to have found a very good balance.

The new Start menu

The first big difference you will recognize in Windows Server 2016 is the Start menu. There is a real Start button that now launches a real Start menu, and one that doesn't take over the entire desktop! Still skeptical? Here's a screenshot to prove it!

Now that is a breath of fresh air. A simple Start menu, and more importantly one that loads quickly over remote connections such as RDP or Hyper-V consoles. No more waiting for screen painting of the full Start screen. If you click on **All Apps**, as expected you see all of the applications installed and available for you to open on the system. Right-clicking inside the blue area of the Start menu gives you options for personalization and properties so that you can adjust the location and presentation of the Start menu and taskbar to your liking.

The hidden Admin menu

As nice as it is to have a functional Start menu, as a server administrator I still very rarely find myself needing to access the traditional menu for my day-to-day functions. This is because many items that I need to access are quickly available to me inside the context menu, which opens by simply right-clicking on the Start button. This menu has been available to us since the release of Windows 8, but many IT professionals are still unaware of this functionality. This menu has become an important part of my interaction with Windows Server operating systems, and hopefully it will be for you as well. Right-clicking on the Start button shows us immediate quick links to do things like open the **Event Viewer**, view the system properties, check **Device Manager**, and even shut down or restart the server. The two most common functions that I call for in this context menu are the Run function and opening the Command Prompt. Even better is the ability from this menu to open either a regular user context Command Prompt, or an elevated/administrative Command Prompt. Using this menu properly saves many mouse clicks and shortens troubleshooting time.

Getting Started with Windows Server 2016

Alternatively, this menu can be invoked using the WinKey + X keyboard shortcut!

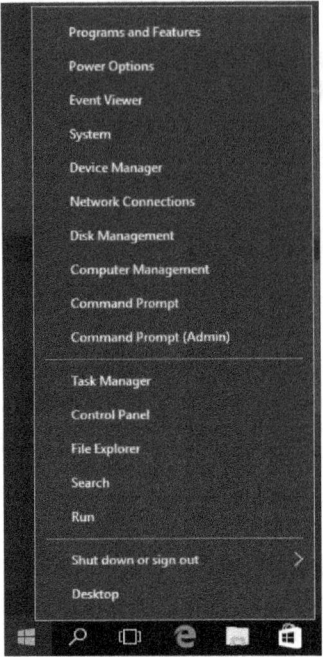

Using the Search function

While the hidden context menu behind the Start button is useful for calling common administrative tasks, using the search function inside the Start menu is a powerful tool for interfacing with literally anything on your Windows Server. Depending on who installed applications and roles to your servers, you may or may not have shortcuts available to launch them inside the Start menu. You also may or may not have desktop shortcuts, or links to open these programs from the taskbar. I find that it is commonly difficult to find specific settings that may need to be tweaked in order to make our servers run like we want them to. The **Control Panel** is much more complex than it used to be, and navigating through it with a mouse in order to find a specific setting can take a lot of extra time. All of these troubles are alleviated with the search bar inside the Start menu. By simply clicking on the Start button, or even easier by pressing the Windows key (WinKey) on your keyboard, you can simply start typing the name of whatever program or setting or document that you want to open up. The search bar will search everything on your local server, and present options to you for which application, program, or even document to open.

As a most basic example, press WinKey on your keyboard, then type `notepad` and press the *Enter* key. You will see that good old Notepad opens right up for us. We never had to navigate anywhere in the `Programs` folder in order to find and open it. In fact, we never even had to touch the mouse, which is music to the ears for someone like me who loves doing everything he possibly can via the keyboard.

An even better example is to pick something that would be buried fairly deep inside **Settings** or the **Control Panel**. How about changing the amount of time before the screen goes to power save and turns itself off? The traditional server admin will open the **Control Panel**, probably navigate to the **Appearance and Personalization** section because nothing else looks obviously correct, and still not find what they were looking for. After poking around for a few more minutes, they would start to think that Microsoft forgot to add in this setting altogether. But alas, these power settings are simply moved to a new container, and are no longer accessible through **Control Panel**, whatsoever. We will discuss the new **Settings** screen momentarily in this chapter, but ultimately for the purposes of this example you are currently stuck at the point where you cannot find the setting you want to change. What is a quick solution? Press your WinKey to open the Start menu, and type `monitor` (or `power`, or just about anything else that would relate to the setting you are looking for).

You see in the list of available options showing in the search menu one called **Choose when to turn off the screen**. Click on that, and you have found the setting you were looking for all along.

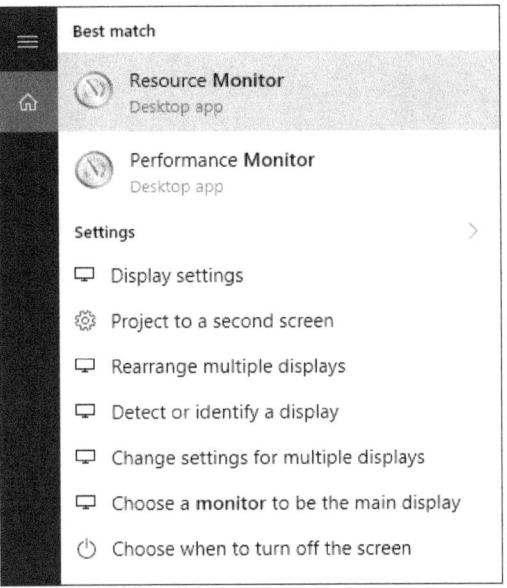

You will also notice that you have many more options on this Search screen than what you were originally searching for. Search has provided me with many different items that I could accomplish, all relating to the word monitor that I typed in. I don't know of a more powerful way to open applications or settings on Windows Server 2016 than using the search bar inside the Start menu. Give it a try today!

Pin programs to the taskbar

While Windows Server 2016 provides great searching capabilities so that launching hard-to-find applications is very easy, sometimes it's easier to have quick shortcuts for commonly used items to be available with a single click, down in the traditional taskbar. Whether you have sought out a particular application by browsing manually through the Start menu, or have used the Search function to pull up the program that you want, you can simply right-click on the program and choose to pin to the taskbar in order to stick a permanent shortcut to that application in the taskbar at the bottom of your screen. Once you have done this, during future logins to your session on the server, your favorite and most used applications will be waiting for you with a single click.

As you can see in the following screenshot, you also have the ability to pin programs to the Start menu, which of course is another useful place from which to launch them regularly.

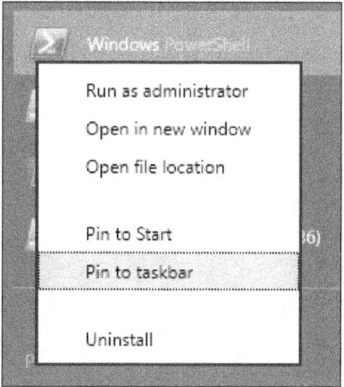

Many readers will already be very familiar with the process to pin programs to the taskbar, so let's take it one step further to portray an additional function you may not be aware is available to you when you have applications pinned.

The power of right-click

We are all pretty familiar with right-clicking in any given area of a Windows operating system in order to do some more advanced functions. Small context menus displayed upon a right-click have existed since the mouse rolled off the assembly line. We often right-click in order to copy text, copy documents, paste the same, or get into a deeper set of properties on a particular file or folder. Many day-to-day tasks are accomplished with that mouse button. What I want to take a minute and point out is that software makers, Microsoft and otherwise, have been adding even more right-click functionality into application launchers themselves, which makes it even more advantageous to have them close at hand, such as inside the taskbar.

The amount of functionality provided to you when right-clicking on an application in the taskbar differs depending on the application itself. For example, if I were to right-click on Command Prompt, I have options to either open Command Prompt, or to **Unpin this program from taskbar**. Very simple stuff. If I right-click again on the smaller menu option for Command Prompt, I have the ability to perform the same functions, but I could also get further into **Properties**, or **Run as administrator**. So I get a little bit more enhanced functionality the deeper I go.

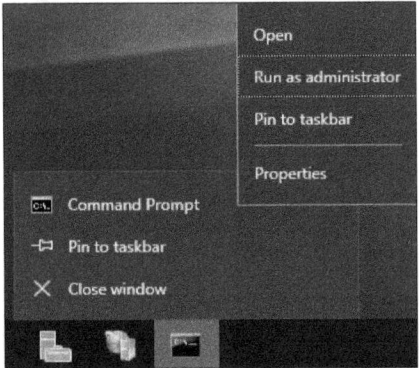

However, with other programs you will see more results. And the more you utilize your servers, the more data and options you will start to see in these right-click context menus. Two great examples are Notepad and the Remote Desktop Client. On my server, I have been working in a few text configuration files, and I have been using my server in order to jump into other servers to perform some remote tasks. I have been doing this using the Remote Desktop Client. Now, when I right-click on Notepad listed in my taskbar, I have quick links to the most recent documents that I have worked on.

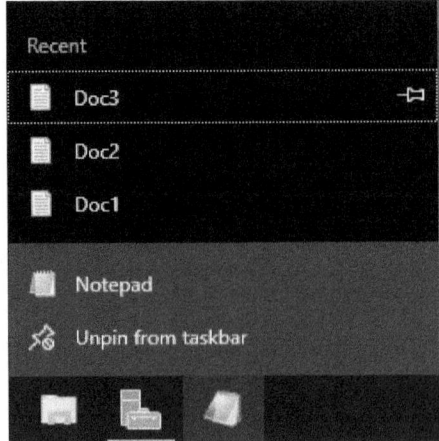

And when right-clicking on my RDP icon, I now have quick links listed right here for the recent servers, which I have connected to. I don't know about you, but I RDP into a lot of different servers on a daily basis. Having a link for the Remote Desktop Client in the taskbar, automatically keeping track of the most recent servers I have visited definitely saves me time and mouse clicks as I work through my daily tasks.

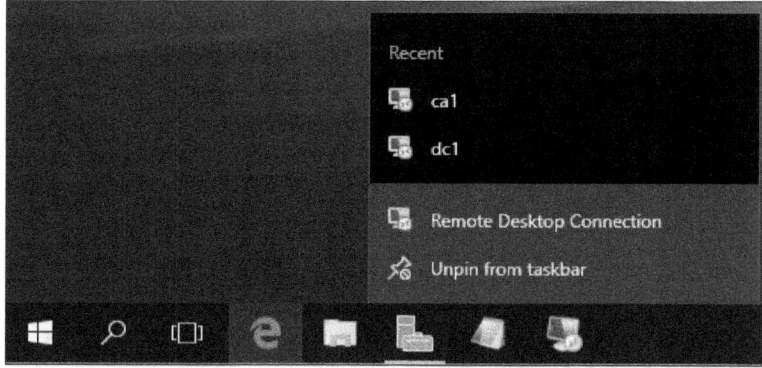

These right-click functions have existed for a couple of operating system versions now, so it's not new technology but it is being expanded upon regularly as new versions of the applications are released. It is also a functionality that I don't witness many server administrators utilizing, but perhaps they should start doing so in order to work more efficiently, which is why we are discussing it here.

Something that is enhanced in the Windows 10 and Server 2016 platforms that is also very useful on a day-to-day basis is the **Quick access** view that is presented by default when you open File Explorer. We all know and use File Explorer and have for a long time, but typically when you want to get to a particular place on the hard drive or to a specific file, you have many mouse clicks to go through in order to get to your destination. Windows Server 2016's **Quick access** view immediately shows us both recent and frequent files and folders, which we commonly access from the server. We as admins often have to visit the same places on the hard drive and open the files time and time again. Wouldn't it be great if File Explorer would lump all of those common locations and file links in one place? That is exactly what it does.

You can see in the following screenshot that opening File Explorer gives you quick links to open both frequently accessed folders as well as links to your recent files. A feature like this can be a real time saver, and regularly making use of these little bits and pieces available to you in order to increase your efficiency portrays to colleagues and those around you that you have a real familiarity and comfort level with this latest round of operating systems.

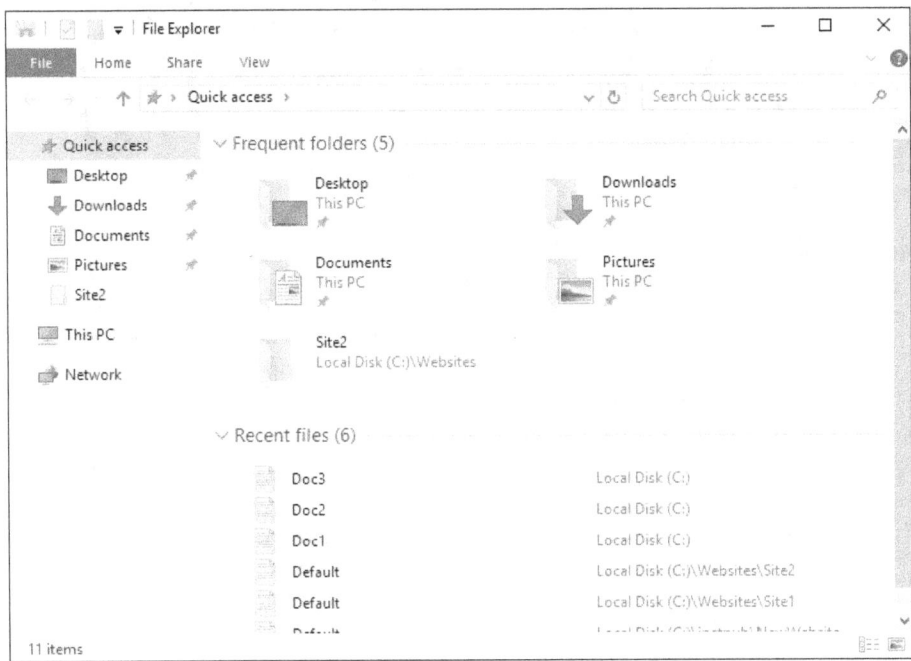

Using the new Settings screen

If you work in IT and have been using Windows 10 on a client machine for any amount of time, it's a sure bet that you have stumbled across the new **Settings** interface. Perhaps accidentally, as was the case for me, the first time I saw it. I have watched a number of people now bump into the **Settings** interface for the first time when trying to view or configure Windows Updates. You see, settings in Windows Server 2016 are just what the name implies, an interface from which you configure various settings within the operating system. What's so hard or confusing about that? Well, we already have a landing platform for all of the settings contained inside Windows that has been around for a zillion years. It's called **Control Panel**.

The **Settings** menu inside Windows isn't a brand new idea, but looks and feels quite new for Server 2016. Our predecessor, Windows Server 2012 and 2012 R2, had a quasi-presence of settings that as far as I know went largely unused by systems administrators. I believe that to be the effect of poor execution as the **Settings** menu in 2012 was accessed and hidden behind the Charms bar, which most folks have decided was a terrible idea. Not to spend too much time on technology of the past, but the Charms bar in Server 2012 was a menu that presented itself when you swiped your finger in from the right edge of the screen. Yes, you are correct, servers don't have touchscreens. Not any that I have ever worked on, anyway. So the Charms bar also presented when you hovered the mouse up near the top-right of the screen. It was quite difficult to access, yet seemed to show up whenever you didn't want it to, like when you were trying to click on something near the right of the desktop and instead you clicked on something inside the Charms bar that suddenly appeared.

I am only giving you this background information in order to segue into this next idea. Much of the user interface in Windows 10, and therefore Windows Server 2016, can be considered a small step backward from the realm of finger swipes and touch screens. Windows 8 and Server 2012 were so focused on big app buttons and finger swipes that a lot of people got lost in the shuffle. It was so different than what we had ever seen before and difficult to use at an administrative level. Because of feedback received from that release, the graphical interface and user controls, including both the Start menu and the **Settings** menu in Windows Server 2016, are sort of smack-dab in the middle between Server 2008 and Server 2012. This backwards step was the right one, and I have heard nothing but praise so far on the new user interface.

So, getting back to the **Settings** menu, if you click on your Start button, then **All Apps**, and then on **Settings**, you will see this new interface:

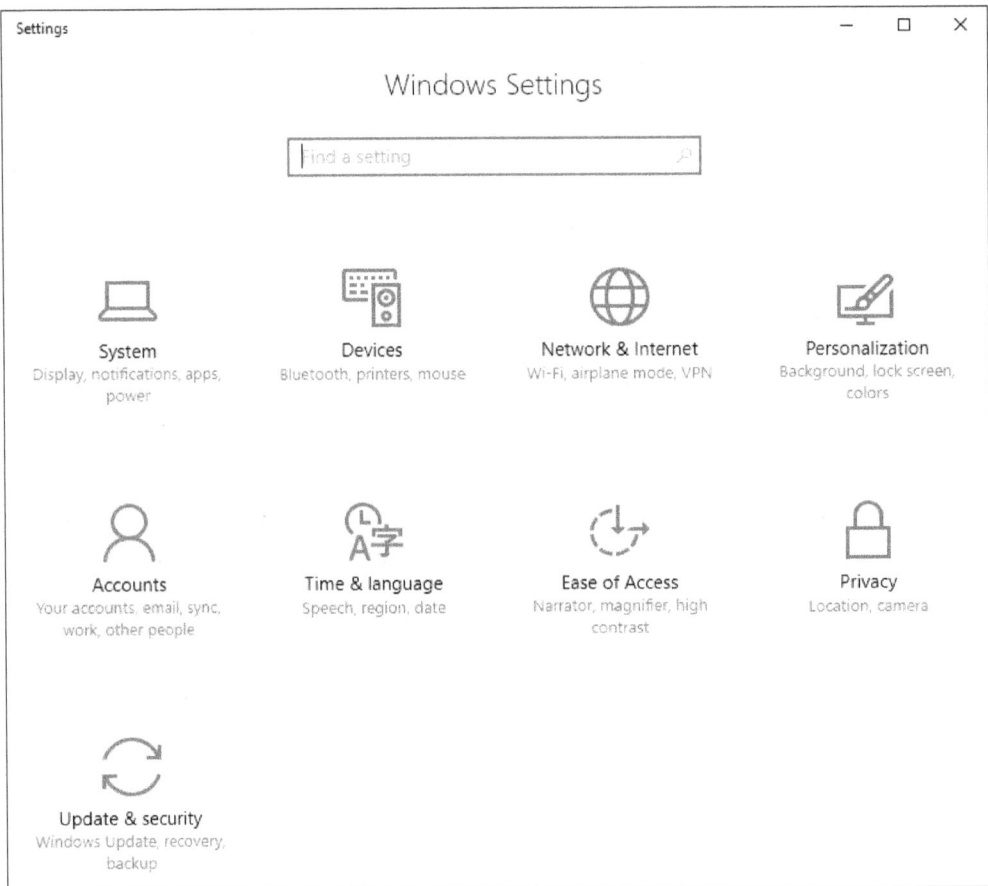

There are many settings and pieces of the operating system that you can configure in this new **Settings** menu. Some settings in Windows now only exist in this interface, but many can still be accessed either here or through the traditional **Control Panel**. The goal seems to be a shift toward all configurations being done through the new menu in future releases, but for now we can still administer most setting changes through our traditional methods if we so choose. I mentioned Windows Updates earlier; that is a good example to look over. Traditionally, we would configure our Windows Update settings via the **Control Panel**, but they have now been completely migrated over to the new **Settings** menu in Windows Server 2016. Search the **Control Panel** for Windows Update, and the only result is that you can view currently installed updates. But if you search the new **Settings** menu for Windows Update, you'll find it right away.

Chapter 1

 Remember, you can always use the Windows search feature to look for any setting! Hit your WinKey and type `Windows Update` and you'll be given quick links that take you straight into the appropriate **Settings** menu.

For the moment, you will have to use a combination of **Control Panel** and the **Settings** menu in order to do your work. It gets confusing occasionally. Sometimes you will even click on something inside the **Settings** menu, and it will launch a **Control Panel** window! Try it out. Open up the **Settings** menu and click on **Network & Internet**. Click on **Ethernet** in the left column. Here you can see the status of your network cards, but you can't change anything, such as changing an IP address. Then, you notice the link for **Change adapter options**. Oh yeah, that sounds like what I want to do. Click on **Change adapter options**, and you are taken right into the traditional **Network Connections** screen:

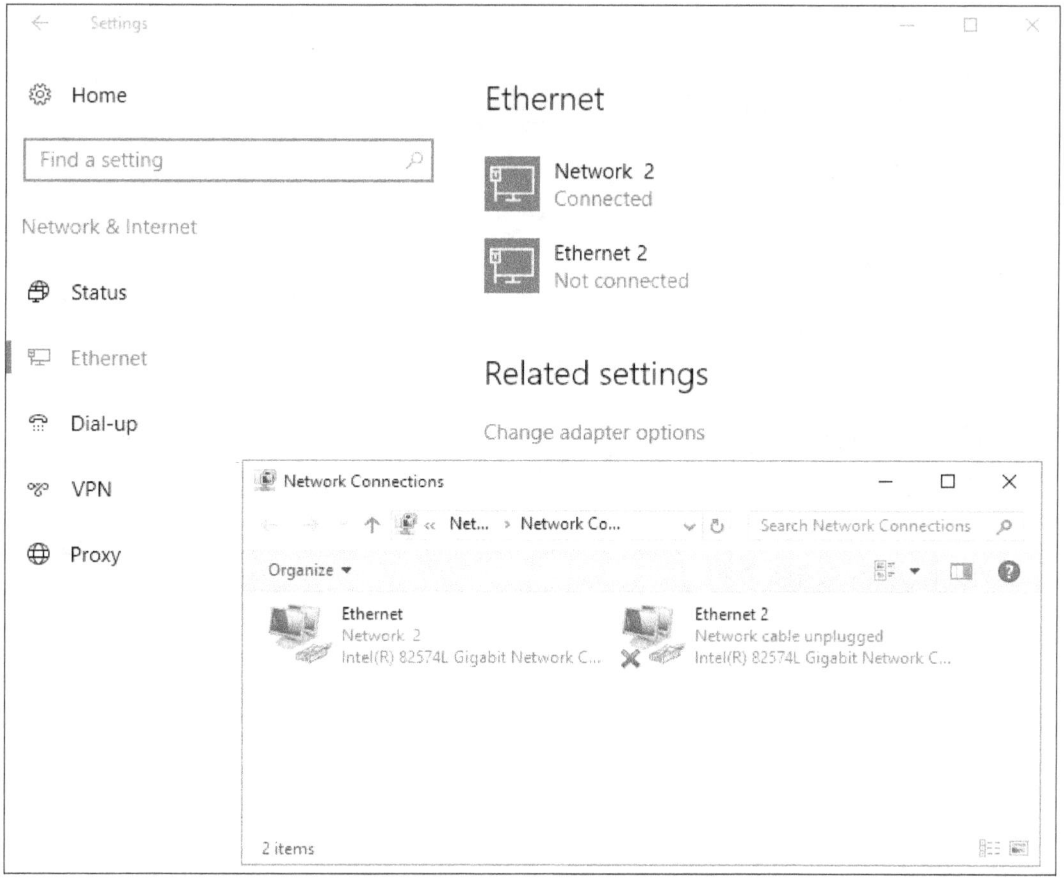

[19]

Two ways to do the same thing

Potentially confusing as well, until you get used to navigating around in here, is that you can sometimes accomplish the same task in either **Control Panel** or **Settings** menu, but the process that you take in each interface can have a vastly different look and feel. Sometimes you can actually accomplish the same task, and sometimes you just think that you can. What do I mean by that? A good example we can follow is to create a new user account.

Creating a new user through the Control Panel

You are probably pretty familiar with this. Open **Control Panel** and click on **User Accounts**. Then, click on the **User Accounts** heading. Now, click on the link to **Manage another account**. Inside this screen is your option to **Add a user account**. Click on that and you get the dialog box where you enter a username and password for your new user.

Add a user
Choose a password that will be easy for you to remember but hard for others to guess. If you forget, we'll show the hint.
Windows can't connect to the Internet right now. Check your Internet connection and try again later if you want to add a Microsoft account.
User name
Password
Reenter password
Password hint

Creating a new user through the Settings menu

Let's take this thing for a test drive. Open the **Settings** menu, and click on **Accounts**. Now, click on **Other People** in the left column. There is clearly an option here that looks like it will allow us to create a new user. I can even see the new testing user account that I created a minute ago with **Control Panel**. Go ahead and click on **Add someone else to this PC**.

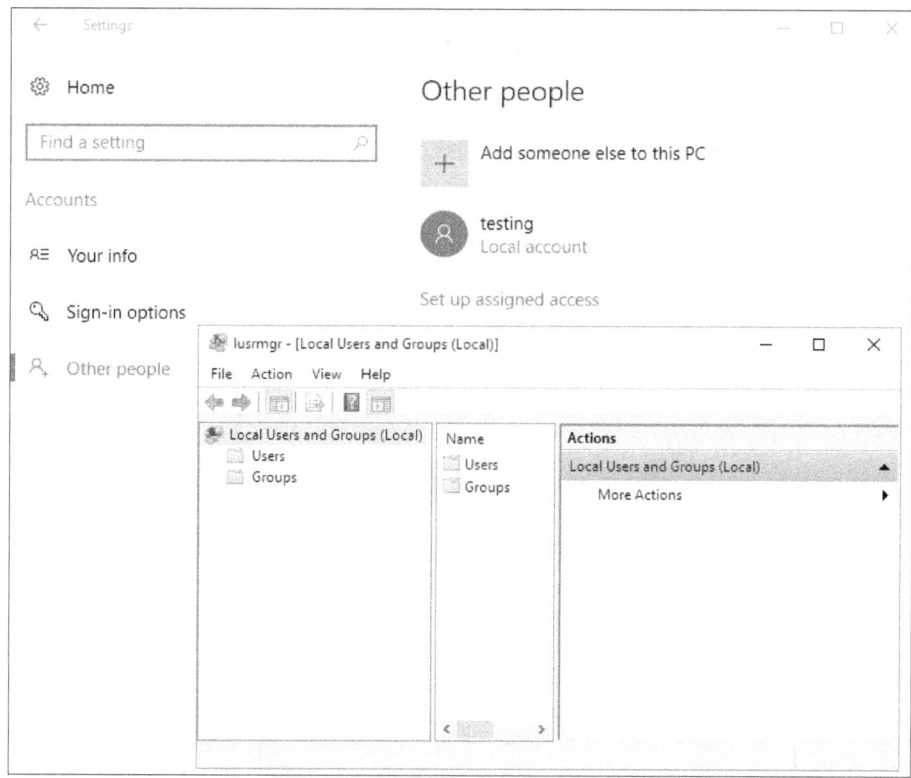

So we also have here the ability to add a new user to this server, but by using the more traditional **Iusrmgr** tool.

We walked through this simple example of attempting to do the same function through two different interfaces to showcase that there are some items which can and must be performed within the new **Settings** menu context, but there are many functions within Windows that still need to be accomplished through our traditional interfaces. While **Control Panel** continues existence, and probably will for a very long time, you should start navigating your way around the **Settings** menu and figure out what is available inside so that you can start to shape your ideas for the best combination of both worlds in order to manage your servers effectively.

Getting Started with Windows Server 2016

Just one last thing to point out as we start getting comfortable with the way that the new **Settings** menu looks. Many of the settings that we configure in our servers are on/off types of settings. By that I mean we are setting something to either one option or another. Typically, these kinds of configurations are handled by either drop-down menus or by radio buttons. That is normal; that is expected; that is Windows. Now you will start to see little swipe bars, or sliders, that allow you to switch settings on or off, like a light switch. Anyone who has used the settings interface of any smart phone knows exactly what I am talking about. This user interface behavior has now made its way into the full Windows operating systems, and is likely here to stay. Just to give you an idea of what it looks like inside the context of the new **Settings** menu, here is a screenshot of the **Windows Defender** page inside the **Update & Security** settings:

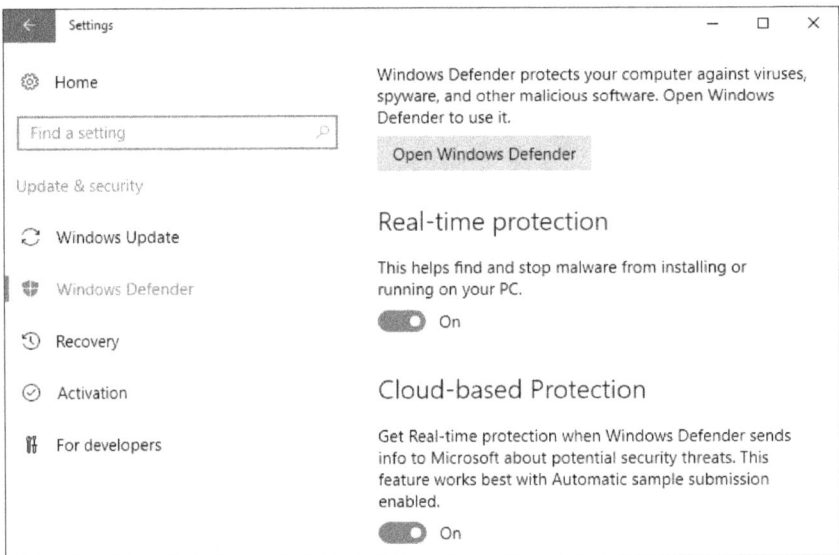

Task Manager

Task Manager is a tool that has existed in all Windows operating systems since the first days of the graphical interface, but it has evolved quite a bit over the years. One of the goals for Windows Server 2016 is to be even more useful and reliable than any previous version of Windows Server has been. So, it only makes sense that we finally remove **Task Manager** altogether, since it simply won't be needed anymore, right?

I'm kidding, of course! While Server 2016 will hopefully prove itself to indeed be the most stable and least needy operating system we have ever seen from Microsoft, **Task Manager** still exists and will still be needed by server administrators everywhere. If you haven't taken a close look at **Task Manager** in a while, it has changed significantly over the past few releases.

Task Manager is still typically invoked by either a *Ctrl + Alt + Delete* on your keyboard and then clicking on **Task Manager**, or by right-clicking on the taskbar and then choosing **Task Manager**. You can also launch **Task Manager** with the key combination *Ctrl + Shift + Esc*, or typing `taskmgr` inside the **Run** or **Search** dialog boxes. The first thing you'll notice is that very little information exists in this default view, only a simple list of applications that are currently running. This is a useful interface for forcing an application to close which may be hung up, but not for much else. Go ahead and click on the **More details** link, and you will start to see the real information provided in this more powerful interface.

We immediately notice that the displayed information is more user-friendly than in previous years, with both **Apps** and **Background processes** being categorized in a more intuitive way, and multiple instances of the same application being condensed down for easy viewing. This gives a faster overhead view of what is going on with our system, while still giving the ability to expand each application or process to see what individual components or windows are running within the application, such as in the following screenshot:

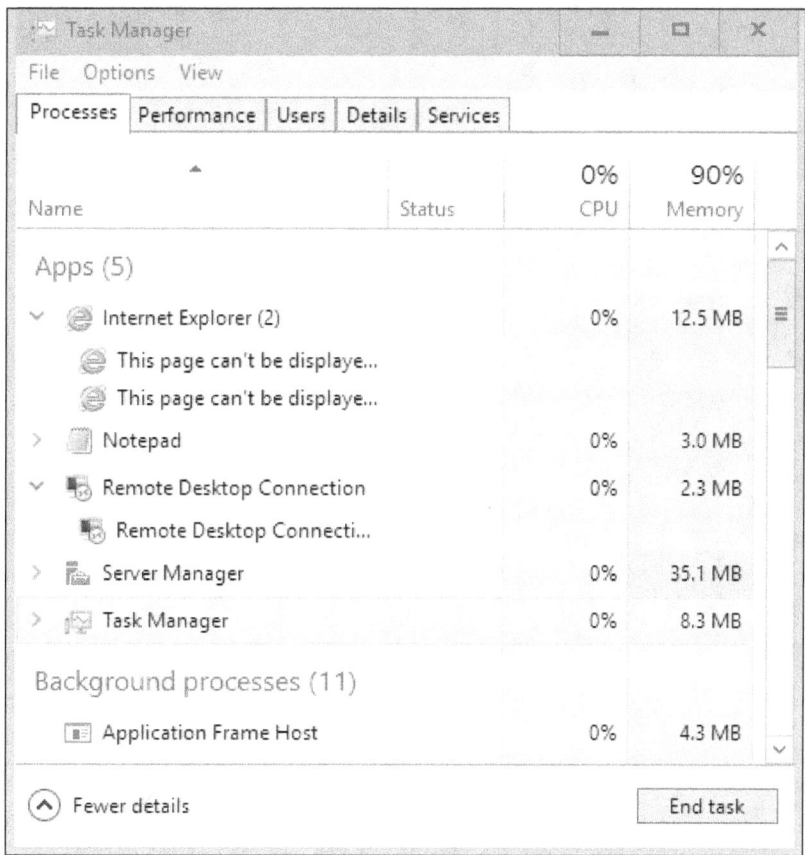

Getting Started with Windows Server 2016

Make sure to check out the other tabs available inside **Task Manager** as well. **Users** will show us a list of currently logged in users and the amounts of hardware resources that their user sessions are consuming. This is a nice way to identify on a Remote Desktop Session Host server, for example, an individual who might be causing a slowdown on the server. The **Details** tab is a little bit more of a traditional view of the **Processes** tab, splitting out much of the same information but in the older style way we were used to seeing it in versions of the operating system long ago. And then the **Services** tab is pretty self-explanatory; it shows you the Windows services currently installed on the server, their status, and the ability to start or stop these services as needed, without having to open the **Services** console separately.

The tab that I skipped over so that I could mention it more specifically here is the **Performance** tab. This is a pretty powerful one. Inside you can quickly monitor CPU, memory, and Ethernet utilization. As you can see in the following screenshot, I haven't done a very good job of planning resources on this particular virtual machine, as my CPU is hardly being touched but I am almost out of system memory:

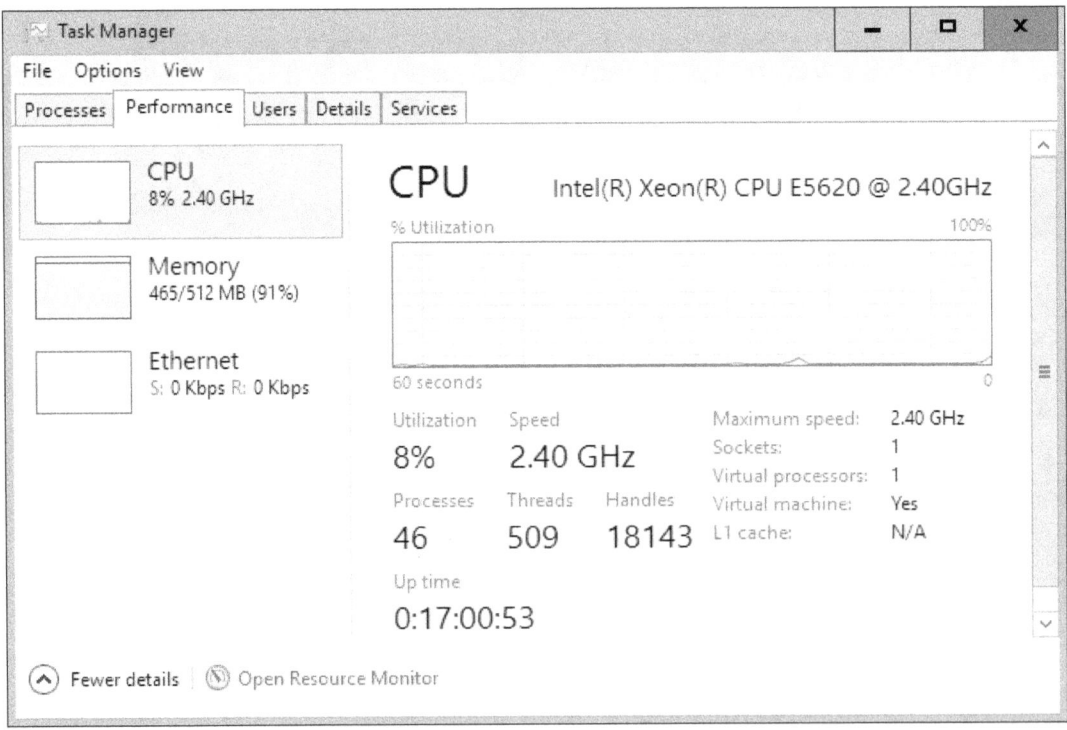

>  Another useful piece of information available inside this screen is server up time. Finding this information can be critical when troubleshooting an issue, and I watch admins time and time again calculating system uptime based on log timestamps. Using **Task Manager** is a much easier way to find that information!

If you are interested in viewing more in-depth data about server performance, there is a link at the bottom of this **Task Manager** window where you can **Open Resource Monitor**. Two technologies provided inside Server 2016 for monitoring system status, particularly for hardware performance, are Resource Monitor and Performance Monitor. Definitely open up these tools and start testing them out, as they can provide both troubleshooting information and essential baseline data when you spin up a new server. This baseline can then be compared against future testing data so that you can monitor how new applications or services installed onto a particular server have affected their resource consumption.

Moving back to **Task Manager**, there is just one other little neat trick I would like to test. Still inside the **Performance** tab, go ahead and right-click on any particular piece of data that you are interested in. I will right-click on the **CPU** information near the left side of the window. This opens up a dialog box with a few options, of which I am going to click on **Summary view**. This condenses the data that was before taking up about half of my screen real-estate down into a tiny little window, which I can move to the corner of my screen. This is a nice way to keep hardware utilization data on the screen at all times as you navigate through and work on your server so that you can watch for any spikes or increases in resource consumption when making changes to the system.

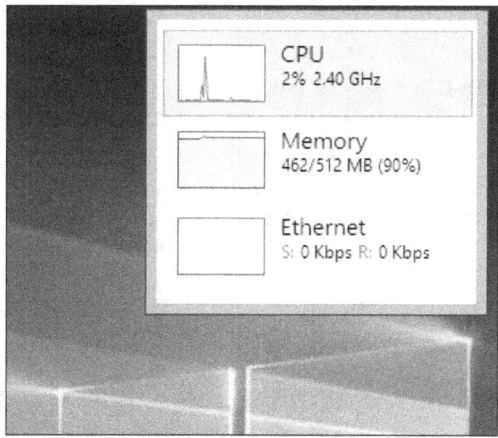

Task View

Task View is a new feature in Windows 10 and Windows Server 2016. It is a similar idea as that of holding down the *Alt* key and then pressing *Tab* in order to cycle through the applications that you currently have running. For anyone who has never tried that, go ahead and hold down those two keys on your keyboard right now. Depending on what version of Windows you are running, your screen might look slightly different than this, but, in effect, it's the same information. You can see all of the programs you currently have open, and you can cycle through them from left to right using additional presses of the *Tab* button. Alternatively, use *Alt + Shift + Tab* in order to cycle through them in reverse order. When you have many windows open, it is perhaps easier to simply use the mouse to jump to any specific window.

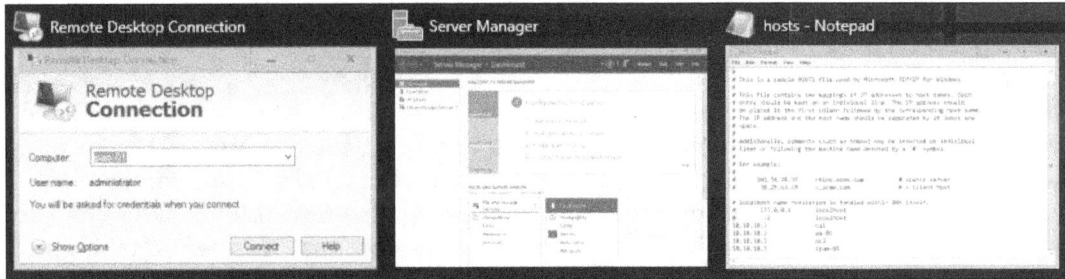

Task View is quite a bit more powerful than this, because it adds the capability of managing multiple full desktops worth of windows and applications. For example, if you were working on two different projects on the same server, and each project required you to have many different windows open at the same time, you would start to burn a lot of time switching back and forth between all of your different apps and windows in order to find what you were looking for. Using Task View, you could leave all of your open windows for the first project on your first desktop, and open all of the windows dealing with the second project on a second desktop. Then, with two clicks you can easily switch back and forth between the different desktops, using the Task View button. By default, Task View is the little button down in the taskbar, immediately to the right of the Start button. Go ahead and click on it now; it looks like this:

You now see a listing of your currently open windows; this looks very similar to the *Alt + Tab* functionality we looked at earlier. The difference is the little button near the bottom-right corner that says **New desktop**. Go ahead and click on that now.

Now, you will see **Desktop 1** and **Desktop 2** available for you to use. You can click on **Desktop 2** and open some new programs, or you can even drag and drop existing windows between different desktops, right on this Task View screen.

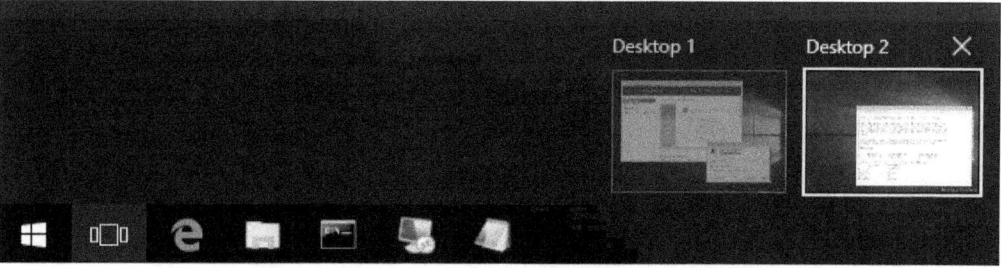

Task View is a great way to stay organized and efficient by utilizing multiple desktops on the same server. I suppose it is kind of like running dual monitors, or three or four or more, all from a single physical monitor screen.

>  If you want to avoid having to click on the icon for Task View, pressing WinKey + *Tab* on your keyboard does the same thing!

Summary

This first chapter on the new Windows Server 2016 is all about getting familiar and comfortable navigating around in the interface. There are various ways to interact with Server 2016 and we will discuss many of them throughout this book, but the majority of server administrators will be interfacing with this new operating system through the full graphical interface, using both the mouse and keyboard to perform their tasks. If you have worked with previous versions of the Windows Server operating system, then a lot of the tools that you will use to drive this new platform will be the same, or at least similar, to the ones that you have used in the past. New operating systems should always be an evolution of the predecessor, and never all new. I think this was a lesson learned with the release of Windows 8 and Server 2012.

With Server 2016, we find a great compromise between the traditional familiarity of the prior versions of Windows, and the new benefits that come with rounded edges and touch-friendly screens that will be used more and more often as we move toward the future of Windows-based devices.

2
Installing and Managing Windows Server 2016

Now that we have taken a look at some of the features inside the graphical interface of Windows Server 2016, I realize that some of you may be sitting back thinking, "That's great to read about, but how do I really get started playing around with this for myself?" Reading about technology is never as good as experiencing it for yourself, so we want some rubber to meet the road in this chapter. One of the biggest goals for this entire book is to make sure we enable you to **use** the product. Rattling off facts about new features and efficiencies is fine and dandy, but ultimately worthless if you aren't able to make it work in real life. So, let's make this chunk of raw server metal do some work for us:

- Installing Windows Server 2016
- Installing roles and features
- Centralized management and monitoring
- Sysprep enables quick server rollouts

Installing Windows Server 2016

The installation process for Microsoft operating systems in general has improved dramatically over the past 15 years. I assume that a lot of you as IT professionals are also the de facto "neighborhood computer guy", being constantly asked by friends and family to fix or rebuild their computers. If you're anything like me, this means you are still regularly rebuilding operating systems such as Windows XP. Looking at the bright blue setup screens and finding a keyboard where the *F8* key actually works are imperative to this process. To spend two hours simply installing the base operating system and bringing it up to the highest service pack level is pretty normal. Compared to that timeline, installation of a modern operating system such as Windows Server 2016 is almost unbelievably fast and simple.

It is very likely that the majority of readers have completed this process numerous times already, and if that is the case feel free to skip ahead a couple of pages. But for anyone who is new to the Microsoft world or new to IT in general, I'd like to take just a couple of quick pages to make sure you have a baseline to get started with. Without earning your "Installing an OS 101" badge on your tool belt, you will get nowhere in a hurry.

Burning that ISO

The first thing you must do is acquire some installation media. The most straightforward way to implement a single new server is to download an .ISO file from Microsoft, burn that .ISO to a DVD disc, and slide that DVD in to be used for installation. Since the website links and URLs are subject to change over time, the most trustworthy way to acquire your .ISO file to be used for installation is to open a search engine, such as **Bing**, and type Download Windows Server 2016. Once you have landed on the official Microsoft downloads page, click on the link to download your .ISO file and save it onto the hard drive of your computer.

The trickiest part of getting an .ISO file to be a workable DVD used to be the need for downloading some kind of third-party tool in order to burn it to a disc while making it bootable. If you are running an older client operating system on your computer, this may still be the case for you. I have watched many who are new to this process take the .ISO file, drag it over to your disc drive, and start burning the disc. This creates a DVD with the .ISO file on it, but that .ISO is still packaged up and not bootable in any way, so the disc would be worthless to your new piece of server hardware. Luckily, the newer versions of the Windows client operating systems have built-in functions for dealing with .ISO files that make the correct burning process very simple.

Once you have your .ISO file for the Windows Server 2016 installation downloaded onto your computer, insert a fresh DVD into your disc drive and browse to the new file. Simply right-click on the .ISO file, and then choose your menu option for **Burn disc image**. This launches a simple wizard that will extract and burn your new .ISO file the correct way onto the DVD, making it a bootable installation media for your new server:

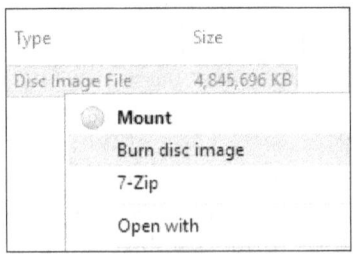

Installing from USB

Alternative to using an actual DVD for this installation process, there are various tools available on the Internet that will take your newly downloaded ISO file and place them onto a USB flash stick that can be used for installation. Now I know you're thinking, "I know how to copy a file onto a USB stick, why would I need a utility for that?" The answer is that you cannot simply copy an ISO onto USB media and expect that it will be bootable. That is the magic of the utilities. They will take your USB stick, format it – yes, you will lose all current data on this USB stick – and then recreate the media from scratch, making it bootable and at the same time injecting all of the installation media from the ISO file. Among the various tools you will come across when searching for a program to use for this, you will probably come across one straight from Microsoft, which is what I typically use. This is called the Windows 7 USB DVD Download Tool. Unless you already have a favorite utility for turning an ISO into a bootable USB, I definitely recommend this one.

Running the installer

Now go ahead and plug your newly created DVD into the drive on the new server hardware. Boot to this disc, and you will finally see the installation wizard for Windows Server 2016. Now, there really are not that many options for you to choose from within these wizards, so we won't spend a lot of time here. For the most part, you are simply clicking on the **Next** button in order to progress through the screens, but there are a few specific places where you will need to make decisions along the way.

After choosing your installation language, the next screen seems pretty easy. There's just a single button that says **Install now**. Yes, that is what you want to click on, but I wanted to make a mention of the text in the lower-left corner of your screen. If you are ever in a position where you have a server that cannot boot and you are trying to run some recovery or diagnostic functions in order to resolve that issue, you can click on **Repair your computer** in order to launch into that recovery console. But for our fresh server installation, go ahead and click on **Install now**:

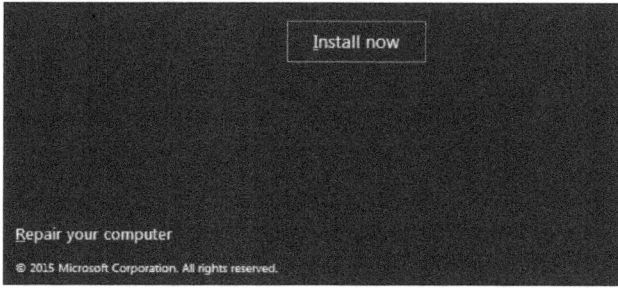

Installing and Managing Windows Server 2016

The next screen is an interesting one, and the first place that you really need to start paying attention. You see two different installation options for Windows Server 2016. There is what seems to be the "regular" installer, and then a second option for Windows Server 2016, including **Desktop Experience**. Typically, in the Microsoft installer world, clicking on **Next** through every option gives you the most typical and common installation path for whatever it is that you are installing. Not so with this wizard. If you simply glide by this screen by clicking on **Next**, you will find yourself in the end with an installation of **Server Core**. We will talk more about Server Core in a later chapter of the book, but for now I will just say that if you are expecting to have a server that looks and feels like what we talked about in *Chapter 1, Getting Started with Windows Server 2016*, this default option is not going to be the one that gets you there. The **Desktop Experience** that the wizard is talking about with the second option is the full Windows Server graphical interface, which you are more than likely expecting to see once we are done with our installation.

So for the purposes of our installation here, where we want to interact with the server using full color and our mouse, go ahead and choose the second option that includes **Desktop Experience** before clicking on the **Next** button.

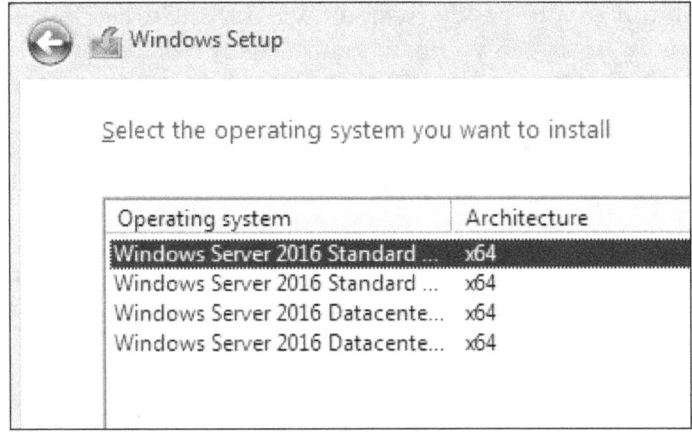

[ In some previous versions of Windows Server, we had the ability to migrate back and forth from a full Desktop Experience to Server Core and back again, even after the operating system was installed. This does not work in Windows Server 2016! The ability to transition between the two modes has disappeared, so it is even more important that you plan your servers properly from the beginning.]

The next screen details licensing terms to which you need to agree, and then we come to another screen where the top option is most likely not the one that you intend to click on. I do understand why the **Upgrade** function is listed first, as that makes the most common sense. In a perfect world where everything always works flawlessly following upgrades, this would be a great way to go. You could have many servers all doing their jobs, and every time that a new operating system is released, you simply run the installer and upgrade them. Voila, magic! Unfortunately, it doesn't quite work like that, and I almost never see server administrators willing to take the risk on doing an in-place upgrade to an existing production server. Much more common is that we are always building brand new servers alongside the currently running production servers. Once the new server is configured and ready to accept its responsibilities, then and only then does the actual work migrate over to the new server from the old one. In a planned, carefully sculpted migration process, once the migration of duties is finished, then the old server is shut down and taken away. If we were able to simply upgrade the existing servers to the newest operating system, it would save an awful lot of time and planning. But this is only feasible when you know that the upgrade is actually going to work without hiccups, and most of the time we are not prepared to take that risk

If an upgrade process goes sideways and you end up with a broken server, now you are looking at a costly repair and recovery process on a business-critical production server. You very well may be looking at working through the night or weekend as well. Would you rather spend your time planning a carefully formed cutover, or recovering a critical server with the business breathing down your neck because they cannot work? My money's on the former.

Installing and Managing Windows Server 2016

So given that, back to the topic at hand. In the Windows Server world, we will almost never use the **Upgrade** option. Maybe someday, but based on everyone I talk to regarding this subject, today is not that day. So go ahead and choose the **Custom: Install Windows only (advanced)** option, which is where we will get into our options for installing this copy of Windows Server 2016 fresh into a new location on the hard drive:

Which type of installation do you want?

Upgrade: Install Windows and keep files, settings, and applications
The files, settings, and applications are moved to Windows with this option. This option is only available when a supported version of Windows is already running on the computer.

Custom: Install Windows only (advanced)
The files, settings, and applications aren't moved to Windows with this option. If you want to make changes to partitions and drives, start the computer using the installation disc. We recommend backing up your files before you continue.

Now we decide where we want to install our new copy of Windows Server 2016. In many cases, you will simply click on **Next** here, because your server will have just a single hard disk drive or maybe a single RAID array of disks, and in either case you will see a single pool of free space onto which you can install the operating system. If you have multiple hard drives installed in your server and they have not been tied together in any way yet, then you will have multiple choices here on where to install Windows Server. We have just a single hard disk attached here, which has never been used, so I can simply click on **Next** to continue. Note here that if your drives had existing or old data on them, you have the opportunity here with some disk management tools where you could format the disk, or delete individual partitions. If you are using some specialized disks that take specific drivers, there is also a **Load driver** button that you can use in order to inject these special drivers into the installation wizard in order to view these kinds of disks.

Also, it is important to note on this screen that there is no need to do anything here with most new server installations. You can see that there is a **New** button below that can be used to manually create hard disk partitions, and so many administrators assume they need to do that in order to install their new operating system. This is not the case. There is no need to create partitions unless you want to set them up manually for some specific reason. If your hard drive is just a bunch of blank, unallocated space, all you need to do is click on **Next** and the Windows Server 2016 installation will set up the partitions for you:

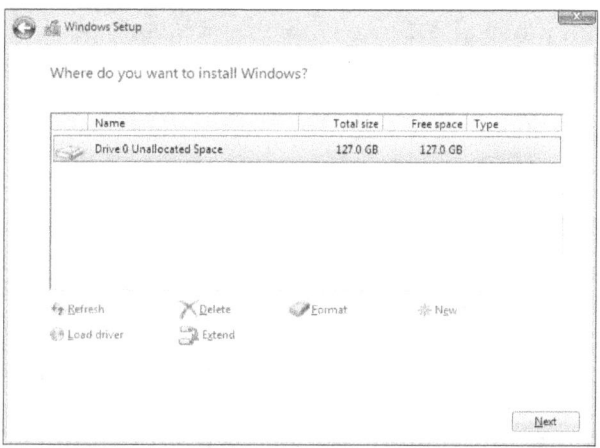

That's it! You will see the server installer start going to town copying files, installing features, and getting everything ready on the hard drive. This part of the installer runs on its own for a few minutes, and the next time you need to interact with the server it will be within the graphical interface where you get to define the administrator password. Once you choose a password, you find yourself on the Windows desktop. Now we are really ready to start making use of our new Windows Server 2016.

Installing roles and features

Installing the operating system itself gets your foot in the door, so to speak, using your server as a server. However, you can't actually do anything useful with your server at this point. On a client desktop system, the base operating system is generally all that is needed in order to start working and consuming data. The server's job is to serve up that data in the first place, and until you tell the server what its purpose is in life, there really isn't anything useful happening in that base operating system. This is where we need to utilize **roles** and **features**. Windows Server 2016 contains many different options for roles.

A role is just what the name implies, the installation of a particular role onto a server defines that server's role in the network. In other words, a role gives a server some purpose in life. A feature, on the other hand, is more of a subset of functions that you can install onto a server. Features can complement particular roles, or stand on their own. They are pieces of technology available in Windows Server 2016 that are not installed or turned on by default, because these features wouldn't be used in all circumstances. Everything in the later chapters of this book revolves around the functionality provided by roles and features. They are the bread and butter of a Windows Server, and without their installation your servers make good paperweights, but not much else. Since we will not be taking the time in each chapter to cover the installation of every particular role or feature that will be used within the chapter, let's take some time right now to cover the most common paths that admins can take in order to get these roles and features installed onto your own servers.

Installing a role using the wizard

Without a doubt, the most common place that roles and features get installed is right inside the graphical wizards available as soon as your operating system has been installed. By default, a tool called **Server Manager** launches automatically every time you log in to Windows Server 2016. We will take a closer look at Server Manager itself coming up shortly in this chapter, but for our purposes here we will simply use it as a launching platform in order to get to our wizard which will guide us through the installation of our first role on this new server we are putting together.

Since you have just logged into this new server, you should be staring at the Server Manager Dashboard. Right in the middle of the Dashboard, you will see some links available to click on, a quick start list of action items numbered one through five. If you haven't already done so, put into place any local server configuration that you may need on this machine through the first link which is called **Configure this local server**. Items that you likely want in place are things such as a permanent hostname for the server, IP addressing, and if you are joining this server to an existing domain, you typically handle that process prior to implementing any new roles on the server. But in our case, we are more specifically interested in the role installation itself, so we will assume that you have already configured these little bits and pieces in order to have your server identified and routing on your network.

Go ahead and click on step 2, **Add roles and features**. Another way you can launch the same wizard is by clicking on the **Manage** menu from the top bar inside Server Manager, and then choosing **Add Roles and Features** from the drop-down list. Selecting either link will bring you into our wizard for installation of the role itself:

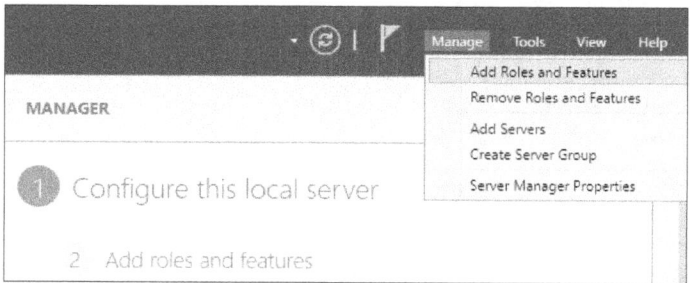

You are first taken to a summary screen about installing roles, go ahead and click on **Next** to bypass this screen. Now we get into our first option, which is an interesting one. We are first asked if we want to continue on with a **Role-based or feature-based installation**, which is exactly what we have been talking about doing. But the second option here, **Remote Desktop Services installation**, is important to note. Most of us consider the **Remote Desktop Services** (**RDS**) components of a Windows Server to be just another role that you can choose when setting up your server, similar to installation of any other role. While that is basically true, it is important to note that RDS is so functionally different from the other kinds of roles that the entry path into installation of any of the RDS components invokes its own wizard, by choosing the second option here. So if you ever find yourself looking for the option to install RDS, and you have glazed over this screen because you are so used to clicking **Next** through it like I am, remember that you need to head back here in order to tell the wizard that you want to deal with an RDS component, and the remainder of the screens will adjust accordingly.

At the moment, I am working on building out a new test lab full of Windows Server 2016 boxes, and I am still in need of a Domain Controller to manage Active Directory in my environment. Prior to installing Active Directory on a server, it is critical that I have a few prerequisites in place, so I have already accomplished those items on my new server. The items that I need to have in place prior to the AD DS role installation are having a static IP address assigned, and making sure that the DNS server setting in my NIC properties points somewhere, even if only to this server's own IP address. I also need to make sure that the hostname of my server is set to its final name, because once you turn it into a Domain Controller it is not supported to change the hostname.

I have already accomplished these items on my server, so I will continue on through my role installation wizard here by leaving the option on for **Role-based or feature-based installation**, and clicking on **Next**:

- **Role-based or feature-based installation**
  Configure a single server by adding roles, role services, and features.

- **Remote Desktop Services installation**
  Install required role services for Virtual Desktop Infrastructure (VDI) to create a virtual machine-based or session-based desktop deployment.

Our **Server Selection** screen is a very powerful one. If you've been through this process before, you have likely glazed over this screen as well, simply clicking on the **Next** button in order to progress through it. But essentially, what this screen is doing is asking you where you would like to install this new role or feature. By default, each server will only have itself listed on this screen, and so clicking on **Next** to continue is more than likely what you will be doing. But there are a couple of neat options here. First of all, if your Server Manager is aware of other servers in your network and has been configured to monitor them, you will have the option here to install a role or feature remotely onto one of the other servers. We will dig a little deeper on this capability coming up shortly. Another feature on this page, which I haven't seen many people utilize, is the ability to specify that you want to install a role or feature onto a virtual hard disk. Many of us work with a majority of virtual servers in this day and age, and you don't even need your virtual server to be running in order to install a role or feature to it! If you have access to the .VHDX file, the hard disk file, from where you are running Server Manager, you can choose this option that will allow you to inject the new role or feature directly into the hard drive. But as is the case with 99% of the times that you will wander through this screen, we are logged directly into the server where we intend to install the role, and so we simply click on **Next**:

Select a server or a virtual hard disk on which to install roles and features.

- Select a server from the server pool
- Select a virtual hard disk

Server Pool

Filter:

Name	IP Address	Operating System
DC1	10.0.0.2	Microsoft Windows Server 2016

Chapter 2

Now we have our list of roles that are available to be installed. Clicking on each role will give you a short description of the purpose of that role if you have any questions, and we will also be talking more about the core infrastructural pieces in our next chapter to give you even more information about what the roles do.
All we need to do here in order to install a role onto our new server is check the box, and click on **Next**. Since this is going to be a Domain Controller, I will choose the **Active Directory Domain Services** role, and I will multipurpose this server to also be a **DNS Server** and a **DHCP Server**. With these roles, there is no need to re-run through this wizard three separate times in order to install all of these roles, I can simply check them all here and let the wizard run the installers together. Whoops, when I clicked on my first checkbox, I got a pop-up message that the
Active Directory Domain Services role requires some additional features in order to work properly. This is normal behavior, and you will notice that many of the roles that you install will require some additional components or features to be installed. All you need to do is click on the **Add Features** button, and it will automatically add in these extra pieces for you during the installation process:

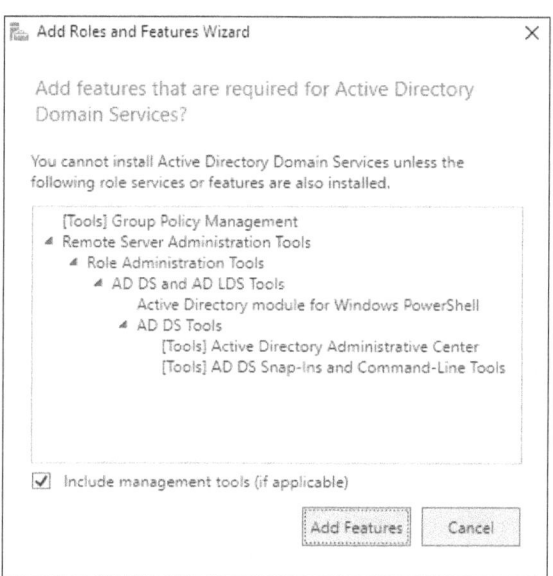

[39]

Installing and Managing Windows Server 2016

Now that we have all three of our roles checked, it's time to click on **Next**. And just to make it clear to all of you readers, I was not required to install all of these roles at the same time, they are not all dependent on each other. It is very common to see these roles all installed onto the same server, but I could split them up onto their own servers if I so desired. In a larger environment, you may have AD DS and DNS installed together, but you might choose to put the DHCP role onto its own servers, and that is just fine. I am configuring this server to support a small lab environment, so for me it makes sense to put these core infrastructure services together in the same box:

```
Roles
    [ ] Active Directory Certificate Services
    [✓] Active Directory Domain Services
    [ ] Active Directory Federation Services
    [ ] Active Directory Lightweight Directory Services
    [ ] Active Directory Rights Management Services
    [✓] DHCP Server
    [✓] DNS Server
    [ ] Fax Server
    [■] File and Storage Services (1 of 12 installed)
    [ ] Host Guardian Service
    [ ] Hyper-V
    [ ] MultiPoint Services
    [ ] Network Controller
    [ ] Network Policy and Access Services
    [ ] Print and Document Services
    [ ] Remote Access
    [ ] Remote Desktop Services
    [ ] Volume Activation Services
    [ ] Web Server (IIS)
    [ ] Windows Deployment Services
```

After clicking on **Next**, we have now landed on the page where we can install additional features to Windows Server 2016. In some cases, you may have originally intended only to add a particular feature, and in these cases, you would have bypassed the role screen altogether, and gone immediately to the features installation screen. Just like with the role installation screen, go ahead and check off any features that you would like to install, and click on **Next** again. For our new Domain Controller, we do not currently require any additional features to be specifically added, so I will just finish out the wizard which starts the installation of our new roles.

After the installation process has been completed, you may or may not be prompted to restart the server, depending on which roles or features you installed and whether or not they require a restart. Once you have landed back inside Server Manager, you will notice that you are now being prompted near the top with a yellow exclamation mark.

Clicking here displays messages about further configurations that may be required in order to complete the setup of your new roles and make them live on the server. For example, in order to finish turning my server into a Domain Controller, I need to run through a promotion process to define my domain, or to specify a domain which I want to join. There are also some loose ends, which I also need to wrap up for putting DHCP into action:

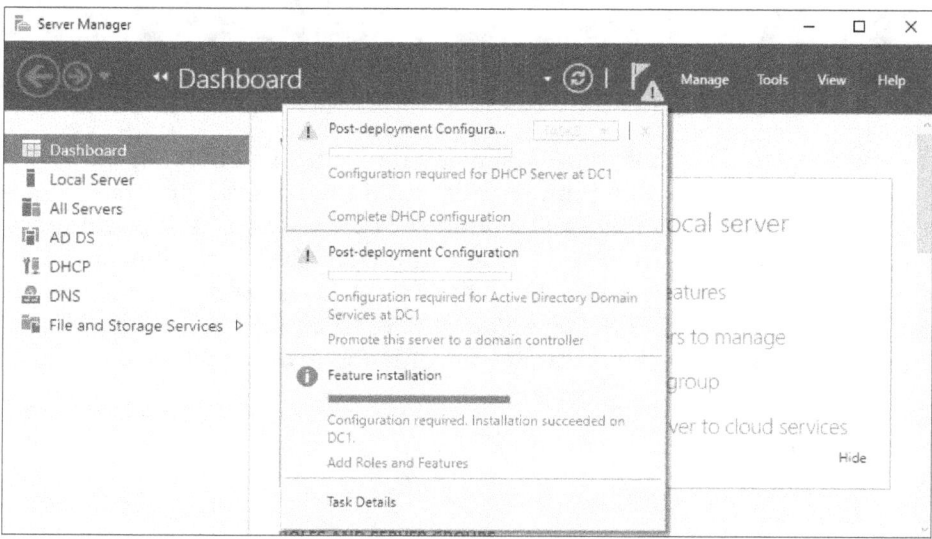

Installing a feature using PowerShell

Now that you have seen the graphical wizards for installing roles and features, you could certainly always use them in order to put these components into place on your servers. But Microsoft has put a big effort into creating a Windows Server environment where almost anything within the operating system can be manipulated using PowerShell, and the addition of roles and features is certainly included in those capabilities. Let's take a look at the appropriate commands we can use to manipulate roles and features on our server right from a PowerShell prompt. We will view the available list of roles and features, and we will also issue a command to install a quick feature onto our server.

Installing and Managing Windows Server 2016

Open up an elevated PowerShell prompt, and use the following command to view all of the available roles and features that we can install onto our server. It will also show you which ones are currently installed:

`Get-WindowsFeature`

```
Windows PowerShell
Copyright (C) 2015 Microsoft Corporation. All rights reserved.

PS C:\Users\Administrator> Get-WindowsFeature

Display Name                                          Name                          Install State
------------                                          ----                          -------------
[ ] Active Directory Certificate Services             AD-Certificate                    Available
    [ ] Certification Authority                       ADCS-Cert-Authority               Available
    [ ] Certificate Enrollment Policy Web Service     ADCS-Enroll-Web-Pol               Available
    [ ] Certificate Enrollment Web Service            ADCS-Enroll-Web-Svc               Available
    [ ] Certification Authority Web Enrollment        ADCS-Web-Enrollment               Available
    [ ] Network Device Enrollment Service             ADCS-Device-Enrollment            Available
    [ ] Online Responder                              ADCS-Online-Cert                  Available
[X] Active Directory Domain Services                  AD-Domain-Services                Installed
[ ] Active Directory Federation Services              ADFS-Federation                   Available
```

What I would like to do on this server is install the Telnet Client feature. I use Telnet Client pretty regularly for testing network connections, so it is helpful to have on this machine. Unfortunately, my PowerShell window currently has pages and pages of different roles and features in it, and I'm not sure what the exact name of the Telnet Client feature is in order to install it. So, let's run `Get-WindowsFeature` again, but this time let's use some additional syntax in the command to pare down the amount of information being displayed. I want to see only the features which begin with the letters `"TEL"`:

`Get-WindowsFeature -Name TEL*`

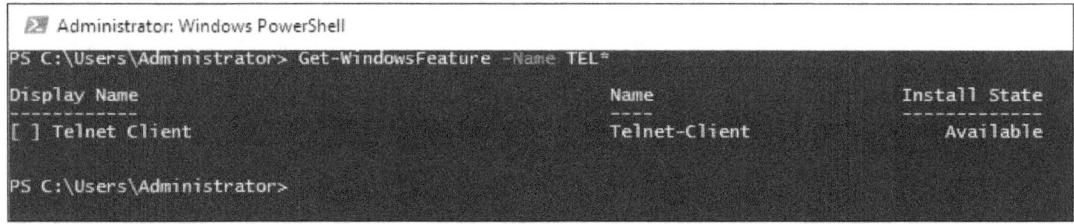

Chapter 2

There it is! Okay, so now that I know the correct name of the feature, let's run the command to install it:

`Add-WindowsFeature Telnet-Client`

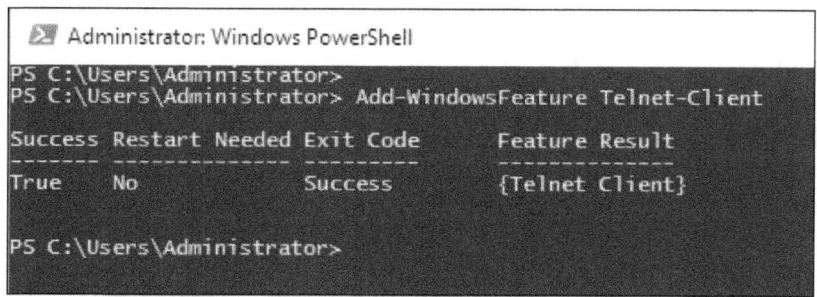

One last thing to show you here, there is also a way to manipulate the `Get-WindowsFeature` cmdlet in order to quickly show which roles and features are currently installed on a server. Typing `Get-WindowsFeature | Where Installed` presents us with a list of the currently installed components. If I run that on my Domain Controller, you can see all the parts and pieces of my roles for AD DS, DNS, and DHCP:

[43]

Centralized management and monitoring

Whether you are installing new roles, running backups and maintenance programs, or troubleshooting and repairing a server, it makes sense that you would log in to the specific server that you will be working on. Long ago this meant walking up to the server itself and logging on with the keyboard and mouse which were plugged right into that hardware. Then, quite a number of years ago, this became cumbersome and since technology had advanced to the point where we had the **Remote Desktop Protocol (RDP)** available to us, we quickly transitioned over to logging in to our servers remotely using RDP. Even though it's been around for many years, RDP is still an incredibly powerful protocol, giving us the ability to quickly connect to servers from the comfort of our desk. And as long as you have proper network topology and routing in place, you can work on a server halfway around the world just as quickly as one sitting in the cubicle next to you.

In fact, I just recently read that mining rights were being granted in outer space. Talk about a co-location for your datacenter! Maybe someday we will be using RDP to connect to servers in outer space. While this might be a stretch in our lifetime, I do have the opportunity to work with dozens of new companies every year and while there are some other tools available for remotely managing your server infrastructure, RDP is the platform of choice for 99% of us out there.

Why talk about RDP? Because I will now tell you that Windows Server 2016 includes some tools, which make it much less necessary to our day-to-day workflow. The idea of centralized management in the server world has been growing through the last few Windows Server operating system rollouts. Most of us have so many servers running that checking in with them all daily would consume way too much time. We need some tools that we can utilize to make our management and monitoring, and even configuration processes, more efficient in order to free up time for more important projects.

Server Manager

If you have worked on a Windows Server recently, you are familiar with the idea that logging in to one of your servers automatically invokes this big window on top of the desktop. This auto-launching program is **Server Manager**. As the name implies, it's here to help you manage your server. So, in my experience, the majority of the server administrators do not utilize Server Manager. Instead, they close it as fast as they can and curse at it under their breath, because it's been popping up and annoying them during every server login for the past 5 years.

Chapter 2

Stop doing that! It's here to help, I promise. Here's a quick screenshot of the default view of Server Manager on my new Domain Controller:

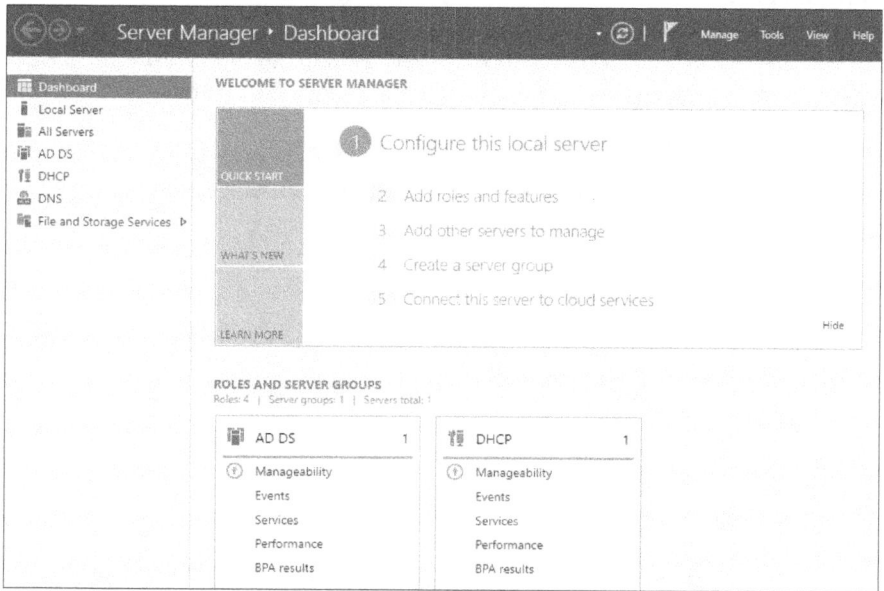

What I like about this opening automatically is that it gives me a quick look into what is currently installed on the server. Looking at the column on the left side shows you the list of roles installed and available for management. Clicking on each of these roles brings you into some more particular configuration and options for the role itself. I often find myself hopping back and forth between many different servers while working on a project, and by leaving Server Manager open it gives me a quick way of double-checking that I am working on the server, which I intend to. The **Roles and Server Groups** section at the bottom is also very interesting. You might not be able to see the colors in the picture, but this gives you a very quick view into whether or not the services running on this server are functioning properly. Right now, both my **AD DS** and **DHCP** functions are running normally, I have a nice green bar running through them. But if anything was amiss with either of these roles, it would be flagged bright red, and I could click on any of the links listed under those role headings in order to track down what the trouble is.

Installing and Managing Windows Server 2016

Up near the top-right corner you see a few menus, the most useful of which, to me, is the **Tools** menu. Click on that, and you see a list of all the available **Administrative Tools** to launch on this server. Yes, this is essentially the same Administrative Tools folder that has existed in each of the previous versions of Windows Server, now stored in a different location. Based on my experience, Server Manager is now the easiest way to access this myriad of tools all from a single location:

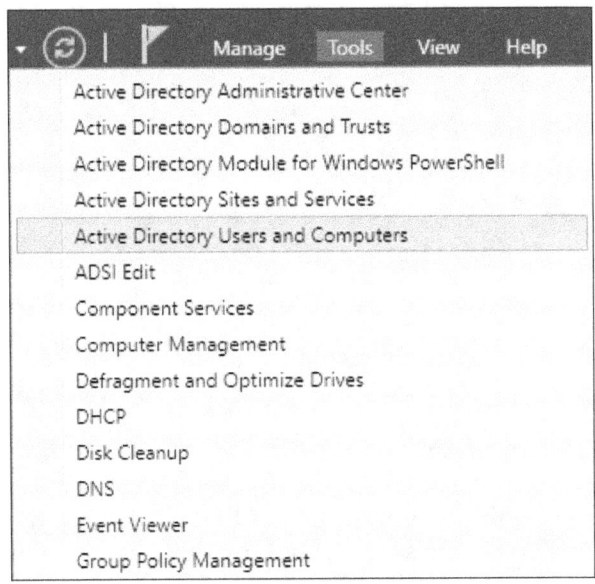

So far the functions inside Server Manager that we have discussed are available on any Windows Server 2016, whether it is standalone or part of a domain. Everything we have been doing is only dealing with the local server that we are logged into. Now, let's explore what options are available to us in Server Manager for centralization of management across multiple servers. The new mentality of managing many servers from a single server is often referred to as "managing from a single pane of glass". We will use Server Manager on one of our servers in the network in order to make connections to additional servers, and after doing that we should have much more information inside Server Manager that we can use to keep tabs on all of those servers.

Chapter 2

Front and center inside the Server Manager console is the section titled **Welcome to Server Manager**. Under that we have a series of steps or links that can be clicked on. The first one lets you configure settings that are specific only to this local server. We have already done some work with the second step when we added a new role to our server. Now we will test out the third step, **Add other servers to manage**. By the way, this same function can also be called by clicking on the **Manage** menu at the top, and then choosing **Add Servers**:

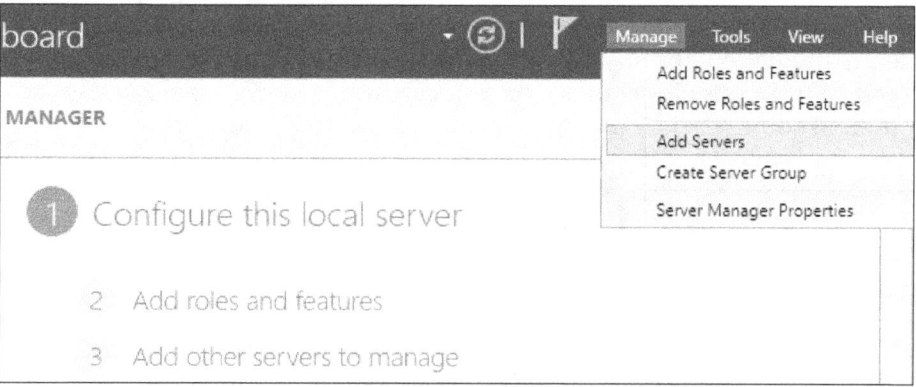

Most of you will be working within a domain environment where the servers are all domain joined, which makes this next part really easy. Simply click on the **Find Now** button, and the machines available within your network will be displayed. From here, you can choose the servers that you want to manage, and move them over to the **Selected** column on the right:

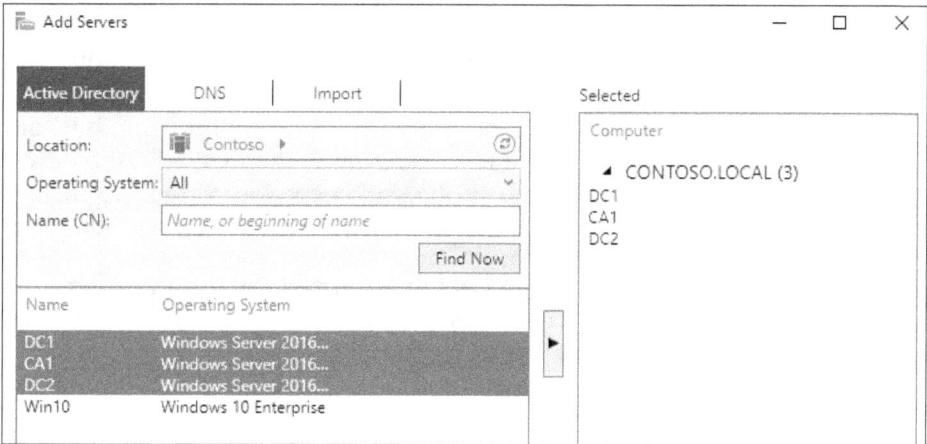

After clicking on **OK**, you will see that Server Manager has transformed in order to give you more information about all of these servers and roles that are installed on them. Now, when you log in to this single server, you immediately see critical maintenance information about all of the systems that you have chosen to add in here. You could even use a separate server, which is only intended for the purposes of this management. For example, I am currently logged into a brand new server called CA1. I do not have any roles installed onto this server, so by default Server Manager looks pretty basic. As soon as I add other servers to manage, I choose my Domain Controllers. My Server Manager on the CA1 server now contains all of the detail about CA1 and my Domain Controllers, so I can view all facets of my infrastructure from this single pane. As you can see, I even have some flags here indicating that some services are not running properly within my infrastructure:

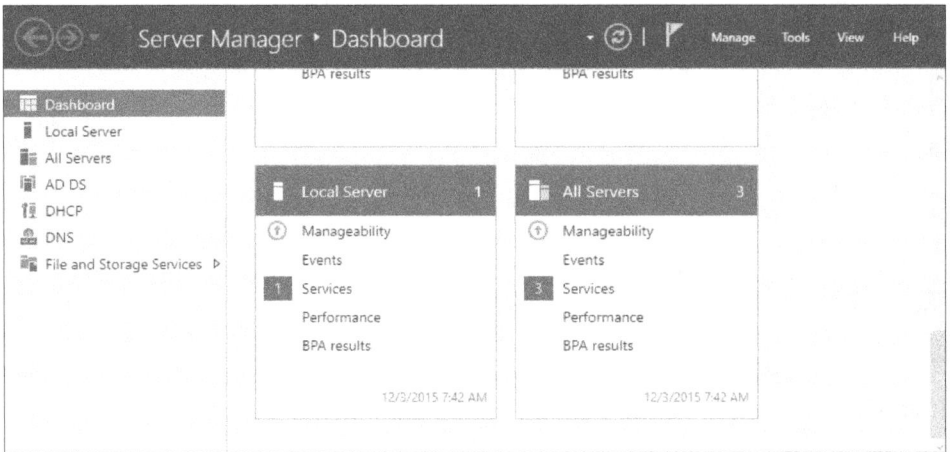

Clicking on the **All Servers** link, or into one of the specific roles, gives you even more comprehensive information collected from these remote servers. Adding multiple servers into Server Manager is not only useful for monitoring, but for future configurations as well. You remember a few pages ago when we added a new role using the wizard? That process has now evolved to become more comprehensive, since we have now "tapped" this server into our other servers in the network.

If I now choose to add a new role, when I get to the screen asking me where I want to install that role, I see that I can choose to install a new role or feature onto one of my other servers, even though I am not working from the console of those servers:

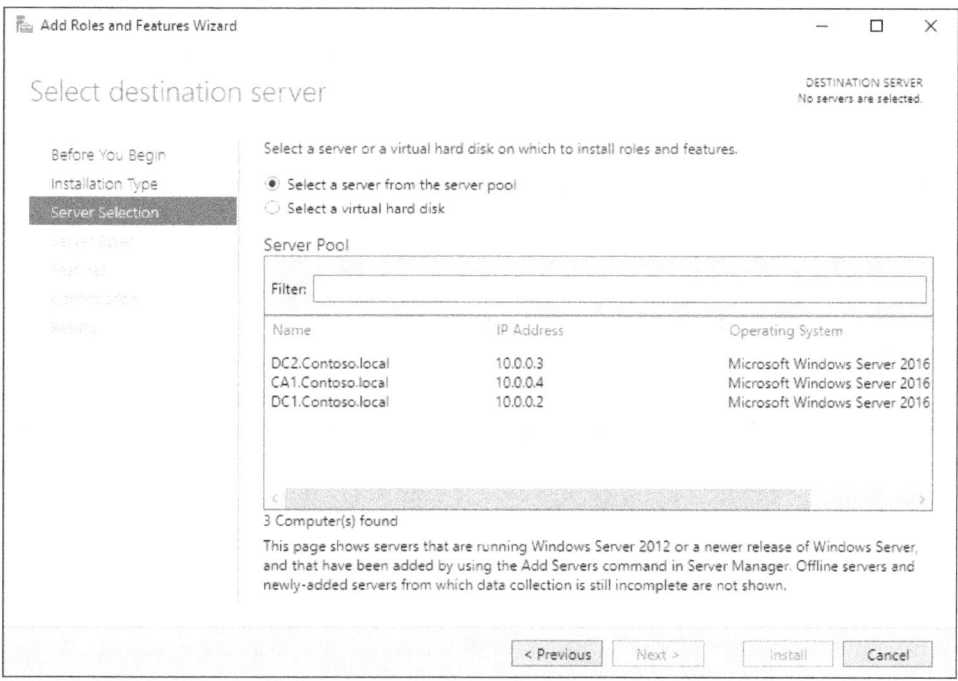

Remote Server Administration Tools

Using Server Manager in order to log in to a single server and have access to manage and monitor all of your servers is pretty handy, but what if we could take one more step out of that process? Wouldn't it make sense if all of these Windows Server boxes could be managed remotely straight from our desktop computer in our office? And we never have to log in to a server in the first place? Yes, that is exactly what we can do.

This is possible by downloading and installing something from Microsoft called the **Remote Server Administration Tools (RSAT)**. I have a Windows 10 regular client computer online and running in our network, also domain joined. The first step is to download this tool, I grabbed it from `https://www.microsoft.com/en-us/download/details.aspx?id=45520`.

After running the installer on my Windows 10 client computer, I can't seem to find any program that is called the Remote Server Administration Tools. That would be correct. Even though the name of this when downloading and installing is RSAT, after installation the program that is actually placed on your computer is called **Server Manager**. This makes sense, except that if you don't realize the name discrepancy, it can take you a few minutes to figure out why you cannot find what you just installed.

So, go ahead and launch Server Manager by finding it in the Start menu, or by using the search bar, or even by saying "Hey Cortana, open Server Manager". Sorry, had to throw that in there. But whatever your method, open up Server Manager on your desktop computer and you will see that it looks and feels just like Server Manager in Windows Server 2016. And in the same way that you work with and manipulate it within the server operating system, you can take the same steps here in order to add your servers for management. In the following screenshot, you can see that within my Windows 10 Server Manager, I now have access to manage and monitor all of the servers in my lab, without even having to log in to them:

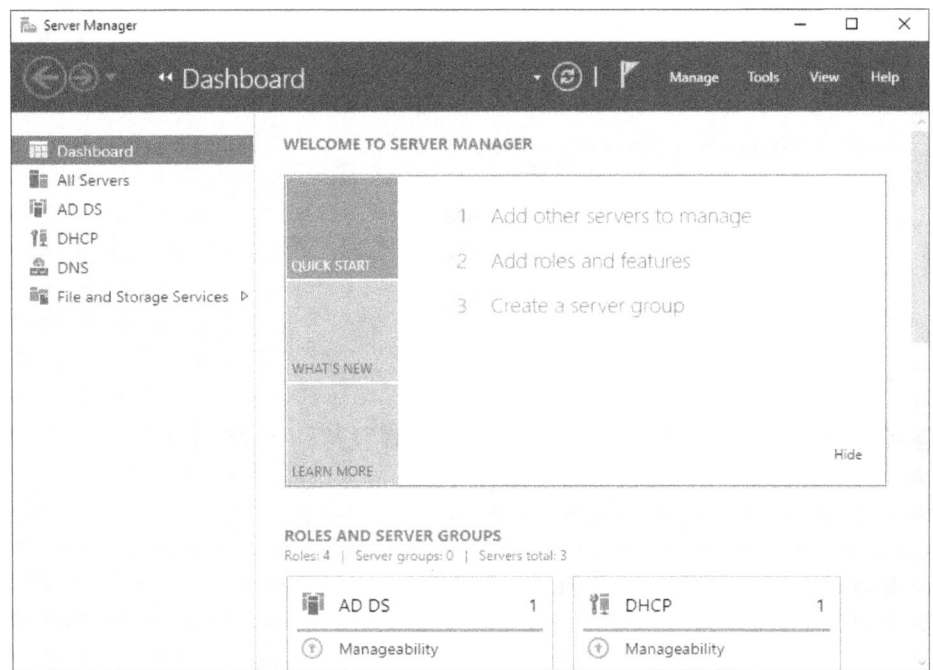

Azure Server Management Tools

Expanding on our last idea of Remote Server Administration Tools, there is a new server management platform coming very soon that will make the word "centralized" take on a whole new meaning. If you have an Azure subscription, you will notice that there is a new toolset when you login called SMT. Server Management Tools is a web-based, centralized server management system that you can access from anywhere. Logging into Azure is as simple as finding a web browser on any computer, anywhere, and so now having remote management capabilities of all your servers is just as easy. The Azure SMT is a free feature of your Azure subscription, so don't start groaning about costs. Simply login, enable the feature, and start using it!

Is SMT only for virtual servers that are running inside Azure? No way! There is an SMT Gateway function that you can install onto a machine running inside your corporate network that has the ability to send server details up into Azure. This way you can manage both your Azure-hosted servers, as well as your on-premise servers, right from the same online SMT interface. The Gateway box does not have any edge or firewall considerations, it is only ever sending data outbound toward Azure. This powerful combination of the Gateway and SMT tools means that you can have full remote management over all of your servers from a single browser session that you are running on any computer, anywhere. While still waiting to be officially released for public preview, I imagine that this will quickly turn into a primary administrative tool for many server admins out there. Perhaps the biggest benefit of SMT is that it gives you a graphical interface for interacting with your Server Core and Nano Servers, which will be critical to the adoption of those headless server platforms.

Does this mean RDP is dead?

With these new and improved ways to manage the underlying components of your servers without having to log in to them directly, does this mean that our age-old friend RDP is going away? Certainly not! We will still have the need for accessing our servers directly sometimes, even if we go all-in with using the newer management tools. And I also expect that many administrators out there will continue using RDP and full desktop-based access for all management and monitoring of their servers simply because that is what they are more comfortable with even if newer, more efficient ways now exist to accomplish the same tasks.

Remote Desktop Connection Manager

Since most of us do still utilize RDP occasionally (or often) when bouncing around between our servers, let's take a quick look at a tool that can at least make this task more manageable and centralized. I won't spend a lot of time looking over individual features or capabilities of this tool, since it is a client-side tool and not something that is specific to Windows Server 2016. You can use this to handle RDP connections for any and all of your servers, or even all of the client computers in your network. However, the **Remote Desktop Connection Manager** is an incredibly useful platform for storing all of the different RDP connections that you make within your environment. You can save connections so that you don't have to spend time trying to remember server names, sort servers into categories, and even store credentials so that you don't have to type passwords when connecting to servers. Though a disclaimer should come with that one, your security folks may not be happy if you choose to employ the password storing feature.

I will leave you with a link for downloading the application, `https://www.microsoft.com/en-us/download/details.aspx?id=44989`, as well as a quick screenshot and then leave it up to you to decide whether or not this tool would be helpful in your daily tasks:

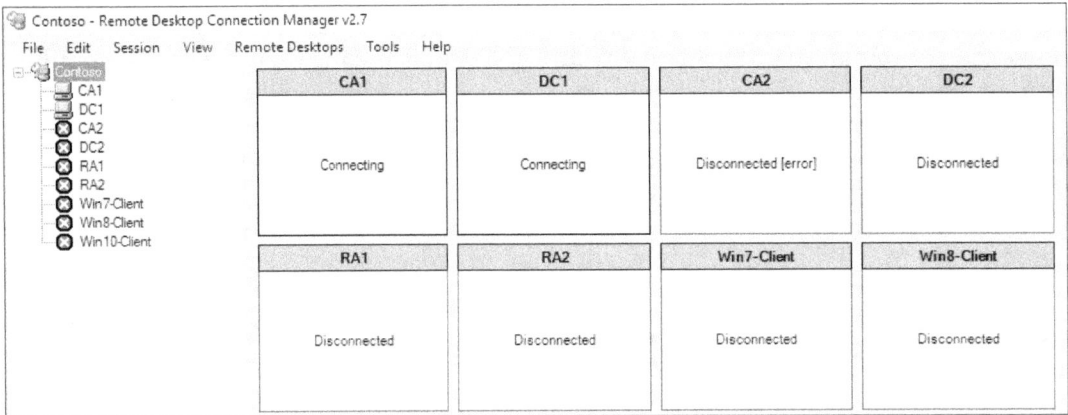

Sysprep enables quick server rollouts

At the beginning of this chapter, we walked through the process for installing the Windows Server 2016 operating system onto your new server. Whether this was a physical piece of hardware or a virtual machine that we were working with, the installation process is essentially the same. Plugging in the CD, booting to it, and letting the installer run its course is an easy enough thing to do, but what if you needed to build out ten new servers instead of just one? This process would start to get tedious in a hurry, and it would seem like you were wasting a lot of time having to do the exact same thing over and over again.

You would be correct, this does waste a lot of time, and there is an easier and faster way to roll out new servers as long as you are building them all from a relatively similar hardware platform. If you are building out your servers as virtual machines, which is so often the case these days, then this process works great and can save you quite a bit of time with new server builds.

Now, before I go too far down this road of describing the sysprep process, I will also note that there are more involved technologies available within the Windows infrastructure that allows automated operating system and server rollouts that can make the new server rollout process even easier than what I am describing here. The problem with some of the automated technologies is that the infrastructure required to make them work properly is more advanced than many folks will have access to if they are just learning the ropes with Windows Server.

In other words, to have a fully automated server rollout mechanism isn't very feasible for small environments or test labs, which is where a lot of us live while we are learning these new technologies.

So anyway, we will not be focusing on an automation kind of approach to server rollouts, but rather we will be doing a few minutes of extra work on our very first server, which then results in saving numerous minutes of setup work on every server that we build afterwards. The core of this process is the **sysprep** tool, which is baked into all versions of Windows, so you can take this same process on any current Windows machine, whether it be a client or a server.

Sysprep is a tool that prepares your system for duplication. Its official name is the **Microsoft System Preparation Tool**, and to sum up what it does in one line, it allows you to create a master "image" of your server that you can reuse as many times as you want in order to roll out additional servers. A key benefit to using sysprep is that you can put customized settings onto your master server and install things such as Windows Updates prior to sysprep, and all of these settings and patches will then exist inside your master image. Using sysprep saves you time by not having to walk through the operating system installation process, but it saves you even more time with not having to wait for Windows Updates to roll all of the current patches down onto every new system that you create. Now, some of you might be wondering why sysprep is even necessary. If you wanted to clone your master server, you could simply use a hard disk imaging tool, or if you were dealing with virtual machines you could simply copy and paste the .VHDX file itself in order to make a copy of your new server, right? The answer is yes, but the big problem is that the new image or hard drive that you just created would be an exact replica of the original one. The hostname would be the same, and more importantly some core identification information in Windows, such as the SID, would be exactly the same. If you were to turn on both the original master server and a new server based off this exact replica, you would cause conflicts and collisions on the network as these two servers fight for their right to be the one and only server with that unique name and SID.

This problem exacerbates itself in domain environments, where it is even more important that each system within your network has a unique SID/GUID, their identifier within Active Directory. If you create exact copies of servers and have them both online, let's just say neither one is going to be happy about it.

Sysprep fixes all of these inherent problems of the system duplication process by randomizing the unique identifiers in the operating system. In order to prepare ourselves to roll out many servers using a master image we create with sysprep, here is a quick-reference summary of the steps we will be taking:

1. Install Windows Server 2016 onto a new server.
2. Configure customizations and updates onto your new server.

3. Run sysprep to prepare and shut down your master server.
4. Create your master image of the drive.
5. Build new servers using copies of the master image.

And now let's cover these steps in a little more detail.

Installing Windows Server 2016 onto a new server

First, just like you have already done, we need to prepare our first server by getting the Windows Server 2016 operating system installed. Refrain from installing any full roles onto the server, because depending on the role or its unique configuration, the sysprep process that we run shortly could cause problems for individual role configurations. Install the operating system and make sure device drivers are all squared away, and you're ready for the next step.

Configuring customizations and updates onto your new server

Next, you want to configure customizations and install updates onto your new server. Each setting or installation that you can do now that is universal to your batch of servers will save you from having to take that step on your servers in the future. This portion may be slightly confusing because I just told you a minute ago not to install roles onto the master server. This is because a role installation makes numerous changes to the operating system, and some of the roles that you can install lock themselves down to a particular hostname running on the system. If you were to do something like that to a master server, that role would more than likely break when brought up on a new server.

Customizations that you can put into place on the master server are things such as plugging in files and folders that you might want on all of your servers, such as an `Admin Tools` folder or something like that. You could also start or stop services that you may or may not want running on each of your servers, and change settings in the registry if that is part of your normal server prep or hardening process. Whatever changes or customizations that you put into place, it's not a bad idea to run a full slew of tests against the first new server that you build from this master image, just to make sure all of your changes made it through the sysprep process.

Now is also the time to let Windows Updates install and to put any patches on this new server that you want to be installed on all of your new servers in the future. There is nothing more frustrating than installing a new operating system in 5 minutes, only to have to sit around and wait 4 hours for all of the current updates and patches to be installed before you can use a new server. By including all of these updates and patches in the master image, you save all of that download and installation time for each new server that you spin up.

> Continue to save yourself time and effort by creating new copies of your master images every few months. This way the newest patches are always included in your master image and it continues to save you more and more time throughout the life of Windows Server 2016.

Running sysprep to prepare and shut down your master server

Now that our master server is prepped how we want, it is time to run the sysprep tool itself. To do that, open up an administrative command prompt and browse to `C:\Windows\System32\Sysprep`. Now you can make use of the `Sysprep.exe` utility inside that folder in order to launch **Sysprep** itself.

As with many executables that you run from command prompt, there are a variety of optional switches that you can tag onto the end of your command in order to make it do specific tasks. From your command prompt window, if you simply run the `sysprep.exe` command, you will see a graphical interface for sysprep, where you can choose between the available options:

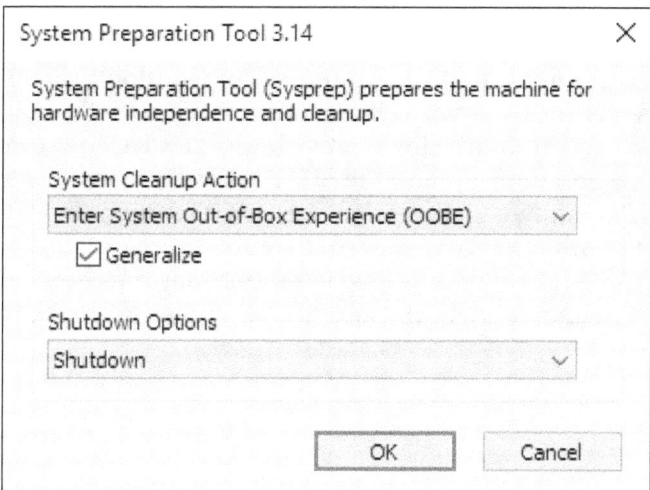

Since I always use the same set of options for sysprep, I find it easier to simply include all of my optional switches right from the command-line input, therefore bypassing the graphical screen altogether. Here is some information on the different switches that are available to use with `Sysprep.exe`:

- `/quiet`: This tells sysprep to run without status messages on the screen.
- `/generalize`: This specifies that sysprep is to remove all of the unique system information (SID) from the Windows installation, making the final image usable on multiple machines in your network, because each new one spun up from the image will get a new, unique SID.
- `/audit`: This restarts the machine into a special audit mode, where you have the option of adding additional drivers into Windows before the final image gets taken.
- `/oobe`: This tells the machine to launch the mini-setup wizard when Windows next boots.
- `/reboot`: This restarts when sysprep is finished.
- `/shutdown`: This shuts down the system (not a restart) when sysprep is finished. This is an important one and is one that I typically use.
- `/quit`: This closes sysprep after it finishes.
- `/unattend`: There is a special `answerfile` that you can create that, when specified, will be used in conjunction with the sysprep process to further configure your new servers as they come online. For example, you can specify in this `answerfile` that a particular installer or batch file is to be launched upon first Windows boot following sysprep. This can be useful for any kind of cleanup tasks that you might want to perform, for example, if you had a batch file on your system that you used to flush out the log files following the first boot of new servers.

The two that are most important to our purposes of wanting to create a master image file that we can use for quick server rollouts in the future are the `/generalize` switch and the `/shutdown` switch. Generalize is very important because it replaces all of the unique identification information, the SID info, in the new copies of Windows that come online. This allows your new servers to co-exist on the network with your original server, and with other new servers that you bring online. The shutdown switch is also very important, because we want this master server to become sysprepped and then immediately shutdown so that we can create our master image from it.

>  Make sure that your server does NOT boot into Windows again until after you have created your master image, or taken your master copy of the .VHDX file. The first time that Windows boots it will inject the new SID information, and you want that only to happen on new servers that you have created based off your new image.

So rather than simply throwing all of the switches at you and letting you decide, let's take a look at the ones that I typically use. I will make use of /generalize so that I make my new servers unique, and I also like to use /oobe so that the mini-setup wizard launches during the first boot of Windows on any of my new systems. Then, I will of course also use /shutdown, because I need this server to be offline immediately following sysprep so that I can take a copy of the hard drive to be used as my master image. So here is my fully groomed sysprep command:

`Sysprep.exe /generalize /oobe /shutdown`

After launching this command, you will see sysprep moving through some processes within Windows, and after a couple of minutes, your server will shut itself down:

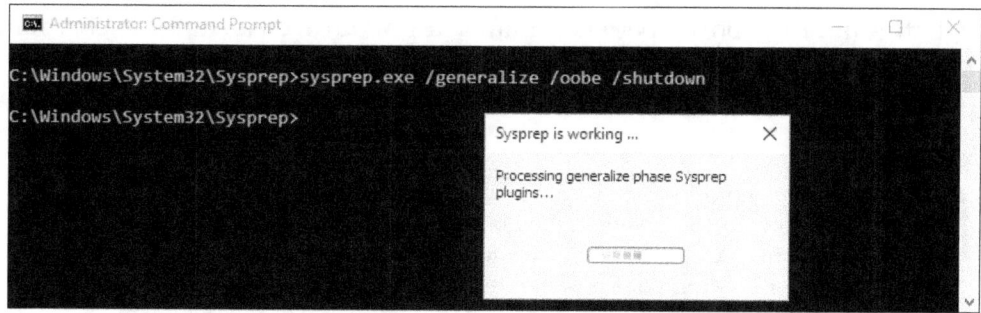

You are now ready to create your master image from this hard disk.

Creating your master image of the drive

Our master server has now shut down, and we are ready to create our master image from this server. If it is a physical server, you can use any hard disk imaging utility in order to create an image file from the drive. An imaging utility like those from the company Acronis will create a single file from your drive, this file contains an image of the entire disk that you can use to restore down onto fresh hard drives in new servers in the future. On the other hand, most of you are probably dealing with virtual servers most often in your day to day work lives, and prepping new servers in the virtual world is even easier. Once our master server has been sysprepped and shutdown, you simply create a copy of the .VHDX file. Log in to your Hyper-V server, copy and paste the hard disk file, and you're done.

This new file can be renamed `WS2016_Master_withUpdates.VHDX` or whatever you would like it to be named in order to help you keep track of the current status on this image file. Save this image file or copy of the .VHDX somewhere safe on your network, where you will be able to quickly grab copies of it whenever you have the need to spin up a new Windows Server 2016.

Building new servers using copies of the master image

Now we get to the easy part. When you want to create new servers in the future, you simply copy and paste your master file into a new location for the new server, rename the drive file to be something appropriate for the server you are creating, and boot your new virtual machine from it. Here is where you see the real benefit for the time that sysprep saves, as you can now spin up many new servers all at the same time, by doing a quick copy-paste of the master image file and booting all of your new servers from these new files.

As the new servers turn on for the first time and boot into Windows, they will run through the out-of-the-box-experience, mini-setup wizard. Also, in the background, the operating system gives itself a new random and unique hostname and SID information so that you can be sure you do not have conflicts on your network with these new servers.

> New servers created from a sysprepped image file always receive a new hostname when they boot. This often confuses admins who might have named their master server something like `MASTER`. After booting your new servers, you can expect to see randomized names on your new servers and you will have to rename them according to their new duties in life.

For example, before running sysprep and creating my master image, the server that I was working on was named `DC1` because I had originally intended to use it as a Domain Controller in my network. However, because I had not installed the role or configured anything domain related on it, this server was a perfect candidate for displaying the sysprep process and so I used it in our text today. You can now see inside the sysprep properties that I am back to having a randomized hostname, and so if I still want to use this server as `DC1`, I will have to rename it again now that it has finished booting through mini-setup:

Computer name, domain, and workgroup settings		
Computer name:	WIN-HM6LA537F59	🛡 Change settings
Full computer name:	WIN-HM6LA537F59	
Computer description:		
Workgroup:	WORKGROUP	

Hopefully, this process is helpful information that can save you time when building out new servers in your own environments. Get out there and give it a try the next time you have a new server to build! You can further benefit yourself with the sysprep tool by keeping many different master image files. Perhaps you have a handful of different kinds of servers that you prep regularly, there is nothing stopping you from creating a number of different master servers, and creating multiple master images from these servers.

Summary

Anyone interested in being a Windows Server administrator needs to be comfortable with installing and managing their servers, and covering those topics establishes an important baseline for moving forward. It is quite common in today's IT world for new operating system releases to be thoroughly tested, both because server hardware resources are so easily available to us through virtualization technologies, and because most business systems are now being designed for 100% uptime. This kind of reliability requires very thorough testing of any platform changes, and in order to accomplish such testing of the Windows Server 2016 operating system in your environment, you will be burning quite a bit of time spinning through the basic installation processes numerous times. I hope that you can put the suggestions provided in this chapter to good use in saving you precious extra minutes when dealing with these tasks in your Windows Server world.

Years ago quite a bit of effort was regularly put into figuring out which roles and services could co-exist, because the number of servers available to us was limited. With the new virtualization and cloud paradigm shift, many companies have virtually unlimited number of servers that can be running, and this means we are running much larger quantities of servers to perform the same jobs and functions. Management and administration of these servers then becomes an IT burden, and adopting the centralized administration tools and ideas available within Windows Server 2016 will also save you considerable time and effort in your daily workload.

3
Core Infrastructure Services

Each of you reading this book is going to have a different acquired skillset and level of experience with the Windows Server environment. As I mentioned previously, being able to make servers run the operating system is great and a very important first step to doing real work in your environment, but until you know and understand what the purposes are behind the main roles available to run on Windows Server 2016, the only thing your new server is doing is consuming electricity.

A server is intended to serve data. The kinds of data that it serves and to what purpose depend entirely on what roles you determine the server must, well, serve. Appropriately, you must install roles within Windows Server 2016 to make it do something. We already know how to get roles installed onto our server, but have not talked about any of the purpose behind these roles. In this chapter, we will take a look at the core infrastructural roles available within Windows Server. This involves discussing the role's general purpose, as well as plugging in some particular tasks dealing with those roles that you will be responsible for doing in your daily tasks as a server administrator. We will also cover new functions that are part of those roles which are being introduced with Windows Server 2016 in particular:

- What is a domain controller?
- Using AD DS to organize your network
- The power of Group Policy
- DNS overview
- DHCP versus static addressing
- Backup and restore
- MMC and MSC shortcuts

What is a domain controller?

If we are going to discuss the core infrastructure services that you need in order to piece together your Microsoft-driven network, there is no better place to start than the domain controller role. A **domain controller**, commonly referred to as a **DC**, is the central point of contact, sort of a central hub that is accessed prior to almost any network communication that takes place. The easiest way to describe it is a storage container for all identification that happens on the network. Usernames, passwords, computer accounts, groups of computers, servers, groups and collections of servers, security policies, file replication services, and many more things are stored within and managed by DCs. If you are not planning to have a domain controller be one of the first servers in your Microsoft-centric network, you might as well not even start building that network. They are essential to the way that our computers and devices communicate with each other and with the server infrastructure inside our companies.

If you've stopped reading at this point in order to go install the domain controller role onto your server, welcome back because there is no role called domain controller. The role that provides all of these capabilities is called **Active Directory Domain Services**, or **AD DS**. This is the role that you need to install on a server. By installing that role, you will have turned your server into a domain controller. The purpose of running a DC really is to create this directory, or database, of items in your network. This database is known as **Active Directory**, and is a platform inside which you build a hierarchical structure to store objects, such as usernames, passwords, and computer accounts.

Once you have created a domain in which you can store these accounts and devices, you can then create user accounts and passwords for your employees to utilize for authentication. You then also join your other servers and computers to this domain so that they can accept and benefit from those user credentials. Having and joining a domain is the secret sauce that allows you to walk from computer to computer within your company and log onto each of them with your own username and password, even when you have never logged into that computer before. Even more powerful is the fact that it enables directory-capable applications to authenticate directly against Active Directory when they need authentication information. For example, when I, as a domain user, log in to my computer at work with my username and password, the Windows running on my computer reaches out to a domain controller server and verifies that my password is correct. Once it confirms that I really am who I say I am, it issues an authentication token back to my computer and I am able to log in. Then, once I am into my desktop and I open an application, let's say I open my Outlook to access my e-mail, that e-mail program is designed to reach out to my e-mail server, called an Exchange Server, and authenticate against it to make sure that my own mailbox is displayed and not somebody else's. Does this mean I need to re-enter my username and password for Outlook, or for any other application that I open from my computer? No. And the reason I do not have to re-enter my credentials over and over is because my username, my computer, and the application servers, are all part of the domain. When this is true, and it is for most networks, my authentication token can be shared among my programs. So, once I log in to the computer itself, my applications are able to launch and open, and pass my credentials through to the application server, without any further input from me as a user. It would be quite a frustrating experience indeed if we required our users to enter passwords all day, every day as they opened up the programs that they need in order to do their work.

The first domain controller you set up in your network will be a fully writeable one, able to accept data from the domain-joined users and computers working within your network. In fact, most DCs in your network will likely be fully functional. However, it's worth taking a quick minute to point out a limited-scope DC that can be installed called a **Read-only domain controller** (**RODC**). Just like the name implies, an RODC can only have its directory data read from it. Writes that might try to be accomplished to the domain-like password changes or new user account creations are impossible with an RODC. Where would a limited-access domain controller like this be beneficial? Many companies are installing them into smaller branch offices or less secure sites, so that the local computers onsite in those smaller offices still have quick and easy access to read from and authenticate to the domain, without the potential security risk of an unauthorized user gaining access to the physical server and manipulating the entire domain in bad ways.

Active Directory itself is a broad enough topic to warrant its own book, and indeed there have been many written on the topic. Now that we have a basic understanding of what it is and why it's critical to have in our Windows Server environment, let's get our hands dirty using some of the tools that get installed onto your domain controller during the AD DS role installation process.

Using AD DS to organize your network

There is not a single tool that is used to manage all facets of Active Directory. Since it is such an expansive technology, our configuration of the directory is spread across a number of different management consoles. Let's take a look at each of them, and a couple of the most common tasks that you will be performing inside these tools. Any of these management consoles can be launched from any of your domain controller servers, and just like we looked at in a previous chapter, the easiest way to launch these consoles are right from the **Tools** menu in the upper-right corner of **Server Manager**.

Active Directory Users and Computers

I'll start with the tool that is alphabetically last in the list of our Active Directory tools, because this is by far the one which the everyday server administrator will use most often. AD Users and Computers is the console from which all of the user accounts and computer accounts are created and managed. Open it up, and you will see the name of your domain listed in the left column. Expand your domain name, and you see a number of folders listed here. If you are opening this on an existing domain controller in a well-grown network, you may have pages and pages of folders listed here. If this is a new environment, there are only a handful. The most important to point out there are **Computers** and **Users**. As common sense would dictate, these are the default containers in which new computer accounts and user accounts that join the domain will be located.

While this window looks quite a bit like File Explorer with a tree of folders, these "folders" really aren't folders at all. Each manila colored folder icon that you see here is known as an **Organizational Unit (OU)**. OUs are the structural containers that we use inside Active Directory in order to organize our objects and keep them all in senseful places. Just like with folders on a file server, you can create your own hierarchy of organizational units here, in order to sort and manipulate the location inside Active Directory of all your domain-joined network objects and devices. In the following screenshot, you can see that instead of having just a plain **Users** and **Computers** OUs, I have created some new OUs including subcategories so that as I grow my environment, I will have a more structured and organized directory.

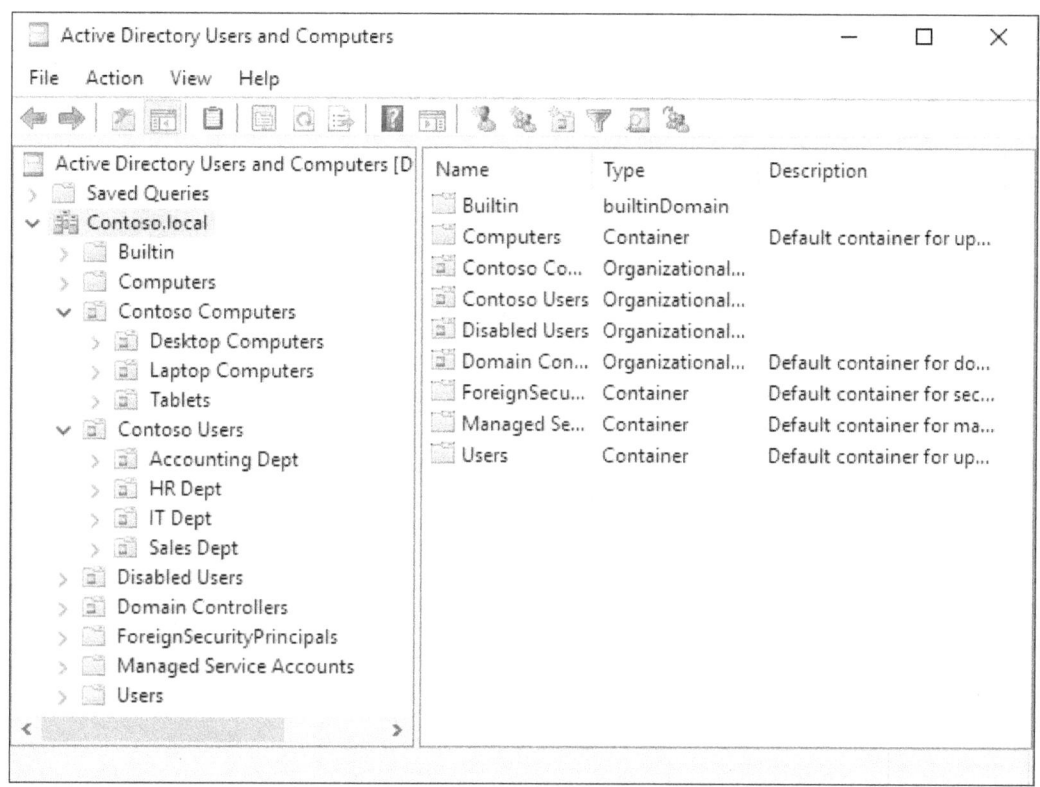

User accounts

Now that we have some OUs ready to structure our objects, let's create a new user. Say we have a new Server Administrator coming onboard, and we need to get him an Active Directory login so that he can start his job. Simply find the appropriate OU for his account to reside within, right-click on the OU, and navigate to **New** | **User**. We are then presented with an information gathering screen about all the things that AD needs in order to create this new account.

Core Infrastructure Services

When finished, our new admin will be able to utilize his new username and password in order to log in to computers and servers on the network, within the security boundaries we have established on those machines, of course. But that is another topic for another chapter.

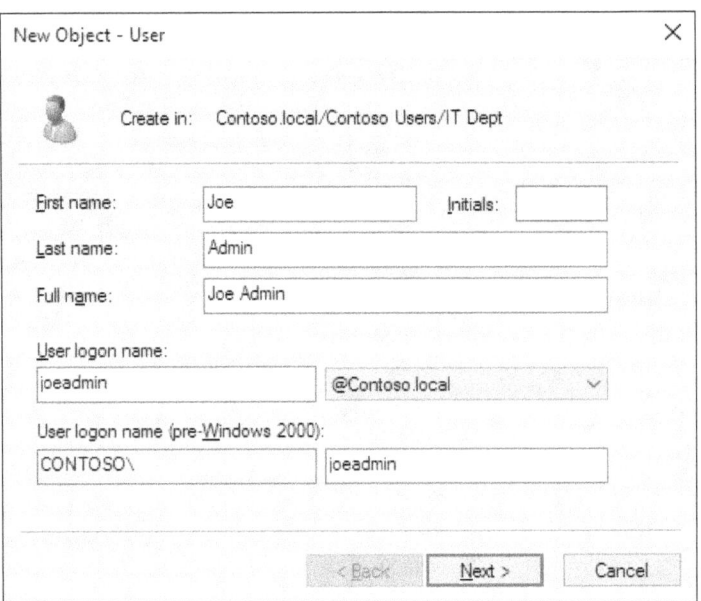

Security Groups

Another useful unit of organization inside Active Directory is **Security Groups**. We can do quite a bit of distinguishing between different types and kinds of users and computer accounts using organizational units, but what about when we need a little cross-contamination in this structure? Perhaps we have an employee that handles some HR and some accounting responsibilities. Maybe it is more likely that we have configured file and folder permissions on our file servers so that only people who are part of certain groups have access to read and write into particular folders. Susie from HR needs to have access to the payroll folder, but Jim from HR does not. By creating Security Groups inside Active Directory, we enable the adding and removing of specific user accounts, computer accounts, or even other groups so that we can granularly define access to our resources. You create new groups in the same way that you create user accounts, by choosing the OU where you want the new group to reside, then right-clicking on that OU and navigating to **New | Group**. Once your group has been created, right-click on it and head into **Properties**. You can then click on the **Members** tab; this is where you add in all of the users that you want to be a part of this new group.

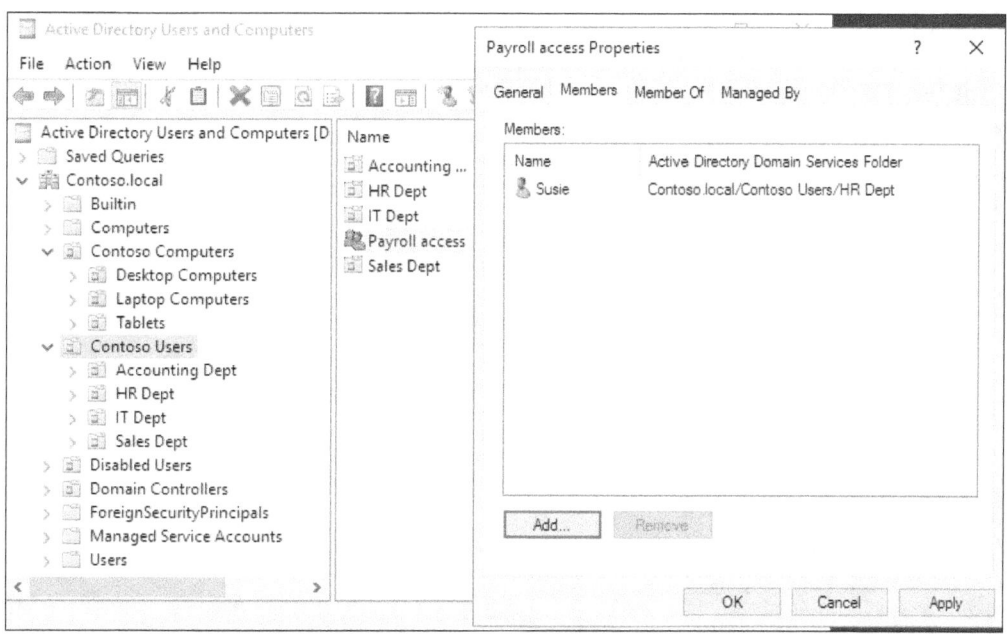

Prestaging computer accounts

While it is very common to utilize Active Directory Users and Computers for creating new user accounts, it is far less common to even think about opening this tool when joining new computers to your domain. This is because the way that the majority of domains are configured, new computers are allowed to the join the domain without any kind of prestaging. In other words, as long as someone knows a username and password that has administrative rights within the domain, they can sit down at any computer connected to the network and walk through the domain-join process on that local computer. It will successfully join the domain, and Active Directory will create a new computer object for it automatically. These auto-generating computer objects place themselves inside the default **Computers** OU, so in many networks if you click on that **Computers** OU, you will see a number of different machines listed, and they might even be a mix of both desktop computers and servers that were recently joined to the domain and haven't been moved to an appropriate, more specific OU yet. In my growing lab environment, I recently joined a client computer called **Win10** and a couple of servers called **CA1** and **DC2** to the domain.

I did nothing in Active Directory prior to joining these machines to the domain, and so you can see that the new computer objects are still sitting inside that default **Computers** container.

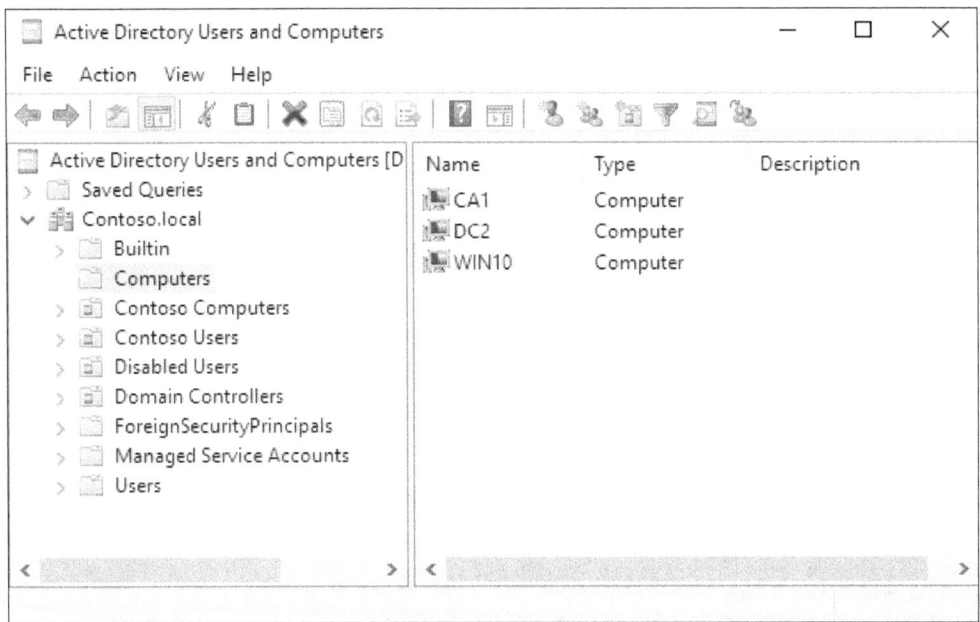

Allowing new computer accounts to place themselves inside the default Computers OU is generally not a big problem for client systems, but if you allow servers to be autogenerated in that folder, it can cause you big issues. Many companies have security policies in place across the network, and these policies are often created in a way that they will be automatically applied to any computer account residing in one of the generalized OUs. Using security policies can be a great way to lock down parts of client machines that the user doesn't need to access or utilize, but if you inadvertently cause these "lockdown" policies to apply to your new servers as soon as they join the domain, you can effectively break the server before you even start configuring it. Trust me, I've done it. And unfortunately your new server accounts that get added to Active Directory will be identified and categorized the same as any client workstation that is added to the domain, so you cannot specify a different default container for servers simply because they are a server and not a regular workstation.

So what can be done to alleviate this potential problem? Prestaging the accounts for your new servers. You can even prestage all new computer accounts as a matter of principle, but I typically only see that requirement in large enterprises. Prestaging a computer account is very much like creating a new user account. Prior to joining the computer to the domain, you create the account for it inside Active Directory.

By accomplishing the creation of the object before the domain-join process, you get to choose which OU the computer will reside in when it joins the domain. You can then ensure that this is an OU which will or will not receive the security settings and policies that you intend to have in place on this new computer or server. I highly recommend prestaging all computer accounts in Active Directory for any new servers that you bring online. If you make it a practice, even if it's not absolutely required all the time, you will create a good habit that may someday save you from having to rebuild a server that you broke simply by joining it to your domain.

Active Directory Domains and Trusts

This tool is generally only used in larger environments that have more than one domain within the same network. A company may utilize multiple domain names in order to segregate resources or services, or for better organizational structure of their servers and namespaces within the company. There is also another tier in the hierarchical structure of Active Directory that we haven't talked about, and that is called a **forest**. The forest is basically the top level of your Active Directory structure, with domains and subdomains coming in under that forest umbrella. Another way to think of the forest is the boundary of your AD structure. If you have multiple domains beneath a single forest, it does not necessarily mean that those domains trust each other. So users from one domain may or may not have permissions to access resources on one of the other domains, based on the level of trust that exists between those domains. When you have a domain and are adding child domains under it, there are trusts placed automatically between those domains, but if you have a need to merge some domains together in a way other than the default permissions, **Active Directory Domains and Trusts** is the management tool you use in order to establish and modify those trust permissions.

Growing organizations often find themselves in a position where they need to regularly manage domain trusts as a result of business acquisitions. If Contoso acquires Fabrikam, and both companies have fully functional domain environments, it is often advantageous to work through an extended migration process in bringing the Fabrikam employees over to Contoso's Active Directory, rather than suffer all the loss associated with simply turning off Fabrikam's network. So for a certain period of time, you would want to run both domains simultaneously, and could establish a trust between those domains in order to make that possible.

If you find yourself in a position where a domain migration of any sort is necessary, there is a tool available that you may want to try out. It is called the **Active Directory Migration Tool (ADMT)** and can be very useful in situations like the one described earlier. If you are interested in taking a closer look at this tool, you can download it from the link `https://www.microsoft.com/en-us/download/details.aspx?id=19188`.

Active Directory Sites and Services

Sites and Services is another tool that is generally only employed by companies with larger Active Directory infrastructures. As is the case with any server, if having one domain controller is good, then having two domain controllers is even better. The larger your company grows, so does your Active Directory infrastructure. Before you know it, you will be looking into setting up servers in a second location, then a third, and so on. In a domain-centric network, having domain controller servers in each significant site is a general practice, and you could soon be looking at dozens of domain controller servers running in your network.

Turning on new domain controllers and joining them to your existing domain so that they start servicing users and computers, is pretty easy. The harder part is keeping all of the traffic organized and flowing where you want it to. If you have a primary datacenter where the majority of your servers are located, you probably have multiple DCs onsite in that datacenter. In fact, in order to make your AD highly available, it is essential that you have at least two domain controllers. But then you build a new office that is significantly sized where it makes sense to install a local DC server in that office also, so that the computers in that office aren't reaching over the **Wide Area Network (WAN)** in order to authenticate all the time. If you were to spin up a server in the new office and turn it into a domain controller for your network, it would immediately start working. The problem is that the client computers aren't always smart enough to know which DC they need to talk to. You may now have computers in the remote office that are still authenticating back to the main datacentres' DCs. Even worse, you probably also have computers in the main office that are now reaching over the WAN to authenticate with the new DC that is in the remote office, even though there are DCs right on the local network with them!

This is the situation where Active Directory Sites and Services become essential. In here, you build out your different physical sites and assign the domain controllers to these sites. Domain-joined users and computers within this network now follow the rules that you have put into place via Sites and Services, so that they are always talking to and authenticating from their local domain controller servers. This saves time as the connections are faster and more efficient, and it also saves unnecessary bandwidth and data consumption on the WAN, which often saves you dollars.

Here's a quick look into Active Directory Sites and Services. There is a good chance you will have to make use of this tool someday if you are part of a growing organization:

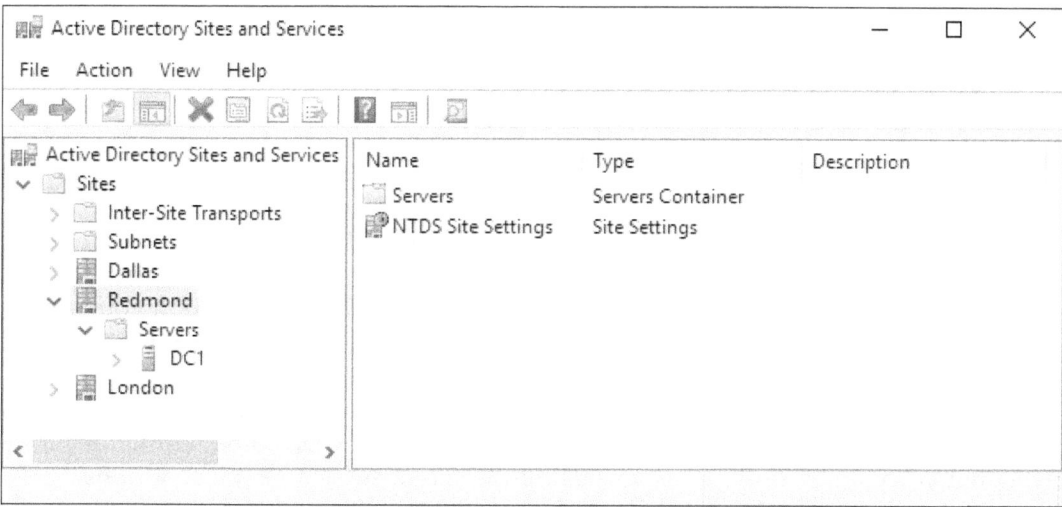

Active Directory Administrative Center

While the tools we have looked at so far are critical to understand and be familiar with in order to manage Active Directory, you can tell that their aesthetics are a bit dated. The **Active Directory Administrative Center**, on the other hand, has a much more streamlined interface that looks and feels like Server Manager that we are all becoming more and more comfortable with. Many of the functions available within the ADAC accomplish the same things that we can do through the other tools already, but it pulls these functions into a more structured interface that brings some of the most commonly utilized functions up to the surface and makes them easier to run.

One great example is right on the landing page of **ADAC**. A common helpdesk task in any network is the resetting of passwords for user accounts. Whether the user forgot their password, changed it recently and mistyped it, or if you are resetting a password during some other sort of troubleshooting, resetting a password for a user account typically involves numerous mouse clicks in order to get the job done. Now there is a quick link called **Reset Password**, shown right here on the main page of the Active Directory Administrative Center. Also useful is the **Global Search** feature right next to it, where you can type in anything to the search field and it will scour your entire directory for results relating to your search.

This is another common task in AD that previously required multiple clicks to accomplish.

If you click on the name of your domain in the left navigational tree, you will dive a little deeper into the capabilities of ADAC. As you can see, the information listed here is being pulled from Active Directory and looks like the same information you would see in AD Users and Computers. That is correct, except instead of having to right-click for every function like new user creations or searches, you now have some quick **Tasks** available on the right that can quickly launch you into accomplishing these functions. Also interesting are the links for raising the forest or domain functional level on this screen. In order to do this using the classic tools, I see most admins accomplish this by launching AD Domains and Trusts. So one of the big benefits of the newer ADAC tool is that it is capable of giving you a centralized management window from which you can accomplish tasks that would normally have taken multiple windows and management consoles. Do you sense a common theme throughout Windows Server 2016 with the centralized management of everything?

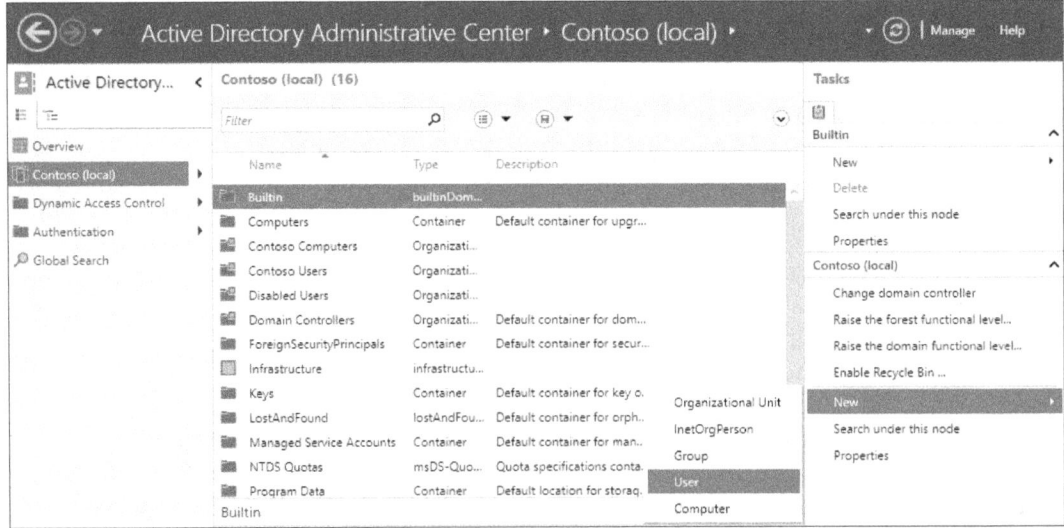

Dynamic Access Control

In addition to teaching the old dogs new tricks, the Active Directory Administrative Center also brings some new functionality to the table that is not available anywhere in the classic tools. If you once again take a look at the tree to the left, you will see that the next section in the list is **Dynamic Access Control (DAC)**. This is a technology that is all about security and governance of your files, the company data that you need to hold onto tightly and make sure it's not falling into the wrong hands. DAC gives you the ability to tag files, thereby classifying them for particular groups or uses. Then you can create Access Control policies that define who has access to these particularly tagged files. Another powerful feature of Dynamic Access Control is the reporting functionality. Once DAC is established and running in your environment, you can do reporting and forensics on your files, like finding a list of the people who have recently accessed a classified document.

DAC can also be used to modify a user's permissions based on what kind of device they are currently using. If our user Susie logs in with her company desktop on the network, she should have access to those sensitive HR files. On the other hand, if she brings her personal laptop into the office and connects it to the network, even when providing her domain user credentials we might not want to allow access to these same files simply because we do not own the security over that laptop. These kinds of distinctions can be made using the Dynamic Access Control policies.

Read-only domain controllers

We can't wrap up our overview of the important Active Directory tools and components without mentioning **Read-only domain controller (RODC)**. Typically, when installing new domain controllers to your network, you add the role in a way that makes them a regular, writeable, fully functional DC on your network so that it can perform all aspects of that DC role. There are some circumstances in which this is not the best way to go, and that is what the RODC is here to help with. This is not a separate role, but rather a different configuration of the same AD DS role that you will see when spinning through the wizard screens during the configuration of your new domain controller. An RODC is a specialized domain controller to which you cannot write new data. It contains a cached, read-only copy of only certain parts of the directory. You can tell an RODC to keep a copy of all the credentials within your domain, or you can even tell it to only keep a list of selective credentials that are going to be important to that particular RODC. Reasons for using an RODC? Branch offices and DMZs are the most common I see. If you have a smaller branch office with a smaller number of people, it may be beneficial for them to have a local domain controller so that their login processing is fast and efficient, but because you don't have a good handle on security in that little office, you would rather not have a full blown DC which someone might walk away with.

This could be a good utilization for an RODC. Another is within a secure DMZ network. These are perimeter networks typically designed for very limited access, because they are touching the public Internet. Some of your servers and services sitting inside the DMZ network might need access to Active Directory, but you don't want to open a communications channel from the DMZ to a full domain controller in your network. You could stand up an RODC inside the DMZ, have it cache the information that it needs in order to service those particular servers in the DMZ, and make a much more secure domain or subdomain environment within that network.

The power of Group Policy

In a network that is based upon Windows Server and Active Directory, it is almost always the case that the primary set of client computers are also based upon the Microsoft Windows operating systems, and that these machines are all domain-joined. Setting everything up this way not only makes sense from an organizational perspective inside Active Directory, but allows centralized authentication across devices and applications, like we have already talked about. I know that in a couple of the examples I gave earlier in the book that I mentioned something like, "What about when a company has a security policy in place that...". or "Make sure your servers don't get those existing security policies because..." So what are these magical "security policies" anyway, and how do I set one up?

This is the power of Group Policy. It enables you to create **Group Policy Objects (GPOs)** that contain settings and configurations which you want to apply to either computers or users in your Active Directory domain. Once you have created and built out a GPO with a variety of settings, you then have the option to steer that GPO in whatever direction you choose. If you have a policy that you want applied to all desktop systems, you can point it at the appropriate OU or groups in Active Directory. Or maybe you created a GPO which only applies to your Windows 7 computers, you can filter it appropriately so that only those systems are receiving the policy. And the real magic is that the issuance of these settings happens automatically, simply by those computers being joined to your domain. You don't have to touch the client systems at all in order to push settings to them via GPO.

So, once again, I'm looking in the list of available roles on my Windows Server 2016, and I am just not seeing one called Group Policy. Correct again, there isn't one. In fact, if you have been following along with the lab setup in this book, you already have Group Policy fully functional in your network. Everything that Group Policy needs in order to work is part of Active Directory Domain Services.

So, if you have a domain controller in your network, then you also have Group Policy on that same server, because all of the information Group Policy uses is stored in the directory. Since the installation of the AD DS role is all we need in order to use Group Policy, and we have already done that on our domain controller, let's jump right in and take a look at a few things which will enable you to start utilizing Group Policy in your environment right away. I have worked with many small businesses over the years that were running a Windows Server simply because that's what everyone does, right? Whoever the IT guy or company was that set this server up for them certainly never showed them anything about GPOs, and so they have this powerful tool just sitting in the toolbox, unused and waiting to be unleashed. If you aren't already using GPOs, I want you to open that box and give it a shot.

The Default Domain Policy

First we need to figure out where we go on our domain controller so that we can create and manipulate Group Policy Objects. As is the case with any of the administrative tools on a Windows Server 2016, Server Manager is the central platform for opening up your console. Click on the **Tools** menu from inside Server Manager, and choose **Group Policy Management**.

Once the console has opened, expand your **Forest** name from the navigational tree on the left, and then also expand out **Domains** and choose your domain name. Inside you will see some familiar-looking objects. This is a list of the organizational units that you created earlier and a couple of other folders alongside your OUs.

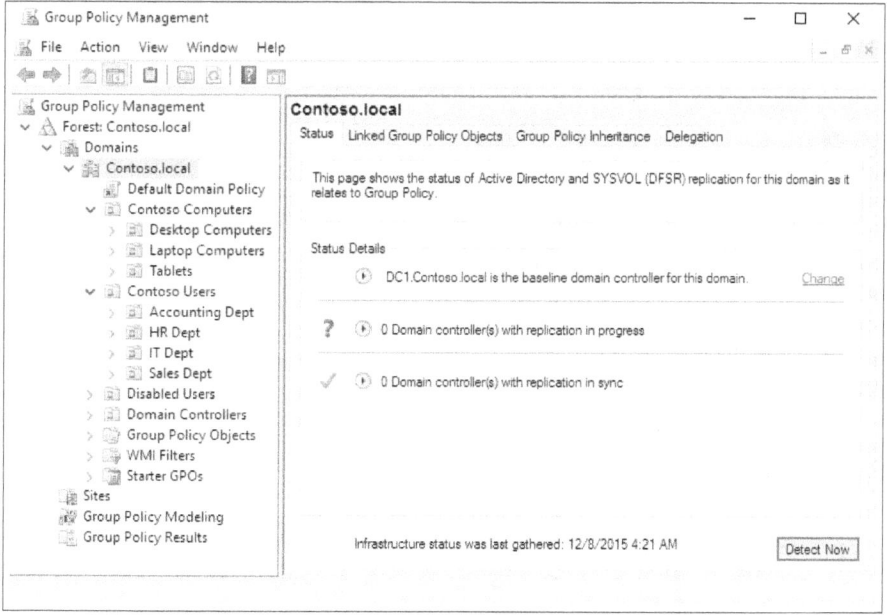

We will talk about why the list of OUs exists here shortly, but for now we want to focus on a particular GPO that is typically near the top of this list, immediately underneath the name of your domain. It is called the **Default Domain Policy**. This GPO is plugged into Active Directory by default during installation, and it applies to every user who is part of your domain directory. Since this GPO is completely enabled right off the bat and applies to everyone, it is a common place for companies to enforce global password policies or security rules that need to apply to everyone.

With any GPO that you see in the management console, if you right-click on that GPO and then choose **Edit…** you will see a new window open, and this GPO Editor contains all of the internals of that policy. This is where you make any settings or configurations that you want to be a part of that particular GPO. So go ahead and edit your **Default Domain Policy**, and then navigate to **Computer Configuration | Policies | Windows Settings | Security Settings | Account Policies | Password Policy**.

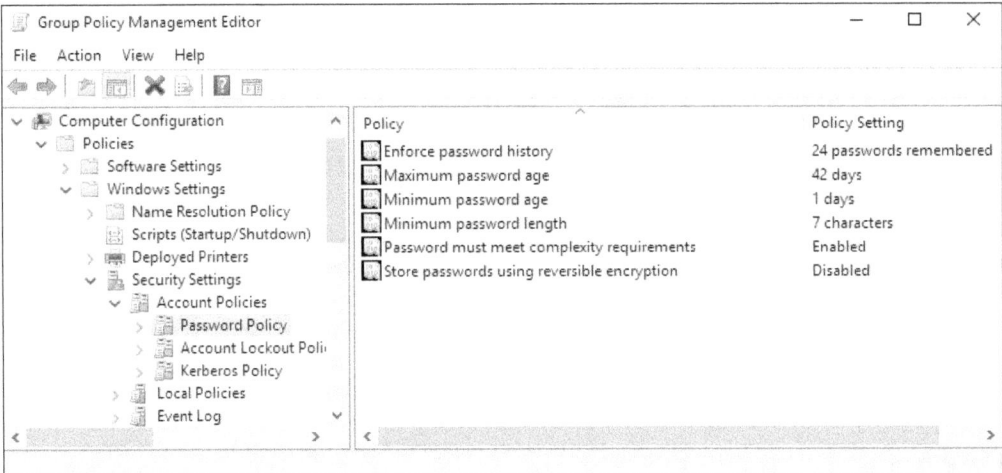

Here, you can see a list of the different options available to you for configuring the **Password Policy** within your domain. Double-clicking on any of these settings lets you modify them, and that change immediately starts to take effect on all of your domain-joined computers in the network. For example, you can see that the default **Minimum password length** is set to `7 characters`. Many companies have already gone through much discussion about their own written policy on the standard length of passwords in the network, and in order to set up your new directory infrastructure to accept your decision, you simply modify this field.

If you look along the left tree of the **Group Policy Management Editor**, you can see that there are an incredibly large amount of settings and configurations that can be pushed out via Group Policy. While the Default Domain Policy is a very quick and easy way to get some settings configured and pushed out to everyone, tread carefully when making changes to this default policy. Every time that you make a setting change in here, remember that it is going to affect everyone in your domain, including yourself. Many times you will be creating policies that do not need to apply to everyone, and in those cases, it is highly recommended that you stay away from the Default Domain Policy, and instead set up a brand new GPO for accomplishing whatever task it is that you are trying to put into place.

Create and link a new GPO

If the best practice in general is to build out a new GPO when we need to apply some settings, we'd better take a minute and cover that process. For this example, we are going to create a new GPO that plugs a list of trusted sites into Internet Explorer on our desktop computers. If you run a web application in your network which needs to run JavaScript or ActiveX controls or something like that, it may be required that the website is part of the trusted sites list inside Internet Explorer in order for it to run properly. You could print off an instructions page for the helpdesk on how to do this on each computer, and have them spend the time doing it for every user who calls in because they cannot access the application. Or you could simply create a GPO that makes these changes for you automatically on every workstation and save all of those phone calls. This is just one tiny example of the power that Group Policy possesses, but it's a good example because it is something useful, and is a setting that is sort of buried way down in the GPO settings, so that you can get a feel for just how deep these capabilities dive.

Inside the **Group Policy Management** console, right-click on the folder called **Group Policy Objects**, and choose **New**. Name your new GPO, mine is called **Adding Trusted Sites**, and then click on **OK**. Your new GPO now shows up in the list of available GPOs, but it is not yet applying to anyone or any computers. Before we assign this new GPO to anyone, let's plug in that list of trusted sites so that the policy contains our configuration information. At the moment, it's void of any settings.

Right-click on the new GPO, and choose **Edit...**. Now navigate to **Computer Configuration** | **Policies** | **Administrative Templates** | **Windows Components** | **Internet Explorer** | **Internet Control Panel** | **Security Page**. See, I told you it was buried in there!

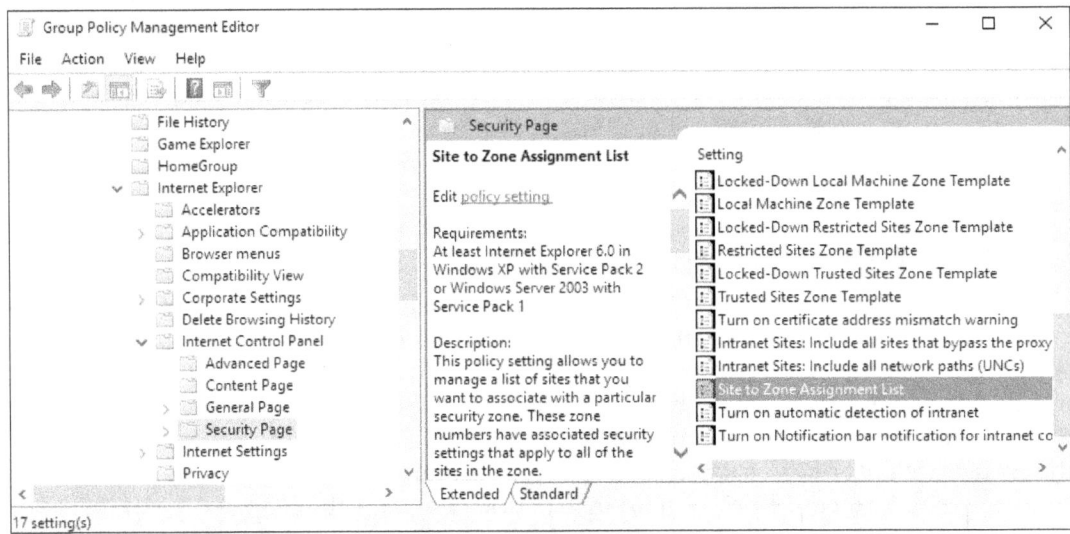

Now double-click on **Site to Zone Assignment List**, and set it to **Enabled**. This allows you to click on the **Show...** button, within which you can enter websites and give them zone assignments. Each GPO setting has a nice descriptive text to accompany it, telling you exactly what that particular setting is for and what the options mean. As you can see in the text for this one, in order to set my websites to be trusted sites, I need to give them a zone assignment value of **2**. And just for fun, I also added in a site which I do not want to be accessible to my users, and gave it a zone value of **4** so that **badsite.contoso.com** is a member of the restricted sites zone on all of my desktop computers. Here is my completed list:

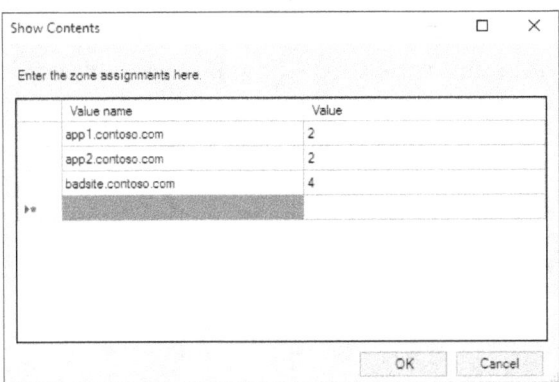

Are we done? Almost. As soon as I click on the **OK** button, these settings are now stored in my Group Policy Object and are ready to be deployed, but at this point in time I have not assigned my new GPO to anything, so it is just sitting around waiting to be used.

Back inside the Group Policy Management console, find the location to which you want to **link** this new GPO. You can link a GPO to the top of the domain similar to the way that the Default Domain Policy works, and it would then apply to everything below that link. So in effect, it would start applying to every machine in your domain network. For this particular example, we don't want the Trusted Site's settings to be quite so global, so we are going to create our link to a particular OU instead. That way this new GPO will only apply to the machines that are stored inside that OU. I want to assign this GPO to my **Desktop Computers** OU that I created earlier. So I simply find that OU, right-click on it, and then choose **Link an Existing GPO...**.

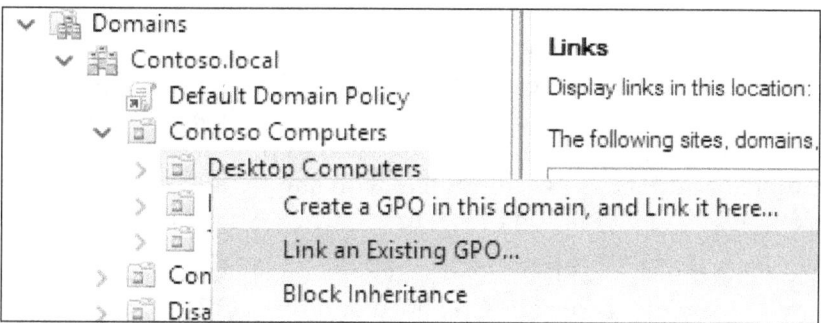

I now see a list of the GPOs that are available for linking. Choose the new **Adding Trusted Sites** GPO, and click on **OK**, and that's it! The new GPO is now linked to the Desktop Computers OU, and will apply those settings to all machines which I place inside that OU.

> You can link a GPO to more than one OU. Just follow the same process again, this time choosing a different OU where you want to make the link, and that GPO will now apply to both OUs which have active links. You can also remove individual links, by clicking on the Group Policy Object itself in order to view its properties.

Filtering GPOs to particular devices

Now that you have created a GPO and linked it to particular OUs, you have enough information in order to really start using Group Policy in your environment. Using links to determine what machines get what policies is the most common method that I see admins use, but there are many circumstances where you might want to take it a step further. What if you had a new GPO and had it linked to an OU that contained all of your desktop computers, but then decided that some of those machines needed the policy and some did not? It would be a headache to have to split those machines up into two separate OUs just for the purpose of this policy that you are building. This is where **GPO Security Filtering** comes into play.

Security Filtering is the ability to filter a GPO down to particular Active Directory objects. On any given GPO in your directory, you can set filters so that the GPO only applies to particular users, particular computers, or even particular groups of users or computers. I find that using groups is especially useful. So, for our preceding example where we have a policy that needs to apply only to some desktop computers, we could create a new Security Group inside Active Directory and add only those computers into the group. Once the GPO has been configured with that group listed in the filtering section, that policy would only apply to machines that are part of that group. In the future, if you needed to pull that policy away from some computers or add it to new computers, you simply add or remove machines from the group itself, and you don't have to modify the GPO at all.

The **Security Filtering** section is displayed when you click on a GPO from inside the Group Policy Management console. Go ahead and open GPMC, and simply click once on one of your GPOs. On the right-hand side, you see the scope open for that policy. The section on top shows you what **Links** are currently active on the policy, and the bottom half of the screen displays the **Security Filtering** section. You can see here that I have linked my GPO to the **Desktop Computers** OU, but I have set an additional security filter so that only machines which are part of the **Accounting Computers** group will actually receive the settings from my GPO.

Chapter 3

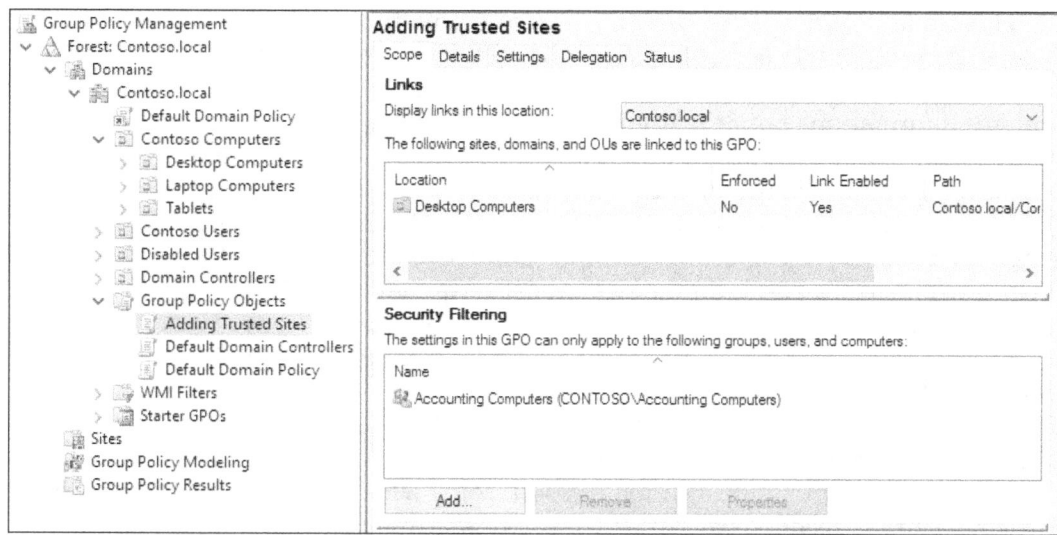

 Another cool feature that is just a click away is the **Settings** tab on this same screen. Click on that tab, and it will display all of the configurations currently set inside your GPO. This is very useful for checking over GPOs that someone else may have created, to see what settings are being modified.

DNS overview

If we consider Active Directory to be the most common and central role in making our Microsoft-centric networks function, then the **Domain Name System** (**DNS**) role slides in at number two. I am yet to meet an admin who has chosen to deploy a domain without deploying DNS at the same time, they always go hand-in-hand.

 DNS is a service that is typically provided by a Windows Server, but doesn't have to be. There are many different platforms available all the way from Linux servers to specialized hardware appliances designed specifically for managing DNS within a network that can be utilized for this role. For most Microsoft-centric networks, and for the purposes of this book, we will assume that you want to use Windows Server 2016 for hosting the DNS role.

[81]

DNS is similar to Active Directory in that it is a structured database which is often stored on domain controller servers, and distributed automatically around your network to other domain controller/DNS servers. Where an AD's database contains information about the domain objects themselves, DNS is responsible for storing and resolving all of the names on your network. What do I mean by names? Whenever a user or computer tries to contact any resource by calling for a name, DNS is the platform responsible for turning that name into something else in order to get the traffic to the correct destination. You see, the way that traffic gets from client to server is via networking, and typically via the TCP/IP stack, using an IP address to get to its destination. When I open an application on my computer to access some data that resides on a server, I could configure the application so that it communicates directly to my server by using the server's IP address on the network. If I plug `10.0.0.15` into my application configuration, it would open successfully. If I set up hundreds of different computers this way, all pointing to the IP address, it would work fine for a while. But the day will come when for whatever reason, that IP address might need to change. Or perhaps I add a second server to share the load and handle my increased user traffic. What to do now? Re-visit every client computer and update the IP address being used? Certainly not. This is one of the reasons that DNS is critical to the way that we design and manage our infrastructures. By using DNS we can employ names instead of IP addresses. With DNS my application can be configured to talk to Server01 or whatever my server name is, and if I need to change the IP address later, I simply change it inside the DNS console to the updated IP address and immediately all of my client computers will start resolving Server01 to the new IP address. Or I can even use a more generic name like Intranet and have it resolve across multiple different servers. We will discuss that a little bit more shortly.

Any time that a computer makes a call to a server, or service, or website, it is using DNS in order to resolve that name to a more useful piece of information in order to make the network connection happen successfully. The same is true both inside and outside of corporate networks. On my personal laptop right now, if I open Internet Explorer and browse to `http://www.bing.com/`, my Internet provider's DNS server is resolving `http://www.bing.com/` to an IP address on the Internet, so that my page opens successfully. When we are working inside our own corporate networks, we don't want to rely on or trust a public provider with our internal server name information, and so we build our own DNS servers inside the network. Since DNS records inside a domain network are almost always resolving names to objects that reside inside Active Directory, it makes sense then that DNS and AD DS would be tightly integrated. That rings true in a majority of Microsoft networks, where it is a very common practice to install both the AD DS role, plus the DNS role, on your domain controller servers.

Different kinds of DNS records

Now having installed our DNS role on a server in the network, we can start using it to create DNS records which resolve names to their corresponding IP addresses, or other pieces of information needed in order to route our traffic around the network. Assuming that you are working in a domain network, you may be pleasantly surprised to see that a number of records already exist inside DNS, even though you haven't created any of them. When you are running Active Directory and DNS together, the domain-join process that you take with your computers and servers self-registers a DNS record during that process. I have not yet created any DNS records on my new lab environment, not purposefully anyway, and yet when I open the **DNS Manager** console from inside the **Tools** menu of Server Manager, I can see a handful of records already existing. This is because when I joined each of these machines to the domain, it automatically registered these records for me so that the new servers and clients were immediately resolvable within our domain.

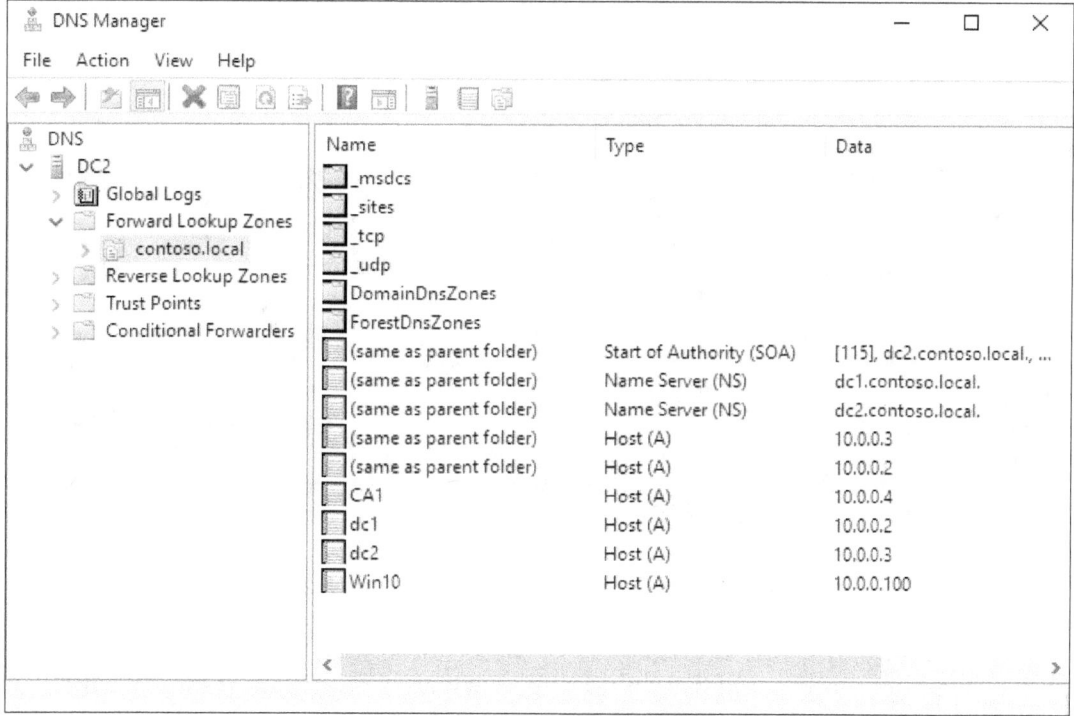

Host record (A or AAAA)

The first kind of DNS record we are looking at is the most common type that you will work with. A **host record** is the one that resolves a particular name to a particular IP address. Pretty simple, and for most of the devices on your network this will be the only kind of record that exists for them inside DNS. There are two different classes of host record that you should be aware of, even though you will likely only be using one of them for at least a few more years. The two different kinds of host records are called an **A record**, and an **AAAA record**, which is pronounced Quad A. The difference between the two? A records are for IPv4 addresses and will be used in most companies for years to come. AAAA records serve the exact same purpose of resolving a name to an IP address, but are only for IPv6 addresses, and will only be useful if you use IPv6 on your network.

In the previous screenshot, you can see some **Host (A)** records that were self-created when those machines joined our domain. I also have another server running on my network which has not yet been domain-joined, and so it has not self-registered into DNS. This server is called `ra1`, but if I log in to any other system on my network, I fail to contact my `ra1` server, since that name is not yet plugged into DNS.

```
Administrator: Command Prompt

Microsoft Windows [Version 10.0.10586]
(c) 2016 Microsoft Corporation. All rights reserved.

C:\Users\administrator>ping ra1
Ping request could not find host ra1. Please check the name and try again.

C:\Users\administrator>
```

For now, I am going to choose not to join this box to the domain, so that we can manually create a DNS record for it and make sure that I am able to resolve the name properly after doing that. Back inside DNS Manager on my DNS server, right-click on the name of your domain listed under the **Forward Lookup Zones** folder, and then choose **New Host (A or AAAA)**. Inside the screen to create a new host record, simply enter the name of your server, and the IP address which is configured on its network interface.

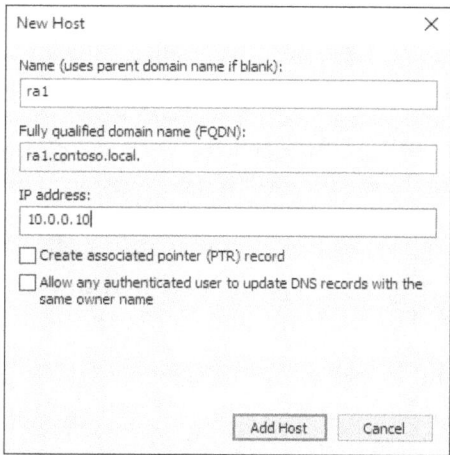

Now that we have created this new host record, we should immediately be able to start resolving this name inside our domain network. Moving back to the client machine from which I was trying to ping `ra1` earlier, I'll try the same command again, and this time it does resolve and reply successfully.

```
C:\Users\administrator>ping ra1

Pinging ra1.Contoso.local [10.0.0.10] with 32 bytes of data:
Reply from 10.0.0.10: bytes=32 time=1ms TTL=128
Reply from 10.0.0.10: bytes=32 time<1ms TTL=128
Reply from 10.0.0.10: bytes=32 time<1ms TTL=128
Reply from 10.0.0.10: bytes=32 time<1ms TTL=128

Ping statistics for 10.0.0.10:
    Packets: Sent = 4, Received = 4, Lost = 0 (0% loss),
Approximate round trip times in milli-seconds:
    Minimum = 0ms, Maximum = 1ms, Average = 0ms

C:\Users\administrator>
```

Alias record – CNAME

Another useful type of DNS record is **CNAME**, or more commonly these days called the **alias record**. This is a record that you can create which takes a name, and points it at another name. Sounds a little silly at first glance, because in the end you are still going to have to resolve your final name to an IP address in order to get the traffic where it needs to go, but the purposes of an alias record can be vast. A good example to portray the usefulness of an alias record is when you are running a web server that is serving up websites within your network. Rather than force all of your users to remember a URL like `http://web1.contoso.local` in order to access a website, we could create an alias record called **Intranet**, and point it at `web1`. This way the more generalized **Intranet** record can always be utilized by the client computers, which is a much friendlier name for your users to remember.

Core Infrastructure Services

In addition to creating a happier user experience with this new DNS record, you have at the same time created some additional administrative flexibility because you can easily change the server components that are running beneath that record, without having to adjust any settings on the client machines or re-train employees on how to access the page. Need to replace a web server? No problem, just point the alias record at the new one. Need to add another web server? That's easy too, as we can create multiple alias records, all with the same Intranet name, and point them at the different web servers that are in play within the environment. This creates a very simple form of load balancing, as DNS will start to round-robin the traffic among the different web servers, based on that Intranet CNAME record.

In fact, rather than continue to talk about this, let's give it a try. I have a website running on exactly that URL in my environment, but currently I can only access it by typing in `http://web1.contoso.local`. Inside DNS I am going to create an alias record that redirects `intranet` to `web1`.

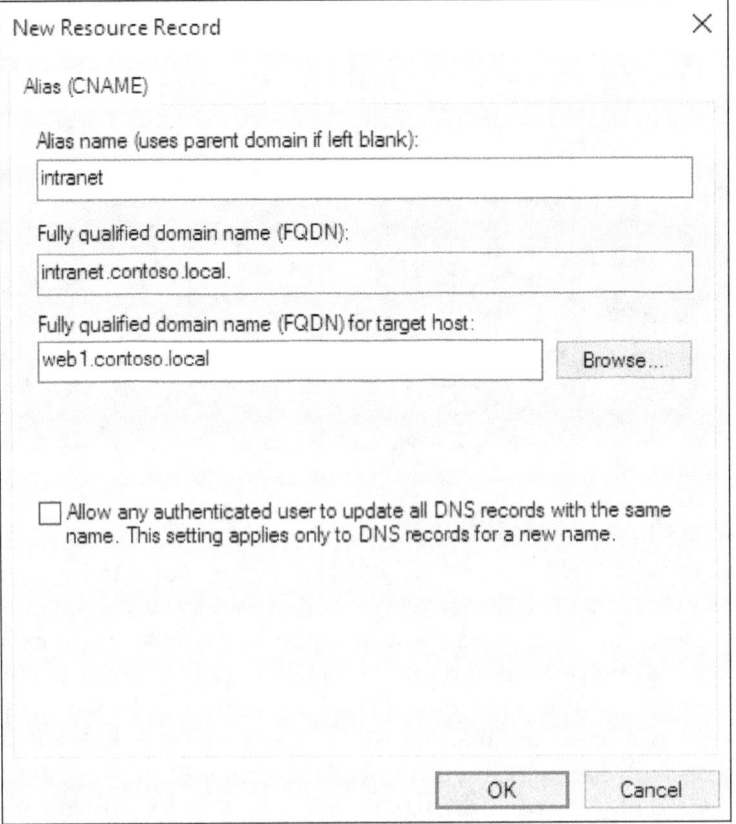

Now when I `ping intranet`, you can see that it resolves to my `web1` server. And when accessing the webpage, I can simply type the word `Intranet` into my address bar inside Internet Explorer in order to launch my page. The website itself is not aware of the name change being made, so I didn't have to make any modifications to the website, only within DNS.

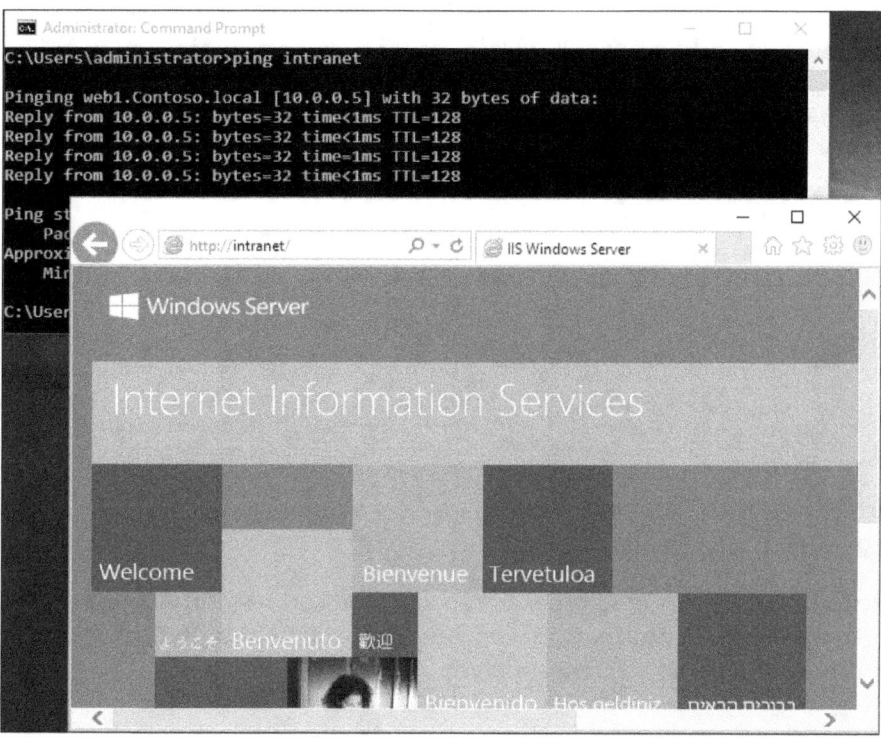

Mail Exchanger record

A third type of DNS record is called a **Mail Exchanger** (**MX**) record. In your everyday duties you would not have to encounter or configure MX records nearly as much as A or CNAME records, but they are important to understand nonetheless. An MX record is all about e-mail services and delivery. Whatever domain name follows the "@" in your e-mail address, the DNS servers who are handling that domain name must contain an MX record telling the domain where to point for its e-mail services. MX records are only used with public DNS, for name resolutions happening over the Internet. For companies hosting their own e-mail on local Exchange servers, your public DNS servers will contain an MX record that points at your Exchange environment. For companies hosting their e-mail in a cloud service, your public DNS records would need to contain an MX record that directs e-mail traffic toward the cloud provider who is hosting your mailboxes.

Name Server record

Here is another that you don't have to deal with on a day-to-day basis, but you should still know what it's there for. An **Name Server** (**NS**) record is an identifier within a DNS zone that tells it which Name Servers, your DNS servers, to use as the authorities for that zone. If you look at the NS records listed in your DNS right now, you will recognize that it is calling out the names of your DNS servers on the network. When you add a new DC/DNS server to your domain, a new NS record for this server will be automatically added into your DNS zone.

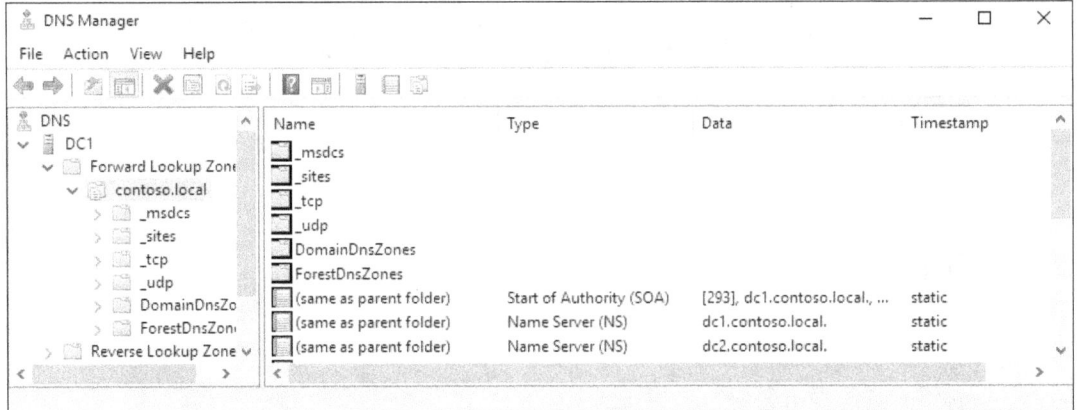

There are many other possible types of records that can be stored and used within a DNS database, but they are not generally relevant to the common server administrator in a typical Microsoft-driven network.

Ipconfig /flushdns

Just one final note to finish out this section. I have been saying things like "now when I do this..." or "immediately following this change..." and if you are creating some of your own records, you may have noticed that it sometimes takes a while for your client computers to recognize these new records. That is normal behavior, and the time that it takes before your change rolls around to the whole network will depend entirely on how large your network is and how Active Directory replication is configured. When you create a new DNS record on one domain controller, your new record needs to replicate itself around to all of the other DCs in your network. This process alone can take up a couple hours if AD is not configured for faster replication. Typically, it only takes a few minutes. And then once the new record exists on all of your DC servers, your clients may still take a little bit of time to utilize the new record, because client computers in a domain network hold onto a cache of DNS data. This way they don't have to reach out to the DNS server for every single name resolution request.

They can more quickly refer to their local cache in order to see what the information was from the last time they checked in with the DNS server. If you are trying to immediately test out a new DNS record that you just created and it's not working, you may want to try to run the command `ipconfig /flushdns` on your client computer. This forces the client to dump its locally cached copies of DNS resolver records, and go grab new information that is current from the DNS server. After flushing your cache, the record will more than likely start working properly.

DHCP versus static addressing

IP addresses on your network are sort of like home addresses on your street. When you want to send a package to someone, you write their address on the front of the package and set it in the mailbox. In the same way, when your computer wants to send data to a server or another device on a network, each of those devices has an IP address which is used for the delivery of those packets. We know that DNS is responsible for telling the machines which name resolves to which IP address, but how do those IP addresses get put into place on the servers and computers in the first place?

Static addressing is simply the process of configuring IP addresses on your system manually, using your own hands as the configuration tool in order to plug all of your IP address information into the NIC settings on that device. While this is a quick and easy way to get network traffic flowing between a few endpoints, by giving them each an IP address, it is not scalable. We do often statically address our servers as a way of making sure that those IP addresses are not subject to change, but what about on the client and device side? Even in a small company with 10 employees, each person may have a desktop and a laptop, there are likely going to be print servers on the network also needing IP addresses, and you may have a wireless network where employees or even guests can connect phones and other devices in order to gain Internet access. Are you going to assign IP addresses by hand to all of these devices? Certainly not.

Our answer to this problem is the **Dynamic Host Configuration Protocol (DHCP)**. This is a protocol which is designed to solve our exact problem by providing the ability for machines and devices on your network to automatically obtain IP addressing information. Almost any user on any device in the entire world uses DHCP every day without even realizing it. When you connect your laptop or smart phone to a Wi-Fi router to gain Internet access, a DHCP server has given you the ability to route traffic on that Wi-Fi network by assigning you IP addressing information. Often in the case of a public Wi-Fi your DHCP server is actually running on the router itself, but in our businesses where Windows Server rules the datacenter, our DHCP services are most often hosted on one or more servers across the network.

The DHCP scope

In the new Windows Server 2016 lab environment I have been building, so far I have been statically assigning IP addresses to all of the servers that are being built. This is starting to get old, and hard to keep track of. When the first domain controller was configured, I actually installed the DHCP role onto it, but haven't told it to start doing anything yet. What does a DHCP server need in order to start handing out IP addresses? It needs to know what IP addresses, subnet mask, default gateway, and DNS server addresses are within your network so that it can package that up and start handing the information out to the computers who request it. This package of information inside the DHCP server is called a **DHCP scope**. Once we define our scope, the DHCP server will start handing out IP addresses from that scope to our new servers and computers which do not already have static addresses defined.

Once again we need to launch a management tool on our Windows Server 2016, and once again the easiest way to launch that is by using the **Tools** menu inside Server Manager. Go ahead and launch the **DHCP** console. Inside, you will see the name of your server where DHCP is running. Expand that, and you have options for both **IPv4** and **IPv6**. Yes, this means that you can use this DHCP server to hand out both IPv4 addresses as well as IPv6 addresses for those of you who are testing out IPv6, or have plans to in the future. For now, we are sticking with good old IPv4, and so I can right-click on **IPv4** and choose to create a **New Scope**. This launches a **New Scope Wizard** which walks you through the few pieces of information that DHCP needs in order to create a scope that is ready to start handing out IP addresses inside your network. As soon as you finish creating your scope, it is immediately active and any computer in your network whose NIC is configured to grab an address automatically from a DHCP server will start doing so against this new DHCP server.

Now that our new scope has been created, you can expand the scope inside the DHCP console and see some additional information about this scope. By clicking on the **Address Leases** folder, you can see all of the DHCP addresses that have been handed out by this DHCP server. As you can see in the following screenshot, I have a Windows 10 client computer on the network which does not have a static address, and so it has grabbed a DHCP address from my DHCP server. It has been given the first IP address that I defined in my scope, 10.0.0.100. The next machine which reaches in to grab an IP address from this DHCP server will receive 10.0.0.101, and so on from there.

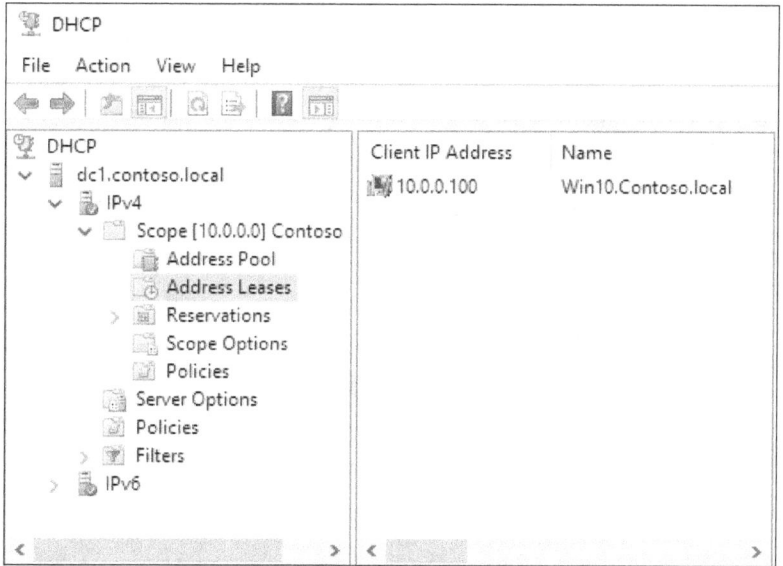

DHCP reservations

Assigning IP addresses from a big pool of available ones is great, but these address leases are subject to expiry and change. This means that a computer who has `10.0.0.100` today might receive `10.0.0.125` tomorrow. Typically this is fine from a desktop computer perspective, as they don't generally care what IP address they have. But what if you have a more permanent fixture in your network, like a Windows Server, but you don't want to have to deal with statically addressing this server. This is where **DHCP reservations** come into play. A reservation is the act of taking a single IP address within your DHCP scope, and reserving it to a particular device. This device will receive the same IP address every time it connects through the DHCP server, and this particular IP address will not be handed out to any other device on your network. By using reservations inside DHCP you can allow the DHCP server to handle the assigning of IP addresses even to your permanent servers, so that you do not have to manually configure the NICs of those servers, yet still maintain permanent IP addresses on those machines.

Core Infrastructure Services

You can see the folder called **Reservations** in the **DHCP** console. Currently there is nothing listed here, but by right-clicking on **Reservations** and choosing **New Reservation...** we will create one for ourselves. Let's work once again with that `web1` server. Right now I have a static IP address assigned to `web1`, but I will instead create a reservation for it on IP address `10.0.0.150`.

Whoa, whoa, whoa...back the train up. Most of the information on this screen makes sense, a quick description of the server name and the IP address itself, but how did I come up with that MAC address? A **MAC address** is a network card's physical address on the network. When your networking equipment tries to send information to a certain IP address, or in this case when the DHCP server needs to hand a certain IP address to a particular NIC on a server, it needs a physical identifier for that network card. So this MAC address is something that is unique to the NIC on my `web1` server. By logging into my `web1` server, I can run an `ipconfig /all` and see the MAC address listed for my NIC right in that output. That is where I got this information. This is how DHCP decides when to invoke reservations. If a network interface asks it for a DHCP address, and that device's MAC address is listed here in the reservations, then the DHCP server will hand the reserved address back to the device, rather than one from the general pool.

```
Ethernet adapter Ethernet:

   Connection-specific DNS Suffix  . :
   Description . . . . . . . . . . . : Microsoft Hyper-V Network Adapter
   Physical Address. . . . . . . . . : 00-15-5D-FA-3E-59
   DHCP Enabled. . . . . . . . . . . : No
```

Now that our DHCP reservation has been created, I will head into the NIC settings on my **WETB1** server, and get rid of all the static IP addressing information by choosing the default option **Obtain an IP address automatically**. After doing that, **WEB1** will reach over to DHCP and ask for an address, and you can see that I have now been assigned the reserved address of 10.0.0.150. This will always be the IP address of the **WEB1** server from this point forward, unless I change my DHCP reservation or somehow change the MAC address of **WEB1**. This could possibly happen if I were to install a new NIC into **WEB1**.

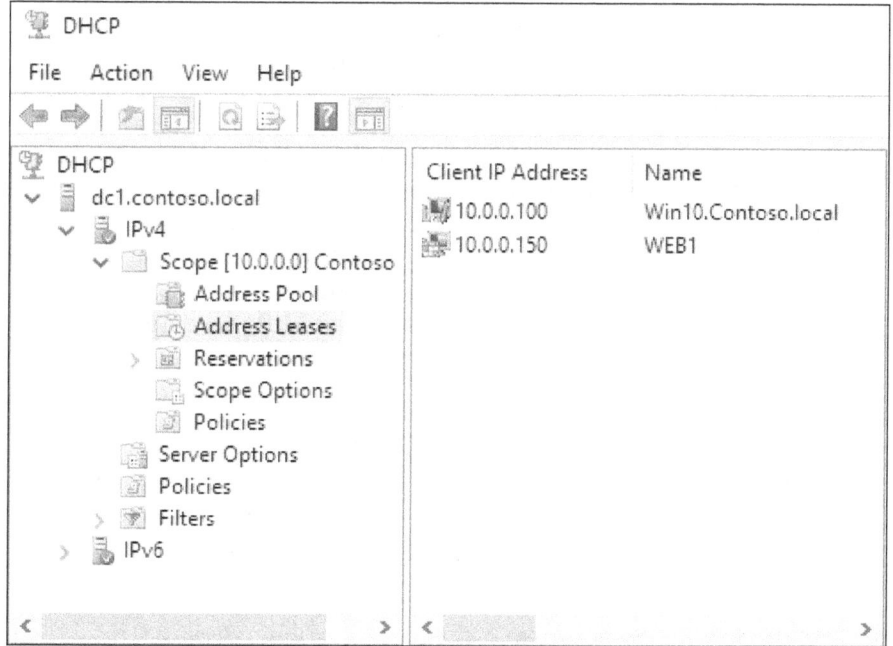

 You can also create DHCP reservations for objects other than Windows devices in your network. Since all you need is the MAC address of the device, it is easy to create reservations for devices like print servers and copy machines as well.

Back up and restore

The need to back up and occasionally to restore your servers is, unfortunately, still present in Windows Server 2016. I dream of a day when servers are 100 percent reliable and stable throughout their lifetimes, unaffected by viruses and rogue software, but today is not that day. While there are many third-party tools available on the market which can improve and automate your backup experience when managing many servers, we do have these capabilities baked right into our own Server 2016 operating system, and we should all be familiar with how to utilize them.

Schedule regular backups

Logging into your servers and launching a manual backup task every day is obviously not feasible for most of our organizations, as the process of running backups would turn into our full time job. Thankfully, the Windows Server Backup feature gives us the option to create a backup schedule. This way we can define what we want to back up, where we want to back it up to, and how often this backup should run. Then we can sit back, relax, and know that our systems are performing this task on their own.

Before we can do anything with backups, we need to install the appropriate feature inside Windows. Using your **Add roles and features** link, go ahead and install the feature called **Windows Server Backup**. Once the feature has finished installing, you can launch the **Windows Server Backup** console which is available inside the **Tools** menu of Server Manager. Once inside, you will see some **Actions** listed on the right side of your screen. Clicking on the **Backup Schedule...** action will launch the wizard which brings us through the configuration of our scheduled backup program.

The first option you come across is deciding what it is that you want to backup. The default option is set for **Full server**, which will take a backup of everything in the operating system. If you want to customize the amount of data that is being backed up, you can choose the **Custom** option and proceed from there. Since I have lots of disk space available to me, I am going to stick with the recommended path of creating full server backups.

Next we get to the real advantage of using the scheduling concept, choosing how often our backup is going to run. The most common way is to choose a particular time of day, and let the backup run every day at that slotted time. If you have a server whose data is being updated regularly throughout the days and you would want to shorten your window of lost information in the event of needing to perform a restore, you can also specify to backup multiple times per day.

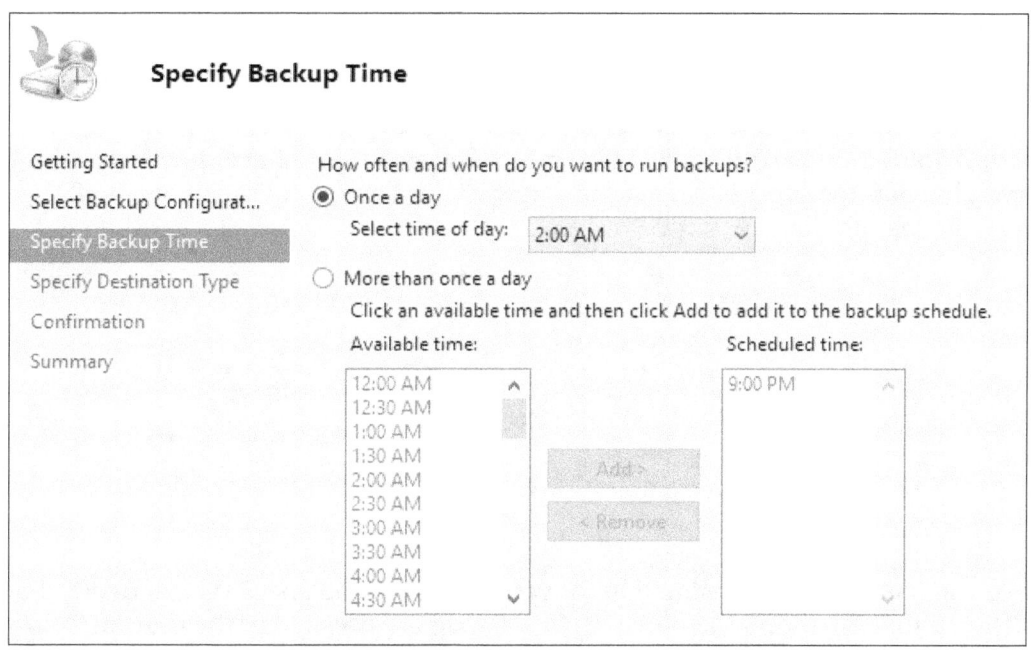

The last screen where we need to make a decision for our scheduled backups is the **Specify Destination Type** screen, where we determine the location that our backup files are going to be stored. You can see there are a couple of different options for storing the backup locally on the physical hard disks of the same server where you are configuring the backups. Storing backup files on a local, dedicated disk, or volume can be advantageous because the speed of the backup process will be increased. For servers that you are trying to backup during the workdays in order to continually backup data, you would likely want to choose a local backup option so that those backups run quickly and smoothly. Another advantage to using a locally connected disk for backups is that you can create multiple rollback points within your backup schema, keeping multiple days' worth of backup information in case you need to roll back to a particular point in time. However, I find that most admins prefer to keep all of their backup files in a centralized location, and that means choosing the third option on this screen, the one entitled **Back up to a shared network folder**. By choosing this option, we can specify a network location, such as a file server or drive mapping to a NAS, and we can set all of our different servers to backup to this same location. That way we have a central, standardized location where we know that all of our backup files are going to be sitting in the event that we need to pull one out and use it for a restore.

Core Infrastructure Services

I cannot tell you which option is best, because it depends on how you are planning to utilize backups in your own environment. The screen where we choose which destination type we want for our backups includes some good text to read over related to these options, such as the important note that when using a shared network folder for backups only one backup file can be stored at a time for your server, because the process of creating a new backup on the following day will overwrite the previous backup.

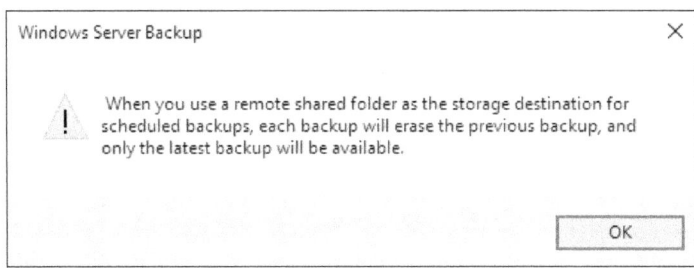

Once you have chosen a destination for your backups, and specified a network share location if that is the option you have chosen, you are finished in the wizard. Your backup jobs will automatically kick off at the allocated time which you specified during the wizard, and tomorrow you will see a new backup file existing for your server. If you are impatient like me and want to see the backup job run right now, you can walk through the other **Action** available in the **Windows Server Backup** console called **Backup Once...** in order to run a manual backup right away.

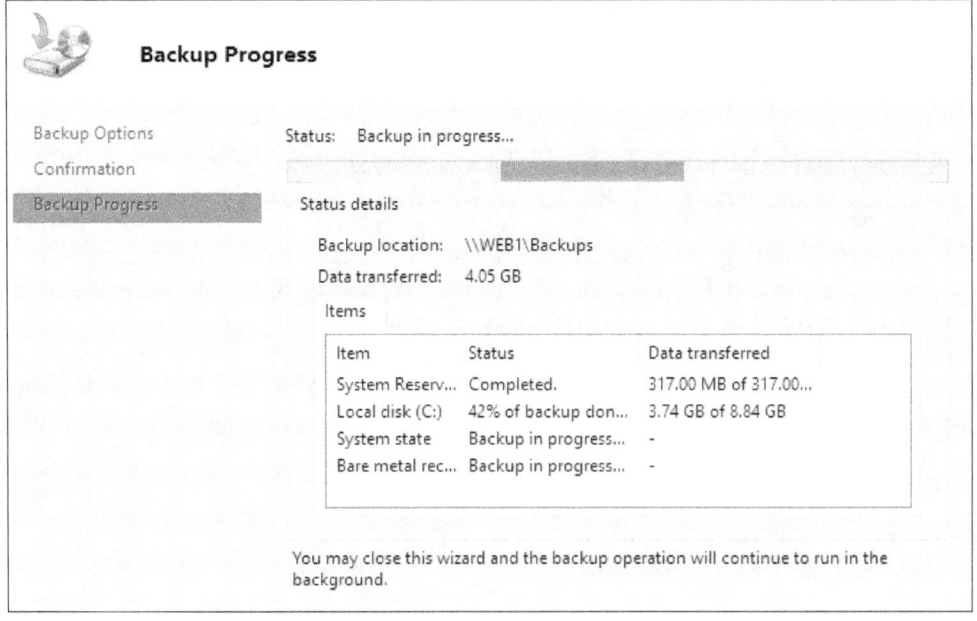

Restoring from Windows

Since you are being diligent and keeping good backups of your servers, the hope is then that you will never have to actually utilize those backup files in order to restore a server. But alas, the time will probably come when you have a server that goes sideways, or some data is accidentally deleted, and you must revisit the process of restoring data or an entire server in your infrastructure. If your server is still online and running, the restore process is quite easy to invoke from the same **Windows Server Backup** console. Open up the console, and choose the **Action** that says **Recover…**.

This invokes another wizard that walks us through the recovery process. First we specify the location of our backup file. If you have a dedicated backup location on the local server it is pretty simple to find, otherwise like in my example where we specified a network location, you choose **A backup stored on another location**, and then choose **Remote shared folder** in order to tell it where to find that backup file.

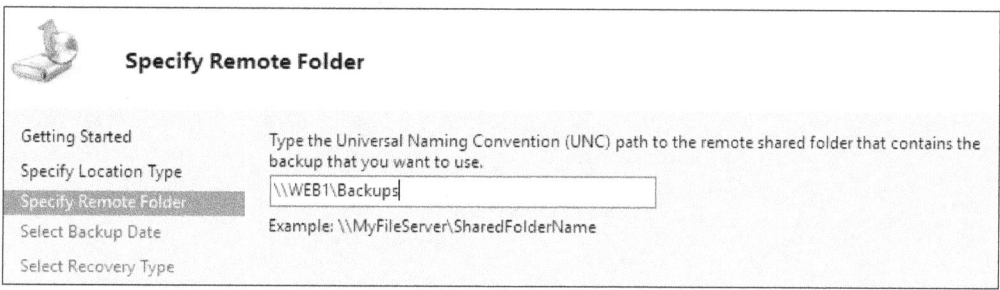

Based on the backup location that you have chosen, the wizard will now identify all available rollback dates that are available within the backup files. If you have stored your backup files on a local disk so that multiple days' worth of rollback points are available, then you will see numerous dates available to click on. For me, since I chose to store my backups on a network location, that means only one day's worth of backup information is available, and yesterday's date is the only one which I can choose. So I will choose to restore yesterday's backup, and continue on through the wizard.

Now that we have identified the specific backup file that is going to be used for recovery, we get to choose what information from that backup is going to be restored. This is a nice piece of the recovery platform, because often when we need to restore from backup it is only for specific files and folders which may have been deleted or corrupted. If that is the case, you choose the top option, **Files and folders**. In other cases, you may want to roll the entire server back to a certain date, and for that functionality you would choose to recover an entire **Volume**. Right now, I am just missing a few files that somehow disappeared between yesterday and today, so I am going to choose the default **Files and folders** option.

Core Infrastructure Services

The **Select Items to Recover** screen is now presented, which polls the backup file and displays to me the entire list of files and folders within the backup file, and I simply choose which ones I want to restore. This kind of recovery can be critical to your daily management of a file server, where the potential is high for users to accidentally delete information.

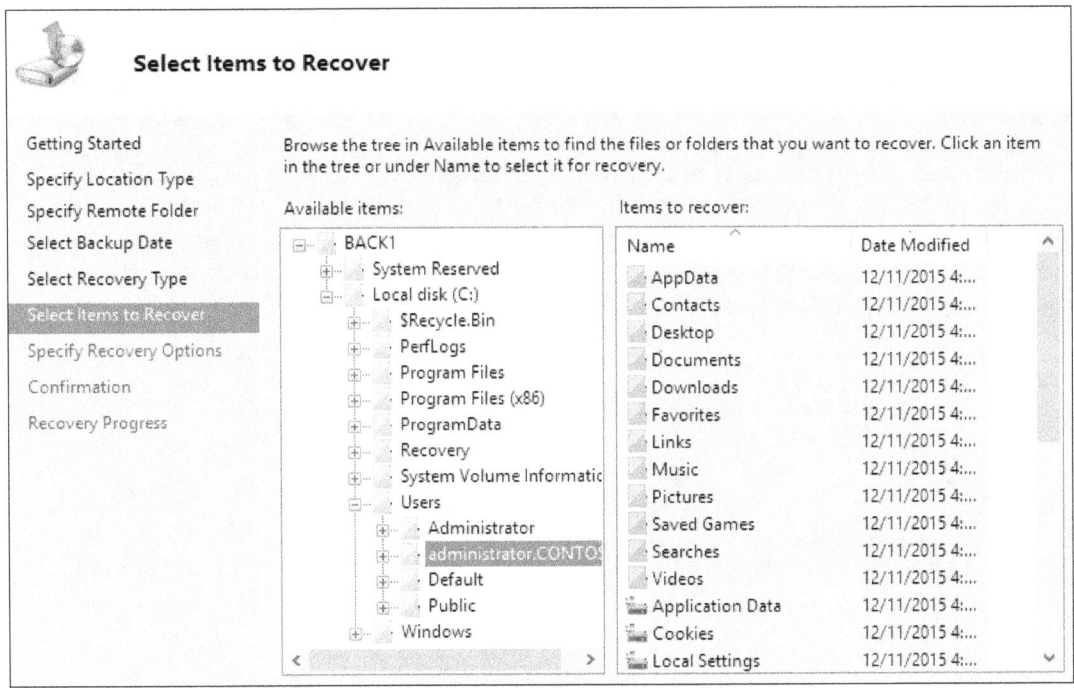

All that remains is to specify where you want these recovered files to be restored. You can choose for the recovered files to be placed back in their original location, or if you are running this recovery process on a different machine, you can choose to restore the files to a new location from which you can grab them and place them manually wherever they now need to reside.

Restoring from the disc

Recovery from the console inside Windows is a nice wizard-driven experience, but what about the case where your server has crashed hard? If you cannot get into Windows on your server, you cannot run the Windows Server Backup console in order to initiate your recovery process. In this case, we can still utilize our backup file that has been created, but we need to use it in combination with a Windows Server 2016 installation disc from which we can invoke the recovery process.

>  It is important to note that this recovery process cannot access locations on the network, and your backup file will have to be stored on a disk attached to your server. You can utilize a USB disk for this purpose during the recovery process, if you did not originally set up your backup job to store onto an existing locally attached disk.

To make things interesting, I'm going to crash my own server. This is the server that we took a backup of a few minutes ago. I accidentally deleted some very important files in my `C:\Windows` directory, whoops! Now this is all I see when I try to boot my server.

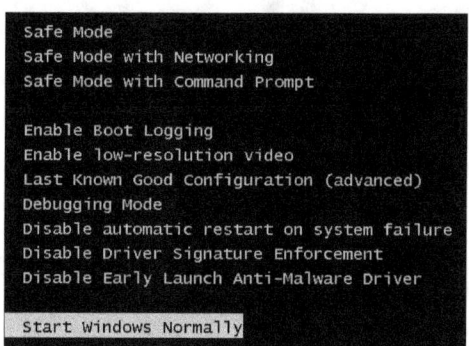

That's not a very friendly screen to see first thing in the morning! Since I seem to be stuck here and unable to boot into Windows, my chances of running the recovery wizard are nil. What to do? Boot to the Windows Server 2016 installer DVD! No, I do not want to install Windows afresh, as all of my programs and data would still be gone. Rather, once I get into the installer screens, you will notice that there is an option down in the corner for **Repair your computer**. Choose this option in order to open up the recovery options that are available to us on the installation DVD.

Core Infrastructure Services

Now you see the screen adjust to a new hue of the color blue, indicating that we have entered a special portion of the installer disc. If we click on the **Troubleshoot** button, we can see all of the options that we have available.

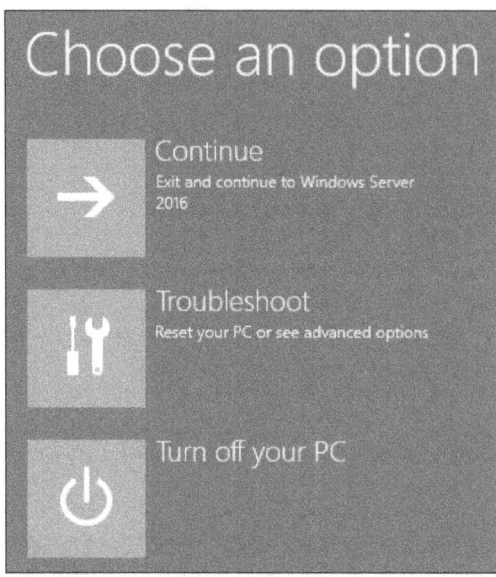

If you think you can fix whatever the issue is from a **Command Prompt**, choose that option and try to fix it yourself. For our example, I am pretty sure that I significantly hosed the operating system, so I am going to do a full **System Image Recovery** and click on that button.

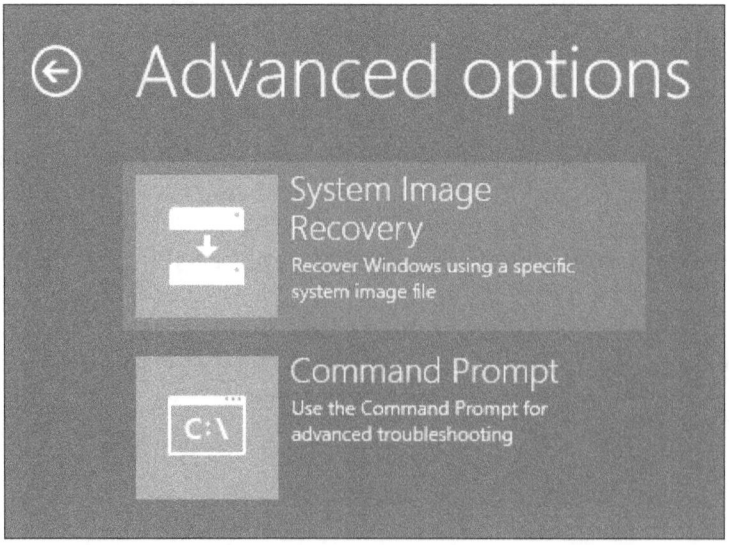

Chapter 3

As long as you have a hard drive connected which contains a Windows Server Backup file, the wizard launches and pulls in the information about the backup. Since I had originally chosen to store my backup file on a network location, I copied the backup files down to a disk and connected it as a second disk into my server. The wizard automatically recognizes that backup file, and displays it in the **Select a system image backup** screen.

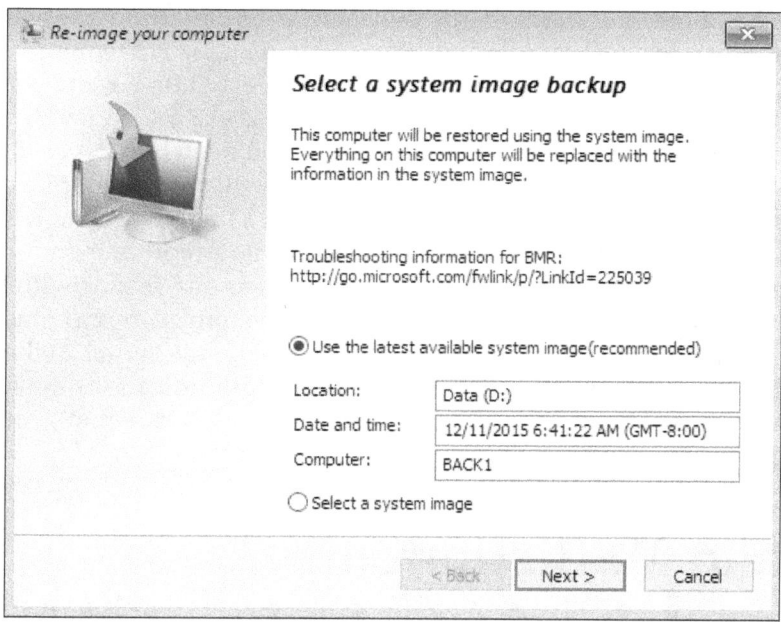

Now by simply clicking on **Next** a few times to progress through the wizard, my backup image is restoring down onto my server.

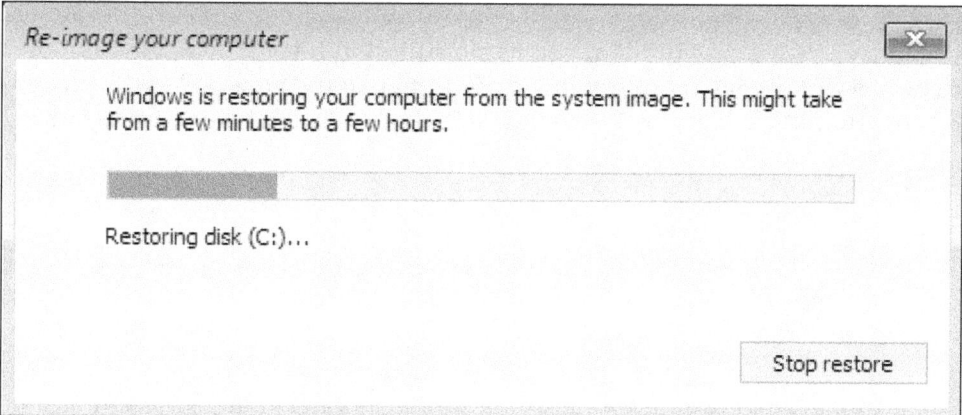

Once the restore process has completed, the system reboots and launches itself right back into Windows where it is fully functional back to the restore point. My test server doesn't have much of anything running on it, so the time that it took to restore was pretty minimal and a production box may take a little longer, but I'd say that 20 minutes from blowing up the server to being fully recovered is a pretty awesome number!

Keeping good and recent backup files is critical to your operation's sustainability. I have worked on quite a few systems where the admins took some manual backups after getting their servers initially configured, but never set up a regular schedule. Even if the data on the server never changes, if you are part of a domain you never want to do this. In the event that a server fails and you need to recover it, restoring a backup that is within a few days old will generally recover great. But if you restore an image that is six months old, Windows itself will come back online with no problems and all of your data will exist, but in that amount of time your computer account for that server would most certainly have fallen out of sync with the domain, causing you authentication errors against the domain controllers. In some cases you may even have to do goofy things like disjoin and re-join the server to the domain following the image restoration in order to recover communications to the domain. If you would have been keeping regular backups from which to restore, you would not have to deal with those issues.

MMC and MSC shortcuts

You have probably noticed that many of the management consoles which we utilize to configure components inside Windows Server 2016 look pretty similar. What happens under the hood with a number of these consoles is that you are actually looking at a snap-in function, a specific set of tools that are snapped into a generic console tool called the **Microsoft Management Console**, or more commonly referred to as **MMC**. In fact, rather than open all of these management functions from inside Server Manager, for many of them you could simply type MMC by navigating to **Start | Run** or in a Command Prompt window, and invoke the generic MMC console. From here you can click on the **File** menu and choose **Add/Remove Snap-in...**.

Chapter 3

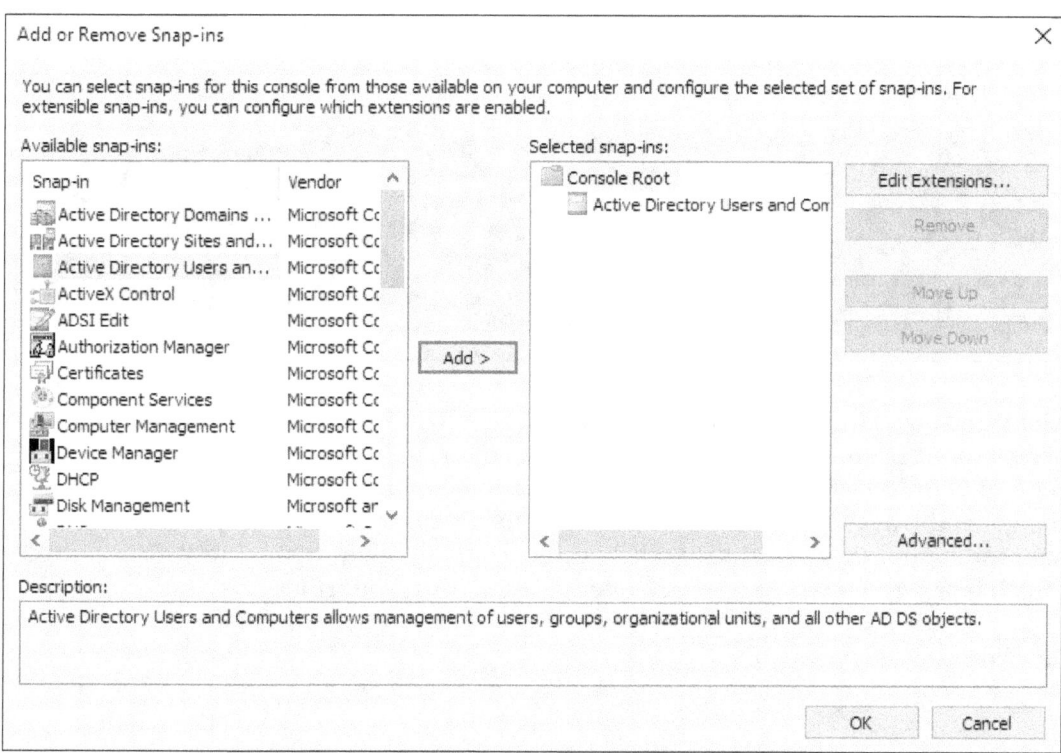

Choose the management snap-in that you would like to work in, and add it to the console. There are a great number of management functions that can be accessed through the standard MMC console, and even some particular functions where MMC is the preferred, or perhaps the only method to interact with some components of Windows. For example, later in our book we will look into certificate stores within Windows Server 2016, and we will be utilizing MMC for some of that interaction.

Another interesting way to open up many of the management consoles is by using their direct **MSC** tool name. An MSC file is simply a saved set of an MMC console session. There are many MSC shortcuts stored in Windows Server 2016 by default. If a given management console provides the capability of being launched by an MSC, all you need to do is type in the name of the MSC by navigating to either **Start | Run** or in a Command Prompt, and it will launch into that particular management console without needing to snap anything in, and without needing to open Server Manager whatsoever. Since I tend to prefer using a keyboard over a mouse, I always have a PowerShell or Command Prompt window open on each system I'm working with, and I can very quickly use that window to open up any of my MSC administrative consoles. Let's show one example so you know exactly how to use this functionality, and then I will provide a list of the common MSCs which I find useful on a day-to-day basis.

Open an elevated PowerShell window, type WF.MSC, and press *Enter*.

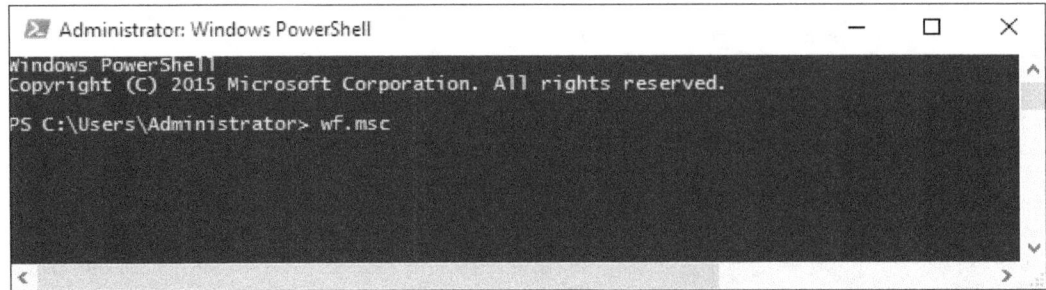

The **Windows Firewall with Advanced Security** window will open, and is ready to accept input from you. We didn't have to poke through **Control Panel**, or open the regular **Windows Firewall** and then click on the **Advanced Settings** link, which are the general ways to get into this console by using a mouse. By knowing our MSC shortcut name, we were able to take a direct route to opening the full WFAS console, which is where I often go to check over particular firewall rules or status.

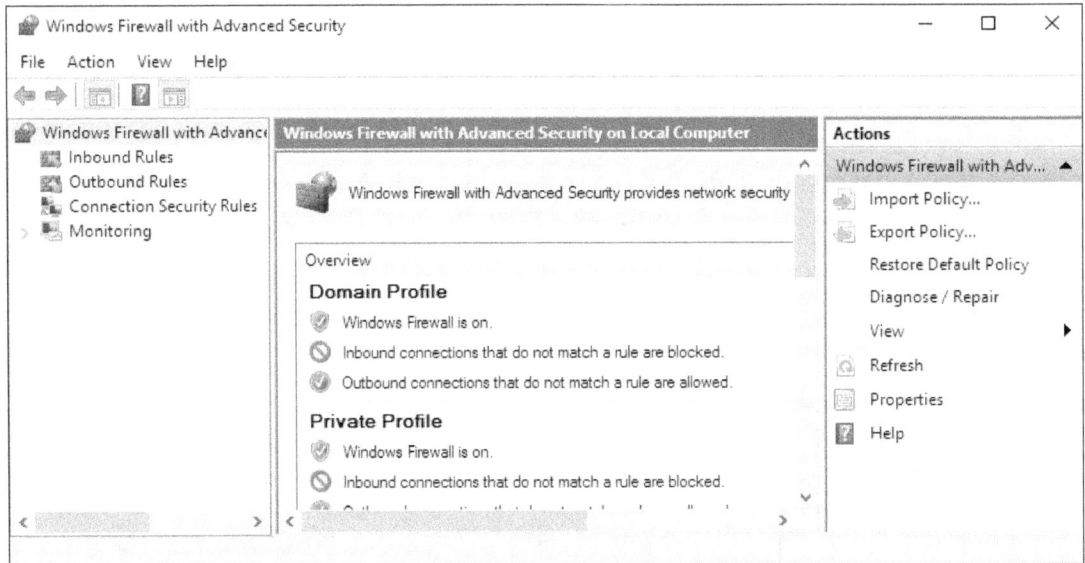

Now that you've seen how an MSC command works, and again there are many different places where you can type in the name of an MSC and invoke it. I want to leave you with a list of common MSC consoles which you can use to quickly gain access to many administrative consoles on your servers:

- DSA.MSC: Active Directory Users and Computers

- `DSSITE.MSC`: Active Directory Sites and Services
- `DNSMGMT.MSC`: DNS Manager
- `GPEDIT.MSC`: Local Group Policy Editor
- `GPMC.MSC`: Group Policy Management Console
- `CERTSRV.MSC`: Certification Authority Management
- `CERTTMPL.MSC`: Certificate Template Management
- `CERTLM.MSC`: Local Computer Certificates Store
- `COMPMGMT.MSC`: Computer Management
- `DEVMGMT.MSC`: Device Manager
- `DHCPMGMT.MSC`: DHCP Manager
- `DISKMGMT.MSC`: Disk Management
- `EVENTVWR.MSC`: Event Viewer
- `PERFMON.MSC`: Performance Monitor
- `SECPOL.MSC`: Local Security Policy Console
- `FSMGMT.MSC`: Shared Folders
- `WF.MSC`: Windows Firewall with Advanced Security

Summary

Today we discussed some of the roles and components inside Windows Server 2016 that you will need to utilize and be familiar with, if you want to run a truly Microsoft-centric infrastructure. Active Directory, DNS, and DHCP are the core services that underlie and support your entire infrastructure. A basic understanding of these technologies is essential to any Windows Server administrator, and an in-depth knowledge of the way these tools work together will open many doors to you as you progress through your IT career. Almost all of the other roles and features available in Windows Server are supported by or hinge on these core services. I hope that you are comfortable with navigating around inside them after following through the examples in this chapter.

Now we continue on our journey through Windows Server 2016 with the next chapter as we dive into one of the scarier topics—for many admins anyway—certificates!

4
Certificates in Windows Server 2016

"Ugh, we need to use certificates to make this work."

– Quote from an anonymous admin who just discovered a new piece of technology they are implementing requires the use of certificates in their organization.

If this sounds familiar, don't scrap that new project just yet! For some reason, the use of certificates seems like a daunting task to many of us, even those who have worked in IT for a lot of years. I think this is probably because there are many different options available on a certificate server, but there is not a lot of common sense or intuitiveness built into the management console for dealing with certificates. This combined with a general lack of requirement for certificates on servers for so many years means that, even though this technology has existed for a long time, a lot of everyday server administrators have not had the opportunity to dig in and deploy certificates for themselves. I regularly deploy a couple of technologies that require a broad use of certificates in an organization, often needing to issue them to every workstation in the network, and I come across these kinds of quotes and concerns all the time. Issuing a certificate to a single business-critical web server sounds daunting enough if you don't have any experience with the process, let alone issuing hundreds or thousands of certificates all at once. Another common scenario is one where a company determined certificates to be in their best interests but lacked the on-staff resources to stand it up themselves, and so hired out a third party to implement certificates within the network. While this gets certificates rolling, it often leaves a knowledge gap that never gets filled, so you may have a certificate server up and running, but not be at all comfortable with modifying or utilizing it.

The broad term for a certificate environment is known as **Public Key Infrastructure** (**PKI**). I call that out specifically because you will probably see *PKI* listed in documentation or requirements at some point, if you haven't already. Your PKI is provided by servers in your network, and configuring those servers to issue certificates for you is the purpose of this chapter. The servers which you determine to be your certificate servers are more technically known as **certification authority** (**CA**) servers, and we will reference them as CA servers throughout this book.

In order to get you rolling with certificates in your own network, here are the topics that we will cover in this chapter:

- Common certificate types
- Planning your PKI
- Creating a new certificate template
- Issuing your new certificates
- Creating an autoenrollment policy
- Obtaining a public authority SSL certificate
- Exporting and importing certificates

Common certificate types

There are a number of different types of certificates that you may find yourself needing to publish. As you will see coming up shortly, when you need a certificate that has a list of particular requirements, you can build that certificate template to whatever specifications you like. So, in a sense, there aren't really certificate *types* at all, but just certificate templates that you scope to contain whatever pieces of information that are needed for that cert to do its job. While this holds true technically, it is generally easier to segment certificates into some different groups, making them more distinguishable for the particular job that they are intended to perform.

User certificates

As the name implies, a user certificate is one used for purposes that are specific to the username itself. One of the platforms that is driving more certificate adoption is the network authentication process. Companies who are looking into stronger authentication in their environments are often looking into certificates as part of that authentication process. Smart cards are one of the specific mechanisms that can be used for this purpose, some sort of physical card to be plugged into a computer in order for the user to gain access to that computer.

Smart cards can also be stored virtually, within a special place on newer machines called the TPM. But that is a different discussion for a different time. The reason we mention smart cards here is that many times the core functionality of the smart card authentication is provided by a user certificate that has been stored on that smart card.

Another authentication form that is becoming more popular is **one-time-passwords** (**OTP**). This requires the user to enter a randomly generated pin number in addition to their regular login criteria, and in some cases when the user enters their pin, they are being issued a temporary user certificate to be used as part of the authentication chain. Yet a third place that user certificates are commonly found is when companies employ file encrypting technologies such as EFS, short for Encrypting File System. If this is something you have been thinking of looking into, it is important to know that you will also be using user certificates as part of this encryption processing.

Computer certificates

Often referred to as computer certificates or machine certificates, these guys get issued to computers in order to assist with the interaction between the network and the computer account itself. Technologies like SCCM that interact with and manage the computer systems regardless of what users are logged into those computers make use of computer certificates. These kinds of certificates are also used for encryption processing between systems on the network, for example, if you were interested in using IPsec to encrypt communications between clients and a highly secure file server, issuing computer or machine certificates to the endpoints within this communication chain would be essential to making that work properly. I issue computer certificates as part of every project in my day job, to be used by the computers as part of the authentication process for a remote access technology called DirectAccess. There are many different reasons and technologies you may be interested in, which would require the issuance of certificates to the client workstations in your environment.

SSL certificates

If you find yourself in the middle of the certificate boat, where you haven't really managed a CA server but you have at one point issued and installed some kind of certificate, then chances are that the certificate you did work with was an SSL certificate. This is by far the most common type of certificate that is used in today's technology infrastructure, and your company is more than likely using SSL certificates, even if you are not aware of them and do not even have a single CA server running inside your network.

SSL certificates are most commonly used to secure website traffic. Any time you visit a website and see HTTPS in the address bar, your browser is using an SSL packet stream to send information back and forth between your computer and the web server that you are talking to. The web server has an SSL certificate on it, and your browser has checked over that certificate before allowing you onto the web page, to make sure that the certificate is valid and really is who it says it is. You see, if we did not use SSL certificates on websites, anyone could impersonate our site.

Let's give a quick example. Let's say one of your users is at a coffee shop, using their public Wi-Fi. An attacker has figured out a way to manipulate DNS on that Wi-Fi network, and so when your user tries to visit `mail.contoso.com` in order to access their Outlook Web Access, the attacker has hijacked that traffic and the user is now sitting on a website that looks like their company portal, but is actually a website hosted by the attacker himself. The user types in their username and password, and bingo, the attacker now has that user's credentials and can use them to access your real network. What prevents this from happening every day in the real world? **SSL certificates**. When you force your externally facing websites, like that e-mail login page, to be HTTPS sites, it requires the client browsers to check over the SSL certificate that is presented with the website. That SSL certificate contains information that only you as a company have, it cannot be impersonated. This way when your user accesses your real login page, the browser checks out the SSL certificate, finds it to be correct, and simply continues on its merry way. The user never even knows they are being protected except for the little lock symbol up near their browser's address bar. On the other hand, if their traffic is being intercepted and redirected to a fake website, the SSL certificate check will fail, and the user will be stopped in their tracks, at least to read through a certificate warning page before being able to proceed. At this point the user should back off and realize that something is wrong, and contact their IT staff to look into the issue.

SSL certificates used by websites on the Internet are almost always provided not by your own internal CA server, but by a public certification authority. You have probably heard of many of them, such as Verisign, Entrust, DigiCert, GoDaddy, and so on. Companies generally purchase SSL certificates from these public authorities because those authorities are trusted by default on new computers that users might purchase in the field. New systems know by default how to interact with certificates issued from these authorities, and you don't have to take any special actions to make your websites function on the Internet. On the other hand, it is possible to issue SSL certificates from a CA server that you have running inside your network, but it requires a couple of things that make it difficult. First, if you want to issue your own SSL certificate to a public website, you need to externalize at least part of your internal PKI, known as the **Certificate Revocation List** (**CRL**), to the Internet. Any time you take a component that is internal to your network, and publicize it on the Internet, you are introducing a security risk and so unless you absolutely have to do this, it is generally not recommended. The second reason it is difficult to utilize your own SSL certificates on public websites is that only your own computers will know how to trust this SSL certificate. So if a user brings their company laptop home and uses it to access their e-mail login page, it will probably work fine. But if a user tries to access the same e-mail login page from their home computer that is not part of your domain or network, they would get a certificate warning message and have to take special steps in order to gain access to the website. What a pain for the users.

These issues can be alleviated by purchasing an SSL certificate from one of those public cert authorities, and so purchasing these kinds of certificates is by far the normal and recommended way to make use of SSL on your publically-facing websites. Websites that are completely inside the network are a different story, since they are not facing the Internet and their security footprint is incredibly smaller. You can certainly use your internal CA server to issue SSL certificates to your internal websites, and not have to incur the cost associated with purchasing certificates for all of those websites.

There are a few different tiers of SSL certificates that you can purchase from a public CA, information for which is listed on the authority's own websites. Essentially, the idea is that the more you pay, the more secure your certificate is. These tiers are related to the way that the authority validates back against the certificate requestor, since that is really where the security comes into play with SSL certificates. The authority is guaranteeing that when you access the page secured by their certificate, the cert was issued to the real company who owns that web page.

Other than the validation tier which you get to choose from when purchasing a certificate, there is another option you have to decide on as well, and this one is much more important to the technical aspect of the way that certificates work. There are different naming conventions available to you when you purchase a certificate, and there is no best answer for which one to choose. Every situation requiring a certificate will be unique, and will have to be evaluated individually to decide which naming scheme works best for the situation at hand. Let's quickly cover these three possibilities for an SSL certificate naming convention.

Single-name certificates

This is the cheapest and most common route to take when purchasing a certificate for an individual website. A single-name certificate protects and contains information about one single DNS name. When you are setting up a new website at `portal.contoso.com` and you want this website to protect some traffic by using HTTPS, you would install an SSL certificate onto the website. When you issue the request to your certification authority for this new certificate, you would input the specific name of `portal.contoso.com` into the **Common name** field of the request form. This single DNS name is the only name that can be protected and validated by this certificate.

Subject Alternative Name certificates

Subject Alternative Name (SAN) certificates generally cost a little bit more than a single-name cert, because they have more capabilities. When you request a SAN certificate, you have the option of defining multiple DNS names that the certificate can protect. Once issued, the SAN certificate will contain a primary DNS name which is typically the main name of the website, and further inside the cert properties you will find listed the additional DNS names that you specified during your request. This single certificate can be installed on a web server and used to validate traffic for any of the DNS names that are contained in the certificate. A use-case example of a SAN certificate is when setting up a Lync server. Lync uses many different DNS names, but all the names that are within the same DNS domain. This is an important note regarding SAN certificates, your names must be part of the same domain or subdomain. Here is an example list of the names we might include in a SAN certificate for the purposes of Lync:

- `Lync.contoso.com` (the primary one)
- `Lyncdiscover.contoso.com`
- `Meet.contoso.com`
- `Dialin.contoso.com`
- `Admin.contoso.com`

Wildcard certificates

Last but certainly not least is the wildcard certificate. This is the luxury model, the one that has the most capabilities, gives you the most flexibility, and at the same time offers the easiest path to implementation on many servers. The name on a wildcard certificate begins with a **star** (*). This star means *any*, as in *anything preceding the DNS domain name is covered by this certificate*. If you own `contoso.com` and plan to stand up many public DNS records that will flow to many different websites and web servers, you could purchase a single wildcard certificate with the name `*.contoso.com`, and it may cover all of your certificate needs. Typically, wildcards can be installed on as many web servers as you need, with no limits on the amount of different DNS names that it can validate. I have run across an exception to this once, when a particular customer's agreement with their certification authority specified that they had to report and pay for each instance of their wildcard certificate that was in use. So watch those agreements when you make them with your CA. Most of the time, a wildcard is meant to be a free-for-all within the company so that you can deploy many sites and services across many servers, and utilize your same certificate everywhere.

The downside of a wildcard certificate is that it costs more, significantly more. But if you have large certificate needs or big plans for growth, it will make your certificate administration much easier, faster, and cost-effective in the long run.

Planning your PKI

Since we are revolving all of our discussion in this book around Windows Server 2016, this certainly means that your CA server can and should be one provided by this latest and greatest of operating systems. As with most capabilities in Server 2016, the creation of a certification authority server in your network is as simple as installing a Windows role. When you go to add the role to a new server, it is the very first role in the list called **Active Directory Certificate Services (AD CS)**. When installing this role, you will be presented with a couple of important options and you must understand the meaning behind these options before you create a solid PKI environment.

Enterprise versus standalone

When configuring your CA role for the first time, you will be presented with a big choice. Do you want this CA server to be an **enterprise CA**, or a **standalone CA**?

Let's start with the enterprise CA. As the wizard will tell you, an enterprise CA server must be a member of your domain, and these certificate servers typically stay online so that they can issue certificates to computers and users who need them. Wait a minute, why in the world would we want to turn a certificate server off anyway? We will discuss that in a minute, but if you intend to utilize this CA to issue certificates, it must obviously remain turned on. Most CA servers within a domain environment will be enterprise CAs. When creating an enterprise CA, your templates and some certificate-specific information is able to store itself within Active Directory, which makes integration between certificates and the domain tighter and more beneficial. If this is your first interaction with the CA role, I recommend that you start with an enterprise CA because this meets the needs better for most organizations.

As you can correctly imply from the preceding text, this means that a standalone CA is less common to see in the wild. Standalones can be members of the domain, or they can remain out of that part of the network and reside on a local workgroup. If you had a security requirement that dictated your certificate server could not be domain joined, that might be a reason you would use a standalone CA. Another reason might be in environments where Active Directory simply does not exist. In my eyes, it would be extremely rare to find a network where someone was trying to use a Windows Server 2016 as their certification authority and at the same time was not running Active Directory Domain Services, but I'm sure there is a corner case somewhere that is doing exactly this.

In that case, you would also need to choose standalone. A third example when you would choose standalone is the event we eluded to already, where you might have a reason to turn off your server. When you run this scenario, it is typically referred to as having an **offline root**. We haven't talked about root CAs yet, but we will in a minute. When you run an offline root, you create the top level of your PKI hierarchy as a standalone root CA, and then you build subordinate CAs underneath it. Your subordinate CAs are the ones who issue the actual certificates, which means that the root can be safely shut down. Why would you want to do this? Well, most companies don't, but I have worked with some that have very high-level security policies, and this is basically the reason why you might visit this topic. If all of a company's CA servers are tied together as enterprise CAs with all of their information being stored inside Active Directory, a compromise to one of the subordinate issuing CAs could spell disaster for your entire PKI. It is possible that the only way to remediate an attack would be to wipe out the whole PKI environment, all of the CA servers, and build them up again. If you had to do this, it would mean not only rebuilding your servers, but also re-issuing brand new copies of all your certificates to every user and device that has them.

On the other hand, if you were running a standalone root CA that was offline, it would not have been affected by the attack. In this case, you could tear down your online certificate servers, but your core root server would have been safe. You could then bring this root back online, rebuild new subordinates from it, and have an easier path to being 100% operational because your root keys that are stored within the CA would not have to be re-issued.

Like I said, I do not see this very often in the field, but it is a possibility. If you are interested in learning more about offline root CAs and their uses, I highly recommend checking out the TechNet article at `http://social.technet.microsoft.com/wiki/contents/articles/2900.offline-root-certification-authority-ca.aspx`.

Root versus subordinate

This is the second big choice you need to make when building a new CA. Is your new server going to be a **root CA** or a **subordinate CA**?

The difference really is just a matter of what you want your CA hierarchy to look like. In a PKI tree, there is a single high-level certificate, self-signed to itself by the root CA, that everything chains up to. A subordinate CA, on the other hand, is one who resides below a root CA in the tree, and it has been issued a certificate of its own from the root above it.

If your plans are to only run a single CA server, then it must be a root. If you are creating a tiered approach to issuing certificates, then the first CA in your environment needs to be a root, and you can slide subordinates in underneath it. You are allowed to have multiple roots, and therefore multiple trees, within a network. So your particular PKI can be structured however you see fit. In smaller companies, it is very common to see only a single CA server, an enterprise root. For the sake of simplicity in administration, these customers are willing to take the risk that if something happens to that server, it won't be that big of a deal to build a new one and re-issue certificates.

For larger networks, it is more common to see a single root with a couple of subordinates below it. Typically, in this case, the root is only responsible for being the top dog, and the subordinate CAs are the ones who do the actual issuing of certificates to the clients.

Can I install the CA role onto a domain controller?

Since the role is officially called the **Active Directory Certificate Services** role, does that mean I should install this role onto one of my domain controller servers? No! Unfortunately, I have run across many small-to-medium businesses that have done exactly this, and luckily they don't have too many problems. So technically, it does work. However, it is not a Microsoft-recommended installation path and you should build your CAs on their own servers; try not to cohost them with other roles whenever possible.

Creating a new certificate template

Enough talk, it's time to get some work done. Now that our CA role has been installed, let's make it do something! The purpose of a certificate server is to issue certificates, right? So maybe do that? Not so fast. When you issue a certificate from a CA server to a device or user, you are not choosing which *certificate* you want to deploy, rather you are choosing which **certificate template** you want to utilize in order to deploy a certificate that is based upon the settings configured inside that template. Certificate templates are sort of like recipes for cooking. On the server side, you build out your templates and include all of the particular ingredients, or settings, that you want to be incorporated into your final certificate. Then, when the users come to request a certificate from the CA server, they are sort of baking a certificate onto their system by telling the CA which template recipe to follow when building that certificate. Certificates relating to food? Maybe that's a stretch, but it's getting pretty late at night and it is the first thing that came to mind.

Certificates in Windows Server 2016

When you walk through the steps to configure your first CA server, it comes with some prebuilt certificate templates right in the console. In fact, one of those templates called **Computer** is typically preconfigured to the point where if a client computer were to reach out and request a computer certificate from your new CA, it would be able to successfully issue one. But where is the fun in using prebuilt templates and certificates? I would rather build my own template so that I can specify the particular configurations and settings inside that template. This way I know exactly what settings are contained within my certificates that will ultimately be issued to my computers in the network.

Once again, the first thing we need to do is launch the proper administrative console in order to do our work. Inside the **Tools** menu of **Server Manager**, go ahead and click on **Certification Authority**. Once inside, you can expand the name of your certification authority and see some folders, including one on the bottom called **Certificate Templates**. If you click on this folder, you will see a list of the templates that are currently built into our CA server. Since we do not want to utilize one of these pre-existing templates, it is common sense that we would try to right-click in here and create a new template, but this is actually not the correct place to build a new template. The reason why new certificate templates are not built right from this screen must be above my pay grade, because it seems silly that they aren't, but in order to get into a second screen where we need to go to actually manage and modify our templates, you need to right-click on the **Certificate Templates** folder, and then choose **Manage**:

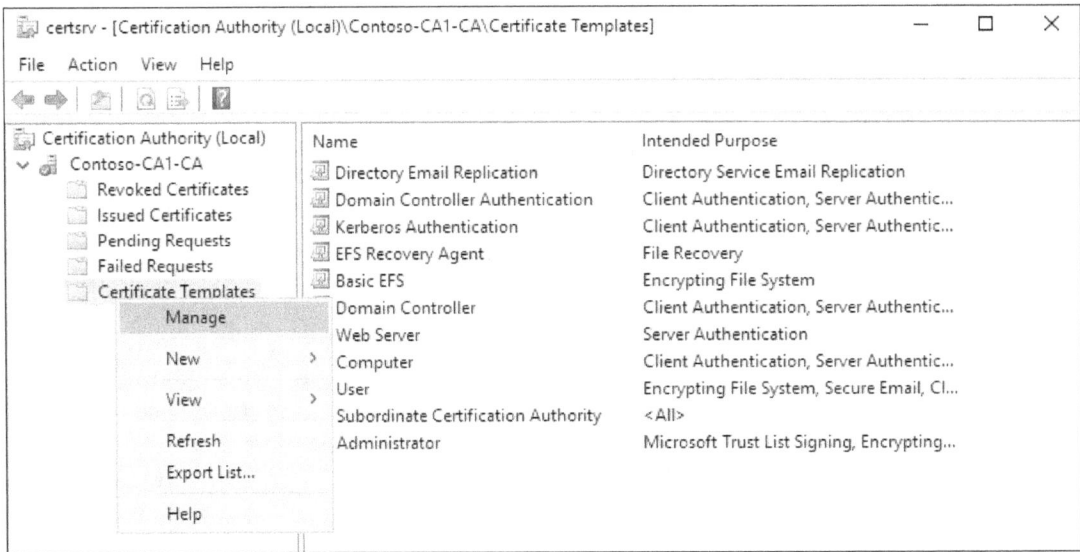

Now you see a much more comprehensive list of templates, including a number of them you couldn't view on the first screen. In order to build a new template, what we want to do is find a pre-existing template that functions similarly to the purpose that we want our new certificate template to serve. Computer templates are becoming commonly issued across many organizations due to more and more technologies requiring these certificates to exist, yet like we talked about we don't want to utilize that baked-in template that is simply called **Computer**, because we want our template to have a more specific name and maybe we want the certificate validity period to be longer than *stock*. What we do then is right-click on the built-in **Computer** template, and click on **Duplicate Template**. This opens the **Properties** screen for our new template, from which we first want to give our new template a unique name inside the **General** tab. In an upcoming chapter, we will discuss DirectAccess, the remote access technology that will be used in our environment. A good implementation of DirectAccess includes machine certificates to be issued to all of the mobile client workstations, so we will plan to make use of this new template for those purposes. The **General** tab is also the place where we get to define our validity period for this certificate, which we will set to 3 years.

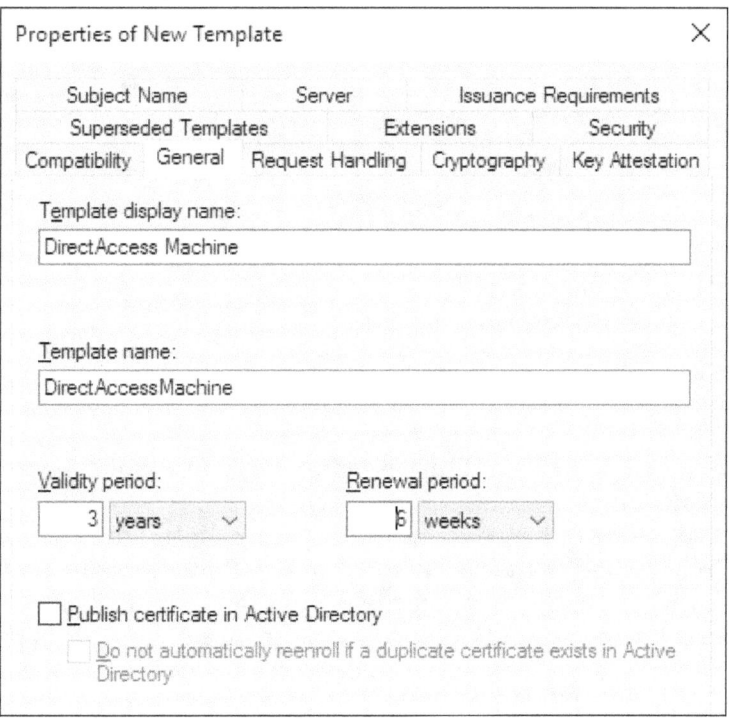

If the certificates that you want to issue require any additional setting changes, you can flip through the available tabs inside properties and make the necessary adjustments. For our example, another setting I will change is inside the **Subject Name** tab. I want my new certificates to have a subject name which matches the common name of the computer where it is being issued, so I have chosen **Common name** from the drop-down list:

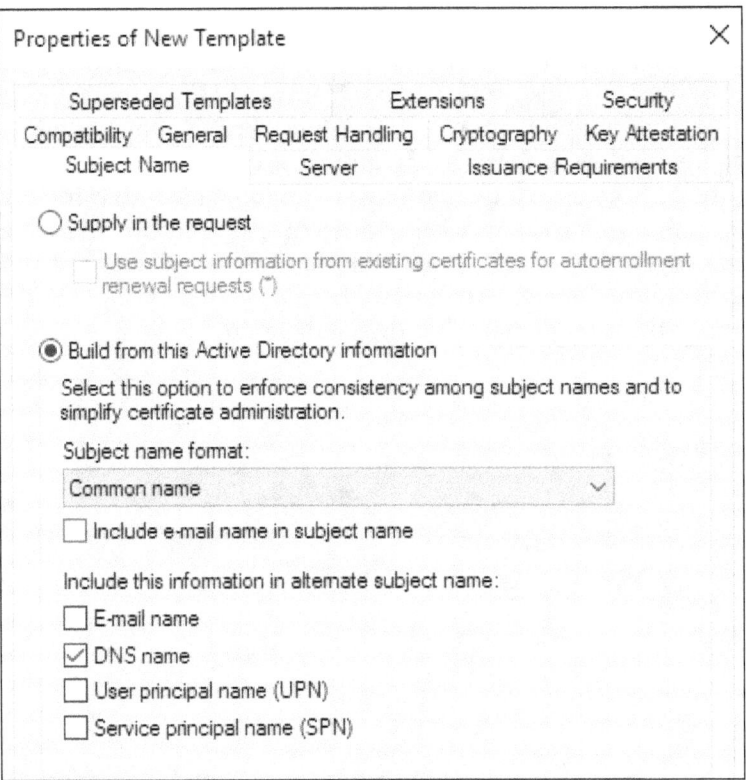

We have one more tab to visit, and this is something you should check over on every certificate template that you build. It is the **Security** tab. We want to check here to make sure that the security permissions for this template are set in a way that allows the certificate to be issued to the users or computers that we desire, and at the same time make sure that the template's security settings are not too loose, creating a situation where someone might be able to get a certificate who doesn't need it. For our example, I plan to issue these DirectAccess certificates to all of the computers in the domain, because this kind of machine certificate I have created could be used for general IPsec authentications as well. So I am just making sure that I have **Domain Computers** listed in the **Security** tab and that they are set for **Enroll** permissions, so that any computer who is joined to my domain will have the option of requesting a new certificate based off my new template.

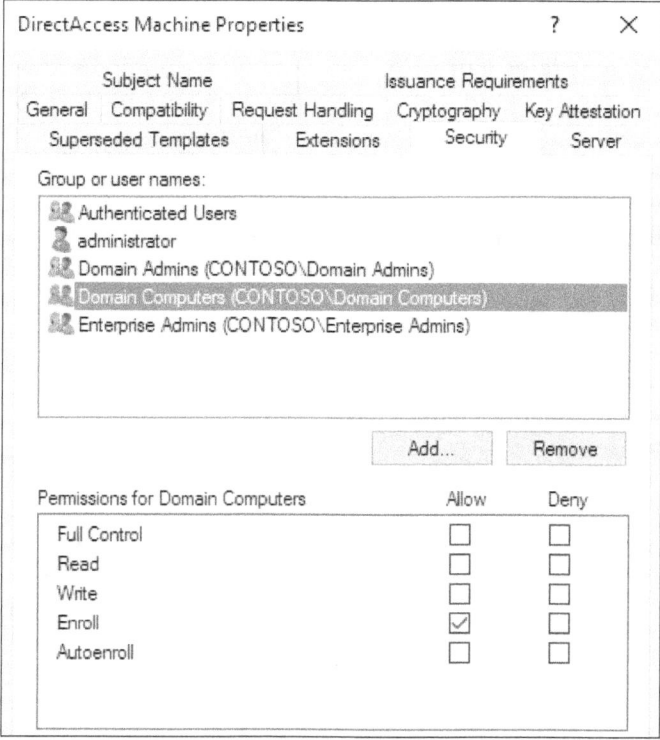

Since that is everything I need inside my new certificate, I simply click on **OK**, and my new certificate template is now included in the list of templates on my CA server.

Issuing your new certificates

Next comes the part that trips up a lot of people on their first attempt. You now have a brand new template to issue, and we have verified that the permissions within that certificate template are appropriately configured so that any computer on your network should be able to request one of these certificates, right? So our logical next step would be to jump onto a client computer and request a certificate, but there is first one additional item that needs to be accomplished in order to make that possible.

Even though the new template has been created, it has not yet been published. So at the moment, the CA server will not offer our new template as an option to the clients, even though security permissions are configured for it to do so. The process to publish a certificate template is very quick, only a couple of mouse clicks, but unless you know about the need to do this, it can be a very frustrating experience.

Publishing the template

If your **Certificate Templates Console** is still open, the one where we were managing our templates, you can go ahead and close that so you are back at the main certification authority management console. Remember how we noticed that the list of available certificate templates that shows up here is much shorter? This is because only these certificate templates are currently published and available to be issued. In order to add additional templates to the published list, including our new one, we simply right-click on the **Certificate Templates** folder, and then navigate to **New | Certificate Template to Issue**:

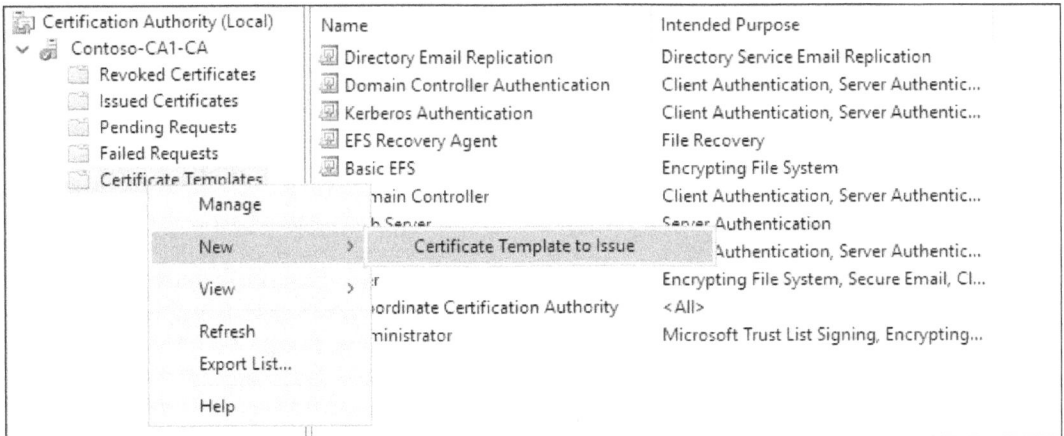

Now we are presented with a list of the available templates that are not yet issued. All you need to do is choose your new template from the list, and click on **OK**. The new template is now included in the list of published certificate templates, and we are ready to request one from a client computer:

Chapter 4

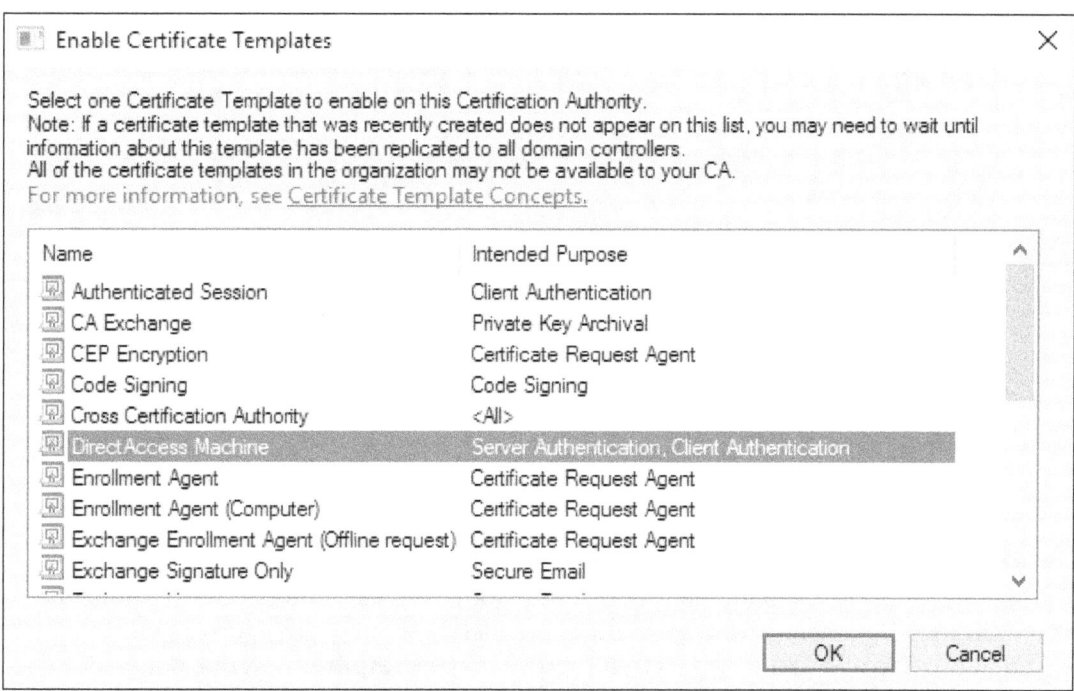

If you look through this list and do not see your newly created template, you may have to take an additional step. Sometimes simply waiting will resolve this behavior, because occasionally the reason that the new template does not show up in the list is because you are waiting for your domain controllers to finish replicating. At other times, you will find that even after waiting for a while, your new template is still not in this list. In that case, you probably just need to restart the certification authority service to force it to pull in the new template information. To restart the CA service, you right-click on the CA's name near the top of the **Certification Authority** management console, and navigate to **All Tasks | Stop Service**. The stopping of that service typically only takes a second, and then you can immediately right-click on the CA name again, and this time navigate to **All Tasks | Start Service**.

Now, try to publish your new template again, and you should see it in the list:

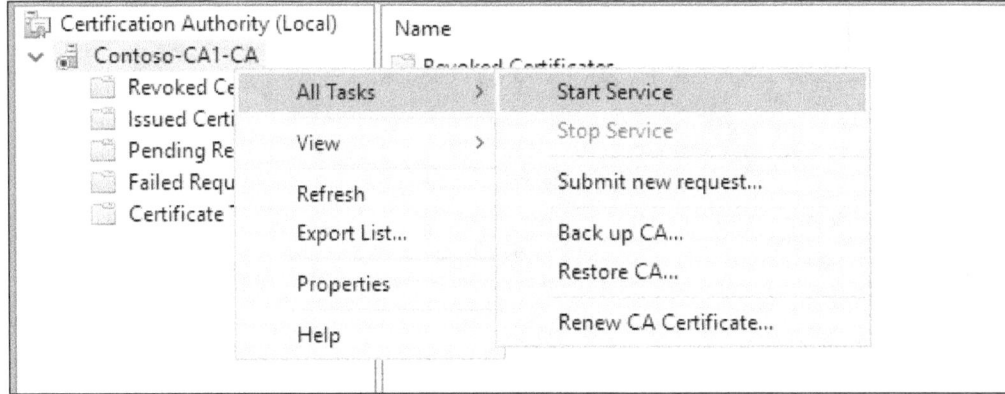

Requesting a cert from MMC

Our new certificate template has been created, and we have successfully published it within the CA console, thereby making it officially ready for issuing. Time to test that out. Go ahead and log in to a regular client computer on your network in order to do this. There are a couple of standard ways which you can utilize in order to request a new certificate on a client computer. The first is by using the good ole MMC console. On your client computer, launch MMC and add the snap-in for **Certificates**. When you choose Certificates from the list of available snap-ins and click on the **Add** button; you are presented with some additional options for which certificate store you want to open. You get to choose between opening certificates for the user account, **Service account**, or **Computer account**. Since we are trying to issue a certificate that will be used by the computer itself, I want to choose **Computer account** from this list, and click on **Finish**:

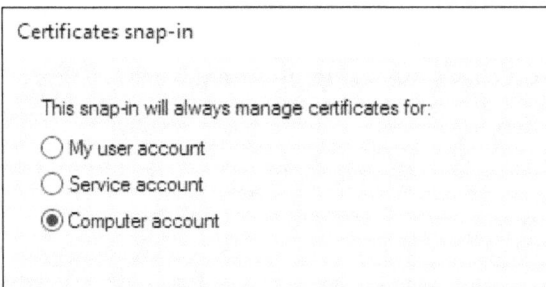

On the next page, click on the **Finish** button again in order to choose the default option, which is **Local computer**. This will snap-in the local machine's computer-based certificate store inside MMC.

 On newer operating systems like Windows 8 and 10, and also with Windows Server 2012, 2012R2, and 2016, there is an MSC shortcut for opening directly into the local computer's certificate store. Simply type CERTLM.MSC into a **Run** prompt, and MMC will automatically launch and create this snap-in for you.

When you are installing certificates onto a computer or server, this is generally the place you want to visit. Inside this certificate store, the specific location that we want to install our certificate into is the **Personal** folder. This is true whether you would be installing a machine certificate like we are doing here, or if you were installing an SSL certificate onto a web server. The local computer's personal certificate folder is the correct location for both kinds of certificates. If you click on **Personal**, you can see that we do not currently have anything listed in there:

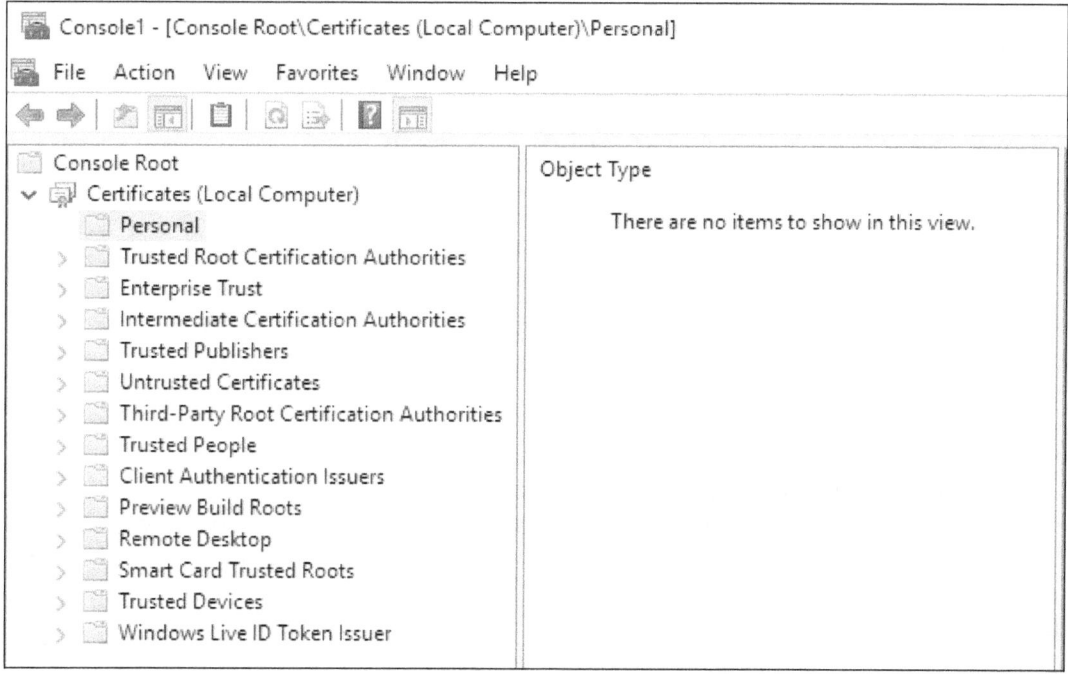

To request a new certificate from our CA server, we simply right-click on the **Personal** folder, and then navigate to **All Tasks | Request New Certificate...**. Doing so opens a wizard; go ahead and click on the **Next** button once.

Certificates in Windows Server 2016

Now you have a screen which looks like something needs to be done, but in most cases because we are requesting a certificate on one of our corporate, domain-joined machines, we actually do not need to do anything on the screen presented in the following screenshot. Simply click on **Next** again on this page, and the wizard will then query Active Directory in order to show all of the certificate templates that are available to be issued:

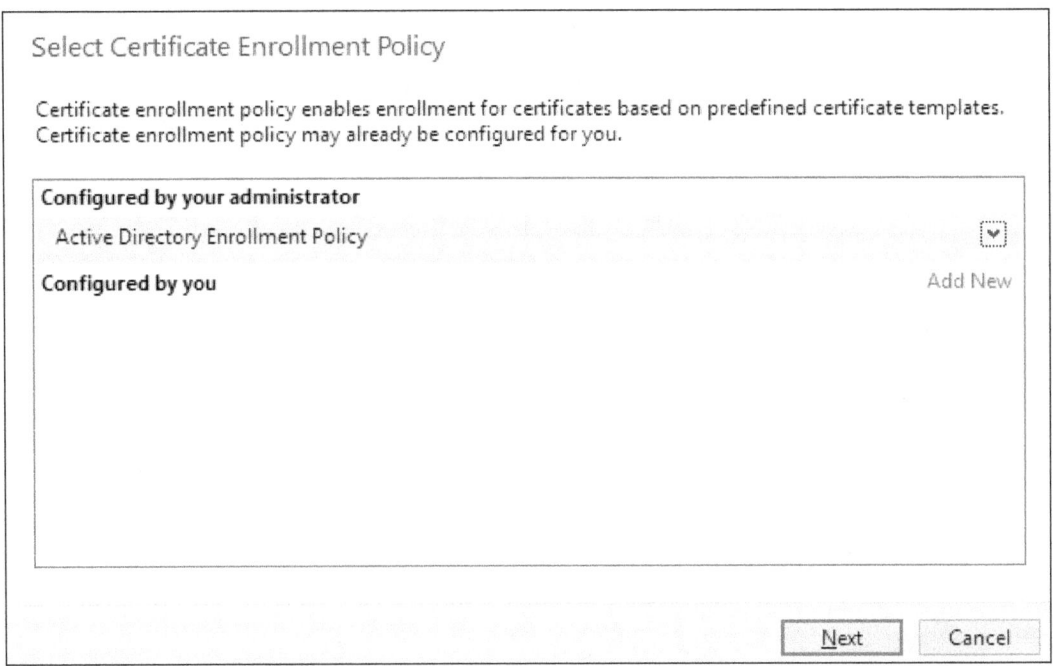

The **Request Certificates** screen is shown, which is our list of templates that are available to us. This list is dynamic based on what computer you are logged into and what your user account permissions are. Remember when we set up the security tab of our new certificate template? It is there that we defined who and what could pull down new certificates based off that template, and if I had defined a more particular group than domain computers, it is possible that my new **DirectAccess Machine** template would not be displayed in this list. But since I did open up that template to be issuable to any computer within our domain, I can see it here:

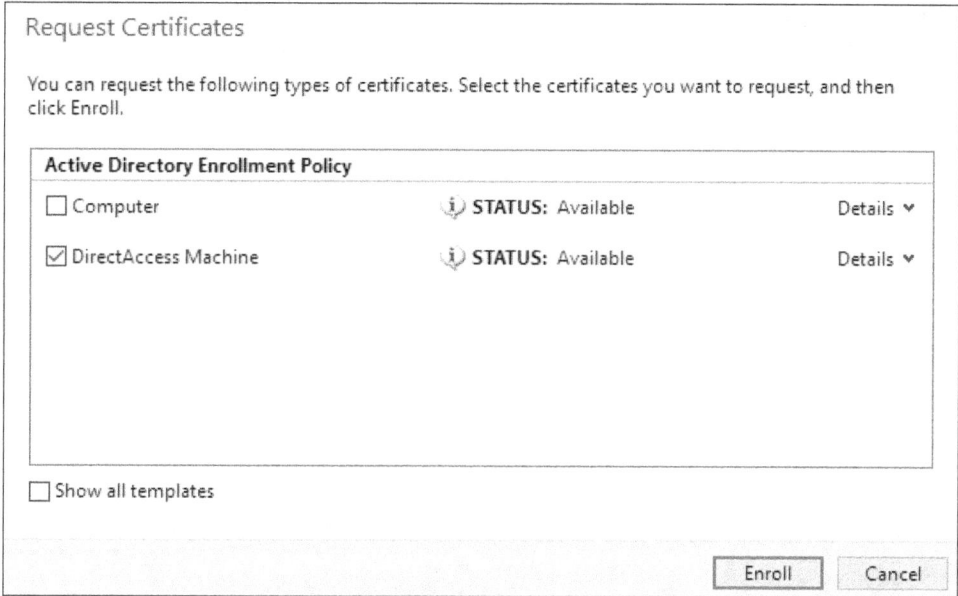

 If you do not see your new template in the list, click on the checkbox for **Show all templates**. This will give you a full list of all the templates on the CA server, and a description on each one as to the reason that it is currently unavailable for publishing.

Put a check mark next to any certificates that you want, and click on **Enroll**. Now the console spins for a few seconds while the CA server processes your request and issues a new certificate that is specific to your computer and the criteria that we placed inside the certificate template.

Once finished, you can see that our brand new machine certificate is now inside **Personal | Certificates** in the MMC. If you double-click on the certificate, you can check over its properties to ensure all of the settings you wanted to be pushed into this cert exist:

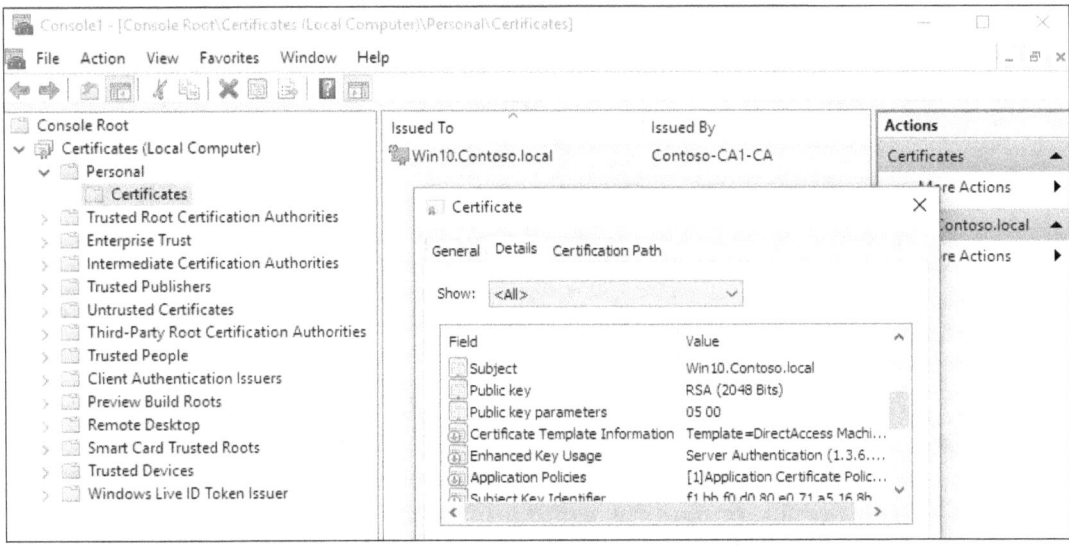

Requesting a cert from the Web interface

I typically use the MMC for requesting certificates whenever possible, but there is another platform available in most cases from which you can request and issue certificates. I say *in most cases* because the existence of this option depends upon how the CA server was built in the first place. When I installed my AD CS role, I made sure to choose the options for both **Certification Authority** and **Certification Authority Web Enrollment**. This second option is important for our next section of text. Without the Web enrollment piece of the role, we would not have a web interface running on our CA server, and this part would not be available to us. If your CA server does not have the Web enrollment turned on, you can revisit the role installation page in **Server Manager** and add it to the existing role:

Roles	Description

▲ ■ Active Directory Certificate Services (2 of 6 installe
  ✓ Certification Authority (Installed)
  ☐ Certificate Enrollment Policy Web Service
  ☐ Certificate Enrollment Web Service
  ✓ **Certification Authority Web Enrollment (Installe**
  ☐ Network Device Enrollment Service
  ☐ Online Responder
☐ Active Directory Domain Services
☐ Active Directory Federation Services
☐ Active Directory Lightweight Directory Services
☐ Active Directory Rights Management Services
☐ DHCP Server
	Certification Authority Web Enrollment provides a simple Web interface that allows users to perform tasks such as request and renew certificates, retrieve certificate revocation lists (CRLs), and enroll for smart card certificates.

Once **Certification Authority Web Enrollment** is installed on your CA, there is now a website running on that server which you can access via a browser from inside your network. Having this website is useful if you have the need for users to be able to issue their own certificates for some reason; it would be quite a bit easier to give them documentation or train them on the process of requesting a certificate from a website, rather than expecting them to navigate the MMC console. Additionally, if you are trying to request certificates from computers that are not within the same network as the CA server, using MMC can be difficult. For example, if you have the need for a user at home to be able to request a new certificate, without a full VPN tunnel the MMC console is more than likely not going to be able to connect to the CA server in order to pull down that certificate. But since we have this certificate enrollment website running, you could externally publish this website like you do with any other website in your network, using a reverse proxy or firewall in order to keep that traffic safe, and present users with the ability to hit this site and request certificates from wherever they are.

Certificates in Windows Server 2016

To access this website, let's use our regular client computer again. This time, instead of opening MMC, I will simply launch Internet Explorer, or any other browser, and log in to the website running at `https://<CASERVER>/certsrv`. For my specific environment, that exact web address is `https://CA1/certsrv`.

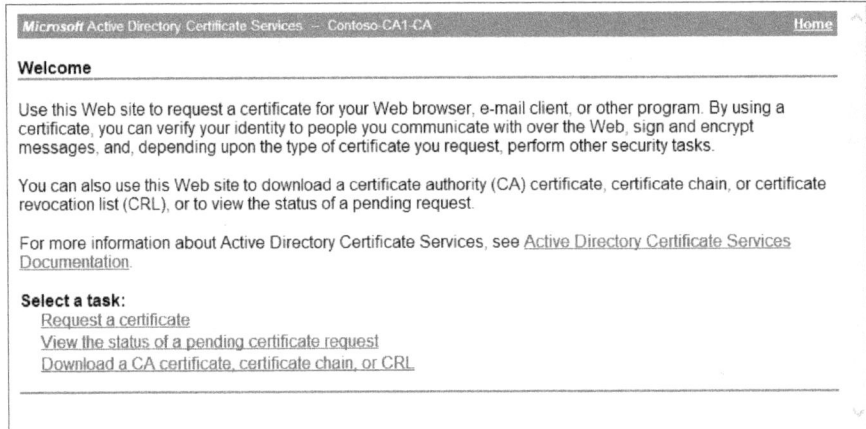

 An important note is that our URL starts with HTTPS. This website must be configured to run on HTTPS instead of regular HTTP in order to allow the website to request certificates. It does not allow issuance of certificates over HTTP because that information would be traveling in clear-text to the client. Enabling the website on the CA server for HTTPS ensures that the certificate issued will be encrypted while it travels.

Clicking on the **Request a certificate** link brings you into our wizard in which we can request a new certificate from the CA server. When you have users driving their own way through this web interface, it is typically for the purpose of a user-based certificate, since we have some pretty easy ways of automatically distributing computer-level certificates without any user interaction. We will discuss that in a moment. However, for this example, since we are asking our users to log in here and request a new **User Certificate**, on the next page I will choose that link:

Chapter 4

 > If you were not interested in a user certificate and wanted to use the web interface to request a machine certificate, a web server certificate, or any other kind of certificate, you could instead choose the link for **advanced certificate request** and follow the prompts to do so.

Next you simply press the **Submit** button, and once the certificate has been generated you will see a link that allows you to **Install this certificate**. Click on that link, and the new certificate that was just created for you has now been installed onto your computer. You can see in the following screenshot the response that the website gave me, indicating a successful installation, and you can also see I have opened up the current user certificates inside MMC in order to see and validate that the certificate really exists.

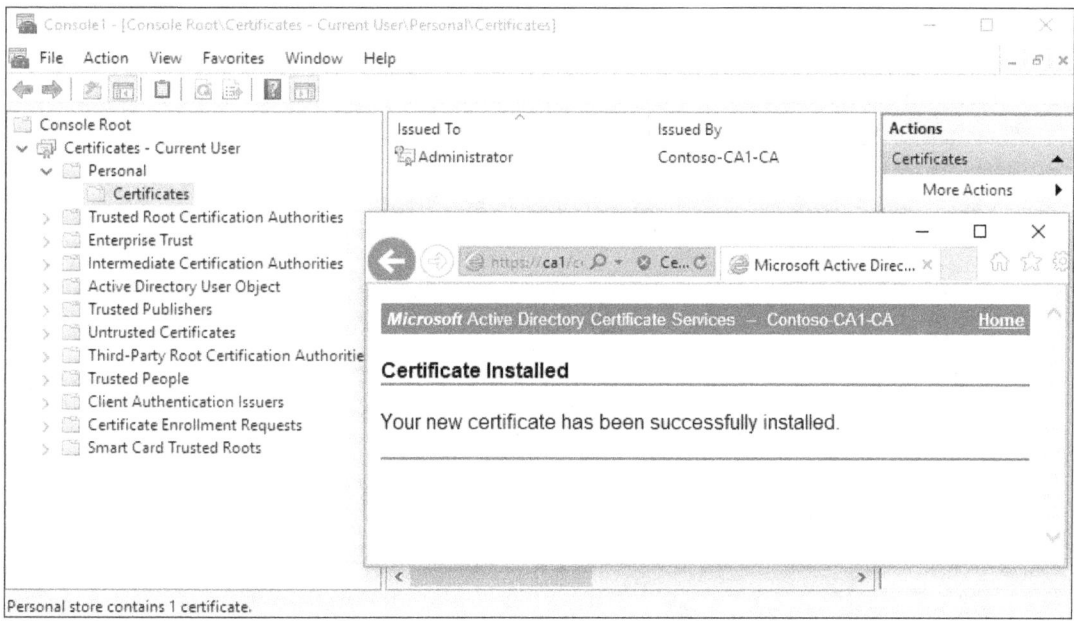

Creating an autoenrollment policy

Our certification authority server is configured and running, and we can successfully issue certificates to the client machines. Great! Now let's pretend we have a new project on our plates, and one of the requirements for this project is that all of the computers in your network need to have a copy of this new machine certificate that we have created. Uh oh, that sounds like a lot of work.

Even though the process for requesting one of these certificates is very quick, only a handful of seconds on each workstation, if you had to do that individually on a couple thousand machines, you are talking about a serious amount of time needing to be spent on this process. And in many cases, the certificates that you issue will only be valid for one year. Does this mean I am facing an extreme amount of administrative work every single year to re-issue these certificates as they expire?

Certainly not! Let's figure out how to utilize Group Policy in order to create a GPO that will **autoenroll** our new certificates to all of the machines in the network, and while we are in there also configure it so that when certificate expiration dates come up, the certificates will autorenew at their appropriate intervals.

Let's pop into the Certification Authority management console on our CA server, and take a look inside the **Issued Certificates** folder. I only want to look here a minute in order to see how many certificates we have issued so far in our network. Looks like just a handful of them, so hopefully once we are done configuring our policy, if we have done it right and it takes effect automatically, we should see more certificates start showing up in this list:

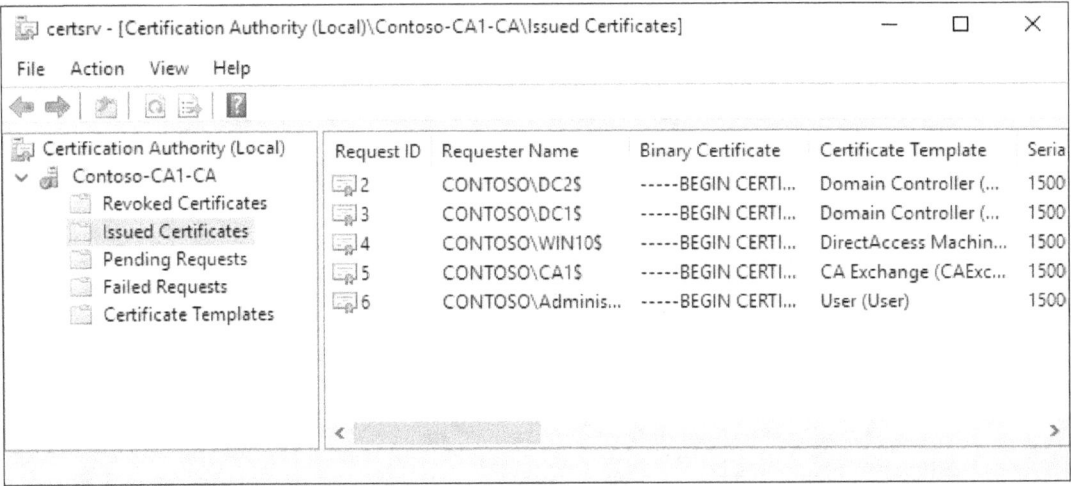

Chapter 4

Log in to a domain controller server, and open up the **Group Policy Management** console. I have created a new GPO called **Enable Certificate Autoenrollment**, and am now editing that GPO to find the settings I need to configure in order to make this GPO do its work.

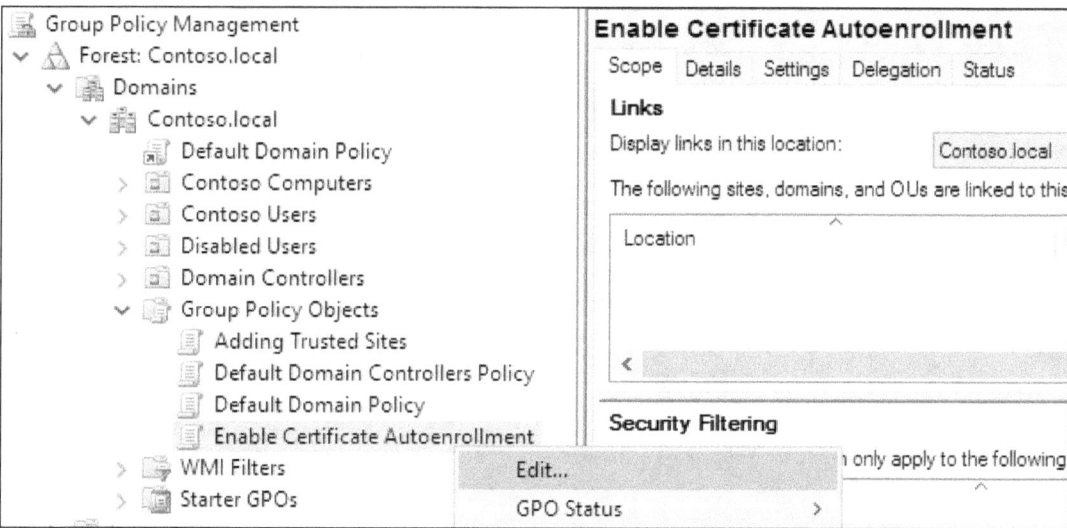

The settings inside this GPO that we want to configure are located at **Computer Configuration | Policies | Windows Settings | Security Settings | Public Key Policies | Certificate Services Client – Auto-Enrollment**.

Double-click on this setting in order to view its properties. All we need to do is change **Configuration Model** to **Enabled**, and make sure to check the box that says **Renew expired certificates, update pending certificates, and remove revoked certificates**. Also check the second box for **Update certificates that use certificate templates**.

Certificates in Windows Server 2016

These settings will ensure that autorenewal happens when the certificates start running into their expiration dates over the next few years.

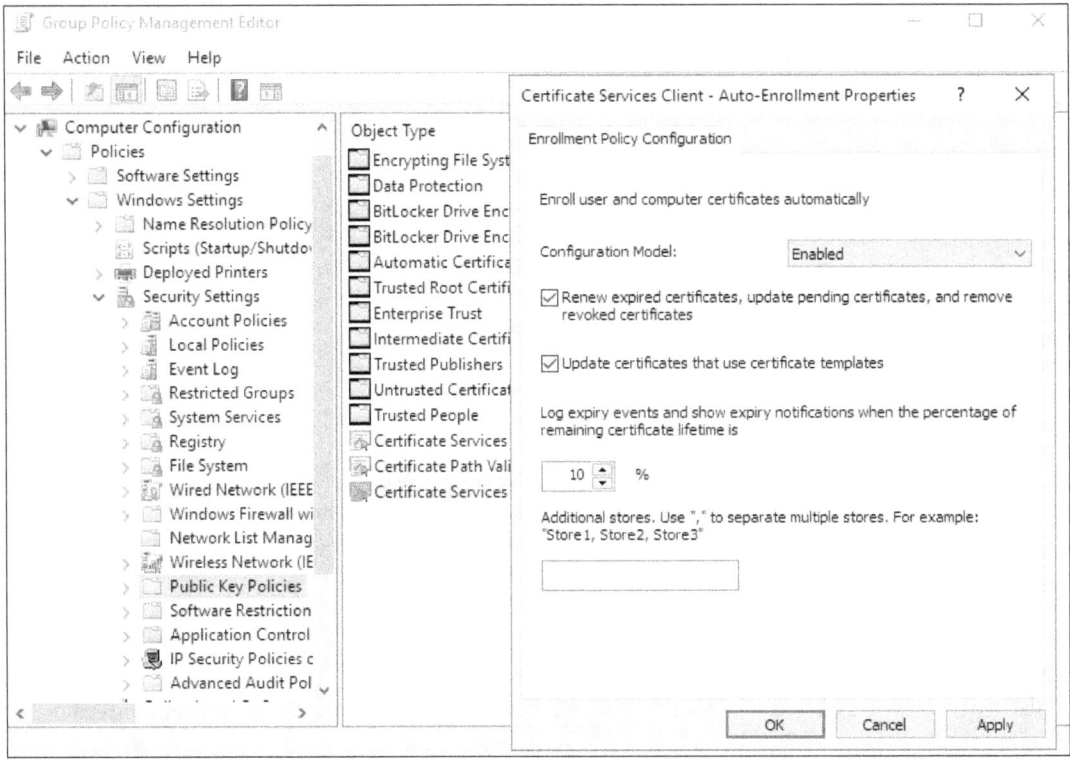

What is the last thing we need to do on our GPO in order to make it live? Create a link so that it starts applying! For your own environment, you will probably create a more specific link to a particular OU like we talked about in the last chapter, but for my lab I want these certificates to apply to every single machine that is joined to the domain, so I will link my new GPO at the root of the domain, so that it applies to all of my clients and servers.

Now that the GPO is created and configured, and we have linked it to the domain, I would think that some new certificates would be issued and there would be more names shown inside my **Issued Certificates** folder inside my certification authority console. But there are not. Wait a minute, in our GPO we didn't really specify anything particular to my DirectAccess Machine cert template, could that be the problem? No, there wasn't really an option for specifying which template I wanted to autoenroll.

When you turn on autoenrollment in **Group Policy**, you simply flip the switch and turn it on for every template. So now that we have a policy that is configured to enable autoenrollment and is linked to the domain, thus making it *live*, autoenrollment has now been enabled on **every certificate template** that is published on our CA server. Yet, none of them are issuing themselves to my computers. This is because we need to adjust the security settings on our new DirectAccess Machine template. Currently, we have it configured so that all domain computers have **Enroll** permissions, but if you remember that security tab within the cert template's properties, there was an additional security identifier called **Autoenroll**. Every certificate template has the autoenroll permission identifier, and it is not allowed by default. Now that the light switch has been flipped ON for autoenrollment in our domain, we need to enable the autoenroll permission on any template that we want to start distributing itself. As soon as we enable that permission, these certificates will start flowing around our network.

If you head into the certificate management section of your CA server and open the **Properties** of your new template, make your way to the **Security** tab and allow **Autoenroll** permissions for the **Domain Computers** group. This should tell the CA to start distributing these certificates accordingly:

And sure enough, if I let my environment sit for a little while, giving Active Directory and Group Policy a chance to update on all of my machines, I now see more certificates have been issued from my CA server!

Request ID	Requester Name	Binary Certificate	Certificate Template
2	CONTOSO\DC2$	-----BEGIN CERTI...	Domain Controller (...
3	CONTOSO\DC1$	-----BEGIN CERTI...	Domain Controller (...
4	CONTOSO\WIN10$	-----BEGIN CERTI...	DirectAccess Machin...
5	CONTOSO\CA1$	-----BEGIN CERTI...	CA Exchange (CAExc...
6	CONTOSO\Admin...	-----BEGIN CERTI...	User (User)
7	CONTOSO\DC2$	-----BEGIN CERTI...	Directory Email Repli...
8	CONTOSO\DC2$	-----BEGIN CERTI...	Domain Controller A...
9	CONTOSO\DC2$	-----BEGIN CERTI...	Kerberos Authenticat...
10	CONTOSO\DC1$	-----BEGIN CERTI...	Directory Email Repli...
11	CONTOSO\DC1$	-----BEGIN CERTI...	Domain Controller A...
12	CONTOSO\DC1$	-----BEGIN CERTI...	Kerberos Authenticat...
13	CONTOSO\BACK1$	-----BEGIN CERTI...	DirectAccess Machin...
14	CONTOSO\WEB1$	-----BEGIN CERTI...	DirectAccess Machin...

Obtaining a public authority SSL certificate

We are now pretty comfortable with grabbing certificates from our own CA server inside our own network, but what about handling those SSL certificates for our web servers that should be acquired from a public certification authority? For many of you, this will be the most common interaction that you have with certificates, and it's very important to understand this side of the coin as well. When you need to acquire an SSL certificate from your public authority of choice, there is a three-step process that needs to be taken. Create a certificate request, submit the certificate request, and install the certificate. We are going to use my WEB1 server, on which I have a website running. Currently the site is only capable of HTTP traffic, but when we turn it loose on the Internet we need to enable HTTPS to keep the information that is being submitted onto the site encrypted. In order to use HTTPS, we need to install an SSL certificate onto the WEB1 server. This web server is running the Microsoft web services platform, **Internet Information Services** (**IIS**). The three-step process we take is the same if you are running a different web server such as Apache, but the particular things that you have to do to accomplish these three steps will be different, because Apache or any other web server will have a different user interface than IIS. Since we are working on a Windows Server 2016 web server, we are utilizing IIS 10.

Creating a Certificate Signing Request (CSR)

When you install an SSL certificate onto a web server, it is very important that the certificate and your server share some information. The information that they share is known as a private key, and without private key information being shared between the server and the cert, your SSL certificate will be good for nothing. If your first step in acquiring an SSL certificate was to log in to the CA's website and try to purchase then immediately download a certificate, you would have a cert that is useless to you because it cannot interact with any of your servers. So before you head into that CA website, we need to generate a CSR from our local web server that we can use when we request the certificate from the authority.

Open up IIS from the **Tools** menu of **Server Manager**, and then click on the name of the web server from the navigational tree on the left side of your screen. This will populate a number of different applets into the center of the console. The one we want to work with is called **Server Certificates**. Go ahead and double-click on that.

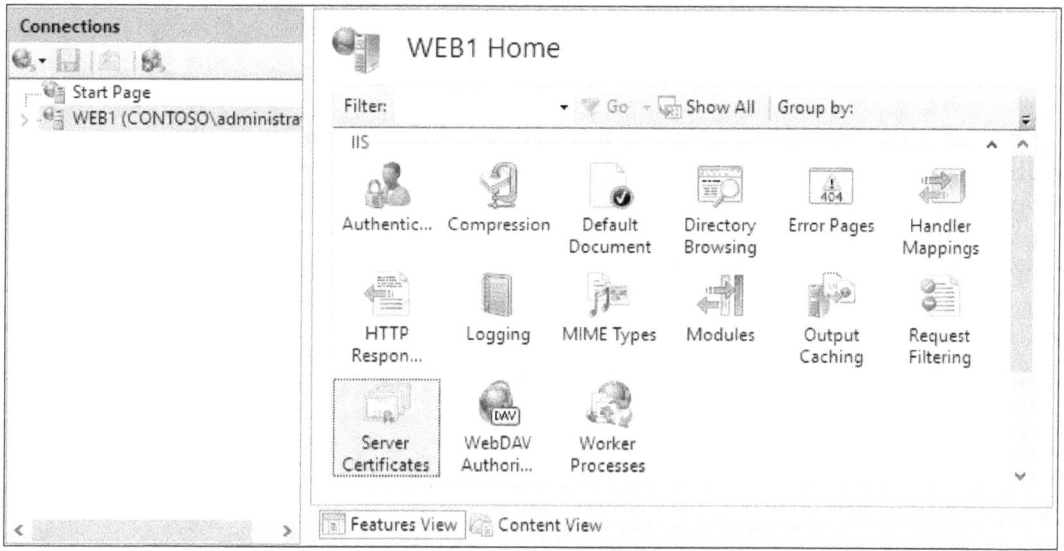

Certificates in Windows Server 2016

Now inside the **Server Certificates** screen, you can see any existing certificates that reside on the server listed here. This is where we ultimately need to see our new SSL certificate, so that we can utilize it inside our website properties when we are ready to turn on HTTPS. The first step to acquiring our new certificate is creating the certificate request to be used with our CA, and if you take a look on the right side of your screen, you will see an **Actions** section, under which is listed **Create Certificate Request...**. Go ahead and click on that **Action**.

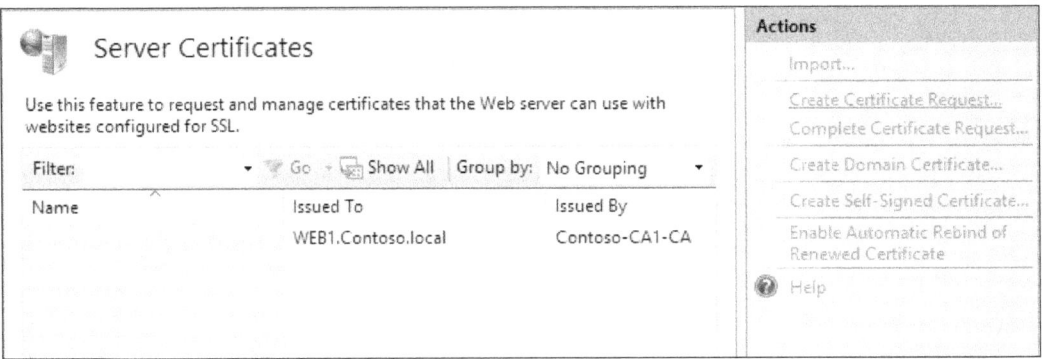

In the resulting wizard, you need to populate the information that will be stored within your SSL certificate. The **Common name** field is the most important piece of information here, it needs to be the DNS name which this certificate is going to protect. So basically, you enter the name of your website here. Then continue with filling out the rest of your company-specific information. A couple of special notes here that often seem to trip up admins are that the **Organizational unit** can be anything at all, I usually just enter the word Web. And then make sure to spell out the name of your **State**, do not use an abbreviation.

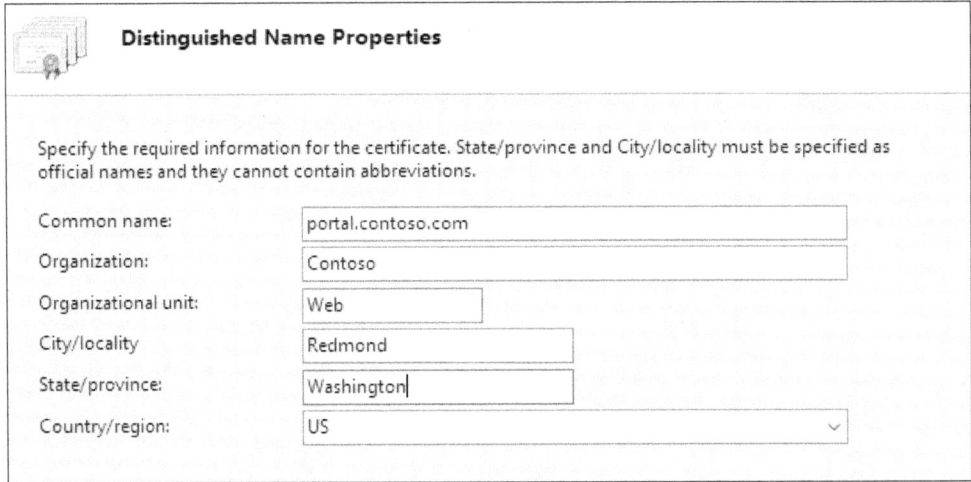

On the **Cryptographic Service Provider Properties** page, you typically want to leave the **Cryptographic service provider** set to its default, unless you have a specialized crypto card in your server and are planning to use it for handling encryption for this website. On an IIS server, you will almost always have **Microsoft RSA SChannel Cryptographic Provider** listed here. What you do want to change, however, is the **Bit length**. The standard bit length for many years was 1024, and that continues to be the default choice in Windows Server 2016. The general industry for SSL encryption though has decided that 1024 is too weak, and the new standard is 2048. When you head onto your CA's website to request a certificate, you will more than likely find that your request needs to have a minimum of 2048 bits. So go ahead and change that drop-down setting to **2048**:

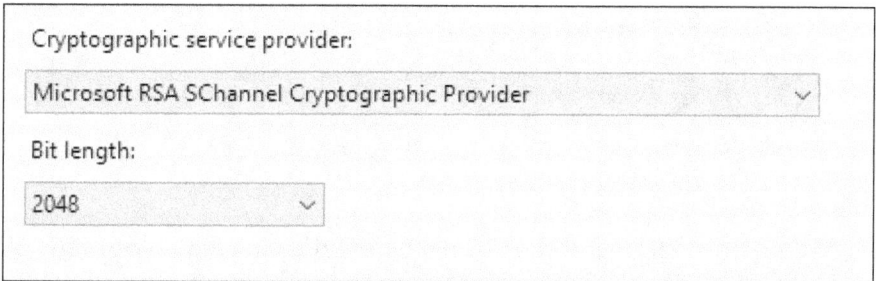

The only thing left to do for our CSR is to give it a location and filename. Saving this CSR as a text file is the normal way to go, and serves our purposes well because all we need to do when we request our certificate is open the file and copy and paste the contents. You have now created your **Certificate Signing Request (CSR)** file, and we can utilize this file to request the certificate from our public CA.

Submitting the certificate request

Next step, head on over to the website for your public certification authority. Again, any of those companies that we mentioned earlier such as GoDaddy or Verisign are appropriate for this purpose. Each authority has its own look and feel for their web interface, so I cannot give you exact steps that need to be taken for this process. Once you have an account and log in to the authority's site, you should be able to find an option for purchasing an SSL certificate. Once that certificate has been purchased, there will be a process for requesting and deploying that certificate.

Once you enter the interface for building your new certificate, generally the only piece of information that the CA will ask you for is the contents of the CSR file. If you open up that text file we saved earlier, you will see a big amount of hogwash:

This mess of data is exactly what the CA needs in order to create your new SSL certificate so that it shares private key info with the web server from which this CSR was generated, and will interact appropriately with IIS. Typically, all you need to do is copy the entire contents of the CSR file and paste them into the CA's website.

Downloading and installing your certificate

Now you wait. Depending on which authority you are using and also depending on how often your company purchases certificates from this authority, your certificate might be available for download almost immediately, or it could take a few hours before that certificate shows up in the available downloads list. The reason for this is that many of the CAs utilize human approval for new certificates, and you are literally waiting for someone to put eyes on the certificate and your information to make sure you really work for the company and that you really own this domain name. Remember, the real benefit to a public SSL cert is that the CA is guaranteeing that the user of this certificate is the real deal, so they want to make sure they aren't issuing a certificate for `portal.contoso.com` to someone in the Fabrikam organization by mistake.

Chapter 4

Once you are able to download the certificate from the CA website, go ahead and copy it over to the web server from which we generated the CSR. It is critically important that you install this new certificate onto the **same server**. If you were to install this new certificate onto a different web server, one that did not generate the CSR this certificate was built from, that certificate would import successfully, but would not be able to function.

Back inside the IIS management console, we can now use the next Action in that list on the right, called **Complete Certificate Request...**. This launches a short little wizard in which you find the new certificate file that you just downloaded, and import it into our server. Now that the certificate resides on the server, it is ready to be used by your website.

There is one additional item that I always check after installing or importing an SSL certificate. You can now see your new certificate listed inside IIS, and if you double-click on your new certificate you will see the properties page for the cert. On the **General** tab of these properties, take a look near the bottom. Your certificate should display a little key icon and the text, **You have a private key that corresponds to this certificate**. If you can see this message, it means your import was successful and that the new certificate file matched up with the CSR perfectly. The server and certificate now share that critical information, and the SSL certificate will be able to work properly to protect our website. If you do not see this message, it means that something in the process to request and download our certificate went wrong. If you do not see the message here, you need to start over with generating a new CSR, because the certificate file that you got back must not have been keyed appropriately against that CSR or something along those lines. Without the text at the bottom of this screen, your certificate will not validate traffic properly. Here is an example of what it should look like when working correctly:

[139]

Exporting and importing certificates

I often find myself needing to use the same SSL certificate on multiple servers. This might happen in the case where I have more than one IIS server serving up the same website and I am using some form of load balancing to split the traffic between them. This need may also arise when working with any form of hardware load balancer, as you sometimes need to import certificates onto not only the web servers themselves, but also into the load balancer box. Yet another example is when using wildcard certificates. When you purchase a wildcard, you typically have the intention of installing it onto multiple servers.

Does this mean that I need to generate a new CSR from each server, and request a new copy of the same certificate multiple times? Definitely not, and in fact doing so could cause you other problems. You see, when a public CA "re-keys" a certificate, or in other words if you have already requested a certificate with a particular name and then come back again later to request another copy of the same certificate, that CA may invalidate the first one as it issues the second copy. This is not always immediately apparent, as there is usually a timer set on the invalidation of the first certificate. If you revisit the CA's web interface and request a new copy of the same certificate using a new CSR for your second web server, you might discover that everything works fine for a few days, but then suddenly the primary web server stops validating traffic because its SSL certificate expired.

What to do then? When you have the need for reusing the same SSL certificate on multiple servers, you can simply export it from one and import it on the next. This process is quite straightforward, and there are two common places from where you can do it. Inside either the MMC snap-in for certificates, or from within IIS itself, you have this capability. It is important to note, though, that the process is slightly different depending on which avenue you take, and you have to be especially aware of what is happening with the private key as you step through these wizards.

Exporting from MMC

Head back into your **Local Computer** certificate store in the MMC, and navigate to **Personal** | **Certificates** so that you can see your SSL certificate listed. Right-click on the certificate, and then navigate to **All Tasks** | **Export...**. When you walk through this export wizard, the important part that I wanted to mention happens right away in the wizard steps. The first choice you have to make is whether or not to export the private key. Again, the private key is the secret sauce that allows the certificate to interact properly with the server on which it is installed.

If you export without the private key, that certificate will not work on another server. So it is important here that if you are exporting this certificate with the intention of installing it onto a second web server and using it for validating SSL traffic, that you do select the top option for **Yes, export the private key**:

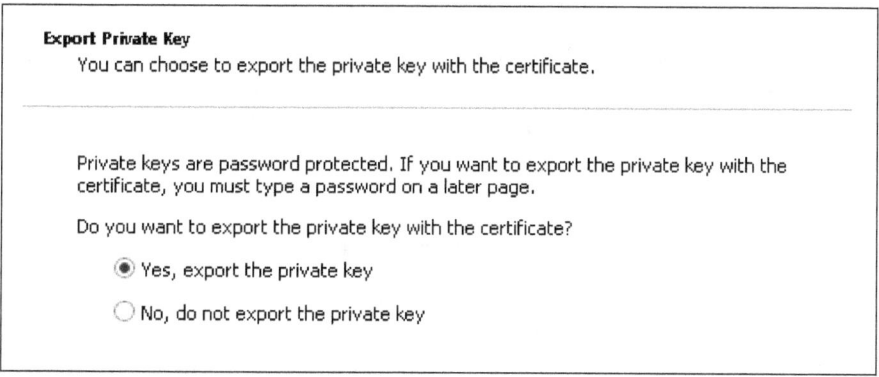

As the wizard sufficiently warns you, when you choose to export a certificate containing the private key information, you are required to supply a password which will be used to protect the exported PFX file. It is important you choose a good password here. If you forget it, your exported file will be completely useless. If you input a password that is very simple or easy to guess, then anyone who gets their hands on this PFX file may be able to use your certificate on their own web servers. That could definitely turn out badly.

Exporting from IIS

Inside the **Server Certificates** applet for IIS, all you need to do is right-click on the certificate and choose **Export...**. This launches a single-page wizard that simply asks you for a location and password:

We had many more options that we could have chosen or denied when we exported using MMC, so why is this so short? IIS makes assumptions for the rest of the settings in order to speed up the export process. When you are exporting an SSL certificate, chances are that you do intend to export the private key also, and that you are going to take the default rest of the settings anyway. So IIS simply bypasses all of those choices. You are forced to enter a password because you don't have a choice about the private key; it will be included with the certificate export automatically. So if you had some reason to export a certificate that did not contain the private key info, then you could not utilize the IIS console for this task. You would need to open up MMC and walk through the more extensive wizard found there.

Importing onto a second server

Whichever direction you take for accomplishing the export, once you have the fully fleshed PFX file available, importing onto your second server is very easy. From within either console, MMC or IIS, you can right-click and choose the **Import** action. Walking through the steps, you simply choose the PFX file and then input the password that you used to protect the file. The certificate then imports, and if you open the properties you will see that the little key icon and the private key message are displayed properly at the bottom of the screen.

Go ahead and try it yourself, find a server with an SSL certificate and test exporting that cert with and without the private key. When you import onto a new server, you will see that importing the certificate file without a private key does not contain this message at the bottom of the properties page, but the export file that does contain the private key results in the proper message here. To take it a step further, try utilizing both certificates on a nonimportant website and see what happens. You will find that the certificate lacking the private key will fail to validate SSL traffic.

Summary

Certificates often get a bad rep, and I believe this is because people think they are a headache to deal with. I see their point. Without knowing how to navigate through the various administrative consoles that deal with your certificate infrastructure, it would be difficult to make even the simplest items function. By talking through the most common certificate-related tasks that any server admin will eventually have to tackle within their own networks, I hope that you have found some comfortability and confidence now to progress with those projects which might be currently sitting on hold, waiting for the certificate infrastructure to be built.

5
Networking with Windows Server 2016

As we have been discussing so far in this book, servers are the tree trunks of our networks. They are the backbone infrastructure that enable us to get work done. If servers are the trunks, then the networks themselves must be the roots. Your network is the infrastructure that supports the company infrastructure; it makes up the channels which any and all devices inside your company use to communicate with each other.

Traditionally there have been *server guys* and *network guys* in the IT profession, and in many places that is still the case today. An administrator who primarily works on servers does not generally have enough time in the day to also support the network infrastructure in an organization of any larger size, and the reverse is also true. Network administrators generally stick to their own equipment and management tools, and wouldn't be interested in diving too deeply into the Windows Server world. However, many of us work in smaller companies where many hats must be worn. Some days both the server admin and the network admin hats sit on top of each other, and so we must understand at least a baseline of networking and tools that we can use to troubleshoot connections that are not working. In addition to that, Windows Server 2016 brings a new networking mindset into focus, the virtualization of your networks. There will always be some semblance of a physical network, using physical switches and routers to move the packets around between different rooms and buildings. But now we are also incorporating the idea of **Software-Defined Networking** into our Windows Servers, which gives us the capability to virtualize some of that configuration. Not only the config itself, we are actually virtualizing the network traffic and building our networks from within a server console, rather than command-line interfaces to configure our routers which was always needed in the past.

Hold the phone, I am getting ahead of myself. First let's talk about some of the new and useful things inside Windows Server 2016 that do involve working with the physical networks, or any networks I suppose, because these are going to be important for any administrator in today's networking world. Later we will take a few moments to further explore this new idea of network virtualization. Here are the items we plan to discuss today:

- Intro to IPv6
- Networking toolbox
- Building a routing table
- Software-Defined Networking

Intro to IPv6

Welcome to the dark side? Unfortunately that is what many people think of IPv6 at the moment. While IPv6 is by no means a new thing, in my experience it is still something that almost no one has deployed in their own networks. In working with hundreds of different companies all over the world over the past few years, I have only found one organization that was running IPv6 over their entire production network, and it wasn't even true native IPv6. Instead, they were using a tunneling technology called ISATAP over their whole network in order to make all of the servers and clients talk to each other using IPv6 packets, but these packets were still traversing an IPv4 physical network. Why does it seem to be so difficult to put IPv6 into place? Because we have been using IPv4 since basically the beginning of time, it's what we all know and understand, and there really isn't a great need to move to IPv6 inside our networks. Wait a minute; I thought there was a big scare being pushed about running out of IPv4 addresses? Yes, that is true for IP addresses on the public Internet, but has nothing to do with our internal networks. You see, even if we run out of public IPv4 addresses tomorrow, our internal networks at our companies are not going to have any impact. We can continue to run IPv4 inside the network for a long time to come, possibly forever and always, as long as we are comfortable using NAT technologies to translate the traffic down into IPv4 as it comes into us from the Internet. We have all been using NAT in one semblance or another for almost as long as IPv4 has existed, so it is obviously something people are very comfortable with doing.

Let me be clear, I am not trying to convince you that sticking with IPv4 is the way of the future. I am just laying out the facts that for most organizations over the next number of years, this will simply be the truth. The reason I want to discuss IPv6 here is that, eventually, you will have to deal with it. And once you do, you'll actually get excited about it! There are some huge advantages that IPv6 has over IPv4, namely, the enormous amount of IP addresses that you can contain within a single network. Network teams in companies around the world struggle every day with the need to build more and more IPv4 networks and tie them together. Think about it, there are many companies now with employee counts in excess of 10,000. Some have many, many times that number. In today's technology world, everyone needs technology and data access. Data is the new currency. Most users now also have at least two physical devices they utilize for work, sometimes more than that. A laptop and a tablet, or a laptop and a cell phone, or a desktop and a laptop and a tablet, you get the idea. In the IPv4 world where you are dealing with comparatively small IP address ranges, you have to get very creative with creating subnets in order to accommodate for all of these physical devices which each need a unique IP address in order to communicate on the network. The biggest advantage to IPv6 is that it resolves all of these problems immediately and by default by providing the capability to have a huge multitude more IP addresses within a single network. How many more addresses are we talking about? Here is some comparison data to give you a little perspective:

- IPv4 addresses look like this—a 32-bit length address:

  `192.168.1.5`

- IPv6 addresses look like this—a 128-bit length address:

  `1111:AABB:CCDD:AB00:0123:4567:8901:ABCD`

As you can see, the IPv4 address is much shorter which obviously means there are fewer possibilities for unique IP addresses. When we set up IPv4 networks, subnetting is extremely important because it is what enables us to have more than one collection of IP addresses within the same network. In the most basic form of networking where you set up some IP addresses and run a subnet mask of 255.255.255.0, which is very common, on that subnet you are limited to only 254 unique IP addresses. Ouch! Some companies have thousands of different servers, let alone all of their client computers and devices that also need to connect to the network. Thankfully, we can build out many different subnets within a single IPv4 network in order to increase our usable IP address scope, but this takes careful planning and calculation of those subnets and address spaces, and is the reason that we rely on experienced network administrators to manage this part of the network for us. One invalid subnet configuration in a routing table can tank network traffic flow. Administration of subnets in an IPv4 network is not for the faint of heart.

When we are talking about IPv6 addressing, the sky almost seems to be the limit. If you were to calculate out all of the unique IPv6 addresses available in that 128-bit space as shown earlier, you would find that there are more than 340 undecillion addresses available to create. In other words, 340 trillion, trillion, trillion addresses. This is the number being touted out there about how many available addresses there are on the Internet, but what does that mean for our internal networks?

To discuss the number of addresses we would have inside a typical internal network running IPv6, let's first step back and look at the address itself. The address I showed earlier is just something I made up, but we will break down the parts of it here.

```
1111:AABB:CCDD:AB00:0123:4567:8901:ABCD
```

Compared to 192.168.1.5, this thing looks like a monstrosity. That is because we are generally not very used to dealing with hexadecimal. But that is all we have here, it is just a different way of looking at data. As we already mentioned, this is a 128-bit address. Since it is broken up into eight different sections, each section being separated by a colon is made up of 16 bits. It is generally the case that companies would dedicate a section of this address as an organizational prefix, something that would be the same across all of their networks and devices. Let's say that is the first 48 bits, or the first three sets of hex. Then the fourth set of information, the next 16 bits, can be our subnet ID. This gives us the flexibility of still having multiple different subnets if we desire in the future, by using multiple numbers here as the subnet ID. After dedicating the first half of the address, we now have the latter half to work with, the last 64 bits. These we can leave for device IDs. This part of the address will be different for every device on the network, and will define the individual static IPv6 addresses that will be used for communication. Let's lay it all out here. We will take the example address from the previous page, and break it out into the following parts:

- **Organizational Prefix**: **1111:AABB:CCDD**:AB00:0123:4567:8901:ABCD

    `1111:AABB:CCDD` is the organizational prefix.

- **Subnet ID**: 1111:AABB:CCDD:**AB00**:0123:4567:8901:ABCD

    `AB00` is the subnet ID.

- **Device IDs**: 1111:AABB:CCDD:AB00:**0123:4567:8901:ABCD**

    `0123:4567:8901:ABCD` is the unique device ID.

How many devices can we have in our network with an IP schema like this? Well, even in our example where we only allocated one 16-bit section for subnetting, and 64 bits for actual IP addresses, that would provide us with the capability to have more than 65,000 subnets and quintillions of unique device IDs in our IP range. Impressive!

If we stick with the aforementioned and use just a single subnet to contain all of our machines, then the first half of our addresses will always be the same, making these long addresses much easier to remember and deal with. It is surprising how quickly you will get used to seeing these large hex numbers in your environment, but even though you will start to recognize them, you still probably are not going to quickly jump into servers or computers in your network anymore by using the static IP addresses. I know a lot of us are still in the habit of saying "I need to quick jump into my web server, I'll just RDP into 192.168.1.5". Just the time that it takes to type out these IPv6 addresses, even if you do remember them, isn't generally worth it. IPv6 will bring with it a much larger reliance on DHCP and DNS to make it more usable.

Now that we understand what sections of the address are going to be used for what purposes, how do we go about assigning the individual device ID numbers for all of the computers, servers, and other devices on our network? You could start with number 1 and go up from there. Another idea that I recently watched someone use is to calculate out the old IPv4 addresses into hex and use this as the last 32 bits of the address. If you open up the **Windows Calculator** on your computer, drop down the menu and change it into the **Programmer** mode. This is a quick-and-easy tool that you can use to convert decimal into hexadecimal, and vice versa. Let's take the example of my web server that is running on 192.168.1.5. I want to implement IPv6 inside my network, and I want my server's IPv6 addresses to reflect the original IPv4 address in the device ID section of the new address. In my calculator, if I type in 192 and then click on **HEX**, it will show me the corresponding hexadecimal to the decimal of 192. If I do that with each of the octets in my IPv4 address, you will see that:

```
192 = C0
168 = A8
1 = 01
5 = 05
```

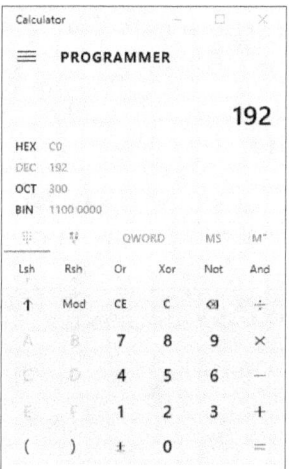

So my 192.168.1.5 factors out to C0A8:0105. I can now utilize that in combination with my organizational prefix and my subnet ID to create a static IPv6 address for my web server.

```
1111:AABB:CCDD:0001:0000:0000:C0A8:0105
```

You'll notice in the preceding IPv6 address that I input the hex for the device ID at the end, but I also made a couple of other changes. Since we are leaving the last 64 bits available for the device ID, but my old IPv4 address only consumes 32 bits, I am left with the 32 bits in the middle. It would be kind of weird to have data in there which didn't mean anything to me, so I simply made it all zeros to simplify my addressing scheme. In addition to that change, I also adjusted my subnet ID to be the number 1, since this is the first subnet in my network.

Our new addressing is starting to look a little cleaner, and makes more sense. Now that we see this new address for our web server laid out, I can see that there are some additional clean-up tasks we can perform on the address in order to make it look even better. Right now the address listed earlier is 100% accurate. I could plug this IP address into the NIC properties of my web server, and it would work. However, there are a whole lot of zeros in my address, and it isn't necessary that I keep them all. Anytime you have unnecessary zeros within a 16-bit segment that are preceding the actual number, they can simply be removed. For example, our subnet ID and the first 32 bits of our device ID have a lot of unnecessary zeros, so I can consolidate the address down to this:

```
1111:AABB:CCDD:1:0:0:C0A8:0105
```

Then to take it even a step further, anytime you have full 16 bit sections that comprise entirely zeros, they can be fully consolidated into a double colon. So the first 32 bits of my device ID that are all zeros, I can replace these with ::. The following is the fully written out address, and the consolidated address. These numbers look quite different. My consolidated address is much easier on the eyes, but from a technology perspective, they are exactly the same number:

```
1111:AABB:CCDD:0001:0000:0000:C0A8:0105
1111:AABB:CCDD:1::C0A8:0105
```

In fact, it is even possible if you are setting up a lab or wanting to quickly test IPv6, that you could use addresses as simple as something like the following example. The two addresses that I will show you here are exactly the same:

```
1111:0000:0000:0000:0000:0000:0000:0001
1111::1
```

>  It is important to note that you can only use a double colon one time within an IP address. If you had two places where it could be applicable within the same address, you can only implement it in one of those places, and you will have to spell out the zeros in the other place.

With the information provided here, you should have enough to put together your own semblance of IPv6 and start issuing some IPv6 addresses to computers or servers in your network. There is so much more that could be learned on this subject that a full book could be written, and indeed multiple ones have been. Here are a couple of references to books about IPv6 from incredibly talented authors if you would like to dig further into this technology:

- *Practical IPv6 for Windows Administrators*, *Apress* by Edward Horley
- *Understanding IPv6 (3rd Edition)*, *Microsoft Press* by Joseph Davies

Networking toolbox

Whether you are a server administrator, a network administrator, or a combination of the two, there are a number of tools that are useful for testing and monitoring network connections within the Windows Server world. Some of these tools are baked right into the operating system and can be used from Command Prompt or PowerShell, and some of the tools are more expansive graphical interfaces that require installation before running. They are all free, though, so you have no excuse to delay getting acquainted with these helpful utilities.

Ping

Even the newest of IT pros is usually familiar with this one. Ping is a command that you can utilize from Command Prompt or PowerShell, and it is simply used to query an IP address to find out whether or not it responds. Ping is and has always been our "go-to" tool for testing network connectivity between two devices on a network. From my Win10 client on the LAN, I can open a prompt and `ping <IP_ADDRESS>`. Alternatively, because I am using DNS in my environment which will resolve names to IP addresses, I can also `ping <SERVERNAME>`, as shown in the following example.

You can see that my server replies to my ping, letting me know that the server is online and responding:

```
Windows PowerShell
Copyright (C) 2015 Microsoft Corporation. All rights reserved.

PS C:\Users\administrator> ping web1

Pinging web1.Contoso.local [10.0.0.150] with 32 bytes of data:
Reply from 10.0.0.150: bytes=32 time=1ms TTL=128
Reply from 10.0.0.150: bytes=32 time<1ms TTL=128
Reply from 10.0.0.150: bytes=32 time=1ms TTL=128
Reply from 10.0.0.150: bytes=32 time<1ms TTL=128

Ping statistics for 10.0.0.150:
    Packets: Sent = 4, Received = 4, Lost = 0 (0% loss),
Approximate round trip times in milli-seconds:
    Minimum = 0ms, Maximum = 1ms, Average = 0ms
PS C:\Users\administrator>
```

Ping traffic is technically called ICMP traffic. This is important because ICMP is being blocked by default more and more often these days, with the existence of firewalls being turned on by default on so many of our systems and devices. Historically, ping was always a tool that we could count on to tell us fairly surely whether or not connectivity was flowing between two devices, but that is not always the case anymore. If you build a brand new Windows box and plug it into your network, that computer may be communicating with the Internet and all of the servers on your network just fine, but if you try to ping that new computer from another machine on your network, the ping might fail. Why would that happen? Because Windows has some security measures built into it by default, including the blocking of ICMP traffic in the Windows Firewall. So in that case, you would need to either turn off the firewall, or provide it with an access rule that allowed ICMP traffic. Once such a rule was enabled, pings would start replying from this new computer. Keep in mind whenever building new systems or servers in your network that ping is not always the most trustworthy tool to depend upon in today's networking world.

Tracert

Tracert, which is pronounced *Trace Route*, is a tool used to trace a network packet as it traverses your network. Really what it's doing is watching all of the places the packet bumps into before hitting its destination. These bumps in the road that a network packet needs to get through are called **hops**. Trace route shows you all of the hops that your traffic is taking as it moves along toward the destination server or whatever it is trying to contact. My test lab network is very flat and boring, so doing a tracert there wouldn't show us much of anything. However, if I open up a PowerShell prompt from an Internet connected machine and tracert to a web service such as Bing, we get some interesting results:

```
PS C:\WINDOWS\system32> tracert www.bing.com

Tracing route to any.edge.bing.com [204.79.197.200]
over a maximum of 30 hops:

  1    <1 ms    <1 ms    <1 ms  192.168.8.1
  2     1 ms    <1 ms    <1 ms  192.168.128.1
  3     8 ms     7 ms     5 ms  172.17.224.1
  4    11 ms     9 ms    15 ms  172.19.253.1
  5    10 ms     9 ms    11 ms  172.31.255.1
  6    20 ms     9 ms    13 ms  ht1-max1-1.iserv.net [206.114.55.1]
  7    15 ms    12 ms     8 ms  69.87.144.9
  8    23 ms    18 ms    19 ms  888-2.iserv.net [206.114.40.2]
  9    23 ms    20 ms    15 ms  g5-0-0.core3.grr.iserv.net [206.114.51.20]
 10    19 ms    11 ms    19 ms  g5-0-0.core1.grr.iserv.net [206.114.51.2]
 11    21 ms    28 ms    19 ms  GigabitEthernet4-1.GW5.DET5.ALTER.NET [152.179.10.81]
 12    25 ms    28 ms    28 ms  0.ae1.XL3.CHI13.ALTER.NET [140.222.225.179]
 13    27 ms    37 ms    54 ms  TenGigE0-6-0-1.GW2.CHI13.ALTER.NET [152.63.65.133]
 14    36 ms    34 ms    34 ms  microsoft-gw.customer.alter.net [152.179.105.130]
 15    58 ms    50 ms    46 ms  104.44.81.58
 16    34 ms    33 ms    36 ms  10.201.194.219
 17    26 ms    29 ms    29 ms  a-0001.a-msedge.net [204.79.197.200]

Trace complete.
PS C:\WINDOWS\system32>
```

 If you utilize tracert but are not interested in seeing all of the DNS information provided in the output, use `tracert -d` to focus only on the IP addresses.

This information can be extremely useful when trying to diagnose a connection that is not working. If your traffic is moving through multiple hops, things like routers and firewalls before it gets to the destination, a tool like tracert can be essential to figuring out where in the connection stream things are going wrong. If the preceding screenshot was a successful trace route to Bing, now let's see what that looks like when things are broken.

I will unplug my Internet router and run the same `tracert www.bing.com` again, and now we can see that I am still able to communicate with my local router, but not beyond:

```
Windows PowerShell
Copyright (C) 2015 Microsoft Corporation. All rights reserved.

PS C:\Users\jkrause> tracert www.bing.com

Tracing route to any.edge.bing.com [204.79.197.200]
over a maximum of 30 hops:

  1     9 ms     1 ms     1 ms  192.168.8.1
  2     *        192.168.8.1  reports: Destination host unreachable.

Trace complete.
PS C:\Users\jkrause>
```

Pathping

Trace route is useful and seems to be the de facto standard for tracing packets around your network, but this next command is even more powerful in my opinion. **Pathping** essentially does exactly the same thing as tracert, except that it provides one additional piece of crucial information. Most of the time with either of these commands you are only interested in figuring out where in the chain of hops something is broken, but often when I'm setting up servers for networking purposes, I am working with servers and hardware that has many different network cards. When dealing with multiple NICs in a system, the local routing table is just as important as the external routers and switches, and I very commonly want to check out the path of a network packet in order to see which local NIC it is flowing out of. This is where pathping becomes more powerful than tracert. The first piece of information that tracert shows you is the first hop away from the local server that you are traversing. But with pathping, it also shows you which local network interface your packets are flowing out. Let me give you an example. I often set up remote access servers with multiple NICs, and during this process we create many routes on the local server so that it knows what traffic needs to be sent in which direction, such as what traffic needs to go out the Internal NIC, and what traffic needs to go out the External NIC. After completing all of our routing statements for the Internal NIC, we test them out by pinging a server inside the network. That ping fails, and we aren't sure why. I can try a tracert command, but it's not going to provide me with anything helpful because it simply cannot see the first hop, it just times out. However, if I try a pathping instead, the first hop will still time out, but I can now see that my traffic is attempting to flow out my External NIC—whoops—we must have set something up incorrectly with our static route on this server. So then I know that I need to delete that route and recreate it in order to make this traffic flow through the Internal NIC instead. Here is the same PowerShell prompt from the same computer that I used in my tracert screenshot. You can see that a pathping shows me the local IP address on my laptop where the traffic is attempting to leave the system, where as the tracert command did not show this information:

Test-Connection

The commands we have discussed so far could be run from either Command Prompt or PowerShell, but now it's time to dive into a newer one that can only be run from the PowerShell prompt. This is a cmdlet called **Test-Connection**, and it is sort of like ping on steroids. If we open up a PowerShell prompt in the lab and Test-Connection WEB1 we get very similar output results as we would with a regular ping, but the information is laid out in a way that I think is a little easier on the eyes. There is also an unexpected column of data here called **Source**:

That is interesting. I am logged in to my DC1 server when I ran this command and so yes, of course my source computer for this command was DC1. But does this mean that I have the ability to manipulate the source computer for the Test-Connection cmdlet? Yes, this is exactly what it means. As with everything in Windows Server 2016 management, the need to be logged in to a local server is being decoupled. Specific to the Test-Connection cmdlet, this means you have the ability to open a PowerShell prompt anywhere on your network, and to test connections between two different endpoints, even if you are not logged in to either of them. Let's test that out. I am still logged in to my DC1 server, but I am going to use a Test-Connection cmdlet in order to test connection between a number of my servers in the network. You see, not only can you specify a different source computer than the one you are currently logged in to, you can take it a step further and specify multiple sources and destinations with this powerful cmdlet. So if I want to test connection from a couple of different source machines to a couple of different destinations, that is easily done with a command like the following:

```
Test-Connection -Source DC1, DC2 -ComputerName WEB1, BACK1
```

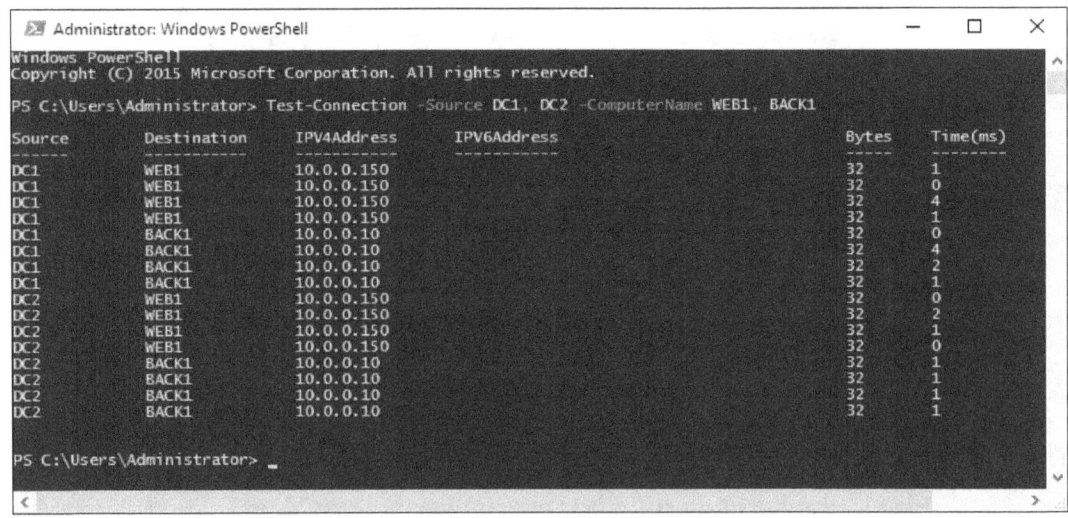

You can see that I have ping statistics from both DC1 and DC2, to each of the servers WEB1 and BACK1 in my network. **Test-Connection** has the potential to be a very powerful monitoring tool!

One more useful function to point out here, you can also clean up the output of the command pretty easily by using the -Quiet switch. By adding -Quiet to a Test-Connection command, it sanitizes the output and only shows you a simple True or False for whether or not the connection was successful, instead of showing you each individual ICMP packet that was sent. Unfortunately it does not seem that you can combine both the -Source switch and the -Quiet switch, but if you are using Test-Connection from the original source computer that you are logged in to, like most of us will be doing anyway, then -Quiet works great. Most of the time all we really care about is Yes or No as to whether or not these connections are working, and don't necessarily care to see all four attempts. By using -Quiet we get exactly that. If I were to use Test-Connection in the standard way to try and contact all of the servers in my network, that would turn into a whole lot of output. But by using the -Quiet switch, I get back a simple True or False on whether or not each individual server could be contacted.

```
Test-Connection -Quiet -ComputerName WEB1, BACK1, DC2, CA1
```

```
Windows PowerShell
Copyright (C) 2015 Microsoft Corporation. All rights reserved.

PS C:\Users\Administrator> Test-Connection -Quiet -ComputerName WEB1, BACK1, DC2, CA1
True
True
True
True
PS C:\Users\Administrator>
```

Telnet

Telnet provides quite a bit of remote management capability, it is essentially the ability to make a connection between two computers in order to manipulate the remote machine through a virtual terminal connection. Surprisingly, we are not here to discuss any of the actual functionality that Telnet provides, because with regards to networking I find it is quite useful as a simple connection testing tool, without knowing anything about what functionality the telnet command itself actually provides.

When we discussed ping earlier, we talked about the downside to ICMP in that it is easily blocked, and it is becoming more standard in today's networks not to allow pings to be successful. This is unfortunate since ping has always been the most common form of networking connection testing, but is the reality of today. If we cannot rely on ping to tell us with certainty whether or not we can contact a remote system, what do we use instead? Another case that I see often is where a server itself might be responding correctly, but a particular service running on that server has a problem and is not responding. A simple ping would show the server to be online, but it can't tell us anything about the service specifically. By using the Telnet Client commands, we can easily query a server remotely. Even more importantly, we can specify to query an individual service on that server, to make sure it is listening as it is designed to do. Let me give you an example that I use all the time. I very often set up new web servers that are facing the Internet. After installing a new web server, it makes sense that I would want to test access to it from the Internet to make sure it's responding, right? But maybe I don't have the website itself online and functional yet, so I can't browse to it with Internet Explorer. It is quite likely that we disabled pings on this server or at the firewall level, because blocking ICMP over the Internet is very common to lower the security vulnerability footprint on the Web. So my new server is running, and we think we have the networking all squared away, but I cannot test pinging my new server because by design it fails to reply. What can I use to test? **Telnet**. By issuing a simple `telnet` command, I can tell my computer to query a specific port on my new web server, and find out whether or not it connects to that port. Doing this establishes a socket connection to the port on that server, which is much more akin to real user traffic than what a ping would be. If a `telnet` command connects successfully, you know your traffic is making its way to the server, and the server service running on the port we queried seems to be responding properly.

The ability to Telnet is not installed by default in Windows Server 2016, or any Windows operating system, so we first need to head into Server Manager and **Add Roles and Features** in order to install the feature called **Telnet Client**:

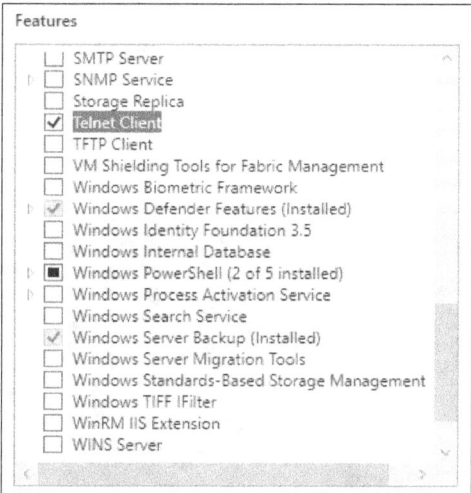

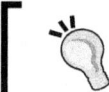 It is important to note that you only need to install Telnet Client on the machine from which you want to do command-line testing. You do not have to do anything on the remote server which you are connecting to.

Now that the Telnet Client feature has been installed, we can utilize it from Command Prompt or PowerShell in order to do work for us, by attempting to make socket connections from our computer to the remote service. All we need to do is tell it what server and port to query. Then telnet will simply connect or time out, and based on that result we can know whether or not that particular service on the server is responding. Let's try it with our own web server. For our example, I have turned off the website inside IIS, so we are now in a position where the server itself is online but the website is dead. If I were to ping WEB1, I can still see it happily responding. You can see where server monitoring tools which rely on ICMP would be showing false positives here, indicating that the server was online and running, even though our website is inaccessible.

Just below the successful ping in the following screenshot, you can see that I also tried querying port 80 on the WEB1 server. The command that I used for that is `telnet web1 80`. That timed out. This shows us that the website, which is running on port 80, is not responding:

```
Windows PowerShell
Copyright (C) 2015 Microsoft Corporation. All rights reserved.

PS C:\Users\administrator.CONTOSO> ping web1

Pinging web1.Contoso.local [10.0.0.150] with 32 bytes of data:
Reply from 10.0.0.150: bytes=32 time<1ms TTL=128
Reply from 10.0.0.150: bytes=32 time<1ms TTL=128
Reply from 10.0.0.150: bytes=32 time<1ms TTL=128
Reply from 10.0.0.150: bytes=32 time<1ms TTL=128

Ping statistics for 10.0.0.150:
    Packets: Sent = 4, Received = 4, Lost = 0 (0% loss),
Approximate round trip times in milli-seconds:
    Minimum = 0ms, Maximum = 0ms, Average = 0ms
PS C:\Users\administrator.CONTOSO>
PS C:\Users\administrator.CONTOSO>
PS C:\Users\administrator.CONTOSO> telnet web1 80
Connecting To web1...Could not open connection to the host, on port 80: Connect failed
PS C:\Users\administrator.CONTOSO>
```

If I go ahead and turn the website back on, then we can try `telnet web1 80` again and this time I do not get a timeout message. This time my PowerShell prompt wipes itself clean and sits waiting on a flashing cursor at the top. While it doesn't tell me anything like "yay, I'm connected" — this flashing cursor indicates that a successful socket connection has been made to port 80 on my web server, indicating the website is online and responding:

Packet tracing with Wireshark or Netmon

Eventually you might run into the need to look a little deeper into your network packets. Now we are entering territory where your network team may also be involved, but if you are familiar with these tools you may be able to solve the problem before needing to make that phone call for assistance. Making use of command-line tools for checking on the status of servers and services is very useful, but occasionally it may not be enough. For example, you have a client application that is not connecting to the application server, but you don't know why. Things like ping and even telnet might be able to connect successfully, indicating that network routing is set up properly, yet the application fails to connect when it opens. If the application's own event logs are not helpful to troubleshoot what is going on, you might want to take a deeper look inside the network packets that the application is trying to push toward the server. This is where the tools **Wireshark** and **Netmon** come in handy. Both are free and easily downloadable, and they both perform basically the same functions. They are designed to capture network traffic as it leaves from or arrives to a system, and they capture the information that is inside the packets themselves so that you can take a deeper look into what is going on. In our example of the application that cannot connect, you could run one of these tools on both the client computer to watch the outgoing traffic, and on the application server to watch for the incoming traffic from the client.

Each tool has quite a bit of individual functionality and we don't have the space to cover all of it here, so I will leave you with the links to get these tools so that you can test them out for yourself:

- Wireshark: `https://www.wireshark.org/download.html`
- Netmon: `https://www.microsoft.com/en-us/download/details.aspx?id=4865`

TCPView

The tools that we have discussed so far are great and can be used on a daily basis for poking and prodding individual resources that you want to test, but sometimes there are situations where you need to step back and figure out what it is you are looking for in the first place. Maybe you are working with an application on a computer and are not sure what server it is talking to. Or perhaps you suspect a machine of having a virus and trying to *phone home* to somewhere on the Internet, and you would like to identify the location that it is trying to talk to or the process that is making the call. In these situations it would be helpful if there was a tool that you could launch on the local computer which tells you all of the network traffic streams that are active on this computer or server. That is exactly what **TCPView** does.

TCPView is a tool originally created by SysInternals, you must have heard of some of their other tools like ProcMon and FileMon. Running TCPView on a machine displays all of the active TCP and UDP connections happening on that computer in real time. Also important is the fact that you do not need to install anything to make TCPView work; it is a standalone executable, making it extremely easy to use and clear off a machine when you are finished with it.

You can download TCPView at `https://technet.microsoft.com/en-us/sysinternals/tcpview.aspx`.

Simply copy the file onto a computer or server that you want to monitor, and double-click on it. Here is a screenshot of the TCPView interface running on my local computer, showing all of the connections that Windows and my applications are currently making. You can pause this output to take a closer look, and you can also set filters to pare down the data and find what you are really looking for. Filters to get rid of the "noise", so to speak, and enable you to look more closely at a particular destination or a specific process ID:

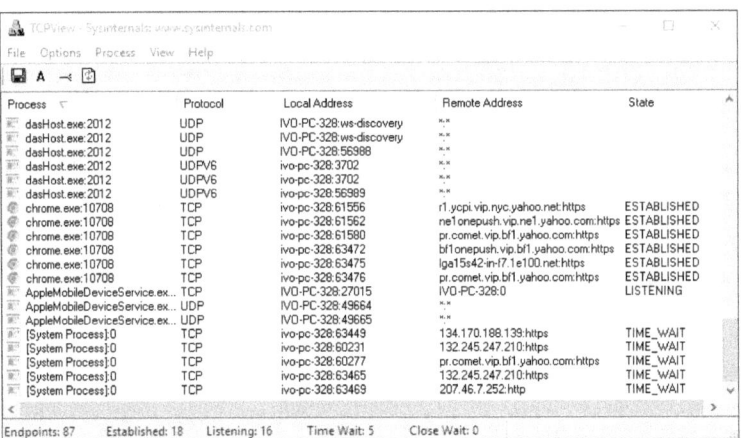

Building a routing table

When you hear the term "routing table" it is easy to pass that off as something the network guys need to deal with, something that is configured within the network routers and firewalls. It doesn't apply to the server admins, right? Networking servers together has been made pretty easy for us by only requiring an IP address, subnet mask, and default gateway, and we can instantly communicate with everything inside the rest of our network. While there is indeed a lot of networking magic going on under the hood of that traffic that has been provided to us by networking equipment and network administrators, it is important to understand how routing inside Windows works because there will be some cases when you need to modify or build out a routing table right on a Windows Server itself.

Multihomed servers

Running multihomed servers is a case where you would certainly need to understand and work with a local Windows routing table, so let's start here. If you think this doesn't apply to you because you've never heard of multihomed before, think again. Multihomed is just a funny looking word meaning your server has more than one NIC. This could certainly be the case for you, even if you are a small shop that doesn't have a lot of servers. Many times Small Business or Essentials Servers have multiple network interfaces, separating internal traffic from Internet traffic. Another instance of a multihomed server would be a remote access server that provides DirectAccess, VPN, or proxy capabilities at the edge of your network. Yet another reason to be interested and understand multihoming is Hyper-V servers. It is very common for Hyper-V servers to have multiple NICs, because the VMs that are running on that server might need to tap into different physical networks within your organization.

Now that we have established what a multihomed server is, simply one that has more than a single network card, you might still be wondering why we are discussing this. If I have more than one NIC, don't I simply configure each NIC individually inside Windows, giving each one an IP address just like I would for any NIC on any server? Yes and no. Yes, you configure an IP address on each NIC, because it needs that for identification and transport of packets on the network. No, you do not set up all of the NICs on your server in the same way. There is one critical item that you need to keep in mind and adhere to in order to make traffic flow work properly on your multihomed server.

Only one default gateway

This is the golden ticket. When you multihome a server by having multiple NICs, you can only have one default gateway. One for your entire server. This means you will have one NIC with a default gateway, and one or many NICs that do NOT have a default gateway inside their TCP/IP settings. This is extremely important. The purpose of a default gateway is to be the *path of last resort*. When Windows wants to send a packet to a destination, it browses over the local routing table—yes there is a routing table even if you haven't configured it or ever looked at it—and checks to see whether or not a specific, static route exists for the destination subnet where this packet needs to go. If a route exists, it shoots the packet out that route and network interface to the destination. If no static route exists in the routing table, then it falls back onto using the default gateway, and sends the traffic to that default gateway address. On all single NIC servers, the default gateway is a router that is designed with all of the routing information for your network, and so the server simply hands it to the router, and the router does the rest of the work.

When we have multiple NICs on a Windows Server, we cannot give each one a default gateway because it will majorly confuse traffic flow from your server. It will be a crap shoot as to which default gateway traffic flows toward with every network transmission. I have helped many people troubleshoot servers in the field with exactly this problem. They needed to use their server as a bridge between two networks, or to have the server plugged into multiple different networks for whatever the reason, and are now struggling because sometimes the traffic seems to work, and sometimes it doesn't. We start looking through the NIC properties to discover that every NIC has its own default gateway address in the TCP/IP properties. Bingo, that's our problem. The system is completely confused when it tries to send out traffic, because it doesn't know which gateway it needs to use at what times.

If you have ever tried adding default gateways to more than one NIC on the same server, you are probably familiar with the warning prompt that is displayed when you do this. Let's give it a try. I have added another NIC to one of my servers, and have IP settings configured on just one of the NICs. Now I will add a new IP address, subnet mask, and default gateway onto my second NIC. When I click on the **OK** button to save those changes, I am presented with the following message:

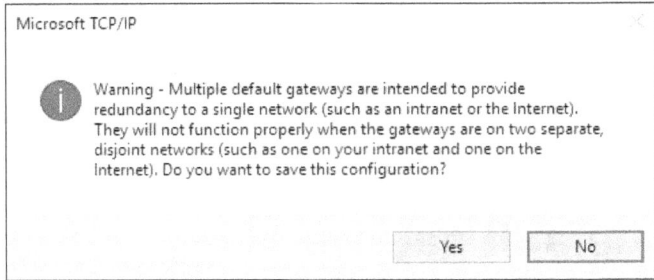

This is one of those warnings that is easy to misread because of its slightly cryptic nature, but you get the essence of it. Proceed at your own risk! And then what do most admins do at this point? Simply click through it and save the changes anyway. Then the routing problems start. Maybe not today, but perhaps the next time you reboot that server, or maybe three weeks down the road, but at some point your server will start to send packets to the wrong destinations and cause you trouble.

Building a route

So what is our answer to all of this? Build a static routing table. When you have multiple NICs on a server, thereby making it multihomed, you must tell Windows which NIC to use for what traffic inside the routing table. This way when network traffic needs to leave the server for a particular destination, the routing table is aware of the different directions and paths that the traffic will need to take in order to get there, and send it out accordingly. You will still be relying on routers to take the traffic the rest of the way, but getting the packets to the correct router by sending them out the proper physical NIC is key to making sure that traffic flows quickly and appropriately from your multihomed server.

Now that we understand why the routing table is important and conceptually how we need to use it, let's dig in and add a couple of routes on my dual-NIC server. We will add a route using Command Prompt, and we will also add one using PowerShell, since you can do so from either platforms but the syntax used is different depending on which you prefer.

Adding a route with Command Prompt

Before we can plan our new route, we need to get the lay of the land for the current networking configuration on this server. It has two NICs, one is plugged into my internal network and one is plugged into my DMZ that faces out toward the Internet. Since I can only have one default gateway address, it goes onto the DMZ NIC because there is no way that I could add routes for every subnet that might need to be contacted over the Internet. By putting the default gateway on my DMZ NIC, this means that the internal NIC does not have a default gateway, and is very limited in what it can contact at the moment. The internal subnet that I am physically plugged into is 10.0.0.0/24, so I can currently contact anything in this small network between 10.0.0.1 through 10.0.0.254. But I cannot contact anything else at the moment through my internal NIC, because the routing table knows nothing about the other subnets that I have inside my internal network. I have an additional subnet that is 192.168.16.0/24, and there are some servers running within this subnet that I need to be able to contact from this new server. Here is the general syntax of the route statement we need to follow in order to make this traffic flow from our server into the new subnet:

```
Route add -p <SUBNET_ID> mask <SUBNET_MASK><GATEWAY> IF <INTERFACE_ID>
```

Before we can type out our unique route statement for adding the 192.168 network, we need to do a little detective work and figure out what we are going to use in these fields. Here is a breakdown of the parts and pieces that are required to build a route statement:

- `-p`: The *dash-P* makes this command persistent. If you forget to put `-p` in the `route add` statement, this new route will disappear the next time you reboot the server. Not good.
- `SUBNET_ID`: This is the subnet we are adding, in our case it is 192.168.16.0.
- `SUBNET_MASK`: This is the subnet mask number for the new route, 255.255.255.0.
- `GATEWAY`: This one is a little confusing. It is very common to mistakenly think it means you need to enter the gateway address for the new subnet, but that would be incorrect. What you are actually defining here is the first hop that the server needs to hit in order to send out this traffic. Or in other words, if you had configured a default gateway address on the internal NIC, what would that address be? For our network it is 10.0.0.1.
- `INTERFACE_ID`: Specifying an interface ID number is not entirely necessary to create a route, but if you do not specify it there is a potential that your route could bind itself to the wrong NIC and send traffic out the wrong direction. I have seen it happen before, so I always specify a NIC interface ID number. This is typically a one- or two-digit number that is the Windows identifier for the internal NIC itself. We can figure out what the Interface ID number is by looking at a `route print` command:

```
C:\Windows\system32>route print
===========================================================================
Interface List
  4...00 15 5d fa 3e 58 ......Microsoft Hyper-V Network Adapter
  9...00 15 5d fa 3e 5a ......Microsoft Hyper-V Network Adapter #2
 13...00 00 00 00 00 00 00 e0 Microsoft 6to4 Adapter
  1...........................Software Loopback Interface 1
  2...00 00 00 00 00 00 00 e0 Microsoft ISATAP Adapter
  3...00 00 00 00 00 00 00 e0 Microsoft ISATAP Adapter #2
===========================================================================
```

At the top of `route print` you see all of the NICs in a system listed. In our case, the internal NIC is the top one in the list, and you can see it is interface ID number 4. So in my `route add` statement, I am going to use IF 4 at the end of my statement to make sure my new route binds itself to that physical NIC.

Here is our completed `route add` statement:

Route add -p 192.168.16.0 mask 255.255.255.0 10.0.0.1 if 4

```
C:\Windows\system32>route add -p 192.168.16.0 mask 255.255.255.0 10.0.0.1 if 4
 OK!

C:\Windows\system32>
```

Still at Command Prompt, if you now run a `route print` command, you can see our new 192.168.16.0 route listed in the `Persistent Routes` section of the routing table, and we can now send packets into that subnet from this new server:

```
===========================================================================
Persistent Routes:
  Network Address          Netmask  Gateway Address  Metric
          0.0.0.0          0.0.0.0          1.1.1.1  Default
     192.168.16.0    255.255.255.0         10.0.0.1        1
===========================================================================
```

Deleting a route

Occasionally, you may key in a route statement incorrectly. The best way to handle this is to simply delete the bad route, then re-run your `route add` statement with the correct syntax. There are possibly other reasons why you might need to delete routes every now and then, so you'll want to be familiar with this command. Deleting routes is much simpler than adding new ones. All you need to know is the subnet ID for the route that you want to remove, that's it. Then simply `route delete <SUBNET_ID>`. For example, to get rid of our 192.168.16.0 route that we created earlier while we were working inside Command Prompt, I would simply issue this command:

Route delete 192.168.16.0

Adding a route with PowerShell

Since PowerShell is king when it comes to most command-line oriented tasks inside Windows Server, we ought to accomplish the same mission from this interface as well. You can utilize the same `route add` command from inside the PowerShell prompt and that will work just fine, but there is also a specialized cmdlet that we can use instead. Let's utilize `New-NetRoute` to add yet another subnet to our routing table, this time we are going to add 192.168.17.0. Here is a command we can utilize:

```
New-NetRoute -DestinationPrefix "192.168.17.0/24" -InterfaceIndex 4 -NextHop 10.0.0.1
```

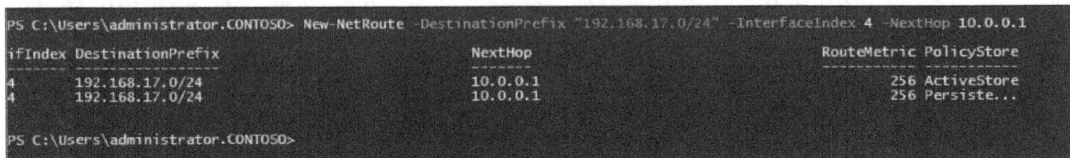

You can see that the structure is similar, but a little bit friendlier. Instead of having to type the word `mask` and specify the whole subnet mask number, you can use the *slash* method for identifying the subnet and mask within the same identifier. Also, where before we were specifying the *gateway* which is always a little confusing, with the `New-NetRoute` cmdlet we instead specify what is called the `NextHop`. This makes a little bit more sense to me.

And where we previously utilized `route print` in order to see our full routing table, the PowerShell cmdlet to display that table for us is simply `Get-NetRoute`:

```
Administrator: Windows PowerShell                                    —    □    ×
PS C:\Users\administrator.CONTOSO> Get-NetRoute

ifIndex DestinationPrefix                               NextHop
------- -----------------                               -------
9       255.255.255.255/32                              0.0.0.0
4       255.255.255.255/32                              0.0.0.0
1       255.255.255.255/32                              0.0.0.0
9       224.0.0.0/4                                     0.0.0.0
4       224.0.0.0/4                                     0.0.0.0
1       224.0.0.0/4                                     0.0.0.0
4       192.168.17.0/24                                 10.0.0.1
1       127.255.255.255/32                              0.0.0.0
1       127.0.0.1/32                                    0.0.0.0
1       127.0.0.0/8                                     0.0.0.0
4       10.0.0.255/32                                   0.0.0.0
4       10.0.0.10/32                                    0.0.0.0
4       10.0.0.0/24                                     0.0.0.0
9       1.1.1.255/32                                    0.0.0.0
9       1.1.1.10/32                                     0.0.0.0
9       1.1.1.0/24                                      0.0.0.0
9       0.0.0.0/0                                       1.1.1.1
9       ff00::/8                                        ::
4       ff00::/8                                        ::
1       ff00::/8                                        ::
9       fe80::b469:d204:780f:6d6f/128                   ::
4       fe80::9d68:a8a6:a4b4:26/128                     ::
3       fe80::200:5efe:1.1.1.10/128                     ::
2       fe80::5efe:10.0.0.10/128                        ::
9       fe80::/64                                       ::
4       fe80::/64                                       ::
13      2002:101:10a::101:10a/128                       ::
13      2002::/16                                       ::
1       ::1/128                                         ::


PS C:\Users\administrator.CONTOSO>
```

Software-Defined Networking

The flexibility and elasticity of cloud computing cannot be denied, and most technology executives are currently exploring their options for utilizing cloud technologies. One of the big stumbling blocks to adaptation is trust. Cloud services provide enormous computing power all immediately accessible at the press of a button, but in order for companies to store their data on these systems the level of trust that your organization has in that cloud provider must be very high. After all, you don't own any of the hardware or networking infrastructure that your data is sitting on when it's in the cloud, and so your control of those resources is limited at some point. Seeing this hurdle, Microsoft has made many efforts in recent updates to bring cloud-like technology into the local datacenter. Introducing server elasticity into our datacenters means virtualization. We have been virtualizing servers themselves for many years now, though the capabilities are still being continually improved. Now that we have the ability to spin up new servers so easily through virtualization technologies, it makes sense that the next hurdle would be our ability to easily move these virtual servers around when we need to.

Have a server that you want to move into a datacenter across the country? Migrating an entire datacenter into a new CoLo across town? Maybe you have recently acquired a new company and need to bring their infrastructure into your network, but have overlapping network configurations. Have you bought into some space at a cloud service provider and are now trying to wade through the mess of planning the migration of all your servers into the cloud? These are all questions that needed an answer, and that answer is **Software-Defined Networking (SDN)**.

SDN is a broad, general term that umbrellas many technologies working together to make this idea possible. Its purpose is to extend your network boundaries whenever and wherever you need them to be. Let's take a look at some of the parts and pieces available in Windows Server 2016 that work in tandem to create a virtual networking environment, the beginning of adoption to our Software-Defined Networking ideology.

Hyper-V Network Virtualization

The biggest component being focused on right now that brings the ability to pick up your networks and slide them around on a layer of virtualization is within Hyper-V. Makes sense, because this is the same place you are touching and accessing to virtualize your servers. With Hyper-V Network Virtualization we are creating a separation between the virtual networks and the physical networks. You no longer need to accommodate for IP scheme limitations on the physical network when you set up new virtual networks, because the virtual networks can ride on top of the physical network, even if the configurations of the two networks would normally be incompatible.

This concept is a little bit difficult to wrap your head around if this is the first time you are hearing about it, so let's discuss some of the real-world situations that would benefit from this kind of separation.

Private clouds

Private cloud is steamrolling through datacenters around the world, because it makes a tremendous amount of sense. Anyone interested in bringing the big benefits of cloud into their environments while at the same time staying away from the cloud negatives can benefit from this. Building a private cloud gives you the ability to have dynamically expanding and shrinking compute resources, the ability to host multiple tenants or divisions within the same compute infrastructure, and provides management interfaces to those divisions so that the nitty-gritty setup and configuration work is able to be done by the tenants themselves and you don't have to spend all kinds of time and resources at the infrastructure provider level making the small detailed configurations.

Private clouds enable all of this capability while staying away from the big scare of your data being hosted in a cloud service provider's datacenter which you have no real control over, and all of the privacy concerns surrounding that.

In order to provide a private cloud inside your infrastructure, particularly one where you want to provide access to multiple tenants, the benefits of network virtualization become apparent, and even a requirement. Let's say you provide computing resources to two divisions of a company, and they each have their own needs for hosting some web servers. No big deal, but these two divisions both have administrative teams who want to use IP schemes that are within 10.0.0.0. They both need to be able to use the same IP addresses, on the same core network that you are providing, yet you need to keep all of their traffic completely segregated and separated. This would have been a nightmare with only a physical network, but by employing the power of network virtualization, you can easily grant IP subnets and address schemes of whatever caliber each division chooses. They can run servers on whatever subnets and IP addresses they like, and all of the traffic is encapsulated uniquely so that it remains separated, completely unaware of the other traffic that is running around on the same physical core network running beneath the virtualization layer. This scenario also plays out very well with corporate acquisitions. Two companies who are joining forces at the IT level often have conflicts with domains and network subnetting. With network virtualization, you can allow the existing infrastructure and servers to continue running with their current network config, but bring them within the same physical network by employing Hyper-V Network Virtualization.

Another simpler example is one where you simply want to move a server within a corporate network. Maybe you have a legacy line-of-business server that many employees still need access to, because their daily workload includes the LOB application to be working at all times. The problem with moving the server is that the LOB application on the client computers has a static IPv4 address configured by which it communicates with the server. When the user opens their app, it does something like "talk to the server at 10.10.10.10". Traditionally that could turn into a deal breaker for moving that server, because moving that server from its current datacenter into a new location would mean changing the IP address of the server, and that would break everyone's ability to connect to it. With virtual networks, this is not an issue whatsoever. With the ability to ride network traffic and IP subnets on the virtualization layer, that server can move from New York to San Diego and retain all of its IP address settings, because the physical network running underneath doesn't matter at all. All of the traffic is encapsulated before it is sent over the physical network, so the IP address of the legacy server can remain at 10.10.10.10, and it can be picked up and moved anywhere in your environment without interruption.

Hybrid clouds

While adding flexibility to your corporate networks is already a huge benefit, the capabilities provided by virtualizing your networks expands exponentially when you do finally decide to start delving into real cloud resources. If and when you make the decision to move some resources to be hosted by a public cloud service provider, you will likely run a hybrid cloud environment. This means that you will build some services in the cloud, but you will also retain some servers and services on-site. At least for a while, though I foresee most companies staying in a hybrid cloud scenario for the rest of eternity, as a 100% movement to the cloud is simply not possible for the ways that many of our companies do business. So now that you want to set up a hybrid cloud, we are again looking at all kinds of headaches associated with the movement of resources between our physical and cloud networks. When I want to move a server from on-site into the cloud, I need to adjust everything so that the networking configuration is compatible with the cloud infrastructure, right? Whatever IP subnet they assigned to me? Wrong—as long as you have your network virtualization infrastructure up and running. Once again Software-Defined Networking saves the day, giving us the ability to retain the existing IP address information on our servers that are moving, and simply run them with those IP addresses in the cloud. Again, since all of the traffic is encapsulated before being transported around, the physical network that is being provided by the cloud does not have to be compatible or distinct from our virtual network, and it gives us the ability to seamlessly shuttle servers back and forth from on-premise to the cloud without having to make special accommodations for networking.

How does it work?

So far it all sounds like a little bit of magic, so how does this actually work and what are the pieces that need to fit together in order to make network virtualization a reality in our organization? Something this comprehensive surely has many moving parts, and cannot be turned on by simply flipping a switch. There are various technologies and components running within a network that have been enabled for network virtualization, let's do a little explaining below so that you have a better understanding of the technologies and terminology that you will be dealing with once you start your work with Software-Defined Networking.

System Center Virtual Machine Manager

Microsoft System Center is a key piece of the puzzle for creating your Software-Defined Networking model, particularly the **Virtual Machine Manager** (**VMM**) component of System Center. The ability to pick up IP addresses and move them to other locations around the world requires some coordination of your networking devices, and VMM is here to help. This is the component that you interface with as your central management point to define and configure your virtual networks. System Center is an enormous topic with many options and datapoints that won't fit in the book you are reading today, so I will leave you with a link as a starting point on VMM learning: https://technet.microsoft.com/en-us/library/gg610610.aspx.

Network Controller

Microsoft's Network Controller is a new role in Windows Server 2016, and as the name implies it is used for control over network resources inside your organization. In most cases, it will be working side-by-side with VMM in order to make network configurations as centralized and seamless as possible. Network Controller is a standalone role and can be installed onto a Server 2016 and then accessed directly, without VMM, but I don't foresee many deployments leaving it at that. Interfacing with Network Controller directly is possible by tapping into its APIs with PowerShell, but is made even better by adding on a graphical interface from which you configure new networks, monitor existing networks and devices, or troubleshoot problems within the virtual networking model. This graphical interface that can be used is System Center VMM.

Network Controller can be used to configure many different aspects of your virtual and physical networks. You can configure IP subnets and addresses, configurations and VLANs on Hyper-V switches, and you can even use it to configure the NICs on your VMs. Network Controller also allows you to create and manage **Access Control List** (**ACL**) type rules within the Hyper-V switch so that you can build your own firewalling solution at this level, without needing to configure local firewalls on the VMs themselves or have dedicated firewall hardware. Network Controller can even be used for configuration of load balancing and providing VPN access through RRAS servers.

Generic Routing Encapsulation

Generic Routing Encapsulation (**GRE**) is just a tunneling protocol, but is imperative to making network virtualization happen successfully. Earlier when we talked about moving IP subnets around and about how you can sit virtual networks on top of physical networks without regard for making sure that their IP configurations are compatible, all of that functionality is provided at the core by GRE.

When your physical network is running 192.168.0.x but you want to host some VMs on a subnet in that datacenter, you can create a virtual network of 10.10.10.x without a problem, but that traffic needs to be able to traverse the physical 192.168 network in order for anything to work. This is where routing encapsulation comes into play. All of the packets from the 10.10.10.x network are encapsulated before being transported across the physical 192.168.0.x network.

There are two different specific routing encapsulation protocols that are supported in our Microsoft Hyper-V Network Virtualization environment. In previous versions of the Windows Server operating system we could only focus on **Network Virtualization Generic Routing Encapsulation** (**NVGRE**), since this was the only protocol that was supported by the Windows flavor of network virtualization. However, there is another protocol called **Virtual Extensible Local Area Network** (**VXLAN**) that has existed for quite some time, and many of the network switches—particularly Cisco—that you have in your environment are more likely to support VXLAN than they are NVGRE. So for the new network virtualization platforms provided within Windows Server 2016, we are now able to support either NVGRE or VXLAN, whichever fits the needs of your company better.

You don't necessarily have to understand how these GRE protocols work in order to make them do work for you, since they will be configured for you by the management tools that exist in Server 2016. But it is important to understand in the overall concept of this virtual networking environment that GRE exists, and that it is the core secret sauce to making all of this work.

Microsoft Azure virtual network

Once you have Hyper-V Network Virtualization running inside your corporate network and get comfortable with the mentality of separating the physical and virtual networks, you will more than likely want to explore the possibilities around interaction with cloud service provider networks. When you utilize Microsoft Azure as your cloud service provider, you have the ability to build a hybrid cloud environment that bridges your on-premise physical network with the remote virtual network stored in Azure. Azure virtual network is the component within Azure that allows you to bring your own IP addresses and subnets into the cloud. You can get a little more info and even sign up for a free trial of Azure virtual network here: https://azure.microsoft.com/en-us/services/virtual-network/.

Windows Server Gateway

When you are working with physical networks, virtual networks, and now virtual networks that are stored in cloud environments, you need some component to bridge those gaps, enabling the networks to interact and communicate with each other. This is where a Windows Server Gateway comes into play.

Windows Server Gateway is the newer term for this piece, it was previously and sometimes still called the Hyper-V Network Virtualization Gateway, so you might see that in documentation as well. A Windows Server Gateway's purpose is pretty simple, to be the connection between virtual and physical networks. These virtual networks can be hosted in your local environment, or up in the cloud. In either case, when you want to connect networks together you will need to employ a Windows Server Gateway. When you are creating a bridge between on-premise and the cloud, your cloud service provider would utilize a gateway on their side, which you would tap into from the physical network via a VPN tunnel.

A Windows Server Gateway is generally a virtual machine, and is integrated with Hyper-V Network Virtualization. A single Gateway can be used to route traffic for many different customers, tenants, or divisions. Even though these different customers have separated networks that need to retain separation from traffic of the other customers, cloud providers, public or private, can still utilize a single Gateway for managing this traffic, because the gateways retain complete isolation between those traffic streams.

Summary

Server administration and network administration used to be segregated pretty distinctively in most organizations, but over time those lines have blurred. There are numerous networking configurations and tasks that now need to be accomplished by Windows Server administrators, without needing to involve a networking team, so it is important that you have a good understanding of how your infrastructure connects together. Familiarity with the tools laid out in this chapter will provide you with the ability to configure, monitor, and troubleshoot the majority of Microsoft-centric networks.

Our introduction to Software-Defined Networking may be a partially confusing section if you have never encountered this idea before, but hopefully it prompts your curiosity to dig a little deeper and prepare yourself for dealing with this in the future. The cloud is here, whether we like it or not, and sometimes executive decisions pull it into our environments faster than we would like to happen on the IT security side. The idea of SDN will grow in popularity over the coming years, it is one of those things that at the moment may seem unknown and daunting, but in five years we may all look back and wonder how we ever made things work without virtual networks. There is much more information both in TechNet and in published books about Hyper-V Virtual Networking and System Center Virtual Machine Manager. I recommend a deeper dive into this material if you are interested in trying this out for yourself.

6
Enabling Your Mobile Workforce

Giving employees the ability to remotely access corporate resources used to be a big benefit to most companies, but not necessarily a requirement. That has certainly changed in the past few years, where most companies and employees have the expectation that they will be able to get their work done from wherever they happen to be. Cell phones are a big part of this equation, but are very limited in scope of what can be done with the small screens and restricted operating systems. In order to grant remote workers the ability to do their jobs from home, the coffee shop, or hotels, we have traditionally used **Virtual Private Networking** (**VPN**), and most of the VPNs that exist in today's businesses are provided by products from companies other than Microsoft. The Remote Access role in Windows Server 2016 is here to change that! With many improvements having been made to the VPN component right in Windows Server, it is now a feasible and secure platform for providing access to corporate resources from remote computers. In addition to VPN, we have a couple of newer technologies baked into Windows Server 2016 that are also designed to provide remote access to corporate resources, in a different way than a traditional VPN.

- DirectAccess – automatic VPN!
- The truth about DirectAccess and IPv6
- Prerequisites for DirectAccess
- Remote Access Management Console
- DirectAccess versus VPN
- Web Application Proxy
- Requirements for WAP
- Server 2016 improvements to WAP

Enabling Your Mobile Workforce

DirectAccess – automatic VPN!

In my experience, Microsoft DirectAccess is the most common reason that administrators deploy the Remote Access role. The easiest way to think about DirectAccess is to think of it as an automatic VPN. Similar to VPN, its purpose is to connect the user's computers into the corporate network when they are outside of the office. Different from VPN, however, is the method that employees use in order to make this connection possible. DirectAccess is not a software component, it is a series of components that are already baked into the Windows operating system, working in tandem to provide completely seamless access for the user. What do I mean by seamless? I mean there is nothing the user has to do in order to make DirectAccess connect. It does that all by itself. As soon as the mobile computer receives an Internet connection, whether that connection is a home Wi-Fi, public Internet at a coffee shop, or a cell phone Mi-Fi style connection, the DirectAccess tunnels automatically build themselves using whatever Internet connection is available, without any user input.

When your computer connects automatically, it saves time and money. Time is saved because the user no longer has to launch a VPN connection. Money is saved because time equals money, but also because having an *always-on* DirectAccess connection means that patching, security policies, and management of these remote computers always happens even when the user is working remotely. You no longer have to wait for users to come back into the office or for them to choose to launch their VPN in order to push new settings and policies down to their computers, it all happens wherever they are, as long as they have Internet access.

DirectAccess has actually been around since the release of Windows Server 2008 R2, and yet I bump into people very regularly who have never heard of it. In the early days, it was quite difficult to deploy and came with a lot of stingy requirements, but much has changed over the past few years and DirectAccess is now easier than ever to deploy, and more beneficial than ever to have running in your environment.

The truth about DirectAccess and IPv6

One of the stingy requirements I mentioned used to be the need for IPv6 inside your network. With the first version of DirectAccess, this was an unfortunate requirement. I say unfortunate because even today in 2016 almost nobody is running IPv6 inside their corporate networks, let alone 8 years ago when this technology released.

A lot of admins didn't even know what IPv6 was. Fortunately, the requirement for IPv6 inside your networks is gone. I repeat, just in case anybody wasn't paying attention or is reading old outdated TechNet documents—*you do not need IPv6 to use DirectAccess*! Why am I shouting? Because I have seen way too many cases where DirectAccess was considered by a company, but the project was tossed aside because reading on TechNet made them believe that IPv6 was a requirement, and because nobody uses IPv6 in their networks yet, they discarded DirectAccess as something that wouldn't work. You absolutely do not have to be running IPv6 in your network to make DirectAccess function, but it is important to understand how DirectAccess uses IPv6, because you will start to encounter it once your deployment gets underway.

When I am sitting at home, working on my company laptop, DirectAccess connects me to the corporate network. My internal network at work has absolutely no IPv6 running inside of it, we are a completely IPv4 network at the moment. This is true for most companies today. However, when I open Command Prompt and ping one of my servers from my DirectAccess laptop, this is what I see—apologies for the sanitized output of the screenshot:

```
Pinging       -vdt-02.     .local [fd63:c3    :4b8:7777::c0a8:    10]
ta:
Reply from fd63:c3    :4b8:7777::c0a8:    10: time=133ms
Reply from fd63:c3    :4b8:7777::c0a8:    10: time=59ms
Reply from fd63:c3    :4b8:7777::c0a8:    10: time=74ms
Reply from fd63:c3    :4b8:7777::c0a8:    10: time=54ms
```

What in the world is that? Looks like IPv6 to me. This is where IPv6 comes into play with DirectAccess. All of the traffic that moves over the Internet part of the connection, between my laptop and the DirectAccess server that is sitting in my datacenter, is IPv6 traffic. My internal network is IPv4, and my DirectAccess server only has IPv4 addresses on it, and yet my DirectAccess tunnel is carrying my traffic using IPv6. This is the core of how DirectAccess works, and cannot be changed. Your DA laptop sends IPsec-encrypted IPv6 packets over the Internet to the DA server, and when the DA server receives the packets it has the capability to spin them down into IPv4 in order to send them to the destination server inside the corporate network. For example, when I open my Outlook and it tries to connect to my Exchange server, my Outlook packets flow over the DirectAccess tunnel as IPv6. Once these packets hit my DirectAccess server, that DA server reaches out to internal DNS to figure out whether that Exchange server is IPv4 or IPv6. If you are actually running IPv6 inside the network and the Exchange server is available via IPv6, the DA server will simply send the IPv6 packets along to the Exchange server.

Enabling Your Mobile Workforce

Connection complete! If, on the other hand, you are running IPv4 inside your network, the DA server will only see a single "A" host record in DNS, meaning that the Exchange server is IPv4-only. The DirectAccess server will then manipulate the IPv6 packet, changing it down into IPv4, and then send it on its way to the Exchange server. The two technologies that handle this manipulation of the packets are **DNS64** and **NAT64**, which you have probably seen in some of the documentation if you have read anything about DirectAccess online. The purpose of these technologies is to change the incoming IPv6 packet stream into IPv4 for the networks where it is required—which is pretty much every network at the moment—and spin the return traffic from IPv4 back up into IPv6 so that it can make its way back to the DirectAccess client computer over the IPv6-based IPsec tunnel that is connecting the DA client to the DA server over the Internet.

It is important to understand that DirectAccess uses IPv6, because any security policies that you might have in place which squash IPv6 on the client computers by default will stop DirectAccess from working properly in your environment. You will have to reverse these policies in order to allow the clients to push out IPv6 packets and get their traffic across the Internet. However, it is also very important to understand that you do not need any semblance of IPv6 running inside the corporate network to make this work, as the DirectAccess server can spin all of the traffic down into IPv4 before it hits that internal network, and most DA implementations that are active today are running in exactly this fashion.

Prerequisites for DirectAccess

DirectAccess has a lot of moving parts, and there are many different ways in which you can set it up. However, not all of these ways are good ideas, so in this section, we are going to discuss some of the big decisions that you will have to make when designing your own DirectAccess environment.

Domain joined

The first big requirement is that the systems involved with DirectAccess need to be domain joined. Your DA server or servers all need to be joined to your domain, and all of the client computers that you want to be DA connected need to be joined to a domain as well. Domain membership is required for authentication purposes, and also because the DirectAccess client settings that need to be applied to the mobile computers come down to these computers via Group Policy. I always like to point out this requirement early in the planning process because it means that users who purchase their own laptops at a retail location are typically not going to be able to utilize DirectAccess—unless you are somehow okay with adding home computers to your domain—and so DA is really a technology that is designed for managing and connecting your corporate assets that you can join to the domain. It is also important to understand this requirement from a security perspective, since your DirectAccess server or servers will typically be facing the edge of your network. It is common for the external NIC on a DA server to sit inside a DMZ, but they also have to be domain joined which may not be something you are used to doing with systems in the perimeter network.

Supported client operating systems

Not all of the Windows client operating systems contain the components that are necessary to make a DirectAccess connection work. Enterprise does, which covers the majority of larger businesses who own Microsoft operating systems, but that certainly does not include everyone. I still see many small businesses using Professional or even Home Premium-style SKUs on their client machines, and these versions do not include the DirectAccess components. Here is a list of the operating systems which do support DirectAccess. During your planning, you will need to make sure that your mobile computers are running one of these:

- Windows 10 Enterprise
- Windows 10 Education
- Windows 8.0 or 8.1 Enterprise
- Windows 7 Enterprise
- Windows 7 Ultimate

DirectAccess servers get one or two NICs?

One big question that needs to be answered even prior to installing the Remote Access role onto your new server—how many NICs are needed on this server? There are two supported methods for implementing DirectAccess.

Single NIC mode

Your DirectAccess server can be installed with only a single NIC. In this case, you would typically plug that network connection directly into your internal network, so that it had access to all of the internal resources that the client computers are going to need to contact during the user's DA sessions. In order to get traffic from the Internet to your DirectAccess server, you would need to establish a Network Address Translation (NAT) from a public IP address into whatever internal IP address you have assigned to the DA server. Many network security administrators do not like this method because it means creating a NAT that brings traffic straight into the corporate network without flowing through any kind of a DMZ.

I can also tell you from experience that single NIC mode does not always work properly. It does a fine job for spinning up a quick test lab or proof of concept, but I have seen too many problems in the field with people trying to run production DirectAccess environments on a single NIC. The ability to use only a single network card is something that was added onto DirectAccess in more recent versions, so it was not originally designed to run like this. Therefore, I strongly recommend that for your production DA install, you do it the right way and go with…

Edge mode with two NICs

Here we have two network cards in the DirectAccess server. The Internal NIC typically gets plugged right into the corporate network, and the External NIC's physical placement can vary depending on the organization. We will discuss the pros and cons for where to place the External NIC immediately following this section of our chapter. Edge mode with two NICs is the way that DirectAccess works best. As you will remember from earlier in this book, implementing a Windows Server with multiple NICs means that you will be multihoming this server, and you need to set up the network settings accordingly. With a Remote Access server, your External NIC is always the one that receives the Default Gateway settings, so you need to make sure and follow this rule and do not configure a Default Gateway on the Internal NIC. On the other hand, you do want to configure DNS server addresses into the Internal NIC properties, but you do not want to configure DNS servers for the External NIC. Since this server is multihomed, you will likely need to create some route statements in order to add your corporate subnets into the Windows routing table of this server before it is able to successfully send and receive traffic. The only networks that would not need to accommodate for adding static routes would be small networks, where all of your internal devices were on a single subnet. If this is the case, then you have no need to input static routes. But most corporate networks span multiple subnets, and in this case you should refer back to the section where we discussed multihoming and how to build out those route statements.

More than two NICs?

Nope, don't go there. If you are familiar with configuring routers or firewalls, you know that you have the potential to install many different NICs on this server and plug them all into different subnets. While there are many reasons why splitting up network access like this on a remote access server might be beneficial, it won't work how you want it to. The DirectAccess configuration itself is only capable of managing two different network interfaces. As you can see in the following screenshot, during the setup wizards you will have to define one NIC as External, and the other as Internal. Any more NICs that exist in that server will not be used by DirectAccess, unfortunately. Maybe this is something that can change in future versions!

```
Select the network adapters on the Remote Access server.

Adapter connected to the external network:        Adapter connected to the internal network:

External          ∨    Details...                 Internal          ∨    Details...
1.1.1.10                                          10.0.0.10

Select the certificate used to authenticate IP-HTTPS connections:
☐ Use a self-signed certificate created automatically by DirectAccess

[                                                                        ] Browse...
```

To NAT or not to NAT?

Now that you have decided to roll with two NICs in your DirectAccess server, where do we plug in the External? There are two common places that this External network interface can be connected to, but depending on which you choose the outcome of your DirectAccess environment can be vastly different. Before we talk about the actual placement of the NIC, I would like to define a couple of protocols that are important to understand, because they pertain very much to answering this question about NIC placement. When your DirectAccess laptop makes a connection to the DirectAccess server, it will do so using one of the three IPv6 transition tunneling protocols. These protocols are **6to4**, **Teredo**, and **IP-HTTPS**. When the DA client connects its DA tunnels, it will automatically choose which of these protocols is best to use, depending on the users, current Internet connection. All three of these protocols perform the same function for a DirectAccess connection; their job is to take the IPv6 packet stream coming out of the laptop, and encapsulate it inside IPv4 so that the traffic can make its way successfully across the IPv4 Internet. When the packets get to the DirectAccess server, they are decapped so that the DA server can process these IPv6 packets.

6to4

DA clients will only attempt to connect using 6to4 when the remote laptop has a true public Internet IP address. This hardly ever happens these days with the shortage of available Internet IPv4 addresses, and so 6to4 is typically not used by any DirectAccess client computers. In fact, it can present its own set of challenges when users are connecting with cell phone cards in their laptops, and so it is common practice to disable the 6to4 adapter on the client computers as a DirectAccess best practice setting.

Teredo

When DA clients are connected to the Internet using a private IP address—
such as behind a home router or a public Wi-Fi router—they will attempt to
connect using the Teredo protocol. Teredo uses a UDP stream to encapsulate these
packets, and so as long as the user's Internet connection allows outbound UDP 3544,
Teredo will generally connect and be the transition protocol of choice for that
DirectAccess connection.

IP-HTTPS

If Teredo fails to connect, such as in the case where the user is sitting in a network that
blocks outbound UDP, then the DirectAccess connection will fall back to using IP-
HTTPS, pronounced *IP over HTTPS*. This protocol encapsulates the IPv6 packets inside
IPv4 headers, but then wraps that up inside an HTTP header and encrypts it with
TLS/SSL before sending the packet out over the Internet. This effectively makes the
DirectAccess connection an SSL stream, just like when you browse an HTTPS website.

Installing on the true edge – on the Internet

When you plug your DirectAccess server's External NIC directly into the Internet,
you grant yourself the ability to put true public IP addresses on that NIC. In
doing this, you enable all three of the above transition tunneling protocols, so
that DirectAccess client computers can choose between them for the best form of
connectivity. When installing in the true edge method, you would put not only
one, but two public IP addresses on that External NIC. Make sure that the public
IP addresses are concurrent, as this is a requirement for Teredo. When your
DirectAccess server has two concurrent, public IP addresses assigned to the external
NIC, it will enable the Teredo protocol to be available for connections.

 The NIC does not necessarily have to be plugged directly into the
Internet for this to work. Depending on your firewall capabilities, you
may have the option to establish a *Bridged DMZ* where no NATing is
taking place. You would need to check with your firewall vendor to
find out whether or not that is an option for your organization.

Installing behind a NAT

It is much more common for the networking team to want to place the external NIC of your DirectAccess server behind a firewall, inside a DMZ. This typically means creating a NAT in order to bring this traffic into the server. While this is entirely possible and better protects the DirectAccess server itself from the Internet, it does come with a big downside. When you install a DA server behind a NAT, Teredo no longer works. In fact, the DirectAccess configuration wizards will recognize when you have a private IP address listed on the external NIC and it will not even turn on Teredo.

When Teredo is not available, all of your DirectAccess clients will connect using IP-HTTPS. So why does it even matter if Teredo is unavailable? Because it is a more efficient protocol than IP-HTTPS. When Teredo tunnels packets, it is simply encapsulating IPv6 inside IPv4. The DirectAccess traffic stream is already and always IPsec encrypted, so there is no need for the Teredo tunnel to be doing any additional encryption. On the other hand, when IP-HTTPS tunnels packets, it takes the already encrypted IPsec traffic stream and encrypts it a second time using SSL. This means all of the packets that are coming and going are being subject to additional processing and CPU cycles, and it makes for a slower connection. It also creates additional hardware load on the DirectAccess server itself, because it is now handling double the encryption processing.

This is a particularly apparent problem when you are running Windows 7 on the client computers, as the double encryption processing will make a noticeably slower connection for the users. DirectAccess still works fine, but if you sit a Teredo connected laptop next to an IP-HTTPS connected laptop, you will notice the speed difference between the two.

In Windows 8 and Windows 10, there have been some counter-measures added to help with this speed discrepancy. These newer client operating systems are now smart enough that they can negotiate the SSL part of the IP-HTTPS tunnel by using the null encryption algorithm, meaning that IP-HTTPS is not doing a second encryption and the performance is much more on par with Teredo. However, this only works for the newer client operating systems, and it still doesn't work in some cases. For example, when you enable your DirectAccess server to also provide VPN connectivity, or if you choose to employ a **One-Time-Password (OTP)** system alongside DirectAccess, then the null algorithm will be disabled because it is a security risk in these situations, and so even your Windows 8 and Windows 10 computers will be doing the double encryption when they connect via IP-HTTPS. You can see where it would be beneficial to have Teredo enabled and available so that any computers that can connect via Teredo, will do so.

Enabling Your Mobile Workforce

To summarize, you can certainly install your DirectAccess server's external NIC behind a NAT, but be aware that all of the DA client computers will be connecting using the IP-HTTPS protocol, and it is important to understand the side effects of implementing in this way.

Network Location Server

This major component in a DirectAccess infrastructure is something that does not even exist on the DA server itself, or at least it shouldn't if you are setting things up properly. The **Network Location Server** (**NLS**) is simply a website that is running inside the corporate network. This website does not need to be available for access over the Internet, in fact it should not be. NLS is used as part of the inside/outside detection mechanism on the DirectAccess client computers. Every time a DA client gets a network connection, it starts looking for the NLS website. If it can see the site, then it knows that you are inside the corporate network, and DirectAccess is not required, so it turns itself off. However, if your NLS website cannot be contacted, it means you are outside of the corporate network, and the DirectAccess components will start turning themselves on.

This prerequisite is easily met; all you need to do is spin up a VM and install IIS on it to host this new website, or you can even add a new website onto an existing web server in your network. There are only two things to watch out for when setting up your NLS website. The first is that it must be an HTTPS site, and so it requires an SSL certificate. We will discuss the certificates used in DA, including this one, in our next section of this chapter. In addition to making sure that the website is accessible via HTTPS, you must also make sure that the DNS name you are using in order to contact this website is unique. You want to do this because whatever name you choose for the NLS website, that name will not be resolvable when the client computers are outside of the corporate network. This is by design, because you obviously don't want your DA clients to be able to successfully contact the NLS website when they are working remotely, as that would then turn off their DirectAccess connection.

The reason I bring up the unique DNS name is that I often see new DirectAccess admins utilize an existing internal website as their NLS website. For example, if you have `https://intranet` running as a SharePoint site, you could simply use this in the DA config as the NLS server definition. However, once you set it up this way, you will quickly realize that nobody who is working remotely can access the `https://intranet` website. This is by design, because the DA environment now considers your intranet website to be the NLS server, and you cannot resolve to it while you are mobile. The solution to this problem? Make sure that you choose a new DNS name to use for this NLS website. Something like `https://nls.contoso.local` is appropriate.

The most important part about the Network Location Server that I want to stress is that you should absolutely implement this website on a server in your network that is not the DirectAccess server itself. When you are running through the DA config wizards, you will see on the screen where we define NLS that it is recommended to do this, but it also gives you the option to self-host the NLS website right on the DirectAccess server itself. There are many things that can go wrong when you cohost NLS on the DA server, so stay away from doing that. Running NLS on your DA server also limits your DirectAccess potential in the future, because some of the advanced DA configurations require you to remove NLS from the DA server anyway, so you might as well do it correctly the first time you set it up. Changing your NLS website after you are running DA in production can be very tricky, and often goes sideways. I have helped numerous companies move their NLS website after realizing that they cannot co-host NLS on the DA server if and when they want to add a second DirectAccess server for growth or redundancy. Here is a screenshot of the section in the DA config wizards where you choose the location of NLS, make sure you stick with the top box!

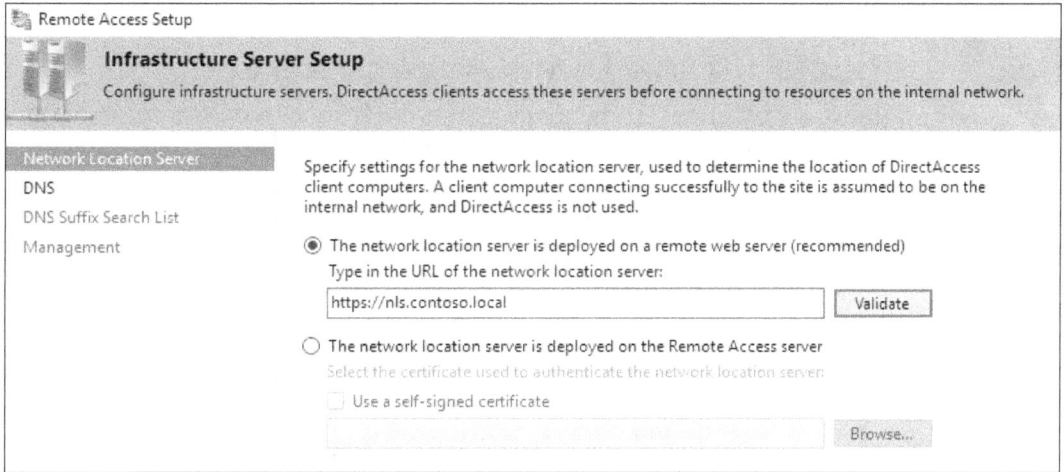

Certificates used with DirectAccess

Aside from reading and misunderstanding about how DirectAccess uses IPv6, here is the next biggest *turn off* for administrators who are interested in giving DirectAccess a try. Once you start to read about how DA works, you will quickly come to realize that certificates are required in a few different places. It is hard to distinguish which certificates need to go where when you are wading through TechNet, so this section is to clear up any confusion that exists surrounding DirectAccess certificates. It really is not very complicated, once you know what does and does not need to be done.

Enabling Your Mobile Workforce

The core prerequisite is that you have a Windows CA server somewhere in your network. The stature of your PKI implementation is not that important to DirectAccess. We simply need the ability to issue certificates to our DA server and clients. There are only three places that certificates are used in DirectAccess, and two of them are SSL certificates.

SSL certificate on the NLS web server

As mentioned just a few minutes ago, your NLS website needs to be running HTTPS. This means that you will require an SSL certificate to be installed on the server that is hosting your NLS website. Assuming that you have an internal CA server, this certificate can be easily acquired from that internal CA, so there are no costs associated with this cert. You do not need to purchase one from a public CA, because this certificate is only going to be accessed and verified from your domain-joined machines, the DirectAccess clients. Since domain-joined computers automatically trust the CA servers in your network, this certificate can simply be issued from your internal CA, and it will do exactly what we need it to do for the purposes of DirectAccess.

SSL certificate on the DirectAccess server

An SSL certificate is also required to be installed on the DirectAccess server itself, but this one should be purchased from your public certification authority. This certificate will be used to validate the IP-HTTPS traffic streams coming in from the client computers, because that is SSL traffic and so we need an SSL certificate to validate it. Since the IP-HTTPS listener is facing the public Internet, it is definitely recommended that you use a certificate from a public CA, rather than try to use a cert from your internal PKI.

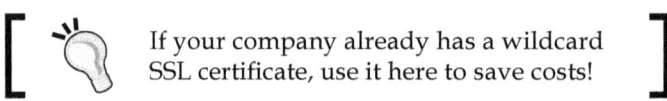

If your company already has a wildcard SSL certificate, use it here to save costs!

Machine certificates on the DA server and all DA clients

The last and most complicated part of the DirectAccess certificate puzzle is the machine certificates. Once you know what is required though, it's really not hard at all. We simply require that a Computer or Machine certificate be installed on the DirectAccess server, as well as each of the DirectAccess client machines. This machine certificate is used as part of the authentication process for the IPsec tunnels. It is a big part of the way that DirectAccess verifies that you really are who you say you are when your computer makes that DA connection happen.

There is a built-in template on a Windows CA server called **Computer**, and this template does exactly what we need it to do for DirectAccess, so often times we simply set up a policy to issue computer certificates to all of the DA machines. If you do not want to use that prebuilt template for some reason, you can certainly create your own custom certificate template for this purpose. When setting up your own certificate template, just make sure that it meets the following criteria:

- The Common Name (subject) of the certificate should match the FQDN of the computer
- The Subject Alternative Name (SAN) of the certificate should equal the DNS Name of the computer
- The certificate should serve the intended purposes—Enhanced Key Usage—of both Client Authentication and Server Authentication

I should note here, though I don't really want to, that issuing these certificates is not absolutely necessary to make DirectAccess work. If you are running Windows 8 or higher on the client side, then it is possible to get DA working without machine certificates. They can instead utilize something called Kerberos Proxy for their computer authentication when the IPsec tunnels are being built, but I highly recommend sticking with certificates. Using certificates as part of the authentication process makes the connection more stable, and more secure. Additionally, like with the placement of NLS, if you want to do any of the advanced functions with DirectAccess like load balancing or Multi-Site, or even if you simply want to make some Windows 7 computers connect through DA, then you would be required to issue certificates anyway. So just stick with the best practice in the first place and issue these certificates before you even get started with testing DirectAccess.

Enabling Your Mobile Workforce

Do not use the Getting Started Wizard!

After making the necessary design decisions and implementing the prerequisites we have talked about so far, it is finally time to install the Remote Access role onto your new DirectAccess server! After you have finished installing the role, similar to many roles in Windows Server 2016, you will be prompted that additional configuration is required in order to use this role. In fact, if you follow the yellow exclamation mark inside Server Manager, the only option that you are presented with is **Open the Getting Started Wizard**. Ugh! This is *not* what you want to click on.

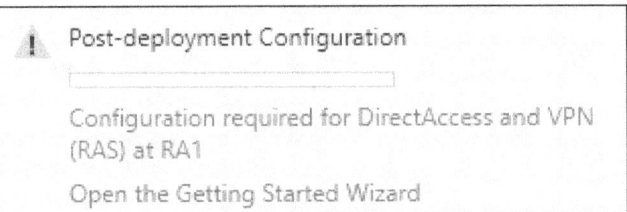

Your home for DirectAccess configurations is the **Remote Access Management Console**, which is available from inside the **Tools** menu of **Server Manager** now that our Remote Access role has been installed. Go ahead and launch that, and now we are presented with a choice:

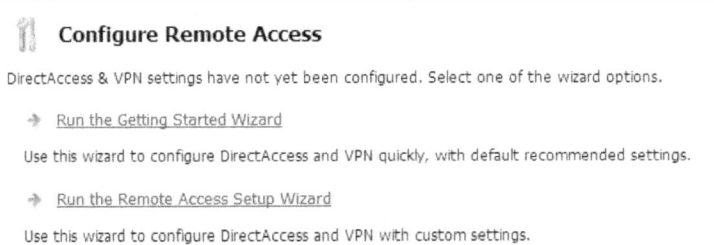

Do not click on **Run the Getting Started Wizard**! The GSW is a shortcut method to implementing DirectAccess, designed only for getting DA up and running as quickly as possible, perhaps for a quick proof of concept. Under no circumstances should you trust the GSW for your production DA environment, because in an effort to make configuration quick and easy, many configuration decisions are made for you that are not best practices.

You want to make sure and click on **Run the Remote Access Setup Wizard** instead when you are first prompted in this console, which will invoke the full set of DirectAccess configuration screens. The setup of DA is a series of four different steps, each containing a handful of screens that you will navigate through to choose your appropriate configuration options. There is good detail on these screens as to what each one of them means and what your options are, so don't be afraid to dive in and set this up the proper way. If you have already configured DirectAccess and used the **Getting Started Wizard**, DA may be working for you but it is not running as efficiently or securely as it could be. The following is a quick list of the reasons why the **Getting Started Wizard** is not in your best interests. These are the things that it does which go directly against a best practices DirectAccess install:

- GSW co-hosts the NLS website on the DA server
- GSW applies the DA client GPO settings to **Domain Computers** — this is a terrible idea
- GSW utilizes self-signed certificates, which is a general security no-no
- GSW automatically disables Teredo
- GSW does not walk you through any of the advanced options for DirectAccess, probably because the way that it sets everything up invalidates your ability to even use the advanced functions

Remote Access Management Console

You are well on your way to giving users remote access capabilities on this new server. As with many networking devices, once you have established all of your configurations on a remote access server, it is pretty common for admins to walk away and let it run. There is no need for a lot of ongoing maintenance or changes to that configuration once you have it running well. However, **Remote Access Management Console** in Windows Server 2016 is useful not only for configuration of the remote access parts and pieces, but for monitoring and reporting as well. Let's take a look inside this console so that you are familiar with the different screens you will be interacting with:

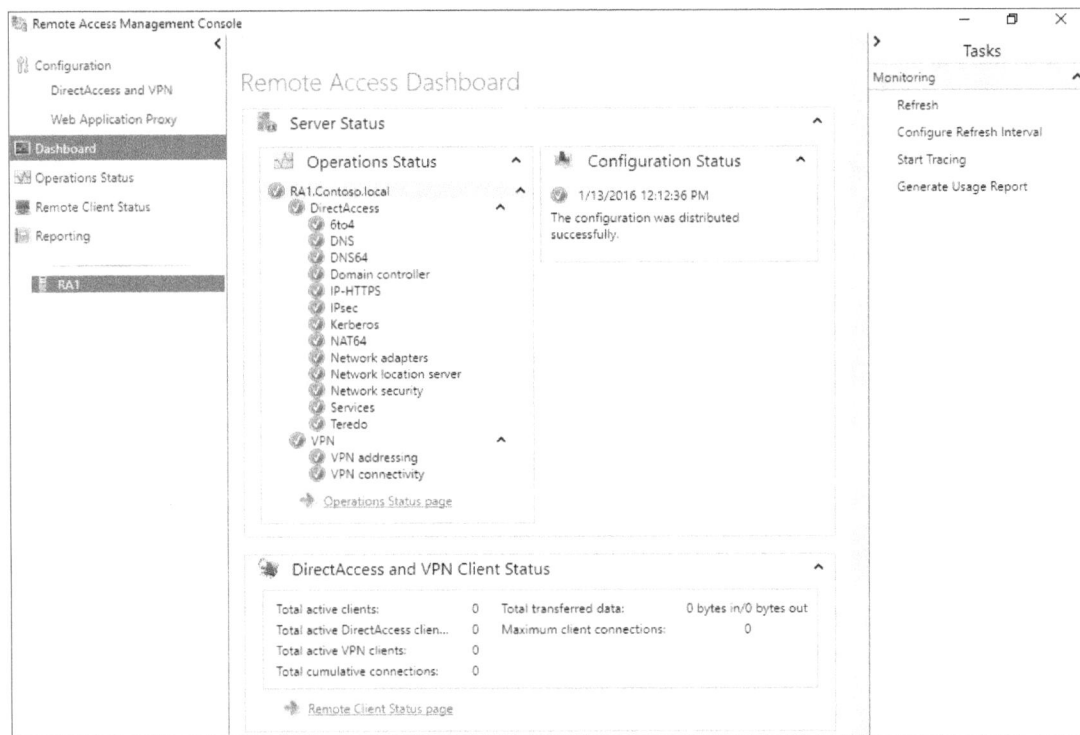

Configuration

The configuration screen is pretty self-explanatory, this is where you would visit in order to create your initial remote access configuration, and where you go to update any settings in the future. As you can see in the screenshot, you are able to configure **DirectAccess**, **VPN**, and the **Web Application Proxy** right from this **Remote Access Management Console**.

There is not a lot to configure as far as the VPN goes, you really only have one screen of options where you define what kind of IP addresses are handed down to the VPN clients connecting in, and how to handle VPN authentication. It is not immediately obvious where this screen is, so I wanted to point it out. Inside the **DirectAccess and VPN** configuration section, if you click on the **Edit...** button listed under **Step 2**, this will launch the Step 2 mini-wizard. The last screen of this mini-wizard is called **VPN Configuration**. This is the screen where you can configure these IP address and authentication settings for your VPN connections:

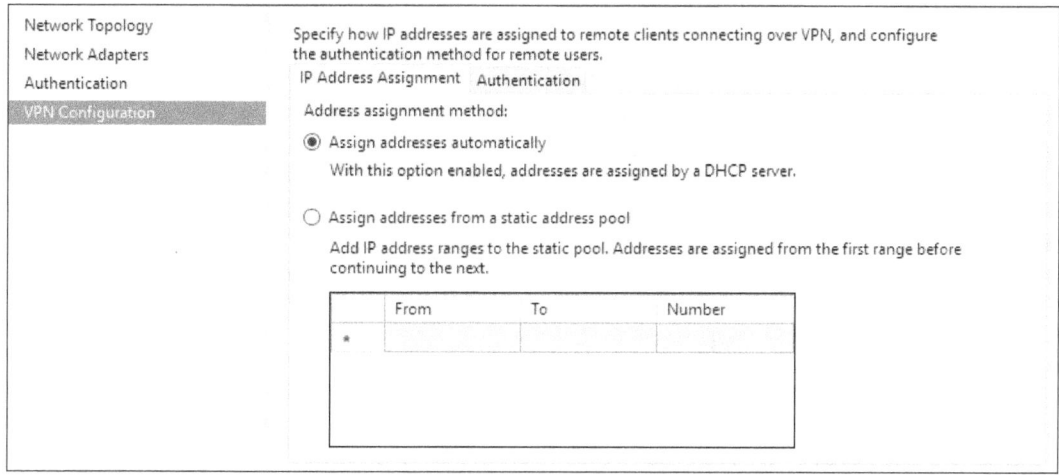

Dashboard

The **Remote Access Dashboard** gives you a 30,000 foot view of the Remote Access server status. You are able to view a quick status of the components running on the server, whether or not the latest configuration changes have been rolled around, and some summary numbers near the bottom about how many DirectAccess and VPN connections are happening.

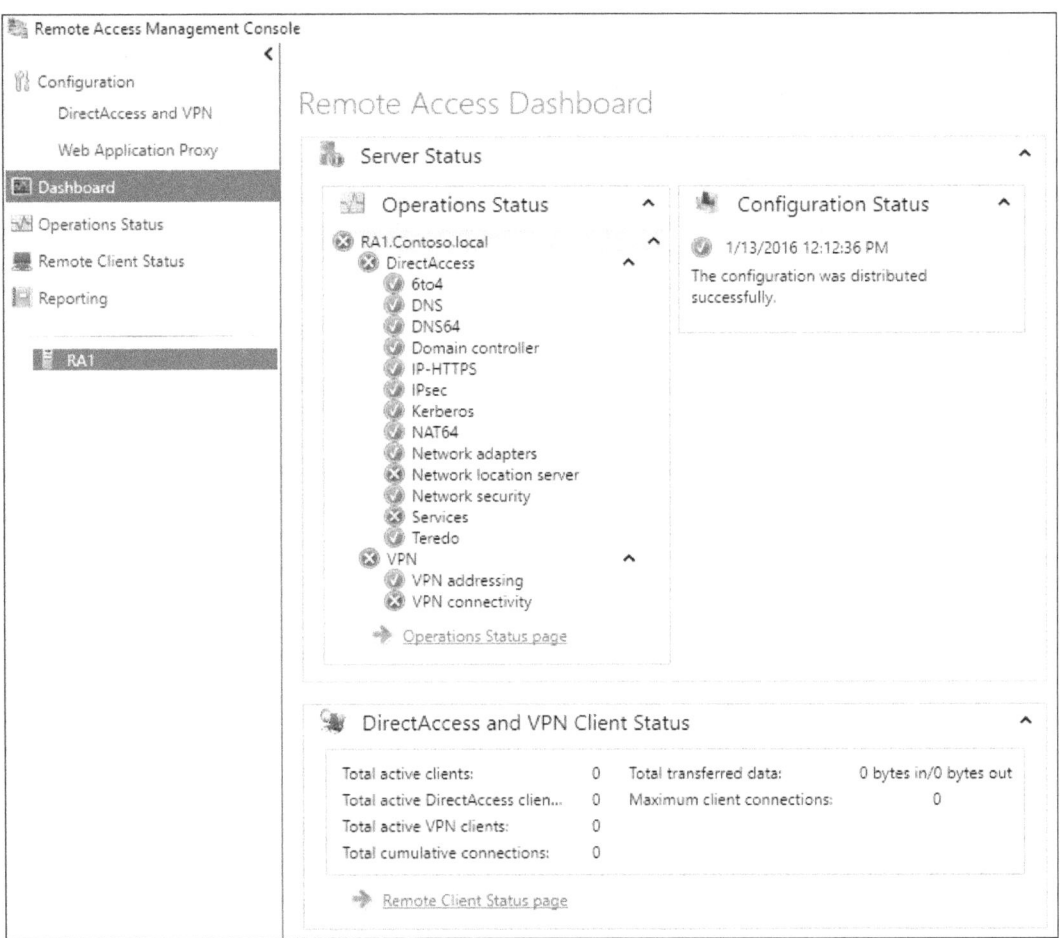

Operations Status

If you want to drill down further into what is happening on the server side of the connections, that is what the **Operations Status** page is all about. Here you can see a little more detail on each of the components that are running under the hood to make your DA and VPN connections happen. If any of them have an issue, you can click on the specific component to get a little more information. For example, as a test, I have turned off the NLS web server in my lab network, and I can now see in the **Operations Status** page that NLS is flagged with an error.

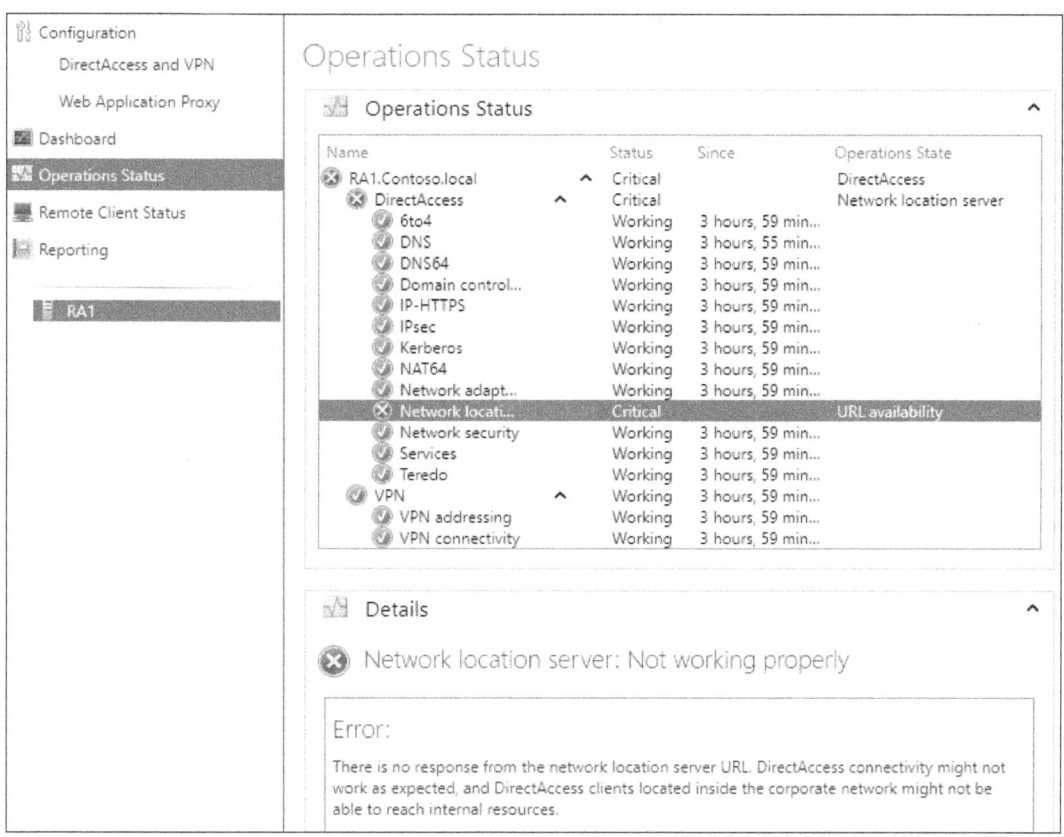

Remote Client Status

Next up is the **Remote Client Status** screen. As indicated, this is the screen where we can monitor the client computers who are connected. It will show us both DirectAccess and VPN connections here. We will be able to see computer names, usernames, and even the resources that they are utilizing during their connections. The information on this screen is able to be filtered by simply putting any criteria into the **Search** bar on the top of the window.

It is important to note that the **Remote Client Status** screen only shows live, active connections. There is no historical information stored here.

Reporting

You guessed it, this is the window you need to visit if you want to see historical remote access information. This screen is almost exactly the same as the **Remote Client Status** screen, except that you have the ability to generate reports for historical data pulled from date ranges of your choosing. Once the data is displayed, you have the same search and filtering capabilities that you had on the **Remote Client Status** screen.

Reporting is disabled by default, but you simply need to navigate to the **Reporting** page and click on **Configure Accounting**. Once that is enabled, you will be presented with options about storing the historical information. You can choose to store the data in the local WID, or on a remote RADIUS server. You also have options here for how long to store logging data, and a mechanism that can be used to clear out old data.

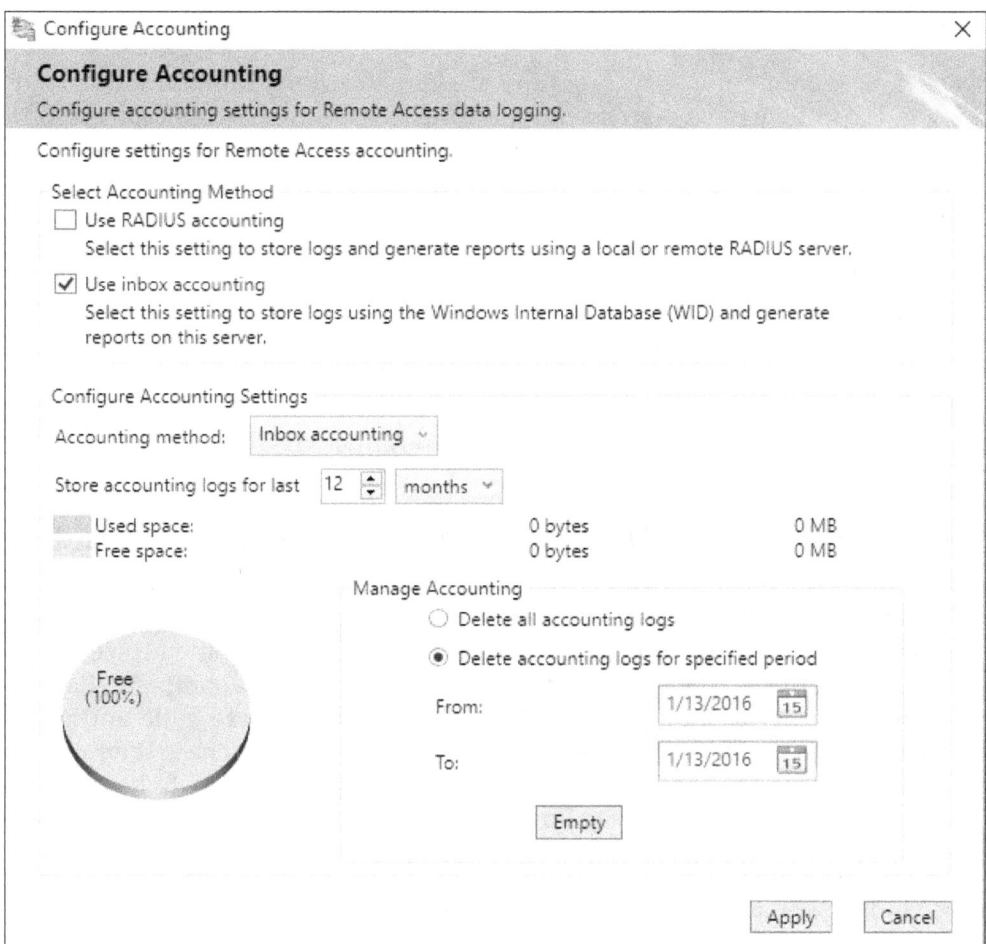

Tasks

The last window pane of **Remote Access Management Console** that I want to point out is the **Tasks** bar on the right side of your screen. The actions and options that are displayed in this taskbar change depending on what part of the console you are navigating through. Make sure to keep an eye on this side of your screen for setting up some of the more advanced functions. Some examples of available tasks are creating usage reports, refreshing the screen, and configuring network load balancing or Multi-Site configurations if you are running multiple remote access servers.

DirectAccess versus VPN

VPN has been around for a very long time, making it a pretty familiar idea to anyone working in IT, and we have discussed quite a bit about DirectAccess today in order to bring you up to speed on this evolution, so to speak, of corporate remote access. Now that you know there are two great solutions built into Windows Server 2016 for enabling your mobile workforce, which one is better?

While DirectAccess is certainly the newer of the technologies, we cannot say that it is better in all circumstances. Each has its pros and cons, and the ways that you use each, or both, will depend upon many variables. Your users, your client computers, and your organization's individual needs will need to factor into your decision-making process. Let's discuss some of the differences between DirectAccess and VPN so that you can better determine which is right for you.

Domain-joined versus non-domain-joined

One of the biggest requirements for a DirectAccess client computer is that it must be domain joined. While this requirement by itself doesn't seem so major, what it implies can be pretty vast. Trusting a computer enough to be joined to your domain more than likely means that the laptop is owned by the company. It also probably means that this laptop was first in IT's hands in order to build and prep it. Companies that are in the habit of allowing employees to purchase their own computers to be used for work purposes may not find DirectAccess to fit well with that model. DA is also not ideal for situations where employees use their existing home computers to connect into work remotely.

In these kinds of situations, such as home and personally-owned computers, VPN may be better suited to the task. You can connect to a VPN from a non-domain-joined machine, and you can even establish VPN connections from many non-Microsoft devices. IOS, Android, Windows Phone — these are all platforms that have a VPN client built into them that can be used to tap into a VPN listener on a Windows Server 2016 remote access server. If your only remote access solution was DirectAccess, you would not be able to provide non-domain-joined devices with a connectivity platform.

Auto versus manual launch

Here, DirectAccess takes the cake. It is completely seamless. DirectAccess components are baked right into the Windows operating system, no software VPN is going to be able to touch that level of integration. With VPN, users have to log in to their computers to unlock them, then launch their VPN, then log in again to that VPN software, all before they can start working on anything. With DirectAccess, all they need to do is log in to the computer to unlock the screen. DirectAccess activates itself in the background so that as soon as the desktop loads for the user, they simply open the applications that they need to access, just like when they are inside the office.

Software versus built-in

I'm a fan of Ikea furniture. They do a great job of supplying quality products at a low cost, all while packaging it up in incredibly small boxes. After you pay for the product, unbox the product, put the product together, and then test the product to make sure it works—it's great. If you can't see where this is going, I'll give you a hint. It's an analogy for VPN. As in, you typically pay a vendor for their VPN product, unbox the product, implement the product at more expense, then test the product. That VPN software then has the potential to break and need reinstallation or reconfiguration, and will certainly come with software updates that need to be accomplished down the road. Maintenance, maintenance, maintenance.

Maybe I have been watching too many home improvement shows lately, but I am a fan of houses with built-ins. Built-ins are essentially furniture that is permanent to the house, built right into the walls, corners, or wherever it happens to be. It adds value, and it integrates into the overall house much better than furniture that was pieced together separately and then stuck against the wall in the corner.

DirectAccess is like a built-in. It is inside the operating system. There is no software to install, no software to update, no software to reinstall when it breaks. Everything that DA needs is already in Windows today, you just aren't using it. Oh, and it's free, well, built into the cost of your Windows license anyway. There are no user CALs, no ongoing licensing costs related to implementing Microsoft DirectAccess.

Password and login issues with VPN

If you have ever worked on a helpdesk for a company that uses VPN, you know what I'm talking about. There are a series of common troubleshooting calls that happen in the VPN world related to passwords. Sometimes the user forgets their password. Perhaps their password has expired and needs to be changed—ugh, VPN doesn't handle this scenario very well either. Or maybe the employee changed their expired password on their desktop before they left work for the day, but are now trying to log in remotely from their laptop and it isn't working.

What is the solution to password problems with VPN? Reset the user's password and then make the user come into the office in order to make it work on their laptop. Yup, these kinds of phone calls still happen every day. This is unfortunate, but a real potential problem with VPN.

What's the good news? DirectAccess doesn't have these kinds of problems! Since DA is part of the operating system, it has the capability to be connected anytime that Windows is online. This includes the login screen! Even if I am sitting on the login or lock screen, and the system is waiting for me to input my username and password, as long as I have Internet access I also have a DirectAccess tunnel. This means that I can actively do password management tasks. If my password expires and I need to update it, it works. If I forgot my password and I can't get into my laptop, I can call the helpdesk and simply ask them to reset my password. I can then immediately log in to my DirectAccess laptop with the new password, right from my house.

Another cool function that this seamlessness enables is the ability to login with new user accounts. Have you ever logged into your laptop as a different user account in order to test something? Yup, that works over DirectAccess as well. For example, I am sitting at home and I need to help one of the sales guys troubleshoot some sort of file permission problem. I suspect it's got something to do with his user account, so I want to log in to my laptop as him in order to test it. The problem is that his user account has never logged into my laptop before. With VPN, not a chance. This would never work. With DirectAccess, piece of cake! I simply log off, type in his username and password, and bingo. I'm logged in, while still sitting at home in my pajamas.

[It is important to note that you can run both DirectAccess and VPN on the same Windows Server 2016 remote access server. If both technologies have capabilities that you could benefit from, use them both!]

Web Application Proxy

DirectAccess and VPN are both great remote access technologies, and combining the two of them together can provide a complete remote access solution for your organization, without having to pay for or work with a third-party solution. Better still, in Windows Server 2016 there is yet another component of the Remote Access role available to use. This third piece of the remote access story is the **Web Application Proxy (WAP)**. This is essentially a reverse proxy mechanism, giving you the ability to take some HTTP and HTTPS applications that are hosted inside your corporate network, and publish them securely to the Internet. Any of you who have been working with Microsoft technologies in the perimeter networking space over the last few years will probably recognize a product called Forefront **Unified Access Gateway (UAG)** that accomplished similar functionality. UAG is a comprehensive SSLVPN solution, also designed for publishing internal applications out to the Internet via SSL. It was considerably more powerful than a simple reverse proxy, including components such as preauthentication, SSTP VPN, and RDS gateway, and DirectAccess itself could even be run through UAG.

If all of your mobile workers have access to launch either DirectAccess or VPN, then you probably don't have any use for something like WAP. However, with the growing cloud mentality, it is quite common for users to expect that they can open up a web browser from any computer, anywhere, and gain access to some of their applications. Document access is now often provided by web services such as SharePoint. E-mail access can be had remotely, from any computer, by tapping into Outlook Web Access. So many applications and so much data can be accessed through only a web browser, and this enables employees to access this data without needing to establish a full-blown corporate tunnel like a VPN. So the real-world use case for WAP? Home computers that you do not want to be VPN connected. This way you don't have to worry as much about the health and status of the home or user-owned computers, since the only interaction they are having with your company is through the web browser. This limits the potential for sinister activity to flow into your network from these computers. As you can see, a technology like WAP does certainly have its place in the remote access market.

In time, I hope that WAP will be a true replacement for Unified Access Gateway. UAG ran on Windows Server 2008 R2, and has now been officially discontinued as a Microsoft product. The official Microsoft replacement for UAG is the WAP role. It is not yet nearly as comprehensive, but they are working on improving it. Currently, WAP is useful for publishing access to simple web applications. You can also publish access to rich clients that use HTTP basic, like ActiveSync. Also included is the ability to publish data to clients that use MSOFBA, such as when users try to pull down corporate data from their Word or Excel applications running on the local computer.

Enabling Your Mobile Workforce

So far, the only real-world uses for WAP that I have seen are publishing remote access to things like Exchange and SharePoint environments. And this is no small thing, as these are technologies that almost everyone uses. So it can certainly be beneficial to your company to implement WAP for publishing secure access to these resources. It's better than NATing directly to your Exchange server. Another useful way that you can utilize a WAP server is when setting up **Active Directory Federation Services** (**AD FS**) in your network. AD FS is a technology designed to enable single sign-on for users and federation with other companies, and so it involves taking traffic coming in from the Internet, into your internal network. Traditionally, there has been a server component called an AD FS Proxy that you install at the edge of your network to handle this traffic, but now you have a choice. You can still implement a standalone AD FS Proxy server, or you can instead provide the AD FS Proxy capabilities from your WAP server. This better unifies the remote access solution, bringing your inbound AD FS traffic through the official remote access server, rather than needing a separate AD FS Proxy server.

Requirements for WAP

Unfortunately, the ability to make use of the Web Application Proxy comes with a pretty stingy requirement. You must have AD FS installed in your environment to be able to use it. Even to test it, because the WAP configuration is stored inside AD FS. None of the WAP configuration information is stored on the remote access server itself, which makes for a lightweight server that can be easily moved, changed, or added to. The downside to this is that you must have AD FS running in your environment so that WAP can have a place to store that configuration information.

While a tight integration with AD FS does mean that we have better authentication options, and the users can take advantage of that AD FS single-sign-on to their applications that are published through WAP, so far this has proven to be a huge roadblock to implementation for any smaller size business. Many folks are not yet running AD FS, and if the only reason they are looking into implementing AD FS is so that they can publish a few web applications to the Internet—they probably aren't going to invest the time and effort just to make that happen.

One thing to keep in mind if you are interested in using WAP, and are therefore looking at the requirement for AD FS, is that AD FS can certainly be used for other functions. In fact, one of the most common uses of it at the present time is integration with Office 365. If you are planning for or thinking of incorporating Office 365 into your environment, AD FS is a great tool that can enhance the authentication capabilities for that traffic.

Server 2016 improvements to WAP

Many consider the Web Application Proxy to be in the toddler phase. It has been alive for a little while now, but is still learning how to do new things. Let's discuss some of the improvements that have been made to WAP inside Windows Server 2016.

Preauthentication for HTTP Basic

There are two different ways that users can authenticate to applications that are being published by Web Application Proxy: Preauthentication or pass-thru authentication. When publishing an application with Preauthentication, this means that users will have to stop by the AD FS interface to authenticate themselves before they are allowed through to the web application itself. In my eyes, preauthentication is a critical component to any reverse proxy, and I would have to be stuck between a rock and a hard place in order to externally publish an application that did not require preauthentication. However, the second option is to do pass-thru authentication, and it does exactly that. When you publish access to an application and choose pass-thru authentication, all WAP is doing is shuttling the packets from the Internet to the application server. The users are able to get to the web application without authentication, so in theory anyone can hit the front website of your application. From there the application itself will likely require the user to authenticate, but there is no man-in-the-middle protection happening, that web application is available for the public to view. As you can tell, I do not recommend taking this route.

We already know that WAP has the capability to authenticate web applications, but in the past versions it could not do any form of preauth on HTTP Basic applications, like when a company wanted to publish access to Exchange ActiveSync. This inability leaves ActiveSync a little bit too exposed to the outside world, and is a security risk. Thankfully, this has changed in Windows Server 2016, as you can now preauthenticate traffic streams that are using HTTP Basic.

HTTP to HTTPS redirection

Users don't like going out of their way or wasting time by having to remember that they need to enter `HTTPS://` in front of the URL when they access applications. They would rather just remember `email.contoso.com`. The inability for WAP to do HTTP to HTTPS redirection has been an annoyance and a hindrance to adoption so far, but that has finally changed. WAP inside Server 2016 brings the capability of WAP itself to handle the HTTP to HTTPS redirection, meaning that users do not need to type "HTTPS" into their browser address bar any longer, they can simply type in the DNS name of the site and let WAP handle the translations.

Client IP addresses forwarded to applications

In the reverse proxy and SSLVPN world, we occasionally run across applications that require knowing what the client's local IP address is. While this requirement doesn't happen very often, and is typically segregated to what we would call legacy applications, it does still happen. When the backend application needs to know what the client's IP address is, this presents a big challenge with reverse proxy solutions. When the user's traffic flows through WAP or any other reverse proxy, it is similar to a NAT, where the source IP address information in these packets changes. The backend application server is unable to determine the client's own IP address, and trouble ensues. The Web Application Proxy now has the ability to propagate the client-side IP address through to the backend application server, alleviating this problem.

Publishing Remote Desktop Gateway

One of the items that UAG is commonly used for is publishing access to Remote Desktop Services. UAG was essentially its own Remote Desktop Gateway, which gave you the ability to publish access to RDSH servers, individual RDP connections to desktop computers such as in a VDI implementation, and even access to RemoteApp applications. Unfortunately, WAP cannot do any of this, even in the new version, but the fact that they have added a little bit of functionality here means movement in the right direction is happening.

What has been improved regarding WAP and Remote Desktop is that you can now use WAP to publish access to the Remote Desktop Gateway server itself. Traditionally, an RD Gateway sits on the edge of the network, and connects external users through to the internal Remote Desktop servers. By placing WAP in front of the RD Gateway, it allows stronger preauthentication for the Remote Desktop services, and creates a bigger separation between the internal and external networks.

All of my fingers are crossed that we will continue to see improvements in this area, and that WAP can be expanded to handle traffic like Remote Desktop natively, without even needing an RD Gateway in the mix.

Improved administrative console

The original version of WAP inside Windows Server 2012 R2 was best served using PowerShell to implement it. You can still certainly use PowerShell in order to create your publishing rules if you so choose, but the Remote Access Management Console has now been improved as it relates to the Web Application Proxy. Before you see it in the console, you need to make sure that the appropriate box was checked during the Remote Access role installation. If you did not select **Web Application Proxy** when you first installed that role, revisit the add/remove Roles function inside Server Manager in order to add WAP to this server:

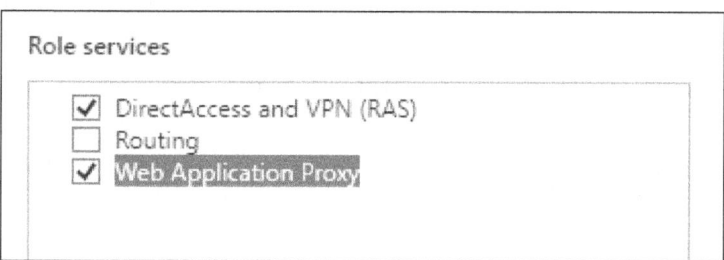

Since we now have a unified management platform for configuring all aspects of our remote access environment, simply visit the same Remote Access Management tool that you use to configure DirectAccess and VPN, and you will see that **Web Application Proxy** is now available under the **Configuration** section near the top-left part of your screen:

Summary

The technology of today demands for most companies to enable their employees to work from wherever they are. More and more organizations are hiring a *work from home* workforce, and need a secure, stable, and efficient way to provide access of corporate data and applications to these mobile workers. The Remote Access role in Windows Server 2016 is designed to do exactly that. With three different ways of providing remote access to corporate resources, IT departments have never had so much remote access technology available at their fingertips, built right into the Windows operating system that they already own. If you are still supporting a third-party or legacy VPN system, you should definitely explore the new capabilities provided here and discover how much they could save for your business.

DirectAccess is particularly impressive and compelling; it's a brand new way of looking at remote access. Automatic connectivity includes always-on machines that are constantly being patched and updated because they are always connected to your management servers. You can improve user productivity and network security at the same time. These two things are usually oxymorons in the IT world, but with DirectAccess they hold hands and sing songs together.

Next we are going to take a look into some of the security functions built into your Windows Server 2016 operating systems, and at some of the ways that your servers can be hardened to provide even better security than what comes out of the box.

7
Hardening and Security

$3.5 *million* dollars. For anyone who read that in the voice of Dr. Evil, my hat goes off to you. For anyone who has no idea what I'm talking about, you may have had a sheltered childhood. Joking aside, that number is significant to IT security. Why? Because $3.5 million dollars is the average cost to a business when they are the victim of a data breach. I recently heard this and other scary statistics at a Microsoft conference in Redmond. Some other statistics that can be used in order to get approval for an increase in your security budget—the average number of days an attacker resides in your network before detection is 243. That is the better part of a year that they camp out before doing anything malicious! What are they typically doing during those 243 days? Siphoning all of your data, bit by bit out the back door. Another number is 76%—as in the percentage of network intrusions that happen as a result of compromised user credentials. Furthermore, it is becoming more and more difficult to identify these attacks in the first place, because attackers are using legitimate IT tools in order to grab what they want. Why use malware when you can use something that is *trusted* and is going to fly under the radar of intrusion detection systems? Makes sense to me.

Data security, network security, credential security—these things are all becoming harder to accomplish, but there are always new tools and technology coming out that can help you fight off the bad guys. Windows Server 2016 is the most secure operating system that Microsoft has produced, let's discuss some of the functionality included that makes that statement true:

- Windows Defender
- Windows Firewall – no laughing matter
- Encryption technologies
- Advanced Threat Analytics
- General security best practices

Windows Defender

Finally! I have to say that I have been waiting for this one for quite some time. Anti-malware platforms have always been such a pain in the neck to deal with, but starting with Windows 8 we finally received a good alternative to the expensive memory-hog third-party applications, at least on the client side. Windows Defender may not be the best thing since sliced bread, but it has one huge benefit over all of the other antivirus platforms—it is built into the Windows operating system. To my great disappointment, this built-in malware protection did not mirror over to the Windows Server side with either 2012 or 2012 R2. Patience has paid off, however, and now in Server 2016 we have Windows Defender installed and running on our server operating systems.

I can't tell you how many times I have tracked memory leaks and random server reboots back to a poorly functioning antivirus software, which is unacceptable in today's server world. Even if Windows Defender might not have all of the bells and whistles that some of the third-party products have, it is anti-malware software, and it is built into the operating system. This means it is going to integrate better than any software-based antivirus that you try to install, and should easily coexist with the operating system, resulting in fewer problems down the road. Updates are also simple as they come down via Windows Update. Like I said, I'm excited about the prospect of automatically having all of my new servers protected against viruses right out of the box.

Installing Windows Defender

You're done! Windows Defender is installed by default in Windows Server 2016. However, the graphical user interface may not be available, depending on what specific SKU of Server 2016 you have installed. If you do not see a configuration console for Windows Defender, you can easily add the Windows Defender feature either from the Add Roles and Features wizard, or by using this PowerShell cmdlet:

```
Install-WindowsFeature -Name Windows-Defender-GUI
```

Exploring the user interface

The interface for Windows Defender is the same as within Windows 10, but if you haven't explored that yet we will take a quick look at it here. Go ahead and launch **Settings** from inside the Start Menu, then click on **Update & Security**. Once inside that section, you will see **Windows Defender** listed on the left. Here you have some quick options for enabling or disabling the active scanning that Defender does, but no advanced options for any further configurations.

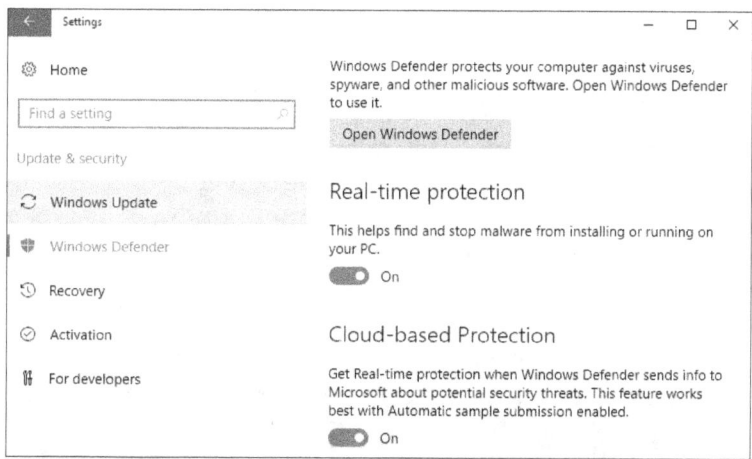

Near the top of this **Settings** screen, you will see a link that allows you to **Open Windows Defender**. Go ahead and click on that now:

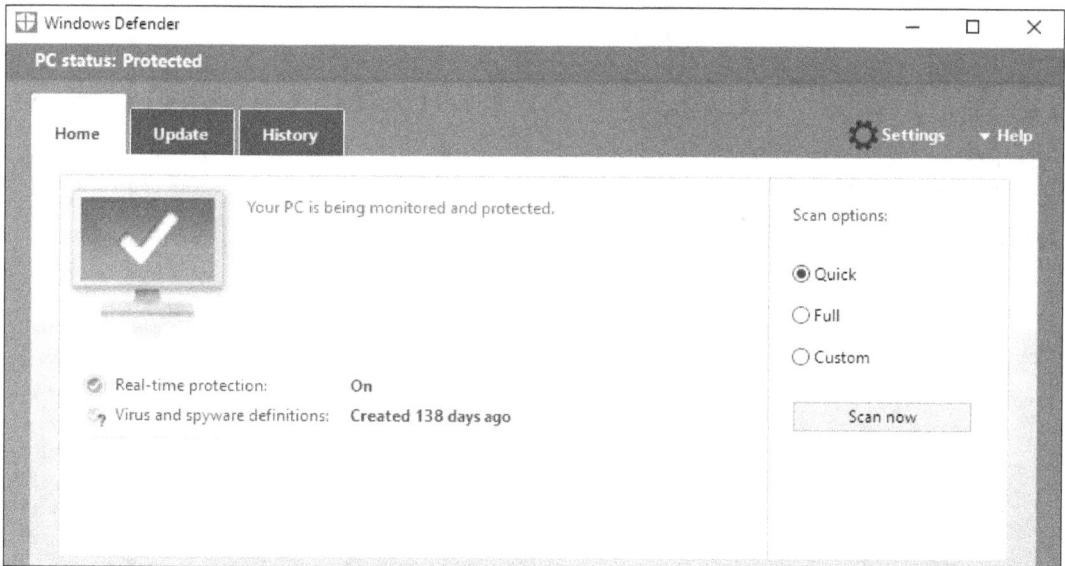

Hardening and Security

Now this looks familiar. As you can see, my definition files are a little out of date, probably because I don't have Windows Updates enabled on this server and that is the mechanism which pulls down Windows Defender updates as well. That is an important note, actually. In order for Defender to get its new definition files, you will want to make sure that Windows Updates are also configured to be running on your server. I know many server administrators that choose not to install Windows Updates on their servers very often in order to minimize reboots and changes, but running your Server 2016 with this mentality will have some adverse side effects, such as your Defender updates never getting installed either.

Disabling Windows Defender

It is important to note that Windows Defender is enabled by default, even though the GUI is only installed by default on some of the Server 2016 SKUs. If you want to disable Defender, you must remove the feature from Windows. This is most easily done via PowerShell, with the following command:

`Uninstall-WindowsFeature -Name Windows-Defender-Features`

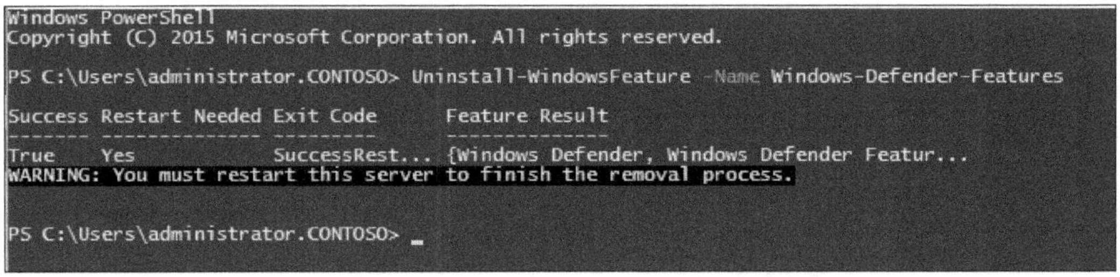

Windows Firewall – no laughing matter

Let's play a word association game. I will say something, and you say the first word that comes to mind.

"Network Security"

Did you say "Firewall"? I think I would have. When we think of securing our devices at the network level, we think of perimeters. Those perimeters are defined and protected by firewalls, mostly at a hardware level with a specialized networking device made to handle that particular task in our networks. Today we are here to talk about another layer of firewalling that you can and should be utilizing in your environments. Yes, we are talking about the Windows Firewall. Stop laughing, it's rude!

It is easy to poke fun at the Windows Firewall based on its history. In the days of Windows XP and Server 2003 it was pretty useless, and caused way more headaches than it solved. In fact, these feelings were so common that I still today find many companies who completely disable the Windows Firewall on all of their domain-joined systems as a matter of default policy. If you ask them, there is usually no specific reason they are doing this, "it's always been this way" or "it's in our written security policy" are standard replies. This is a problem, because the **Windows Firewall with Advanced Security (WFAS)** that exists in Windows operating systems of today is much more robust and advanced than ever before, and can absolutely be used to enhance your security architecture. I would go as far as to say that it is entirely silly to disable WFAS on a current operating system, unless you have a very good, very specific reason to do so.

Two Windows Firewall administrative consoles

First it is important to know that there are two different consoles from which you can configure Windows Firewall settings, and one is much more capable than the other.

Windows Firewall settings

Opening up the **Control Panel** and navigating to **System and Security | Windows Firewall** will get you a basic layout of what is going on with the built-in firewall in Windows Server 2016. You can see whether or not the firewall is turned on, and some current status information. You also have the ability here to disable the firewall, or to do something simple like allow a particular application to have access through the Windows Firewall.

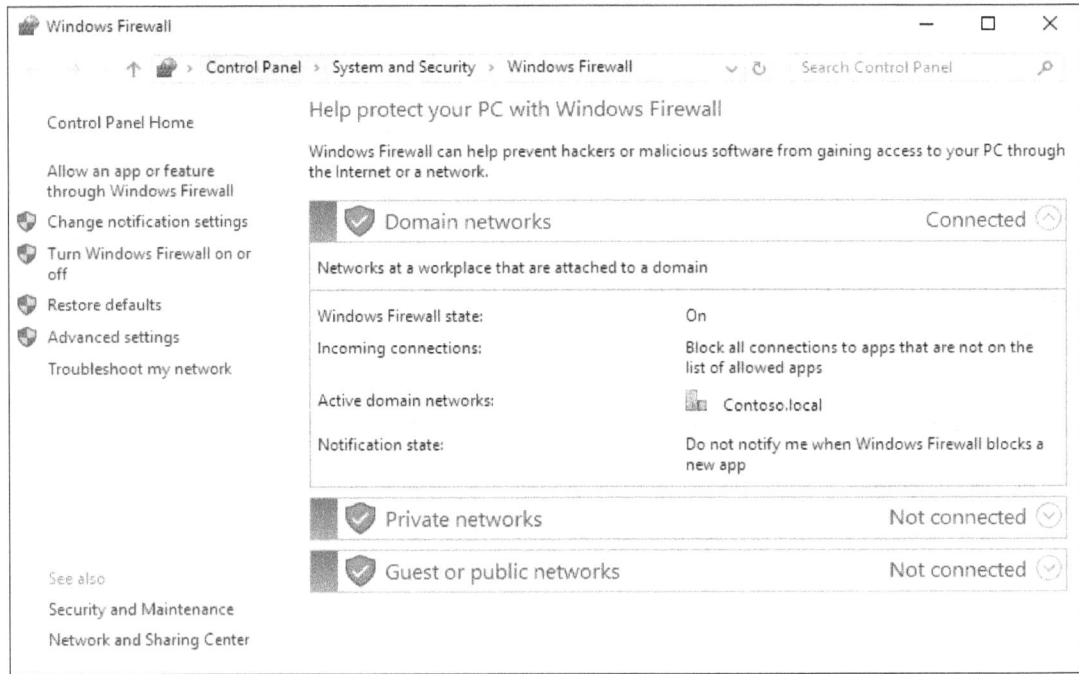

Windows Firewall with Advanced Security

If you are anything like me, you won't be satisfied with this information and will want to see what is going on under the hood with this thing, and so you will want a little more information than the Windows Firewall tool alone can give you. You can either click on the **Advanced settings** link shown in the previous screenshot, or simply open a command prompt or a **Start | Run** prompt and type wf.msc. Either of these functions will launch the full **Windows Firewall with Advanced Security (WFAS)** administration console.

Chapter 7

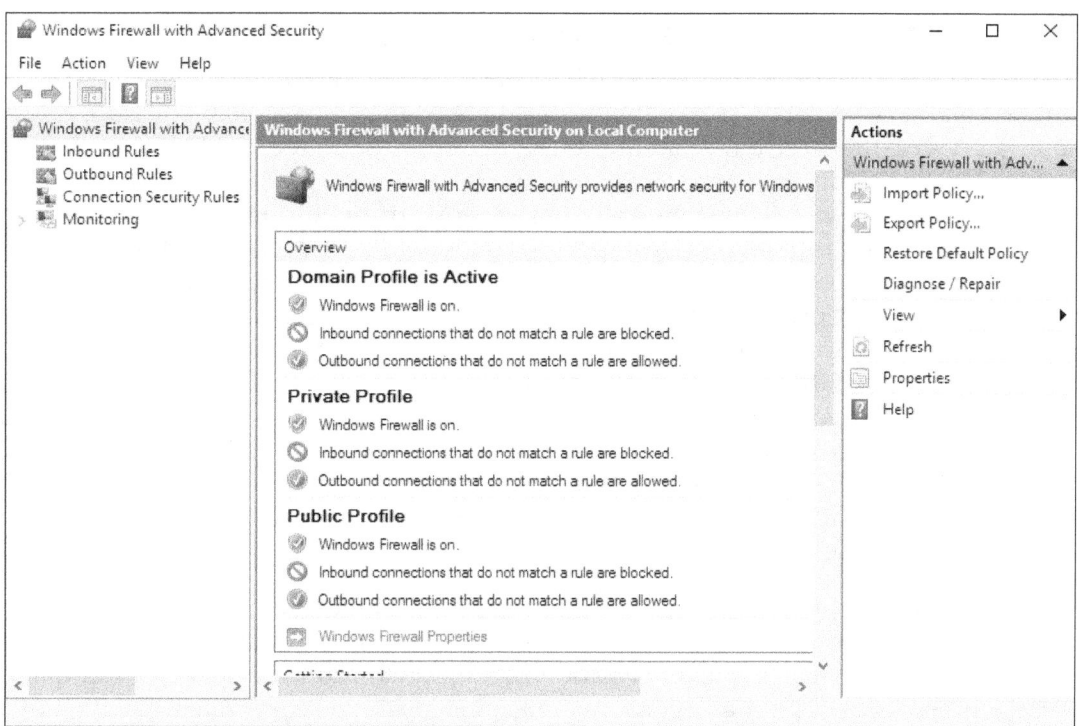

Here you can see much more in-depth information about the activity and rules that are in play with the Windows Firewall, and make more acute adjustments in your allowances and blocks. There is also a **Monitoring** section where you can view actively engaged rules, including **Connection Security Rules**. This is an important section because it highlights the fact that WFAS does much more than block network traffic. It is not only a firewall, it is also a connectivity platform. If you plan to utilize IPsec for encryption of network traffic, whether it be native IPsec inside your network or through the remote access technology DirectAccess, you will see rules populated in this section that are the definitions of those IPsec tunnels. The Windows Firewall is actually responsible for making those encrypted connections and tunnels happen. This is way more advanced than the Windows Firewall of yesteryear.

Three different firewall profiles

When any NIC on a server is connected to a network, the Windows Firewall will assign that connection one of the three different profiles. You have probably interfaced with this decision-making process before without even realizing it. When you connect your laptop to the Wi-Fi at your local coffee shop, did Windows prompt and ask you if you were connecting to a home, work, or public network? This is your Windows Firewall asking you which profile you would like to assign to the new network connection. The reason that you can assign NICs and network connections to different firewall profiles is that you can assign different access rules and criteria for what is or is not allowed over those different profiles. For example, when your laptop is connected to the corporate network you can probably be a little bit more lax than when that same laptop is connected at a hotel down the street. By assigning more intense firewall rules to the profile that is active when you are in the hotel, you build bigger walls for attackers to face when you are out working on that public Internet. Let's take a look at the three different types of profiles that are available, with a quick description of each:

- **Domain Profile**: This is the only one that you cannot choose to assign. The Domain Profile is only active when you are a domain-joined computer that is currently connected to a network where a domain controller for your domain is accessible. So for any corporate machine inside the corporate network, you can expect that the Domain Profile would be active.

- **Private Profile**: When connecting to a new network and you are prompted to choose where you are connected, if you choose either "Home" or "Work", that connection will be assigned the Private Profile.

- **Public Profile**: When prompted, if you choose "Public" then of course you are assigned the Public firewall profile. Also, if you are not prompted for some reason, or if you do not choose an option at all and simply close that window which is asking you what to assign to your new connection, this Public Profile will be the default profile that is given to any connections which do not have a different profile already assigned.

Because each network connection gets assigned its own profile definition, you could certainly have more than one firewall profile active at the same time on the same system. For example, my RA1 server is connected to both the corporate network as well as the public Internet. Inside WFAS, you can see that both the Domain Profile and the Public Profile are active.

Alternatively, if you open up **Network and Sharing Center** on this server, we can also see the profiles listed here, and you can easily tell which NIC is using which profile.

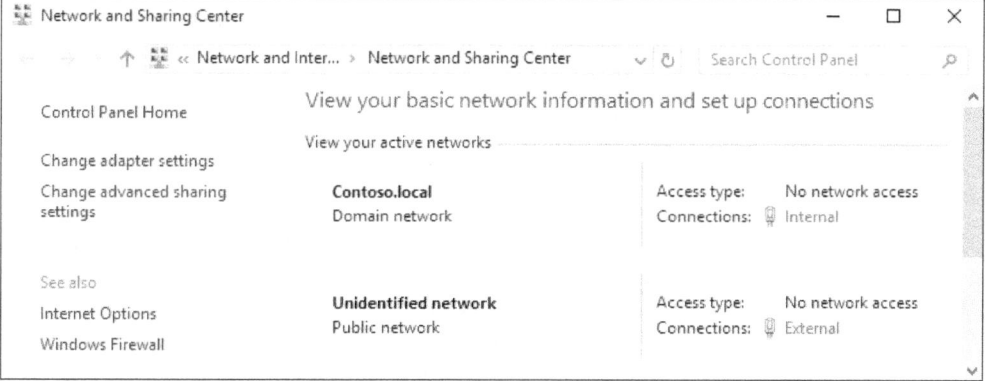

Building a new Inbound Rule

Now we know that the real meat and potatoes of the Windows Firewall is inside the WFAS console, so let's use WFAS to build ourselves a new rule. On this RA1 server, I have enabled RDP access so that I can more easily manage this server from my desk. However, by turning on RDP I have now allowed RDP access from all of the networks on this server. That means I can RDP into RA1 from inside the network, but I can also RDP into RA1 from the Internet. This is a big problem, because now any yahoo on the Internet could potentially find my server, find the RDP login prompt, and try to brute force their way into RA1.

Hardening and Security

To alleviate this problem, I want to squash RDP only on my External NIC. I want it to remain active on the inside so that I can continue to access the server, but is there an easy way inside WFAS to create a firewall rule which blocks RDP access only from the outside? Yes, there certainly is.

Open up `wf.msc` in order to launch the Windows Firewall with Advanced Security, and navigate to the **Inbound Rules** section and you will see all of the existing inbound firewall rules that exist on this server. Right-click on **Inbound Rules**, and choose **New Rule...** This launches a wizard from which we will create our new firewall rule. The first screen is where we identify what kind of a rule we want to create. You can create a rule that modifies traffic for a particular program, or you can look through the list of **Predefined** protocols. However, I like knowing exactly what my rule is doing because of the way that I defined it, not because of a pre-existing protocol definition, and I know that RDP runs over TCP port 3389. So I am going to choose **Port** on this screen, and after I click on **Next**, I will define **3389** as the specific port which I want to modify.

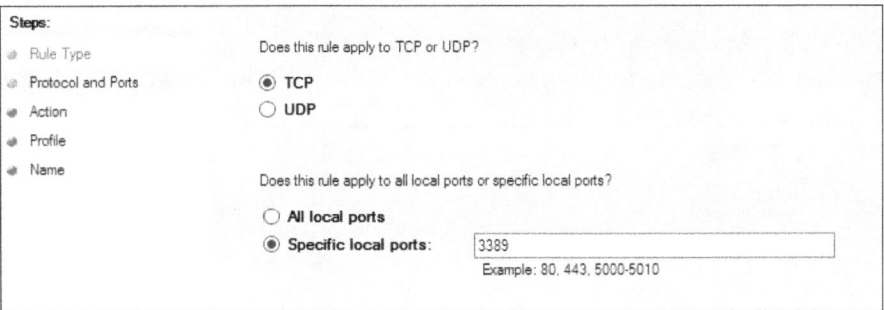

Our third step is to decide whether we want to **Allow** or **Block** this particular port. There is a third option listed about only allowing the connection if it is authenticated by IPsec, which is a powerful option, but necessitates having IPsec established in our network already. Because of that requirement, this option doesn't apply to most people. For our example, we already have RDP working, but we want to block it on one of the NICs, so I am going to choose **Block the connection**.

Chapter 7

> What action should be taken when a connection matches the specified conditions?
>
> ○ **Allow the connection**
> This includes connections that are protected with IPsec as well as those are not.
>
> ○ **Allow the connection if it is secure**
> This includes only connections that have been authenticated by using IPsec. Connections will be secured using the settings in IPsec properties and rules in the Connection Security Rule node.
>
> Customize...
>
> ● **Block the connection**

We don't want to block RDP for all of the NICs though, so this next screen is very important. Here we need to reference back to our knowledge about those firewall profiles we talked about. Remember that internal NICs connected to our domain network will have the Domain profile assigned to them. But any NICs that are not connected to an internal network where a domain controller resides will have either Public or Private profiles active. That is the knowledge we need to employ on this screen. If we want to disable RDP only on the External NIC, we need this rule to be active for only the **Private** and **Public** profiles. In fact, in looking back at the screenshots we already took, we can see that the External NIC is assigned the Public profile specifically, and so we could check only the **Public** box here and RDP would then be blocked on the External NIC. But in case we add more NICs to this server in the future over which we want to make sure RDP access is not possible, we will leave both **Public** and **Private** checked, to ensure better security for the future. Make sure that you **uncheck Domain**! Otherwise you will block RDP access to the entire server, and if you are currently using RDP in order to connect to this server, you will kick yourself out of it and be unable to reconnect.

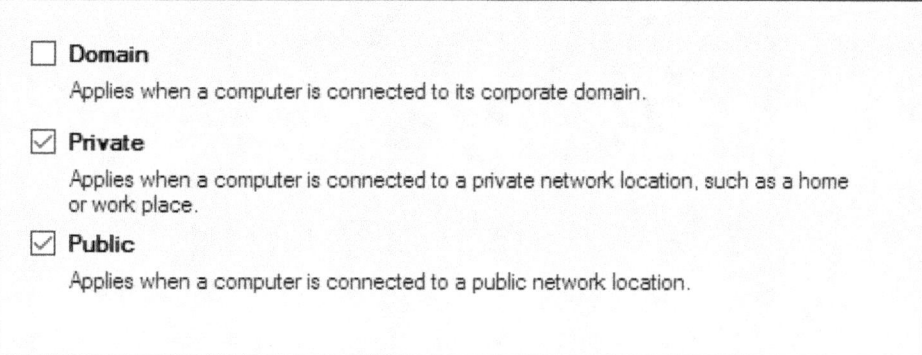

And now we simply create a name for our new rule, and we are done! Our ability to RDP into this server from the Internet has immediately been disabled, and we can rest much easier tonight.

How to build a rule for ICMP?

Very often I find myself needing to create either an allow or a block rule for ICMP. In other words, I often find myself needing to adjust the firewall on servers in order to enable or disable their ability to reply to ping requests. You must have noticed with newer server operating systems that it is pretty normal for the firewall to automatically block pings (ICMP) out of the box. When we need to create a new rule that allows pings to happen, we set up a rule just like we did for RDP, but there is one big catch. On that very first **Rule Type** screen when creating the new rule where you have to identify what kind of rule you are creating, there are no options or predefinitions for ICMP. I find this strange because this is a very common type of rule to put into place, but alas—choosing ICMP from the drop-down list would just be too easy. Instead, what you need to do is create an incoming rule that is configured for something else, and then modify that rule. Let's walk through that together.

Go ahead and create a rule similar to the way we did a minute ago for RDP. Create the new rule and tell it to use TCP port 3389, but this time define it as an **Allow** rule and to be active on all of the firewall profiles. Or if you intend to only allow ICMP on certain profiles, then certainly go ahead and choose whichever ones are appropriate for your situation. Then on the last screen where you type a name for this new rule, make sure to make it something about pings or ICMP so that you can easily identify it in the list of rules later. Once your new rule is created, what it is currently doing is allowing TCP 3389 for RDP access, even though this is redundant because we are already allowing RDP. Now find your new rule in the **Inbound Rules** list, right-click on it, and head into **Properties**.

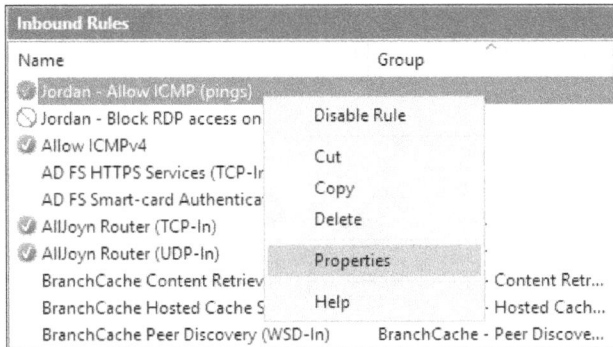

Now navigate into the **Protocols and Ports** tab, and expand the drop-down menu for **Protocol type**. Now you can see an option for ICMP as the protocol. Go ahead and choose appropriately for your network ICMPv4 or ICMPv6. Since my internal network is all IPv4 based, I am going to choose **ICMPv4**.

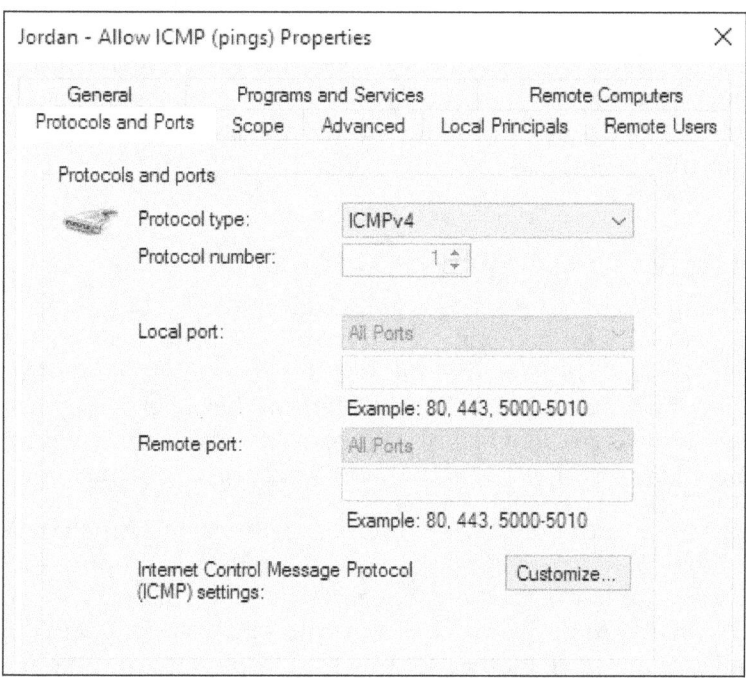

After clicking on **OK**, the new rule that was originally created for RDP access has now been changed to be an Allow rule for ICMPv4, and this server will now respond to ping requests successfully.

```
C:\Users\Administrator>ping ra1

Pinging ra1.Contoso.local [10.0.0.10] with 32 bytes of data:
Reply from 10.0.0.10: bytes=32 time=1ms TTL=128
Reply from 10.0.0.10: bytes=32 time=1ms TTL=128
Reply from 10.0.0.10: bytes=32 time=5ms TTL=128
Reply from 10.0.0.10: bytes=32 time=3ms TTL=128
```

While this feels like sort of a goofy way to create a simple rule, it's the most efficient way I have found so far. Sometimes you need to dig into the more extensive properties of a rule in order to make it do what you want. While you are in those properties, feel free to poke around a little and see what other options you have available to you. For example, we discussed how you can determine what firewall profiles a particular rule applies to, but what if you wanted to make the rule even more specific? If you look at the **Scope** tab inside the **Properties** of a certain rule, you can see that you could even identify particular IP addresses or subnets and make it so that your rule only applies to traffic that comes from or goes to specific networking information such as this.

Managing WFAS with Group Policy

Managing firewall rules on your servers, and clients, can be a huge step toward a more secure environment for your company. The best part? This technology is enterprise class, and free to use since it's already built into the operating systems that you use. The only cost you have associated with firewalling at this level is the time it takes to put all of these rules into place, which would be an administrative nightmare if you had to implement your entire list of allows and blocks on every machine individually.

Thank goodness for Group Policy. As with most settings and functions inside the Microsoft Windows platform, setting up a firewall policy that applies to everyone is a breeze for your domain-joined machines. Or maybe you break it up a little bit, and have a GPO that applies firewall rules to your clients, and a separate GPO that applies firewall rules to your servers. Or however you see fit, but the point is—you can group many machines together in categories, create a ruleset for that category just once, and automatically apply it to every other machine by making use of Group Policy's powerful distribution capabilities.

Chapter 7

You are already familiar with creating GPOs, so go ahead and make one now that will contain some firewall settings for us to play with. Link and filter that GPO accordingly so that only the machines you want to have these settings will actually get them. Perhaps a good place to start is a group of test machines, so that you can make sure all the rules you are about to place inside the GPO work well together and with all of your other existing policies.

Once your new GPO is created, right-click on it from inside the Group Policy Management Console, and click on **Edit...**.

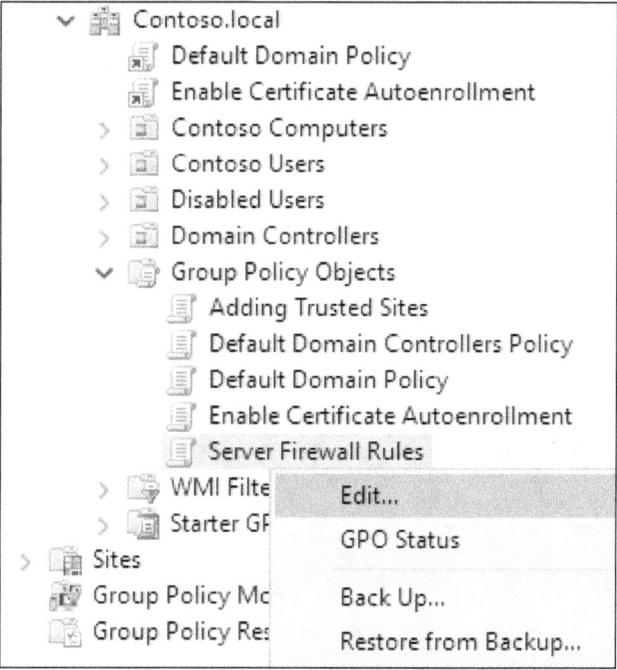

Hardening and Security

Now that we are looking at the insides of this new GPO, we just need to figure out where the correct location is in order for us to create some new firewall rules. As when you are looking inside the rules on the local machine itself, everything is listed under a **Windows Firewall with Advanced Security** heading, and that is located at **Computer Configuration | Policies | Windows Settings | Security Settings | Windows Firewall with Advanced Security | Windows Firewall with Advanced Security**.

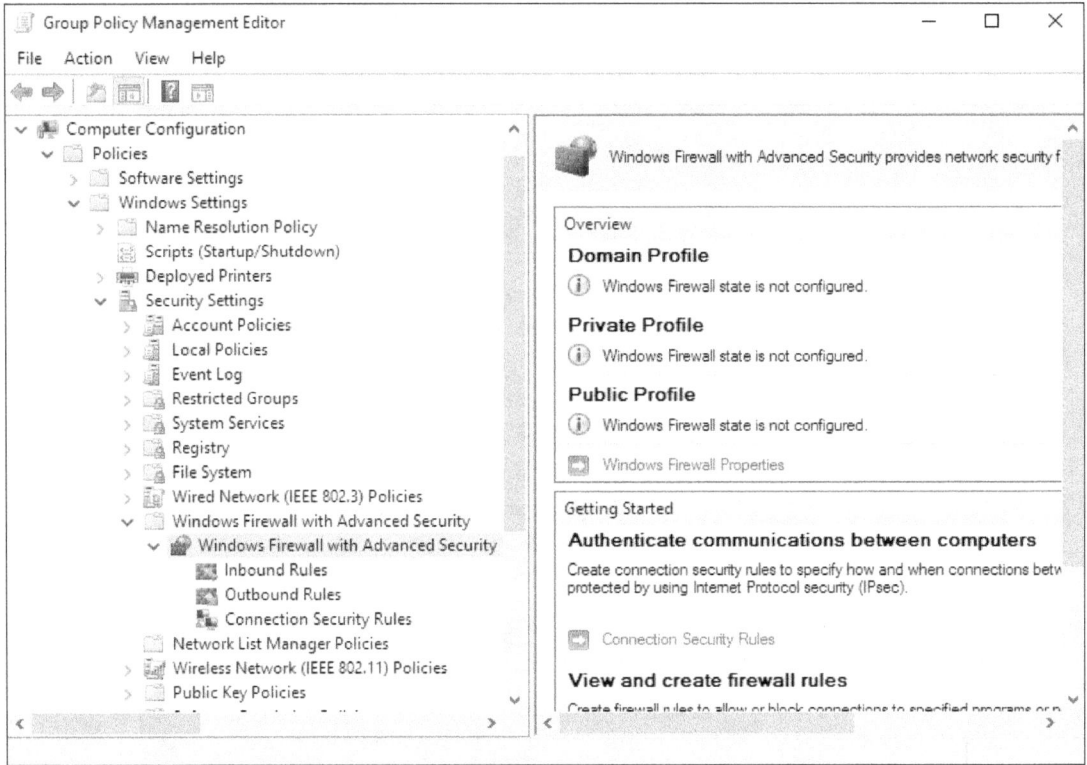

As you can see, this is also the place to go when you want to make sure that particular firewall profiles, or the Windows Firewall as a whole, are specifically turned on or off. So this is the same place that you would go if you wanted to disable the Windows Firewall for everyone. By clicking on the **Windows Firewall Properties** link shown earlier, you can determine the status of each firewall profile individually.

Chapter 7

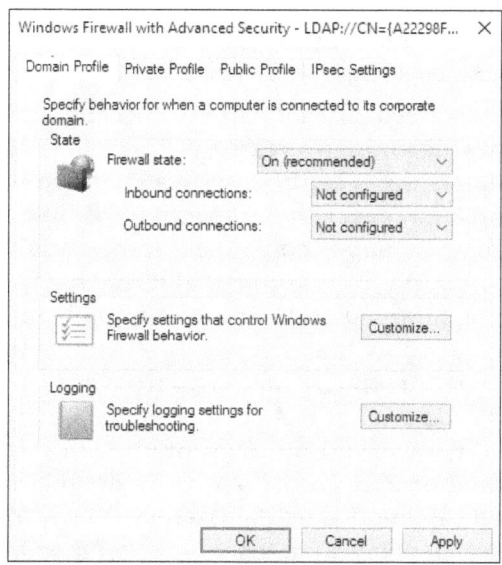

Once you are finished setting your profiles according to your needs, click on **OK** and you find yourself back at the WFAS part of the GPO. Just like inside the local WFAS console, you have categories for **Inbound Rules** and **Outbound Rules**. Simply right-click on **Inbound Rules**, and click on **New Rule...** in order to get started with building a rule right into this GPO. Walk through the same wizard that you are already familiar with from creating a rule in the local WFAS console, and when you are finished your new inbound firewall rule is shown inside the GPO. This firewall rule is already making its way around Active Directory, and installing itself onto those computers and servers which you defined in the policy's links and filtering criteria.

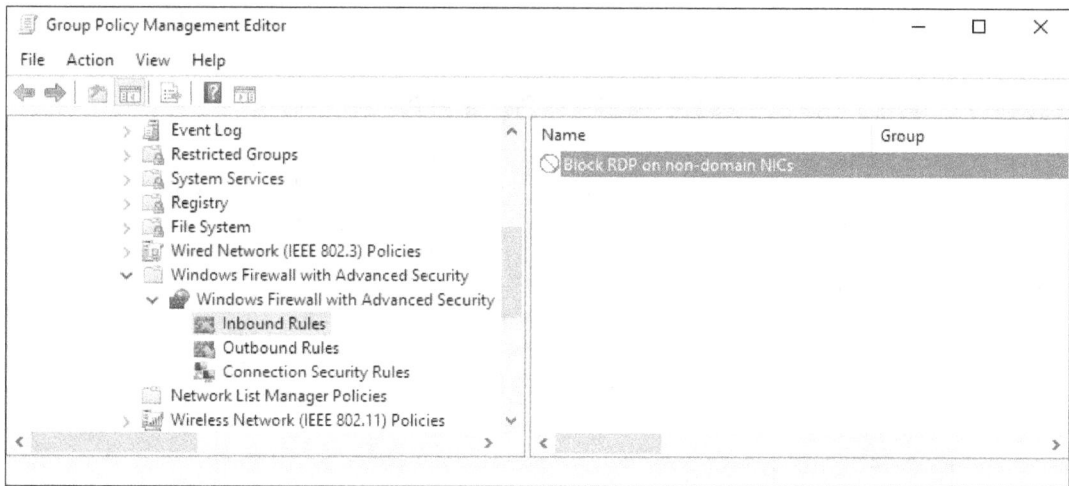

[221]

Encryption technologies

An idea that has taken a fast step from "something the big organizations are playing around with" to "everybody needs it" is the use of encryption. Most of us have been encrypting our website traffic for many years by using HTTPS websites, but even in that realm there are surprising exceptions with a lot of the cheap web hosting companies still providing login pages that transmit traffic in clear text. This is terrible, because with anything that you submit over the Internet now using regular HTTP or an unencrypted e-mail you HAVE to assume that it is being read by someone else. Chances are you are being paranoid and nobody is actually intercepting and reading your traffic, but you need to know that if you are accessing a website that says HTTP in the address bar, or if you are sending an e-mail from any of the free e-mail services, any data that is being entered on that webpage or in that e-mail can easily be stolen by someone halfway around the world. Data encryption is an absolute requirement these days for corporate information that needs to traverse the Internet, though at the same time I say that the back of my mind is telling me that the vast majority of companies are still not using any kind of encryption technology on their e-mail system and so that is still a potential disaster waiting to happen for most.

While we are getting better and better at protecting Internet browser traffic, we are traditionally still not paying a lot of attention to data that is "safe" within the walls of our organization. The bad guys aren't dumb, though, and they have a very large toolbox of tricks to socially engineer their way into our networks. Once inside, what do they find? In most cases, it's a big free-for-all. Get ahold of one user account or one computer and you've got keys to a large part of the kingdom. Fortunately, there are several technologies built into Windows Server 2016 that are designed to combat these intrusions and protect your data even while it sits within the four walls of your datacenter. Let's look at some information on them so that you can explore the possibility of using these encryption technologies to further protect your data.

BitLocker and the Virtual TPM

BitLocker is a technology that has become pretty familiar to see on our client systems within corporate networks. It is a full drive encryption technology, giving us the advantage of making sure our data is fully protected on laptops or computers that might be stolen. If a thief gets his hands on a company laptop, claws out the hard drive and plugs it into their computer—sorry Charlie, no access. The entire volume is encrypted. This makes all kinds of sense for mobile hardware that could be easily lost or stolen, but in the beginning stages of this technology the server side of the equation was never really a consideration.

With our new cloud mentality coming into play, suddenly it makes much more sense to want BitLocker on our servers. More particularly when talking about the cloud, what we really want is BitLocker on our virtual machines. Whether you are storing your VMs in a true cloud environment provided by a public cloud service provider or are hosting your own private cloud where tenants reach in to create and manage their own VMs, without the possibility of encrypting those virtual hard drives—the VHD and VHDX files—your data is absolutely **not** secure. Why not? Because anyone with administrative rights to the virtualization host platform can easily gain access to any data sitting on your server's hard drives, even without any kind of access or user account on your network. All they have to do is mount your virtual hard disk on their system, and bingo—they have access. This is a big problem for data security compliance.

Why has it historically not been feasible to encrypt VMs? Because BitLocker comes with an interesting requirement. The hard drive is encrypted, which means that it can't boot without the encryption being unlocked. How do we unlock the hard drive so that our machine can boot? One of two ways. The best method is to store the "unlock keys" inside a Trusted Platform Module (TPM). This is a physical microchip that is built right into a computer. Storing the BitLocker unlock key on this chip means that you do not have to connect anything physically to your computer in order to make it boot, you simply enter a pin to gain access to the TPM. On the other hand, if you choose to deploy BitLocker without the presence of a TPM, to unlock a BitLocker volume and make it bootable you need to plug in a physical USB stick that contains the BitLocker unlock keys. Do you see the problem with either of these installation paths in a virtual machine scenario? VMs do not have a TPM, and you also have no way of plugging in a USB stick! So how do we encrypt those VMs so that prying eyes at the cloud hosting company can't see all my stuff?

Enter the **Virtual TPM**. Brand new in Windows Server 2016, we now have the capability of giving our virtual servers a virtual TPM that can be used for storing these keys! This is incredible news, and means that we can finally encrypt our servers, whether they are hosted on physical Hyper-V servers in our datacenter, or sitting in the Azure cloud.

Shielded VMs

BitLocker and the Virtual TPM are the secret sauce that enable this next piece of technology that is also new in Server 2016, **Shielded VMs**. I am going to leave all the details about Shielded VMs for a later chapter that is focused on all things Hyper-V, but let's just say that you are going to want all of your virtual machines to be shielded from this point forward.

Encrypting File System

The **Encrypting File System (EFS)** is a component of Microsoft Windows that has existed on both client and server operating systems for many years. Where BitLocker is responsible for securing an entire volume or disk, EFS is a little more particular. When you want to encrypt only particular documents or folders, this is the place you would turn. When you choose to encrypt files using EFS, it is important to understand that it needs to use a user certificate as part of the encrypt/decrypt process, and so the availability of an internal PKI is pretty key to a successful deployment. Also important to note is that authentication keys are tied to the user's password, so a fully compromised user account could negate the benefits provided by EFS.

I think that many companies don't employ EFS because you are leaving the decision on what documents to encrypt up to the user. This also means that you are depending on them to remember to do the encryption in the first place, which means they will have to understand the importance of it in order to make it worthy of their time. I wanted to mention EFS because it is still alive and is still a valid platform for which you can encrypt data, but most administrators are landing on BitLocker as a better solution. Lack of responsibility on the user's part and a good centralized management platform do put BitLocker a solid step ahead of EFS. Both the technologies could certainly co-exist, though, keeping data safe at two different tiers instead of relying on only one of the data encryption technologies available to you.

IPsec

A lot of the encryption technology built into operating systems revolves around data at rest. But what about our data on the move? We talked about using SSL on HTTPS websites as a way of encrypting web browser data that is on the move across the Internet, but what about data that is not flowing through a web browser? And what if I'm not even concerned about the Internet, what if I am interested in protecting traffic that could even be flowing from point to point inside my corporate network? Is there anything that can help with these kinds of requirements? Certainly.

IPsec is a protocol suite that can be used for authenticating and encrypting the packets that happen during a network communication. IPsec is not a technology that is particular to the Microsoft world, but there are various ways in Windows Server 2016 that IPsec can be utilized in order to secure data that you are shuttling back and forth between machines.

The most common place that IPsec interaction shows up on a Windows Server is when using the Remote Access role. When configuring VPN on your RA server, you will have a number of different connection protocols that the VPN clients can use to connect to the VPN server. Included in this list of possible connection platforms is IPsec (IKEv2) tunnels. The second remote access technology that uses IPsec is DirectAccess. When you establish DA in your network, every time that a client computer creates a DirectAccess tunnel over the Internet to the DirectAccess server, that tunnel is protected by IPsec. Thankfully the Remote Access Management Console that you use to deploy both VPN and DirectAccess is smart enough to know everything that is needed to make IPsec authentication and encryption work, and you don't need to know a single thing about IPsec in order to make these remote access technologies work for you!

The big missing factor with IPsec provided by the Remote Access role is traffic inside your network. When you are talking about VPN or DirectAccess you are talking about traffic that moves over the Internet. But what if you simply want to encrypt traffic that moves between two different servers inside the same network? Or the traffic that is flowing from your client computers inside the office to their local servers, also located in the office? This is where some knowledge of the IPsec policy settings comes in handy, because we can specify that we want traffic moving around inside our corporate networks to be encrypted using IPsec. It's just a matter of putting the right policies into place.

Configuring IPsec

There are two different places that IPsec settings can be configured in a Microsoft Windows environment. Both old and new systems can be supplied with IPsec configurations through the traditional **IPsec Security Policy snap-in**. If you are running all systems that are newer, like Windows 7 and Server 2008 and above, then you can alternatively employ the **Windows Firewall with Advanced Security** for setting up your IPsec policies. WFAS is the most flexible solution, but isn't always an option depending on the status of legacy systems in your environment.

First let's take a glance at the older IPsec policy console. We will start here because the different options available will help to build a baseline for us to start wrapping our minds around the way that IPsec interaction works between two endpoints. There are three different classifications of IPsec policy that can be assigned to your machines that we will encounter in this console. Let's take a minute to explain each one, because the policy names can be a little bit misleading. Understanding these options will put you a step ahead for understanding how the settings inside WFAS work as well.

Server policy

The Server policy should probably be renamed to Requestor policy, because that is really what this one does. When a computer or server makes a network request outbound to another computer or server, it is requesting to establish a network connection. On these requesting computers—the ones initiating the traffic—this is where we tell the Server policy to apply. Once applied, the Server policy tells that computer or server to request IPsec encryption for the communication session between the initiating machine and the remote computer. If that remote system supports IPsec, then the IPsec tunnel is created in order to protect the traffic flowing between the two machines. The Server policy is pretty lenient though, and if the remote computer does not support IPsec, then the network connection is still successful, but remains unencrypted.

Secure Server policy

The difference here is that the Secure Server policy **requires** IPsec encryption in order to allow that network communication to happen whatsoever. The regular Server policy that we talked about earlier will encrypt with IPsec when possible, but if not possible it will continue to flow that traffic unencrypted. The Secure Server policy, on the other hand, will fail to establish the connection at all if IPsec cannot be supplied between the two machines.

Client policy

The Client policy needs to be renamed to Response policy, because this one is on the other end of the connection. The Client policy does not care about requesting an IPsec session, it only cares about **receiving** one. When a computer makes a network request to a server, and that computer has the Server or Secure Server policy so it is requesting IPsec, then the server would need to have the Client policy assigned to it in order to accept and build that IPsec tunnel. The Client policy responds by allowing the encryption to happen on that session.

IPsec Security Policy snap-in

The original console for manipulating IPsec settings is accessed via MMC. Open that up, and add the **IP Security Policy Management** snap-in. Interestingly, when adding this snap-in you will notice that you can view either the local IPsec policy of the machine which you are currently logged in, or you can open the IPsec policy for the domain itself. If you are interested in configuring a domain-wide IPsec implementation, this would be your landing zone for working on those settings. But for the purposes of just sticking our head in here to poke around a little, you can choose the **Local computer** in order to take a look at the console.

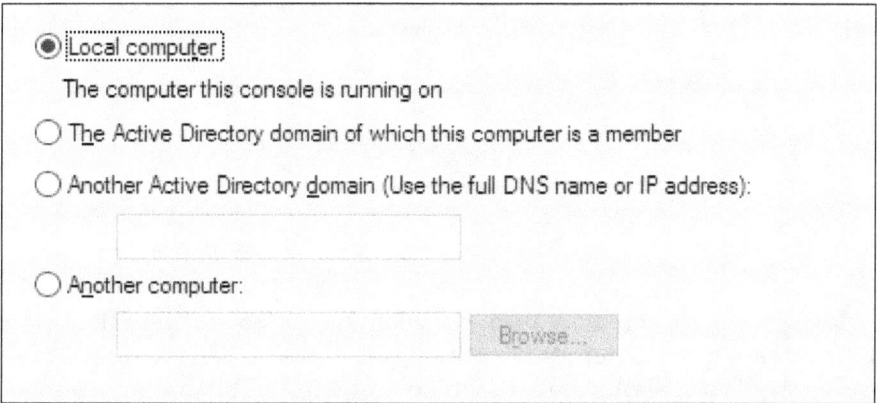

Once inside, you can see any existing IPsec policies that might be in place, or you can start creating your own by using the **Create IP Security Policy...** action available when right-clicking on **IP Security Policies**. Doing this would invoke a wizard which will walk through the configuration of your particular IPsec policy.

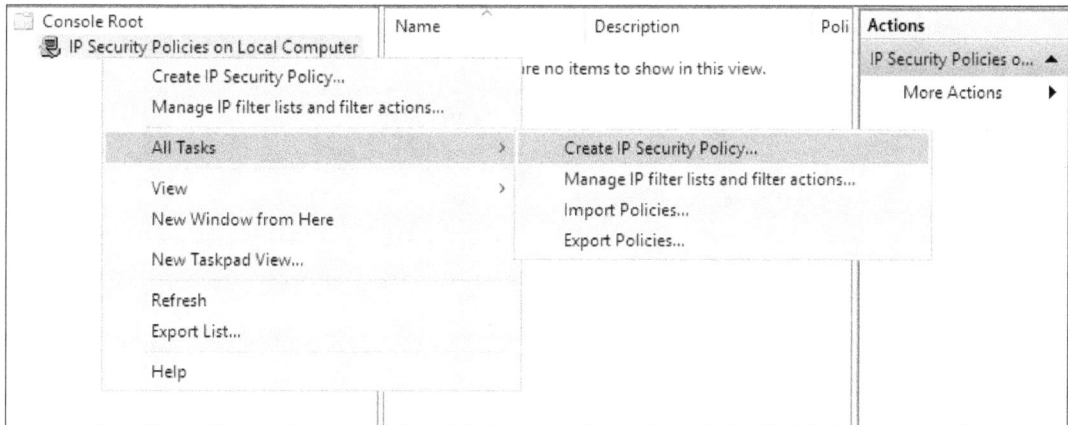

Using WFAS instead

The newer platform used for establishing IPsec connection rules is the **Windows Firewall with Advanced Security**. Go ahead and open that up, as you are already familiar with doing. Once inside, navigate to the **Connection Security Rules** section, which is listed immediately below **Inbound Rules** and **Outbound Rules**. **Connection Security** Rules is where you define IPsec connection rules. If you right-click on **Connection Security Rules** and choose **New Rule...** you will then walk-through a wizard which is similar to creating a firewall rule.

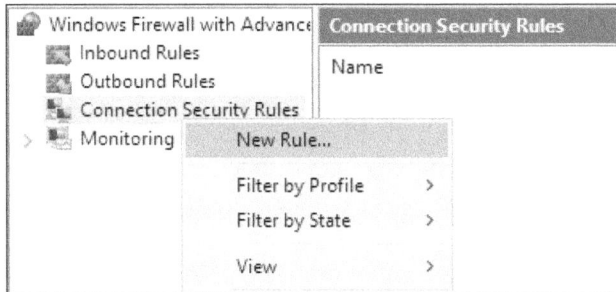

Once inside the wizard to create your new rule, you start to see that the options available to you are quite different from the ones shown when creating a new firewall rule. This is the platform from which you will establish IPsec connection security rules that define what the IPsec tunnels look like, and on what machines or IP addresses they need to be active.

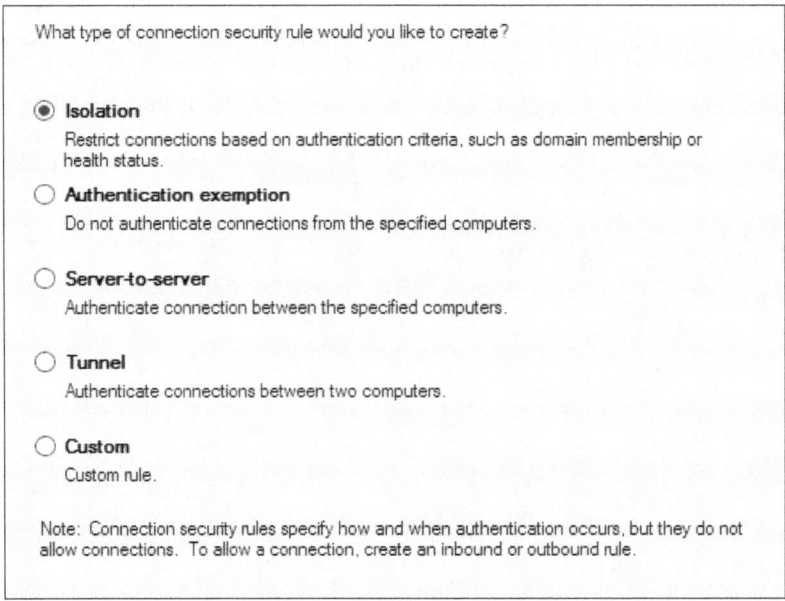

We do not have space here to cover all of the available options in this wizard, but I definitely recommend picking up from here and taking it a step further with some added knowledge on TechNet, as given in the link `https://technet.microsoft.com/en-us/library/hh831807.aspx`.

Advanced Threat Analytics

In my opinion, one of the coolest security features to come out of Microsoft this past year is **Advanced Threat Analytics (ATA)**. It's not a feature or function built into the Windows Server operating system, not yet anyway, but is a software that rides on top of Windows to produce some amazing functionality. Essentially what ATA does is monitor all of your Active Directory traffic, and warns you of danger or unusual behavior in real time, immediately as it is happening.

The idea of ATA is pretty simple to understand and makes so much common sense that it's something we are all going to wonder why it took so long to put into place. The reason for that, though, is because under the hood the processing and learning that ATA is doing is very advanced. Yes, I said learning. This is the coolest part of ATA. What you do is set up port mirroring on your switches so that all of the packets moving in or out of your Domain Controllers get mirrored over to the first piece of the ATA puzzle, the collection servers. These are called ATA Gateways. The ATA Gateways then send this traffic onward to a centralized ATA Center. The Center receives this data and starts to find patterns. If Betty uses a desktop computer called BETTY-PC and a tablet called BETTY-TABLET, Advanced Threat Analytics will see that pattern and associate her user account with those devices. It also watches for her normal traffic patterns. Betty usually logs in around 8 a.m. and her traffic usually stops somewhere around 5 p.m.. She typically accesses a few file servers and a SharePoint server. After a week or so of collecting and monitoring data, ATA has a pretty good idea of Betty's standard MO.

Now one night something happens. ATA sees a bunch of password failures against Betty's account. That in itself might not be something to get too excited about, but then all of a sudden Betty logs into a terminal server that she doesn't typically access. From there her credentials are used to access a Domain Controller. Uh oh, this clearly sounds like an attack to me. With the tools built into Active Directory that we currently have at our disposal, what do we know? Nothing, really. We might see the password failures if we dig into the event logs, and based on that we could try poking around other servers' event logs in order to find out what that account was accessing, but we really wouldn't have any reason to suspect anything. This could be the beginning of a very large breach, and we would never see it. Thankfully, ATA knows better.

The management interface for ATA is like a social media feed, updated almost in real time. During the events I laid out above, if we had been looking at the ATA media feed, we would have seen all of these items that I pointed out happen, as they happened, and it would be immediately obvious that someone compromised Betty's account and used it to gain access to a Domain Controller. There has never been a technology that watches Active Directory traffic so intensely, and there has certainly never been anything that learns patterns and behavioral diversions like this. It is truly an amazing technology, and I don't say that only because I happen to know the guys who built it. But since I do, I can tell you that they are brilliant, which is already pretty obvious since Microsoft scooped them up.

At this point ATA is still new enough that most of the IT community hasn't had any interaction with it, and I strongly encourage you to change that. It may save your bacon one day. The following is a screenshot of the ATA web interface so you can get a visual on that social media-style feed. This screenshot was taken from a Microsoft demo where they purposefully stole the Kerberos ticket from a user, and then utilized it on another computer in order to access some confidential files that only Demi Albuz should have been able to access. While ATA did not stop this activity, it immediately — and I mean within seconds — alerted inside this feed to show the Pass-the-Ticket attack!

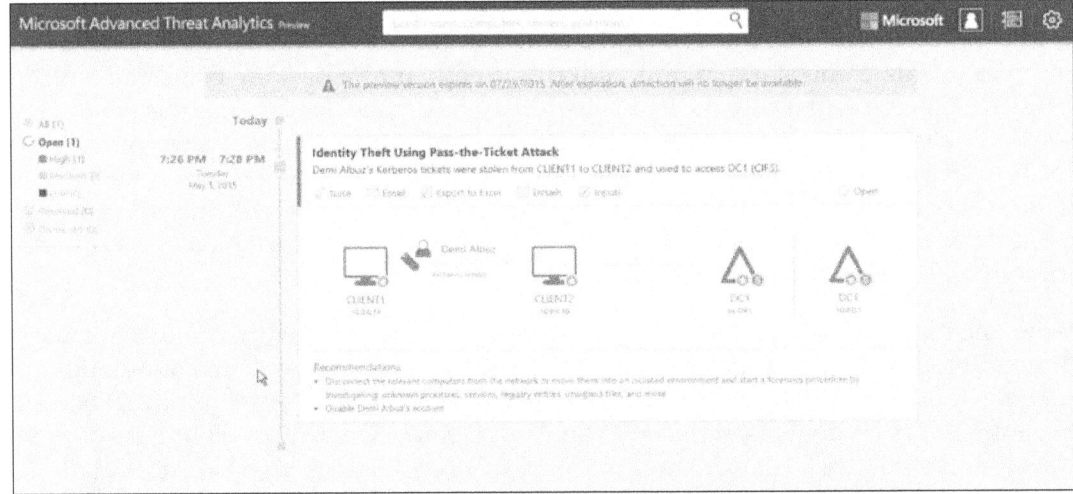

Lightweight Gateway

If port mirroring data to the ATA Gateway sounds too complicated or too involved for you, make sure to check out the new ATA Lightweight Gateway. This is an ATA Gateway component that installs directly onto your domain controllers, so you don't have to make changes to your networking equipment. While this is a much easier approach to getting the data from your DCs into ATA, it does come with some drawbacks that I wanted to take a minute and point out.

If your environment flows more than 10,000 packets per second from the domain controllers, then you should run a real ATA Gateway, with the port mirroring setup. Typical domain controllers will be well under this number, but in large environments it will be a consideration. There is a sizing tool available on the ATA website which runs in your environment and captures these numbers on your DCs. You can download that here: https://aka.ms/atasizingtool.

If your intended purpose in having ATA is to be SUPER secure, then you should really go with the port mirrored gateway setup. One of the huge advantages of running ATA is that it is completely invisible to an attacker who might be inside your network, because of the port mirroring configuration. On the other hand, if you install the Lightweight Gateway onto your domain controller servers, that installer will be obvious to the attacker and they could try to shut it down.

General security best practices

Sometimes we need only to rely on ourselves, and not necessarily functionality provided by the operating system, to secure our systems. There are many common sense approaches to administratorship, if that is a word, that are easy to accomplish but are rarely being used in the field. The following are a few tips and tricks that I have learned over the years and have helped companies implement. Hopefully, you as the reader, will have even more to add to this list as to what works well for you, but if nothing else this section is intended to jog your thinking into finding creative ways which you can limit administrative capability and vulnerability within your network.

Get rid of perpetual administrators

Do all of your IT staff have domain admin rights the day they are hired? Do any of your IT staff have access to the built-in domain administrator account password? Do you have regular users whose logins have administrative privileges on their own computers? You know where I'm going with this—these are all terrible ideas!

Unfortunately, the above was the status quo for many years in almost every network, and the trend continues today. I still regularly watch engineers use the "administrator" domain account for many tasks when we set up new servers. This means they not only have access to potentially the most important account in your network and are using it for daily tasks, but it also means that anything being set up with this user account is not actually accountable. What do I mean by that? When I set up a new server or make changes to an existing server-using administrator, and I end up causing some kind of big problem, nobody can prove that I did it. Using agnostic user accounts is a sure way to thwart responsibility in the event that something goes wrong. I'm not trying to imply that you are always on the lookout for "who did that?", but if I mess something up on an application server which I don't normally administer, it would be nice if the guys trying to fix it could easily figure out that it was me and come ask me what I did so that they can reverse it. There are many reasons that using the built-in administrator account should be off-limits for all of us.

To address the client side, do your users really need administrative rights on their computers? Really? I think you could probably find ways around it. Bringing regular users down to User or even Power User rights on their systems can make a huge impact on the security of those computers. It gives viruses a much harder time installing themselves if the user needs to walk through a prompt asking for admin privs before they can proceed with the install. It also keeps all of your machines in a much more consistent behavioral pattern, without new and unknown applications and settings being introduced by the user.

Use distinct accounts for administrative access

This idea piggy-backs off the last one, and is something that I have started employing even on all of the home computers that I install for friends and family members. It really boils down to this—have two different user accounts. One with administrative access, and one without. When you are logged in for daily tasks and chores, make sure that you are logged in with your regular user account that does not have administrative privileges, either on the local computer or on the domain. That way if you attempt to install anything, or if something attempts to install itself, you will be prompted by the User Access Control (UAC) box, asking you to enter an administrative username and password before the installer is allowed to do anything. I can tell you that this works, as I have stopped a number of viruses on my own computer from installing themselves as I'm browsing around the Internet trying to do research for one project or another. If I get a UAC prompt asking me for an admin password and I haven't clicked on an installer file, I know it's something I don't want.

All I have to do is click on No, and that installer will not get ahold of my computer. On the other hand, if it is something that I am intending to install, then it is a minor inconvenience to simply enter the password of my administrative account, and allow the installer to continue.

Use a different computer to accomplish administrative tasks

If you want to progress even further on the idea of separate user accounts, you could make your computing experience even more secure by utilizing a separate computer altogether when accomplishing administrative-level tasks. One computer for regular knowledge worker tasks, and another computer for administration. This would certainly help to keep your administrative system secure, including the remote systems that it has access to. And while it does seem cumbersome to have two physical computers at your desk, remember that with most SKUs in Windows 10 we have the ability to run Hyper-V right on our desktop computers. I actually do exactly this with my own computer. I have my computer that is running Windows 10, and then inside that computer I am running a virtual machine via Hyper-V from which I do all administrative tasks on the sensitive servers. This way a compromise of the normal computer doesn't necessitate a compromise of the entire environment.

Whether you choose to split up administrative access at the user account level or the computer level, remember this simple rule—**never administer Active Directory from the same place that you browse Facebook**. I think that pretty well sums this one up.

Never browse the Internet from servers

Seems like a no-brainer, but everyone does it. We spend all day working on servers, and very often have to reach out and check something from a web browser. Since Internet Explorer exists on Windows Servers, sometimes it is just quicker and easier to check whatever it is that we need to check from the server console where we are working, rather than walk back over to our desks. Resist the temptation! It is so easy to pick up bad things from the Internet, especially on servers because if any machines in our network are running without antivirus protection, it is probably on the server side. The same is true for Internet filters. We always make sure that the client traffic is flowing through our corporate proxy (if we have one), but we don't always care whether or not the server traffic is moving outward the same way.

Don't even do it for websites that you trust. A man-in-the-middle attack or a compromise of the website itself can easily corrupt your server. It's much easier to rebuild a client computer than it is a server.

Role-Based Access Controls

The phrase **Role-Based Access Control (RBAC)** is not one that is limited to Microsoft environments. It also is not a particular technology that can be utilized inside Windows Server 2016, but rather it is an ideology that is all about separating job roles and duties. When we think about separating our employees' job roles from an IT perspective, we traditionally think in terms of Active Directory groups. While adding user accounts to groups does solve many problems about splitting up levels of permissions and access, it can be complicated to grow in this mentality, and ultimately AD groups still empower administrators with full access to the groups themselves. RBAC technologies divide up roles at a different level, caring about more than permissions. RBAC focuses more on employee job descriptions than access restrictions. There are a number of different technologies that take advantage of RBAC tools integrated into them, and there are even third-party RBAC solutions which ride on top of all your existing infrastructure, making it widely accessible across your entire organization, and not restricted to working in the confines of a single domain or forest.

Just Enough Administration

A great example of an RBAC technology that is included in Windows Server 2016 is **Just Enough Administration (JEA)**, which is part of PowerShell 5.0. JEA provides you with a way to grant special privileged access for people, without needing to give them administrative rights which would have been required to accomplish the same duties in the past. The necessity to add someone to the Administrators group on a server so that they can do their job is quite common, but JEA is a first step away from that necessity.

In our old way of thinking, it might be easy to think of JEA as doing something like allowing users to have administrative access within PowerShell even when they don't have administrative access to the operating system itself, but it's even more powerful than that. The design of JEA is such that you can permit users to have access only to run particular PowerShell commands and cmdlets at an administrative level, leaving other commands that they do not need access to in the dark. In fact, if a user is working within a JEA context of PowerShell and they try to invoke a cmdlet that is not part of their "allowed" cmdlets, PowerShell pretends like it doesn't even recognize that cmdlet. It doesn't say, "sorry, you can't do this"—it just ignores your command! This definitely helps to keep prying fingers out of the cookie jar, unless you want to let them in.

Let's take it a step further. Maybe you are a DNS administrator, and you might occasionally need to restart the DNS services. Since we are adopting the JEA/RBAC mentality, you are not going to have administrative rights on the operating system, but you will have JEA-based rights within PowerShell so that you can run the tools that you need in order to do your work. Restarting the DNS service requires access to use the `Restart-Service` cmdlet, right? But doesn't that mean I would be able to restart any service on that server, and could potentially do all sorts of things that I don't need to do? JEA is even powerful enough to deal with this scenario. When setting up the level of access that the user needs to get, you can even dive into particular cmdlets and divide up permissions. In our example, you could provide the user with access to the Restart-Service cmdlet, but only give permissions to restart particular services, like those pertaining to DNS. If the user tried to Restart-Service on winrm, they would be denied.

Device Guard

A new device security mechanism that exists in Windows 10, and now Server 2016, is Device Guard. This is a technology that is all about limiting which applications are allowed to run and install on your systems. Effectively, you can have a white-list of allowed applications, but even if you don't want to manually specify each application you can do things like enforce that only applications which have a code signing certificate are allowed to run. Apps that are not trusted natively by Microsoft, or are not explicitly trusted by you, simply don't run. While there are other technologies that accomplish similar functionality already, like AppLocker, Device Guard is unique in that it manages both user and kernel mode processes. Even if an attacker gains access to the operating system of your server, if you have Device Guard policies in place, they will not be able to launch and run malicious software.

Credential Guard

Having some similarities to Device Guard, a new function called Credential Guard also makes use of virtualization-based security in order to keep information stored off in isolation so that only specific parts of the system can access it. Specifically with Credential Guard, we are talking about storing password hashes and Kerberos tickets. Prior to Windows 10 and Windows Server 2016, password hashes and tickets were stored on the hard drive of a machine, in something called the Local Security Authority (LSA). Those hashes were very easily stolen by using simple, free tools available on the Internet. This is exactly how attackers accomplish pass-the-hash and pass-the-ticket attacks, by gaining access to a machine, sucking out the hashes or tickets by using a utility like klist, and then attempting to use those tickets against other machines on the network. With Credential Guard running on your systems, this is absolutely no longer possible! That sensitive information is now stored in a protected virtual hardware environment that is completely isolated from the operating system itself. Using a tool like klist now shows you nothing, and gains you nothing from which you can accomplish these age-old attacks.

Summary

The number one agenda item for many CIOs this year is security. Security for your client machines, security for your networks, security for your cloud resources, and most importantly security for your data. There is no single solution to secure your infrastructure, it requires many moving parts and many different technologies all working together in order to provide safety for your resources. The purpose of this chapter was to provide examples of security measures and technologies that can be utilized in anyone's environments, as well as to reprioritize the importance that security has in today's IT world. Concerns about privacy and security need to be discussed for any and every technology solution that we put into place. Too many times do I find new applications being implemented inside organizations without any regard to how secure that application platform is. Apps which transmit or store data unencrypted need to be modified or dumped. Protection of information is essential to the longevity of our businesses. When discussing security in Windows Server 2016, it is also critical to talk about a couple of completely different installation paths that you can take when implementing your servers, but those topics are large enough to warrant their own chapter. Turn the page to dive into Nano Server and Server Core.

8
Tiny Servers

"Honey, I shrunk the server!" Another chapter, another outdated movie reference. Terribly sorry about that. Moving on to the topic—over the past 20 or more years we have seen nothing but growth out of the Microsoft operating systems. Growth can be good, like new features and enhancements to make our lives easier. Growth can also be bad, like bloated file structures and memory-hog graphical interfaces. If you were to graph chronologically Windows and Windows Server operating systems by terms of their footprints, based on factors like disk space consumption and memory requirements, it would show a steady upward grade. Every new release requires just a little more processing power, and just a little more hard drive space than the previous version. That was the case, until—I'm guesstimating a little bit here—maybe Windows 8 and Server 2012. We saw some surprising steps taken with lowering these threshold numbers, a welcome change. But the change wasn't too dramatic. I mean, what can you glean from the fact that a brand new Windows Server 2016 box has all kinds of core items that are still running inside `C:\Windows\System32`? We're not even going to talk about what's in the registry. Clearly there are still cutbacks that could be made, and at some level the new operating systems are still just being built and patched on top of the old ones.

Until now, perhaps. Today we are going to talk about a couple of alternate ways to use Windows Server 2016 on a much, much smaller scale. Server Core has been around for quite some time now, but I'm hard pressed to find people that actually use it. Nano Server, on the other hand, is brand new. These miniaturized versions of Server 2016 have some very specific purposes, and some very large benefits. Let's explore a little together:

- Why Server Core?
- Interfacing with Server Core
- Roles available in Server Core

- Nano Server versus Server Core
- Setting up your first Nano Server
- Administering Nano Server

Why Server Core?

Why am I even talking about Server Core? Hasn't it been around since 2008? Yes, that is exactly why I am talking about it. The Server Core variant of the Windows Server operating system has been around for quite some time, but it seems like many admins are scared to trust it. I work with many different companies from many different industries. They all have one big thing in common—they use a lot of Windows Servers, and all of these Windows Servers are running the full GUI. Have they heard of Server Core? Sure. Have they tested it out in a lab? Sometimes. Everyone seems to have a slightly different experience level with Core, but it's quite rare to find one in production. Maybe I'm just talking to the wrong people, but I have to assume that there is a majority of us out there, myself included, that need to start using Server Core on a more regular basis.

Why do we need to start using Server Core? Because GUI-less servers are the future, says Microsoft. Would you believe that early in the previews for Windows Server 2016, the Desktop Experience option wasn't even there? You couldn't run a full GUI desktop shell on a Server 2016 if you wanted to, save for a quasi, mini shell that could be plopped on top of Server Core. There was so much user feedback, more commonly known as **flack**, about this that the full Desktop Experience was added back in during one of the Technical Preview rollouts. But you still notice that Server Core is the default option when installing the operating system. Remember back to the beginning of our book where we did a quick covering of the actual Server 2016 installation? The default option for installation is not the Desktop Experience, that top option in the following screenshot is the option for installing the command-line driven Server Core:

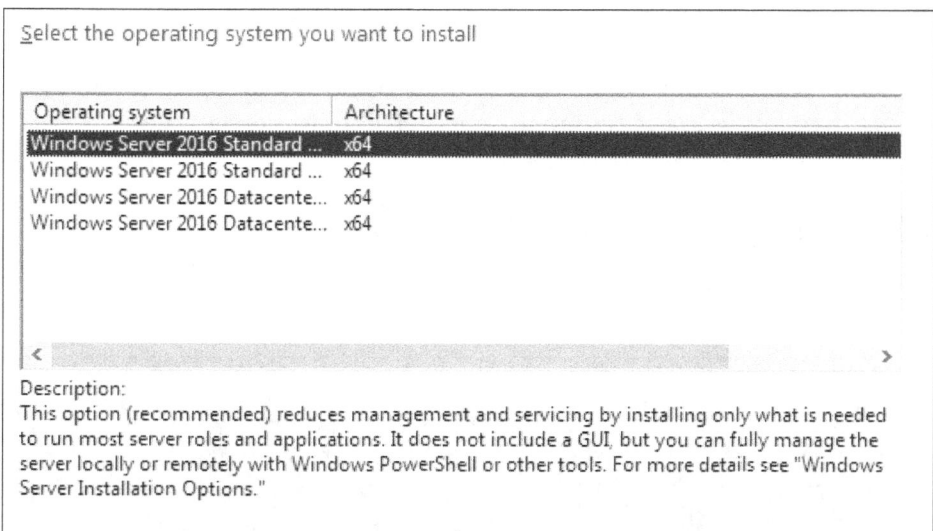

Microsoft wants to move away from a graphical interface because the GUI gets in the way of automation and scalability. When all of our servers are built very similarly, it means that we can do more cloud-like functions with them. Automatic spinning up and down of resources as they are needed, rolling out dozens of servers at the click of a switch, these kinds of automations and sizings are possible in the cloud, but they are only possible because the infrastructure is set up in a way that it is so standardized. Cloud hardware resources need to be so streamlined that the operations and automation tools can make them do what is needed, without worrying about all of the variables that would be present in a user-tweaked graphical interface.

There are other obvious advantages to running all of your servers as this limited, restricted version. Server Core boasts reduced hard drive space, reduced memory consumption, and a reduced attack surface when compared to a traditional, full-blown server experience. Now you can see why I made the hefty statements a minute ago about how we all need to start becoming more comfortable with Server Core!

No more switching back and forth

There is a very important note that I wanted to point out here. Those of you who have worked with Server Core in Windows Server 2012 R2 know that we had the option of changing a server *on the fly*. What I mean is that if you created a new server as the full Desktop Experience, you could later change it to be Server Core. The opposite approach was equally capable, you could take a Server Core and flip it over to a full Desktop Experience.

Not anymore! This capability to move servers back and forth between platforms has been removed/erased/deleted/nullified. I repeat, this is no longer possible. So plan carefully from here on out when installing these operating systems. If you install a Server Core, that guy is going to remain a Server Core for its lifetime.

Interfacing with Server Core

After running through your first installation of Server Core, you will be presented with the following lock screen:

Is that really a Command Prompt window that says **Press Ctrl-Alt-Del to unlock**? Yes, yes it is. This usually draws a few chuckles when an admin sees it for the first time. I know it did for me, anyway. It reminded me a little of when we used to code if/then games on our TI-83 calculators during high school math class. Stop me, I'm getting off on a rabbit trail again. Go ahead and press *Ctrl + Alt + Del*, and you will be prompted to change your administrator password for the first time, just like in the case if this were the GUI version of Windows Server. Except, of course, that you do it all from within the Command Prompt window using only your keyboard. Once you are officially logged into the server, you will find yourself sitting at a traditional C:\Windows\system32\cmd.exe prompt, with a flashing cursor awaiting instructions.

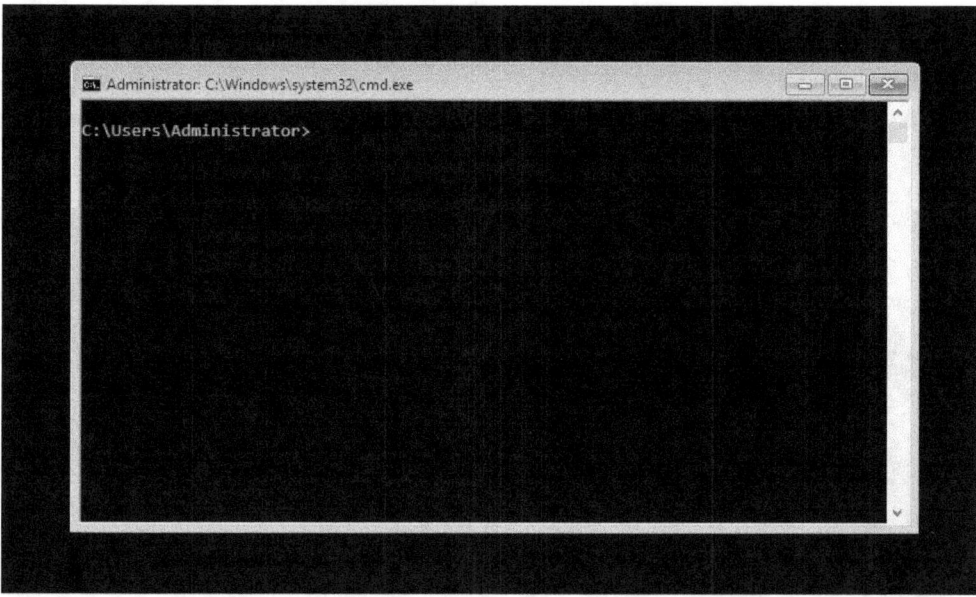

Interestingly, the Command Prompt window isn't consuming the full screen, it is clear that there is black background that cmd.exe is riding on top of. I only find this interesting because you can tell that the Core operating system itself is something other than Command Prompt, and that cmd.exe is just an application that autolaunches. You can even utilize the mouse here and resize or move that Command Prompt window around. I do wonder if and when this will be replaced with a PowerShell prompt as the default, and if it will consume the full screen in future versions.

Tiny Servers

Even more interesting and good to know is that you can launch some actual GUI-like applications from this prompt. For example, you can open up Notepad and utilize it with both keyboard and mouse, just like you would from any version of Windows. If you have the Notepad open, create a note and then save it; you can see that there is in fact a real-file structure and a set of relatively normal-looking system folders. So rather than some form of black magic, Server Core is actually the real operating system, wrapped up in a smaller and more secure package.

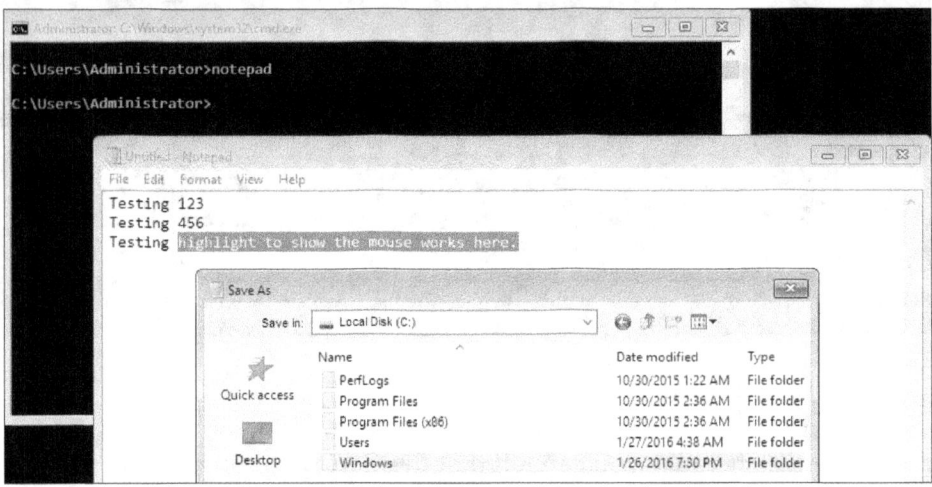

PowerShell

So, as far as managing a Server Core, you can obviously use Command Prompt. In reality though, the commands and functions available from inside Command Prompt are going to be limited. It makes much more sense that, if you are working from the console of a Windows Server Core box, you would use Command Prompt for just one purpose—to invoke PowerShell, and then use it to accomplish whatever tasks you need to do on that server. The quickest way I know to move into PowerShell from the basic Command Prompt is to simply type the word `powershell`, and press *Enter*. This will bring the PowerShell capabilities right into your existing Command Prompt window, so that you can start interfacing with the PowerShell commands and cmdlets that you need in order to really manipulate this server:

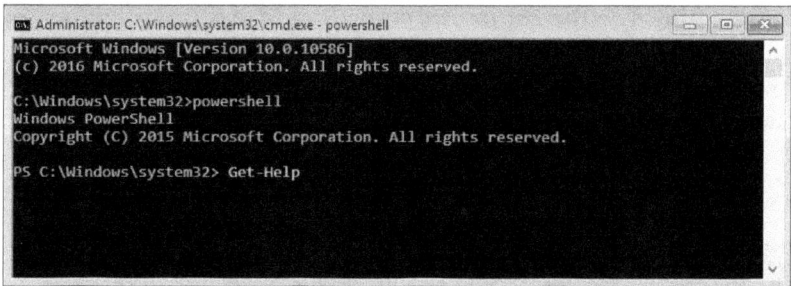

What is the first thing we typically do on new servers? Give them an IP address, of course. Without network connectivity there isn't much that we can do on this server. You can assign IP address information to NICs using PowerShell on any newer Windows Server, but most of us are not in the habit of doing so. Since we can't just open up the Control Panel and get into the Network and Sharing Center like we can from inside the Desktop Experience GUI of Windows Server, where do we begin with getting network connectivity on this new Server Core?

Cmdlets to manage IP addresses

Here are cmdlets that you can use to view and manipulate IP address settings from within PowerShell. Again, these same cmdlets can be used in the full GUI version of Windows Server, Server Core, or in Nano Server, which we will be talking about very shortly. Currently, working from Server Core where we only have command-line interfacing available to us, these cmdlets are essential to getting network connectivity flowing on our new server:

- `Get-NetIPConfiguration`: This displays the current networking configuration.
- `Get-NetIPAddress`: This displays the current IP addresses.
- `Get-NetIPInterface`: This shows a list of NICs and their interface ID numbers. This number is going to be important when setting an IP address, because we want to make sure we tell PowerShell to configure the right IP onto the right NIC.
- `New-NetIPAddress`: This is used to configure a new IP address.
- `Set-DNSClientServerAddress`: This is used to configure DNS Server settings in the NIC properties.

Tiny Servers

Let's quickly walk through the setup of a static IP address on my new Server Core instance to make sure this all makes sense. I want to assign the IP address 10.0.0.30 to this new server, but first I need to find out which NIC interface ID number it needs to be assigned to. The output of Get-NetIPInterface tells us that the **ifIndex** I am interested in is number **2**:

```
PS C:\Windows\system32> Get-NetIPInterface

ifIndex InterfaceAlias              AddressFamily NlMtu(Bytes) InterfaceMetric
------- --------------              ------------- ------------ ---------------
2       Ethernet                    IPv6                  1500               5
7       isatap.Contoso.local        IPv6                  1280              50
1       Loopback Pseudo-Interface 1 IPv6            4294967295              50
2       Ethernet                    IPv4                  1500               5
1       Loopback Pseudo-Interface 1 IPv4            4294967295              50

PS C:\Windows\system32>
```

Now that we know the interface number, let's build the commands which are going to assign the new IP address settings to the NIC. I am going to use one command to assign the IP address, subnet mask prefix, and default gateway. I will use a second command in order to assign DNS server addresses:

```
New-NetIPAddress -InterfaceIndex 2 -IPAddress 10.0.0.30 -PrefixLength 24
-DefaultGateway 10.0.0.1
```

```
Set-DNSClientServerAddress -InterfaceIndex 2 -ServerAddresses
10.0.0.2,10.0.0.3
```

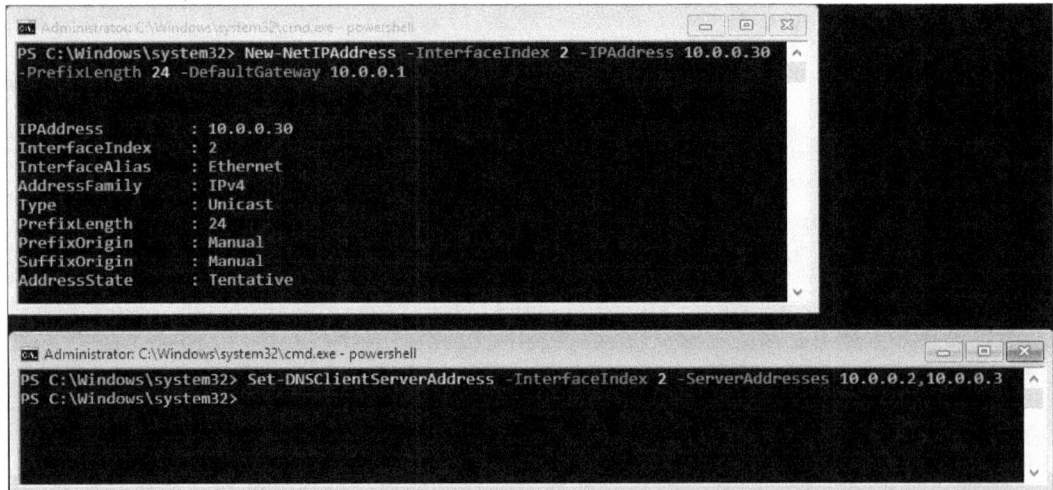

[244]

Now, all of these settings should be in place on the NIC. Let's double-check that with a `Get-NetIPConfiguration` command. Alternatively, you could use good old `ipconfig` to check these settings, but where's the fun in that?

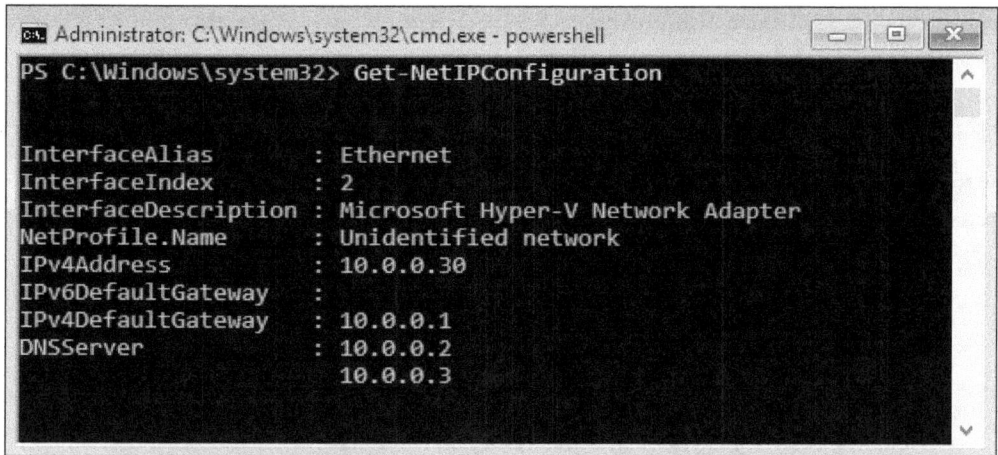

 Remember, you can always utilize DHCP reservations to make this a little bit easier. If you were to run a simple `ipconfig /all` from your Server Core and jot down the MAC address, you could use this address in order to create a reservation in DHCP and assign a specific IP address to the new server that way.

Setting the server hostname

Now that we have network connectivity, a good next step is setting the hostname of our server and joining it to the domain. First things first, let's see what the current name of the server is, and change it to something that fits our standards. When you fresh install Windows, it self-assigns a random hostname to the server. You can view the current hostname by simply typing `hostname` and pressing *Enter*:

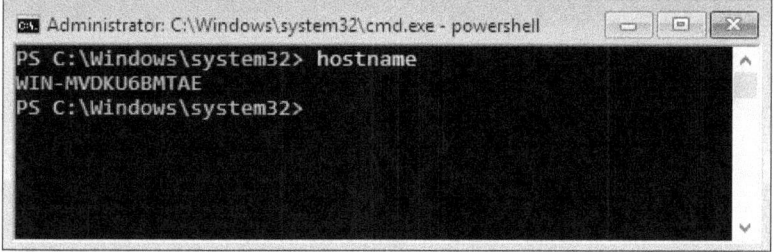

Tiny Servers

To change the hostname of your server, we need to use PowerShell. Bring yourself into a PowerShell prompt if not already there, and all we need to do is use the `Rename-Computer` cmdlet in order to set our new hostname. I have decided to name my new server CORE1 — whew, I put a lot of thought into that one — so I would issue the command as follows. Remember, after renaming your computer just like in the GUI version of Windows Server, a system restart is necessary to put that change into action. So following your `Rename-Computer` command, you can issue a `Restart-Computer` to reboot the box:

```
Rename-Computer CORE1
```

```
Restart-Computer
```

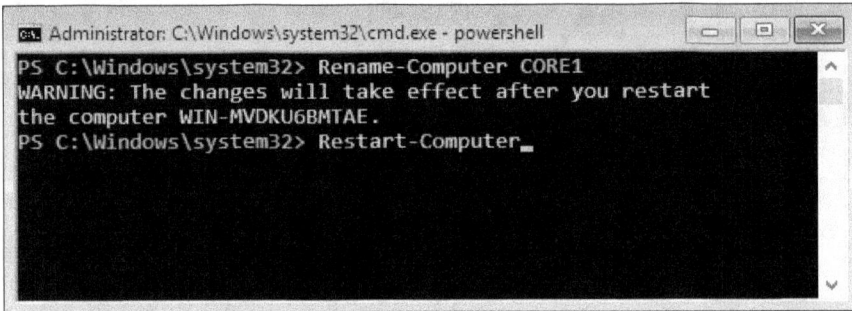

Joining your domain

The next logical step is, of course, joining your domain. These are the standard functions that we would perform on any new server in our environment, but done in a way that you may have never encountered before, since we are doing all of this strictly from the Command Prompt and PowerShell interfaces. To join a Server Core to your domain, head into PowerShell and then use the `Add-Computer` cmdlet. You will be asked to specify both the domain name as well as credentials for joining the domain, the same information you would have to specify if you were joining a Windows Server 2016 in Desktop Experience mode to a domain. First you specify the credentials needed:

Then you tell it what domain you would like to join:

Alternatively, you could utilize the -DomainName parameter in combination with the original Add-Computer cmdlet in order to specify the name of the domain in the original command. And of course, after joining the domain, you need to Restart-Computer once again to finalize this change.

Server Manager

While the initial configuration of your server will be somewhat handled from the command-line interfaces available at the console, once your server has been established on the network it will likely be more advantageous for you to expand the horizons a little. By using tools like Server Manager to manage many different servers from a single point, you will start conforming to the new Microsoft "centralized management mentality". Yes, this remote management capability in Server Manager that we explored earlier in the book allows you to tap into not only GUI-based Windows Servers, but Server Core instances as well.

I want to install a role onto my new CORE1 server. I could do that with PowerShell right on the server console, but instead let's try adding CORE1 into Server Manager that is running on another one of my servers. I am going to log in to WEB1, and use Server Manager from there. Just like we have already seen, I can add a new server into Server Manager using the **Manage** menu and choosing **Add Servers**:

Add the new CORE1 server into our list of managed machines, and it is now manageable from inside this instance of Server Manager. Getting back to what my original intentions were, I want to install a role onto CORE1. If I use the **Add roles and features** function inside Server Manager, I can now choose to manipulate the CORE1 server:

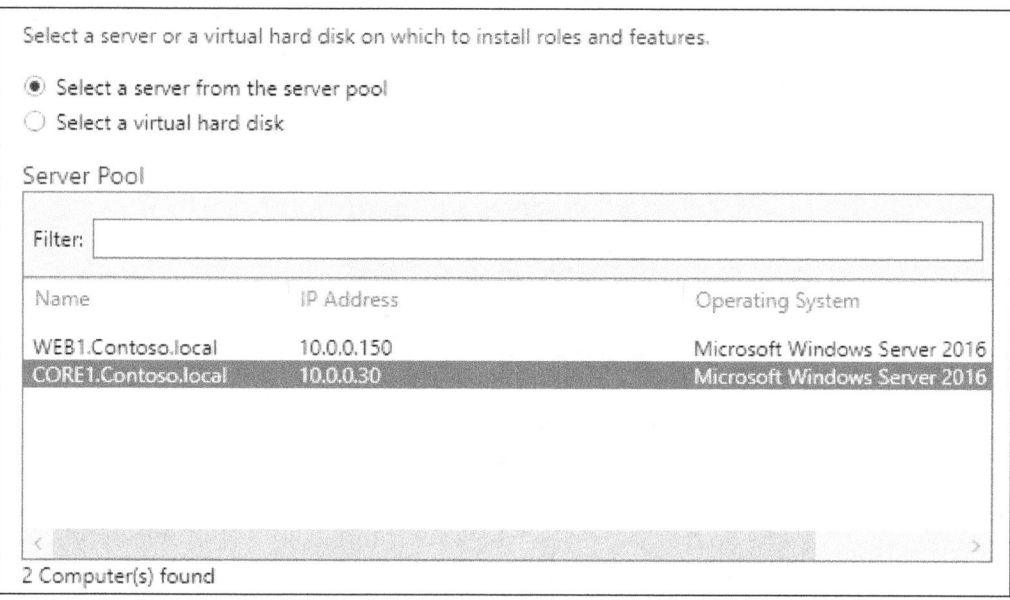

Just like with any server running the full Desktop Experience version of Windows Server, we can now finish walking through the role installation wizard, and the new role will be installed on CORE1.

Remote Server Administration Tools

Also true is the fact that you can manage Server Core instances with the **Remote Server Administration Tools (RSAT)** in Windows 10. RSAT is essentially just a copy of Server Manager that is designed to run on the client operating system. In our case, I already have a Windows 10 machine on which I installed RSAT earlier in the book, so I will prove this out by logging into that guy and adding CORE1 into the interface. I just finished installing the IIS role on CORE1 in our previous task, so I should be able to see that listed inside RSAT when I connect it to CORE1.

If you haven't used RSAT before and haven't read over that section of our text, it is important to know that there is no application called "Remote Server Administration Tools". Instead, after the RSAT installation has completed, take a look inside your Start Menu for the application called **Server Manager**. This is how you utilize a Windows 10 client to remotely manage Windows Server 2016 instances.

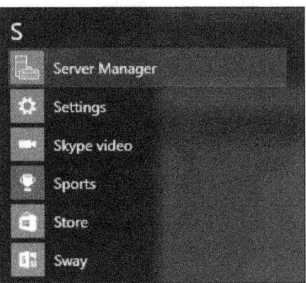

Exactly like you would do from a Server Manager interface of Windows Server 2016, go ahead and walk through the wizard to add other servers to manage. Once I have added CORE1 into Server Manager, I can now see IIS listed inside my Dashboard. This indicates that my IIS service running on CORE1 is visible, accessible, and configurable right from my Windows 10 desktop computer. For the majority of the tasks that I need to accomplish on CORE1, I will never have to worry about logging into the console of that server. If I right-click on the CORE1 server name from within this RSAT console, you can see that I have many features available to me that I can use to manage this remote Server Core instance.

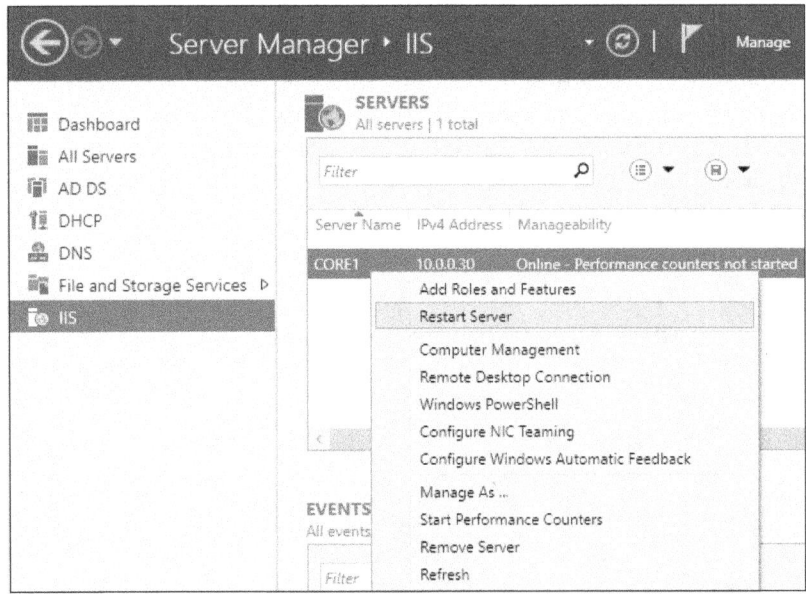

So you can see that there are ways to use the GUI tools in order to manage our GUI-less instances of Windows Server. It's just a matter of putting your mind into a place where you are thinking of servers as headless, and that the tools like PowerShell or Server Manager really don't care at all whether the server they are changing is local or remote. The processes and tools are the same either way.

Accidentally closing Command Prompt

This is a common hurdle to overcome if you haven't utilized Server Core much. It is our tendency to close windows and applications that are no longer being used, and so you might unconsciously close out of the Command Prompt window that is serving your entire administrative existence within a Server Core. Now you're sitting at a large blank screen, with seemingly no interface and nowhere to go from here. How do you get back to work on this server? Do we have to turn the server off and back on in order to reset it? That would interrupt any roles or traffic that this server might be serving up to users, so obviously it isn't the ideal approach.

There is a simple way to get Command Prompt back, by using Task Manager to launch a new instance of Command Prompt. When sitting at the empty black screen of a Server Core console, you can press *Ctrl* + *Alt* + *Del* and you will be presented with the following options:

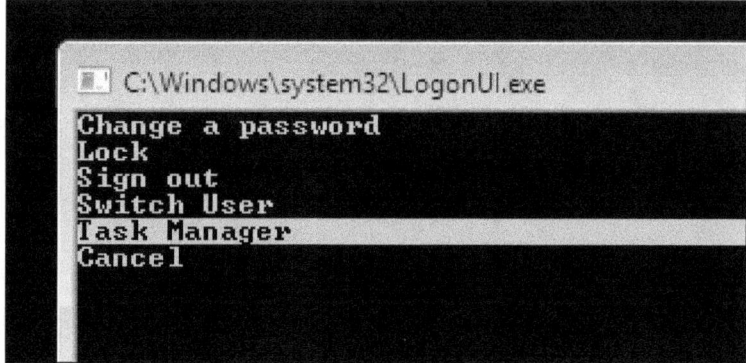

Tiny Servers

There are actually a few different functions you can perform here, which is pretty neat. But to get our Command Prompt window back, arrow-down to **Task Manager**, and press *Enter*. This will launch the Task Manager application that we are all familiar with. Now click on **More details** in order to expand Task Manager's screens. Drop down the **File** menu, and click on **Run new task**:

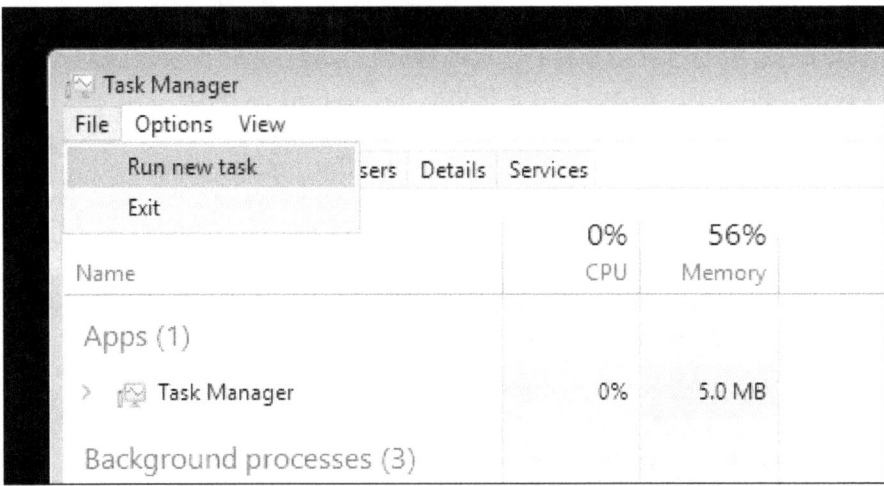

In the **Create new task** box, type cmd and then click on **OK**:

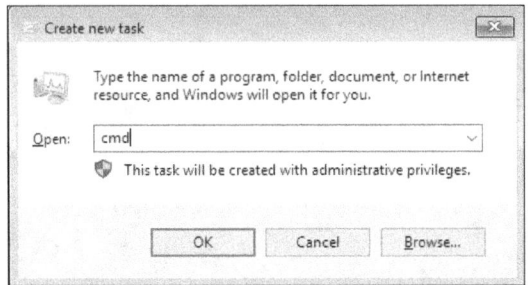

Alternatively, you could specify to launch any application directly from this **Create new task** prompt. If you were interested in moving straight into PowerShell, instead of typing cmd, you could instead simply type powershell into that prompt, and it would open directly:

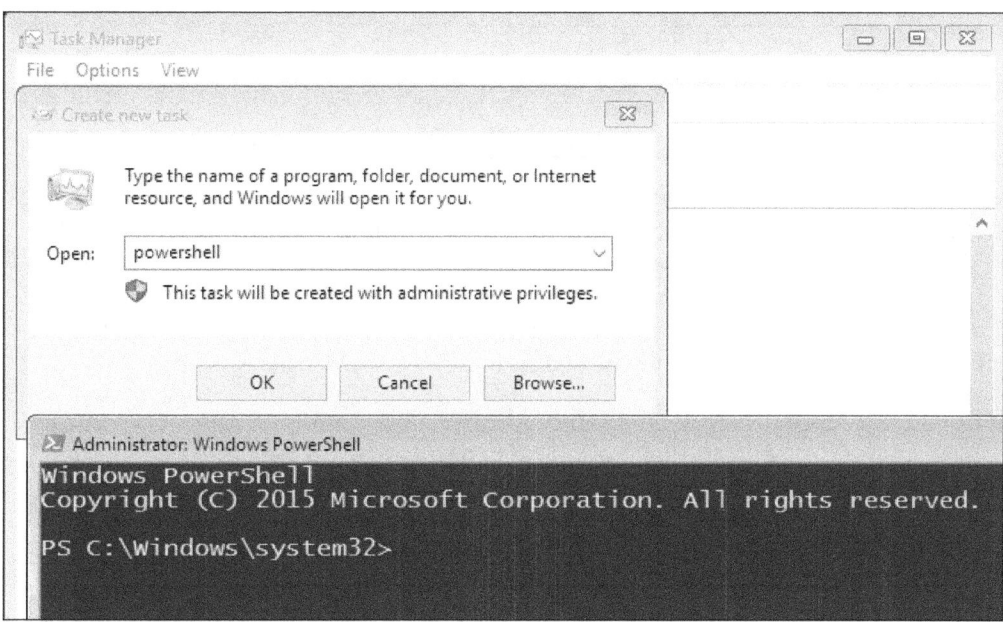

Roles available in Server Core

Server Core is obviously a restricted form of the operating system, and some of the roles inside Windows Server are just not designed to work properly within that limited context. Here is a list of the roles which are supported to run on a Windows Server 2016 — Server Core instance:

- Active Directory Certificate Services
- Active Directory Domain Services
- Active Directory Lightweight Directory Services
- Active Directory Rights Management Server
- DHCP Server
- DNS Server
- File Services
- Print and Document Services

- Routing and Remote Access
- Streaming Media Services
- Hyper-V
- Web Server
- Windows Server Update Server

Nano Server versus Server Core

Imagine you own two cars, the family SUV and a mid-size sedan. The SUV has all of the bells and whistles, and can do pretty much whatever you want. The sedan gets you where you need to go, but it is smaller, and maybe a little more limited. The upside is that it was cheaper to acquire and consumes fewer resources as you roll down the road. You can see where this is going, the SUV is **Windows Server Desktop Experience** (GUI), and the sedan is our **Server Core**.

Now picture a moped. Super small, incredibly efficient on fuel, and very simple when compared to a car, so that build and repair times are considerably lower. The potential for it to break in the first place is lower as well, as all of the components are simplified and aren't put through a lot of stress. **Nano Server** is your moped. Well, that analogy is lacking one thing—the intense security provided by Nano Server. Safety and security are not generally associated with mopeds, so let's rethink this. Perhaps if the moped had airbags, or if it could fly. Or maybe better yet—the moped is invisible. There you go—**Nano Server is your invisible moped**. Yes Microsoft, you have permission to pull that quote and use it on your website.

All joking aside, there is a brand new Windows Server installation option this year with Server 2016. **Nano Server** is similar to Server Core, but it takes a big step further in terms of size and security. Let's take a look at some of the specifics on Nano Server and how it differs from Server Core.

Sizing and maintenance numbers

Nano Server is tiny! It is said to be 20 times smaller than Server Core. Here are some numbers from Microsoft intended to impress:

93 percent smaller VHD size means no more hard drive space being consumed by parts of the operating system that you don't need.

92 percent fewer security bulletins means much less time spent patching and maintaining Nano Servers.

80 percent fewer reboots. This is incredible, especially considering that our number of reboots has already decreased significantly over the past few years with the changes happening in the Windows Update mechanisms. The reboot process is also significantly faster than with the larger versions of Windows Server 2016.

64-bit applications only. It is important to understand when you start using Nano Server that they can only support 64-bit applications.

452 MB — this number is from me. This is the actual size of the Nano Server that we are going to build together in just a few minutes. While the size of your Nano Servers will differ depending on what roles you intend to use them for, seeing virtual disks smaller than 1 GB is going to be standard in Nano Server environments. On the other hand, the basic Server Core box that we built earlier has a disk footprint of 7 GB. Ouch!

35 seconds is all the time that it takes to set up a new Nano Server, as opposed to roughly 300 seconds for a Server Core – and that's only if you have automated the setup of Server Core. A standard installation takes even longer.

Nano Server boots in approximately 9 seconds. Even the snappy, lightweight Server Core seems slow by comparison, as he clocks in around 85 seconds for boot time.

Accessibility

Unlike Server Core, Nano Server is not intended to be configured from the console. Well, that was the original idea anyway. At one point, the plans for Nano Server were to be completely headless, so that any administration done to the box needed to be done remotely. That has changed a little bit, I assume because of negative feedback from testing users and customers. There is a very limited console function that can be performed with a monitor and your keyboard. You can assign some network settings and configure pieces of the firewall from this console. However, Nano is definitely designed to be accessed and administered remotely, so you will have to become familiar with the remote administration tools that can be used to interact with Nano Server. Many of the existing Microsoft remote management tools are now compatible to be used with Nano Server. It is assumed that PowerShell will be the most popular way that folks will interface with Nano Server, but you could also use tools such as Server Manager, WinRM, WMI, VMM, SCOM, and the new SMT running in Azure in order to perform maintenance on these servers.

An important one that is missing is RDP. Remember, there is no GUI on these kinds of servers, so the most popular administration tool of all time—the Remote Desktop Protocol—is not going to do anything for you here.

Capability

Where Server Core is a restricted but almost fully capable operating system for most roles in the Windows world, Nano Server was created, so far, with a limited scope of usability. I fully expect that the capabilities Nano Server provides will grow as we start adopting these headless, minute servers, so this list should grow in the future. Currently, here is the list of scenarios that Microsoft has deemed worthwhile to run on a Nano Server:

- **Hyper-V**: To be used as a computing host for Hyper-V virtual machines
- **File Server**: To be used as a storage host for file servers
- **DNS Server**: To be used as a DNS server
- **Web Server**: To be used as an IIS web server
- **Cloud Application Server**: To be used as a host for cloud-developed applications

Installation

When installing a Windows Server 2016 with Desktop Experience or a Windows Server 2016 Server Core instance, all you need to do is throw the ISO onto a DVD or USB stick, run the installer, and choose the installation option that you want. As you can see during that installation process, or rather—as you cannot see—there is no option to select for installing a Nano Server. This could certainly change in the future as more and more people get interested in using Nano, but for the time being, we need to take some special steps in order to build an image that we will be using to boot into our new Nano Server.

Immediately following this text we will take a more specific look at the step-by-step actions you need to perform in order to build your first Nano Server, but when comparing Server Core and Nano Server it is important to understand that the setup is quite different. For Nano, you will be building a VHD file, your virtual hard disk that will be used to boot, outside the scope of a Windows installation process. Once the VHD is created, mounted, and filled with data, then you move that VHD to the virtual machine you are planning to use as your Nano Server, and simply boot it up. Here, let the upcoming steps (sections) speak for themselves…

Setting up your first Nano Server

Let's get a Nano Server rolling so that we can take a real look at it. We are going to build a VHD file using tools that are available in the Windows Server 2016 installation ISO. Once built, we will use this new VHD to boot a new virtual machine that will be our Nano Server.

Preparing the VHD file

Here is the bulk of what we need to do in order to take a look at Nano Server, we need to build our VHD file. First we need to grab some files off the Windows Server 2016 installation media. Before we can grab these files, go ahead and mount the ISO to a drive letter on your computer. Simply double-clicking on the ISO file typically auto-mounts it to the next available drive letter. For example, when I double-clicked on the ISO installer, it mounted the ISO onto my drive letter D. I can now access the files in that ISO as if it were a DVD that was sitting inside the DVD drive (D:) of my machine. If you open up the ISO file, you want to copy the entire NanoServer folder onto the drive of the computer you are working from. For example, copy D:\NanoServer to C:\NanoServer, so that these tools and files from the ISO are now sitting on your own hard drive.

From the computer or server where those files now reside, go ahead and launch an administrative PowerShell session.. Then navigate into the directory where you stored these files. For my example, I stored them in C:\NanoServer on my computer and so this is the directory I am sitting inside from my PowerShell prompt.

Now we need to import the Generator script into our PowerShell session. Do that using the following command:

```
Import-Module -Name C:\NanoServer\NanoServerImageGenerator\NanoServerImageGenerator.psm1 -Verbose
```

Tiny Servers

Next we run a command to build our VHD file. There are a number of different switches that can be specified within this command, so let's take a minute and explain some of them. Here is the base command we will be working from:

```
New-NanoServerImage -MediaPath <MEDIAPATH> -DeploymentType <DEPLOYMENT_
TYPE> -Edition <EDITION> -TargetPath <TARGETPATH> -ComputerName
<HOSTNAME>
```

- `MEDIAPATH`: This is used to specify the path to the Server 2016 ISO. Access to this file is needed in order to pull installation information out of it during the VHD building process.
- `DEPLOYMENT_TYPE`: Here you decide whether this NanoServer will be a "guest" or a "host".
- `EDITION`: This determines whether your NanoServer will be Server 2016 Standard or Datacenter.
- `TARGETPATH`: This is used to specify a path where the VHD file will be output. Make sure to specify both the path and the actual filename, including the extension.

> It is important to note that you can create either a VHD file or a VHDX file. VHD will create this as an MBR disk. If you create a VHDX file, it will bump the disk up to GPT. Depending on what you plan to do with this server, you will need to choose accordingly.

- `COMPUTERNAME`: This is used to specify the hostname that you want to assign to your new Nano Server.

After defining all of the preceding items, the specific command that I will be running is as follows:

```
New-NanoServerImage -MediaPath D:\ -DeploymentType Guest -Edition
Standard -TargetPath C:\NanoServer\NANO1.vhd -ComputerName NANO1
```

![Administrator Windows PowerShell screenshot showing the New-NanoServerImage command execution prompting for AdministratorPassword]

Chapter 8

After pressing *Enter* on the preceding command, you will be asked to supply an administrator password for this new server. Supply the password, and your VHD creation process begins! As the process gets rolling you can see that numerous steps are being taken in order to prep this new VHD file for us to use.

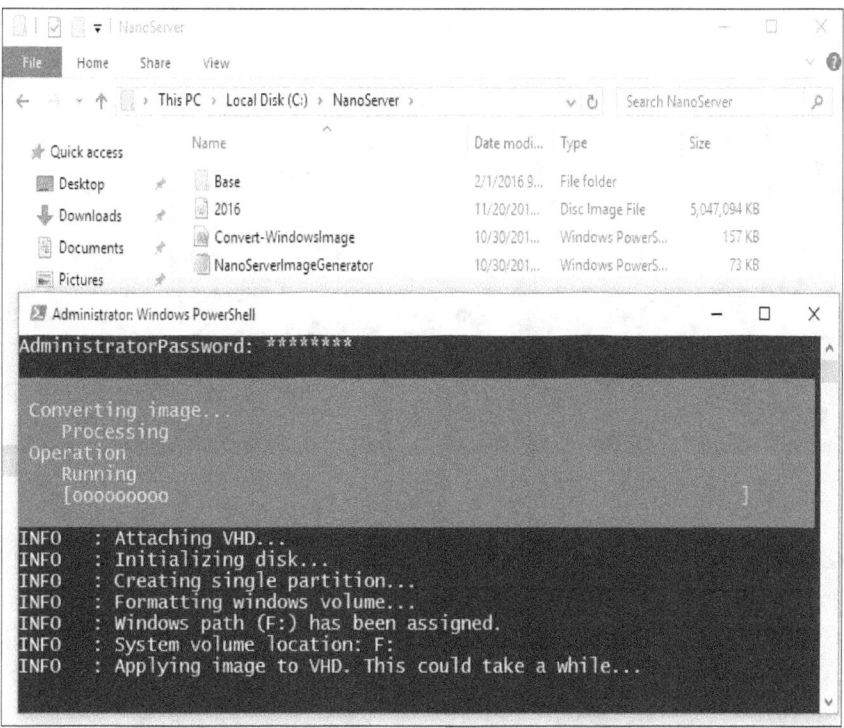

Once complete, a brand new `NANO1.vhd` file is sitting inside the `C:\NanoServer` folder on my computer, right where I programmed it to go. As you can see, the output VHD file is not even 500 MB, I told you these servers were tiny!

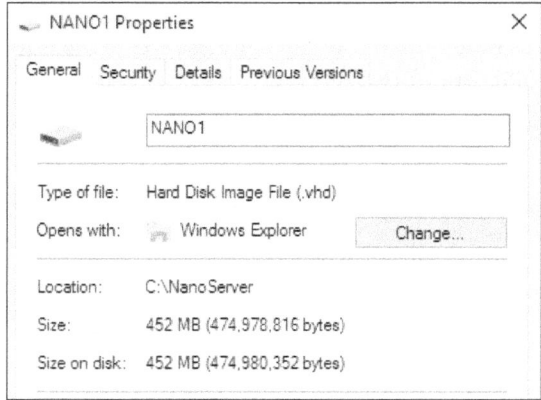

[259]

Creating a virtual machine

With a new VHD file in our hands, the next step is using this virtual hard disk in order to create a new virtual machine. I am going to create a new, very simple virtual machine to take a look at this. Simply boot the VM to my new VHD file, and I am sitting at the console of my brand new Nano Server!

Nano Server Image Builder

The process we just stepped through in order to create our new NANO1 server isn't overly complicated once you get familiar with it, but there are still a lot of IT admins out there who are not using PowerShell regularly. Thankfully for those folks, there is a brand new graphical utility called the Nano Server Image Builder. This tool allows you to select and specify options about the Nano Server you want to create right from a graphical interface, using your keyboard and mouse, and upon completion it spits out a VHD file for you. No PowerShell required! The Nano Server Image Builder is also a really nice way to implement Nano Server onto physical hardware, as you can easily spit out a USB stick installer rather than exporting a VHD file. The installation options for Nano are evolving very quickly, and I recommend you stay on top of the TechNet articles for the latest and greatest methods for implementing Nano. Here is a good starting point: https://technet.microsoft.com/en-us/windows-server-docs/get-started/deploy-nano-server.

Administering Nano Server

Working with a Nano Server is quite different than our other flavors of Windows Server 2016, primarily because Nano is designed to be headless, without the need to access the console whatsoever. Here are some of the options that are currently available to you for monitoring, maintaining, and otherwise administering a Nano Server.

Nano Server Recovery Console

As seen when we first launched our new Nano Server, there is a very limited console with which you can interface to configure network settings. This is the **Nano Server Recovery Console**. The purpose of this console is pretty singular. If you somehow mess up the networking configuration on your Nano Server when using the remote administration tools, this is your get-out-of-jail-free card where you can login and reset IP address settings, allowing you to once again get back into the server with the remote administration tools. Let's log in to this console for a minute and take a look at our available options. By entering our username and password, we find ourselves at the following screen:

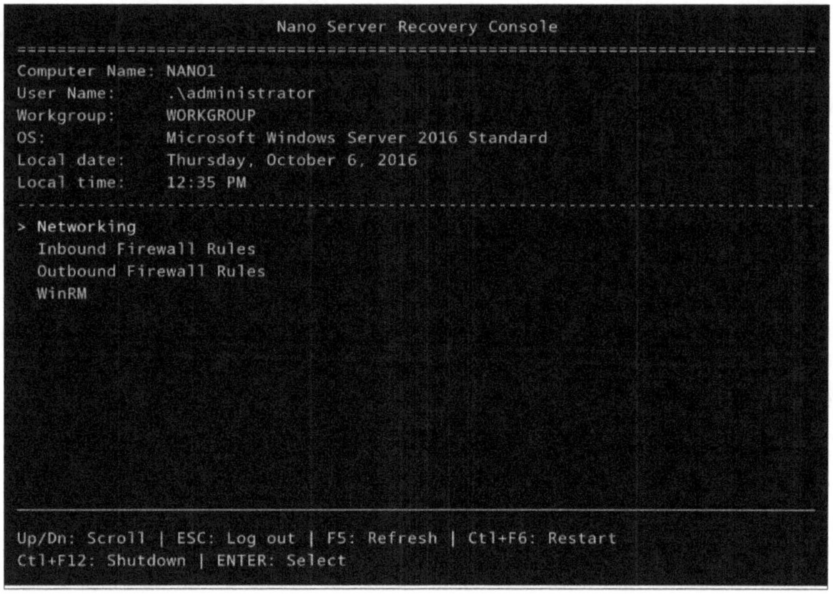

Tiny Servers

You can see that we have currently picked up an IP address from the DHCP server running in our environment, which is great. However, if you were having problems getting into this Nano Server from a remote administration tool and suspected something was wrong with the local IP configuration, you can press *Tab* in order to highlight the **Networking** option near the bottom of the screen, and then press *Enter* to see the networking configuration. Once inside the IP address settings, you can press *F11* on the keyboard to change or update your IPv4 config.

```
DHCP               [ Disabled  ]
IP Address         10.0.0.25
Subnet Mask        255.255.255.0
Default Gateway    10.0.0.1
```

Other than **Networking**, the only other option inside this recovery console is **Firewall**. Inside this section of the Nano console you will see a list of in-built **Firewall Rules**. Select a rule, and you have the ability to enable or disable that particular rule using your *F4* key.

```
                        Firewall Rules
================================================================
Select a rule to view
> File and Printer Sharing over SMBDirect (iWARP-In)
> Connected User Experiences and Telemetry
> Windows Remote Management (HTTP-In)
> Windows Remote Management (HTTP-In)
> Windows Remote Management - Compatibility Mode (HTTP-In)
> File and Printer Sharing (NB-Session-In)
> File and Printer Sharing (NB-Session-Out)
> File and Printer Sharing (SMB-In)
> File and Printer Sharing (SMB-Out)
> File and Printer Sharing (NB-Name-In)
> File and Printer Sharing (NB-Name-Out)
> File and Printer Sharing (NB-Datagram-In)
> File and Printer Sharing (NB-Datagram-Out)
> File and Printer Sharing (Spooler Service - RPC)
```

Remote PowerShell

Once you have figured out the IP address of your new Nano Server, whether by looking inside the recovery console or by peeking inside your DHCP leases to figure out what IP it grabbed, it's time to start really administering your new server. This requires the use of an external remote management tool. The most common? PowerShell. Let's try out some commands that should get our local PowerShell prompt remotely managing our new NANO1 server.

First we need to add NANO1 to our machine's list of trusted hosts. Open up an elevated PowerShell prompt on the computer from which you want to establish this remote PowerShell connection, and utilize the following command:

`Set-Item WSMan:\localhost\Client\TrustedHosts "10.0.0.25"`

(Obviously, you will want to replace `10.0.0.25` with the IP address of your Nano Server.)

```
PS C:\> Set-Item WSMan:\localhost\Client\TrustedHosts "10.0.0.25"

WinRM Security Configuration.
This command modifies the TrustedHosts list for the WinRM client. The
computers in the TrustedHosts list might not be authenticated. The client
 might send credential information to these computers. Are you sure that
you want to modify this list?
[Y] Yes  [N] No  [S] Suspend  [?] Help (default is "Y"): y
PS C:\>
```

Tiny Servers

Now we just need to start the remote PowerShell session. Still inside that elevated prompt, this one-liner should get you connected. When you enter this command, you will be prompted for the administrator password, and will then be able to issue remote PowerShell commands against the NANO1 server.

```
Enter-PSSession -ComputerName 10.0.0.25 -Credential administrator
```

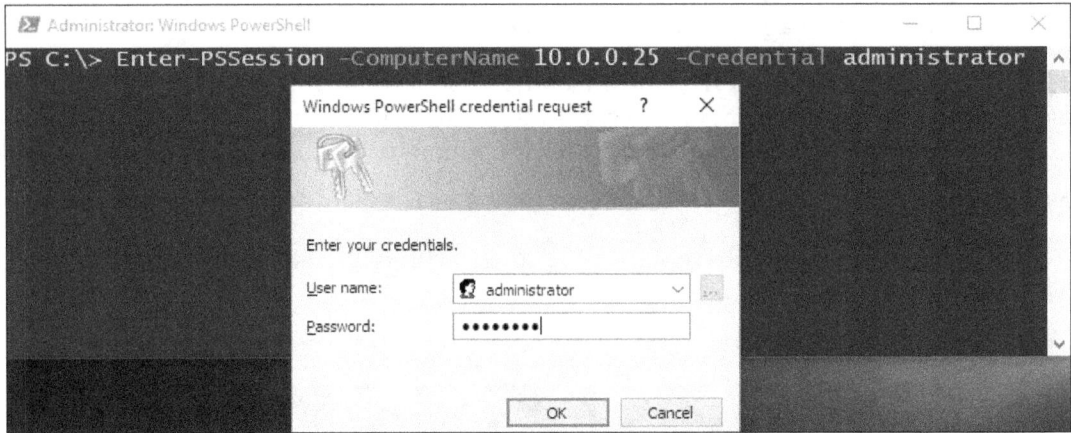

Now you are sitting at a PowerShell prompt, remotely connected to the NANO1 server. Want to prove it's really NANO1? Try something like a simple `hostname` or `ipconfig` command.

```
PS C:\> Enter-PSSession -ComputerName 10.0.0.25 -Credential administrator
[10.0.0.25]: PS C:\Users\Administrator\Documents> hostname
NANO1
[10.0.0.25]: PS C:\Users\Administrator\Documents> ipconfig

Windows IP Configuration


Ethernet adapter Ethernet:

   Connection-specific DNS Suffix  . :
   Link-local IPv6 Address . . . . . : fe80::f8f2:b8:8961:2bac%2
   IPv4 Address. . . . . . . . . . . : 10.0.0.25
   Subnet Mask . . . . . . . . . . . : 255.255.255.0
   Default Gateway . . . . . . . . . : 10.0.0.1
[10.0.0.25]: PS C:\Users\Administrator\Documents>
```

Since you now have full PowerShell access to this new Nano Server, you can do pretty much whatever you want with that server, right from this console. It is important to note, however, that PowerShell in a Nano Server is not as fully comprehensive as on a regular version of Windows Server. Some commands and cmdlets will work, and some will not. If you want to see a list of the PowerShell cmdlets that are included with Nano Server, simply run the following command to display that list:

```
Get-Command -CommandType cmdlet
```

Windows Remote Management

If you need to run WinRM applications remotely onto a Nano Server, you're in luck. This too is possible. In order to use WinRM, a few simple commands are necessary on the Nano Server in order to get you started:

```
winrm quickconfig
winrm set winrm/config/client@{TrustedHosts="*"}
chcp 65001
```

That should be it! You should now be able to run WinRM commands remotely on your Nano Server.

Other management tools

There are a few more management tools that are less commonly used, from what I have seen in the field, but it is still possible to use them in order to work with Nano Server. If you are used to working with **Windows Management Instrumentation** (**WMI**), Nano can be interfaced with that tool set. Additionally, if your organization is using **Virtual Machine Manager** (**VMM**) or **System Center Operations Manager** (**SCOM**), both of these interfaces have the capability to interact with Nano Server.

Brand new in the mix is the Server Management Tools (SMT) that we mentioned earlier in the book. This is part of your Azure subscription, but one without cost, thankfully. If you choose to utilize SMT, you will be able to manage and manipulate many aspects of your Nano Servers right from your Azure login!

Summary

I have to be honest with you, writing this chapter has been exactly the kick in the pants that I needed to start thinking about shrinking my own servers. I am in the same boat as many of you. I know what Server Core is and have played around with it, but have never taken the steps to really use it in the production environment that I support. The new Nano Server will absolutely start to find a place in this environment, but might take a little bit longer to really become mainstream because of its limited capabilities at the present time. Rehashing all of the advantages that Server Core itself has, really changed my perspective, and made me a believer about it making sense to be the default option when installing new servers. The core and essential baseline to making either Server Core or Nano Server work in your environments is a good, thorough understanding of the PowerShell interface. So make sure that you take some time to familiarize yourself with all of the possibilities in that tool.

The largest real-world benefit that I see companies gaining out of using Nano Server is as a compute host for their virtualization infrastructure. Rather than installing the Hyper-V role onto a traditional Windows Server, why not make that Hyper-V host much more secure and cause it to reboot far less often by putting Hyper-V on a Nano Server instead? You can continue to utilize any storage you desire for keeping the VM data, that doesn't have to be managed by the Nano Server, and you can continue to use good old Hyper-V Manager for all of your Hyper-V tasks. The difference is that you will now run Hyper-V Manager from a different server, or even right from your desktop computer by using RSAT. There is absolutely no reason that every new Hyper-V server being built on Windows Server 2016 couldn't be installed onto Nano Server!

9
Redundancy in Windows Server 2016

"Multiply that by two." This is a phrase I hear all the time when planning rollouts for work. I'm sure you have done it as well. Anytime you are rolling out a new technology, you want to plan that rollout very carefully. Figure out what servers you need, where they need to be placed, and how the networking needs to be configured for those guys. And then once the planning is all said and done—oh yeah, I want two of everything, in case one breaks. We live in a world of always-on technology. Services going down is unacceptable, particularly if we are hosting cloud or private cloud services. Really, any application or service that our users depend on to get their work done is mission critical, and needs 100% uptime, or darn close to it. The problem with redundancy is that it's much easier to talk-the-talk than to walk-the-walk. Maybe someday we will be blessed with a magic "Press here to make this server redundant" button—but that day is not today. We need to understand the technologies that are available to us that enable us to provide redundancy on our systems. This chapter will introduce us to some of those technologies. Since cloud adoption is not mainstream as of yet, we are setting that idea aside for the purposes of this section of text. The technologies we will discuss today are the ones that you can utilize in your own local datacenters, on the real (physical or virtual) servers that you are responsible for building, configuring, and maintaining yourself. Yes, the cloud can provide us with some magical scalability and redundancy options, but those are easy, and we don't even need to know how they work. When we are using our own servers within our own walls, how can we add some increased reliability to our systems? The following are the topics we will cover in this chapter:

- Network Load Balancing
- Configuring a load balanced website
- Failover clustering
- Clustering tiers

- Setting up a failover cluster
- Clustering improvements in Windows Server 2016

Network Load Balancing

Many times when I hear people discussing redundancy on their servers, the conversation includes many instances of the word "cluster". Such as "If we set up a **cluster** to provide redundancy for those servers…" or "Our main website is running on a **cluster**…" While it is great that there is some form of resiliency being used on the systems for which these conversations pertain, it is often the case that *clustering* is not actually involved anywhere. When we boil down into the particulars of how their systems are configured, we discover that it is **Network Load Balancing** (**NLB**) doing this work for them. We will discuss real clustering further along in this chapter, but first I wanted to start with the more common approach to making many services redundant. NLB distributes traffic at the TCP/IP level, meaning that the server operating systems themselves are not completely aware of or relying on each other, but the redundancy is being provided at the network layer itself. This can be particularly confusing, NLB versus clustering, because sometimes Microsoft themselves even refer to something as a **cluster**, when in fact it is using NLB to make those connections happen. A prime example is DirectAccess. When you have two or more DA servers together in an array, there are TechNet documents and even places inside the console itself where it is referred to as a cluster. But there is no actual failover clustering going on here, the technology under the hood that is making connections flow to both nodes is actually Windows Network Load Balancing.

You've probably heard some of the names in the hardware load balancer market—F5, Cisco, Kemp, Barracuda. These are dedicated boxes that can take traffic headed toward a particular name or destination, and split that traffic up smartly between two or more application servers. While this is generally the most robust way that you can establish NLB, it is also the most expensive and makes the overall environment more complex. One feature these guys offer that the built-in Windows Network Load Balancing cannot provide is SSL termination, or SSL offloading as we often call it. These specialized appliances are capable of receiving website traffic from user computers that is SSL, and decrypting the packets before sending them on their way to the appropriate webserver. This way the webserver itself is doing less work, since it doesn't have to spend CPU cycles encrypting and decrypting packets. However, today we are not going to talk about hardware load balancers at all, but rather the same NLB capabilities that are provided right inside Windows Server 2016 itself.

Not the same as round-robin DNS

I have discovered over the years that some people's idea of Network Load Balancing is really round-robin DNS. Let me give an example of that. Say you have an intranet website running which all of your users access daily. It makes sense that you would want to provide some redundancy to this system, and so you set up two web servers, in case one goes down. However, in the case that one does go down, you don't want to require manual cutover steps to fail over to the extra server, you want it to happen automatically. In DNS, it is possible to create two Host (A) records that have the same name, but point to different IP addresses. If Server01 is running on 10.0.0.5 and Server02 is running on 10.0.0.6, you could create two DNS records both called "INTRANET", pointing one host record at 10.0.0.5, and the other host record at 10.0.0.6. This would provide round-robin DNS, but not any real-load balancing. Essentially, what happens here is that when the client computers reach out to INTRANET, DNS will hand them one or the other IP address to connect. DNS doesn't care whether or not that website is actually running, it simply responds with an IP address. So even though you might set this up and it appears to be working flawlessly because you can see that clients are connecting to both Server01 and Server02, be forewarned. In the event of a server failure, you will have many clients who still work, and many clients who are suddenly getting **Page cannot be displayed** when DNS decides to send them to the IP address of the server that is now offline.

Network Load Balancing is much more intelligent than this. When a node in an NLB array goes down, traffic moving to the shared IP address will only be directed to the node that is still online. We'll get to see this for ourselves shortly, when we set up NLB on an intranet website of our own.

What roles can use NLB?

Network Load Balancing is primarily designed for "stateless" applications, in other words, applications that do not require a long-term memory state or connection status. In a stateless application, each request made from the application could be picked up by Server01 for a while, then swing over to Server02 without interrupting the application. Some applications handle this very well (such as websites), and some do not.

Web Services (IIS) definitely benefits the most from the redundancy provided by Network Load Balancing. NLB is pretty easy to configure, and provides full redundancy for websites that you have running on your Windows Servers, without incurring any additional cost.

Another role that commonly interacts with NLB is the remote access role. Specifically, DirectAccess can use the Windows in-built Network Load Balancing to provide your remote access environment redundant entry point servers. When setting up DirectAccess to make use of load balancing, it is not immediately obvious that you are using the NLB feature built into the operating system because you configure the load balancing settings from inside the Remote Access Management Console, rather than the NLB console. When you walk through the Remote Access Management wizards in order to establish load balancing, that Remote Access console is actually reaching out into the NLB mechanism within the operating system and configuring it, so that its algorithms and transport mechanisms are the pieces being used by DirectAccess in order to split traffic between multiple servers.

One of the best parts about using NLB is that you can make changes to the environment without affecting the existing nodes. Want to add a new server into an existing NLB array, no problem. Slide it in without any downtime. Need to remove a server for maintenance? No issues here either. NLB can be stopped on a particular node, in fact, it is actually NIC-particular, so you can run different NLB modes on different NICs in a particular server. You can tell NLB to stop on a particular NIC, removing that server from the array for the time being. Even better, if you have a little bit of time before you need to take the server offline, you can issue a **drain-stop** command instead of an immediate stop. This allows the existing network sessions that are currently live on that server to finish cleanly. No new sessions will flow to the NIC that you have drain-stopped, and old sessions will evaporate over time. Once all sessions have been dropped from that server, you can then yank it and bring it down for maintenance.

Virtual and dedicated IP addresses

The way that Network Load Balancing uses IP addresses is an important concept to understand. A static IP address on an NIC is referred to as a **Dedicated IP Address** (**DIP**). These DIPs are unique per NIC, obviously meaning that each server has its own DIP. For example, in my environment WEB1 is running a DIP address of 10.0.0.40, and my WEB2 server is running a DIP of 10.0.0.41.

Each server is hosting the same website, on their respective DIP addresses currently. What is important to understand is that when establishing NLB between these two servers, I need to retain the individual DIPs on the boxes, but I will also be creating a brand new IP address that will be shared between the two servers. This IP is called the **Virtual IP Address** (**VIP**). When we walk through the NLB set up shortly, I will be using the IP address of 10.0.0.42 as my VIP, which is so far unused in my network.

Here is a quick layout of the IP addresses that are going to be used when setting up my network load balanced website:

```
WEB1 DIP = 10.0.0.40
WEB2 DIP = 10.0.0.41
Shared VIP = 10.0.0.42
```

When establishing my DNS record for `intranet.contoso.local`, which is the name of my website, I will be creating just a single Host (A) record, and it will point at my 10.0.0.42 VIP.

NLB modes

Shortly, we will find ourselves into the actual configuration of our load balancing, and will have a few decisions to make inside that interface. One of the big decisions is what NLB mode we want to use. Unicast is chosen by default, and is the way that I see most companies set up their NLB—maybe just because it is the default and they've never thought about changing it. Let's take just a minute and discuss each of the available options here, to make sure you can choose the one that is most appropriate for your networking needs.

Unicast

Here we start to get into the heart of how NLB distributes packets among the different hosts. Since we don't have a physical load balancer that is receiving the traffic first and then deciding where to send it, how do the load balanced servers decide who gets to take which packet streams?

To answer that question, we need to back up a little bit and discuss how traffic really flows around inside your network. When you open up a web browser on your computer and visit `HTTP://WEB1`, DNS resolves that IP address to 10.0.0.40, for example. When the traffic hits your switches and needs to be directed somewhere, the switches need to decide where the 10.0.0.40 traffic needs to go. You might be familiar with the idea of MAC addresses. Each NIC has a MAC address, and when you assign an IP address to a NIC, it registers its own MAC address and IP with the networking equipment. These MAC addresses are stored inside an ARP table, which is a table that resides inside most switches, routers, and firewalls. When my WEB1 server was assigned the 10.0.0.40 IP address, it registered its MAC address corresponding to 10.0.0.40. When traffic needs to flow to WEB1, the switches realize that traffic destined for 10.0.0.40 needs to go to that NIC's particular MAC address, and shoots it off accordingly.

So in the NLB world, when you are sending traffic to a single IP address that is split between multiple NICs, how does that get processed at the MAC level? The answer with unicast NLB is that the physical NIC's MAC addresses get replaced with a *virtual MAC address*, and this MAC is assigned to all of the NICs within the NLB array. This causes packets flowing to that MAC address to be delivered to all of the NICs, therefore all of the servers, in that array. If you think that sounds like a lot of unnecessary network traffic is moving around the switches, you would be correct.

The best part about unicast is that it works without having to make any special configurations on the switches or networking equipment in most cases. You set up the NLB config, and it handles the rest. The downsides to unicast are that, because the same MAC address exists on all the nodes, it does cause some intranode communication problems. In other words, the servers that are enabled for NLB will have trouble communicating with each other's IP addresses. If you really need those web servers to be able to talk with each other consistently and reliably, the easiest solution is to install a separate NIC on each of those servers, and use that NIC for those intra-array communications, while leaving the primary NICs configured for NLB traffic.

The other downside to unicast is that it can create some uncontrollable switch flooding. The switches are unable to learn a permanent route for the virtual MAC address, because we need it to be delivered to all of the nodes in our array. Since every packet moving to the virtual MAC is being sent down all avenues of a switch so that it can hit all of the NICs where it needs to be delivered, it has the potential to overwhelm the switches. If you are concerned about that or are having complaints from your networking guys about switch flooding, you might want to check out one of the multicast modes for your NLB cluster.

Multicast

Choosing multicast as your NLB mode comes with some upsides, and some headaches. The positive is that it adds an extra MAC address to each NIC. Every NLB member then has two MAC addresses, the original and the one created by the NLB mechanism. This gives the switches and networking equipment an easier job with learning the routes and sending traffic to its correct destinations, without an overwhelming packet flood. In order to do this, you need to tell the switches which MAC addresses need to receive this NLB traffic, otherwise you will cause switch flooding just like with unicast. Telling the switches which MACs need to be contacted is done by logging into your switches and creating some static ARP entries to accommodate this. For any company with a dedicated networking guy, usually proficient in Cisco equipment, this will be no sweat.

If you are not familiar with modifying ARP tables and adding static routes, it can be a bit of a nuisance to get it right. In the end, multicast is generally better than unicast, but it can be more of an administrative headache. My personal preference still tends to be unicast, especially in the smaller businesses. I have seen it used in many different networks without any issues, and going with unicast means we can leave the switch programming alone.

Multicast IGMP

Better yet, but not always an option, is **Multicast with Internet Group Membership Protocol (IGMP)**. Multicast IGMP really helps to mitigate switch flooding, but it only works if your switches support HGMP snooping. This means that the switch has the capability to look inside multicast packets in order to determine where exactly they should go. So where unicast creates some amount of switch flooding by design, multicast can help to lower that amount, and IGMP can bake that down even smaller.

The NLB mode that you choose will depend quite a bit upon the capabilities of your networking equipment. If your servers have only a single NIC, try to use multicast or you will have intra-array problems. On the other hand, if your switches and routers don't support multicast, you don't have a choice—unicast will be your only option for configuring Windows Network Load Balancing.

Configuring a load balanced website

Enough talk, it's time to set this up for ourselves and give it a try. I have two web servers running on my lab network, WEB1 and WEB2. They both use IIS to host an intranet website. My goal is to provide my users with a single DNS record for them to communicate with, but have all of that traffic be split between the two servers with some real load balancing. Follow along for the steps on making this possible.

Enabling NLB

First things first, we need to make sure that WEB1 and WEB2 are prepared to do Network Load Balancing, because it is not installed by default. NLB is a feature available in Windows Server 2016, and you add it just like any other role or feature, by running through the **Add roles and features** wizard. Add this feature on all of the servers that you want to be part of the NLB array.

Enabling MAC address spoofing on VMs

Remember when we talked about unicast NLB and how the physical MAC address of the NIC gets replaced with a virtual MAC address that is used for NLB array communications? Yeah, virtual machines don't like that. If you are load balancing physical servers with physical NICs, you can skip over this section. But many of you will be running web servers that are VMs. Whether they are hosted with Hyper-V, VMware, or some other virtualization technology, there is an extra option in the configuration of the virtual machine itself that you will have to make, so that your VM will happily comply with this MAC addressing change.

The name of this setting will be something along the lines of *Enable MAC Address Spoofing*, though the specific name of the function could be different depending on what virtualization technology you use. The setting should be a simple checkbox that you have to enable in order to make MAC spoofing work properly. Make sure to do this for all of your virtual machines on which you will install NLB.

The VM needs to be shut down in order to make this change, so I have now shut down my WEB1 and WEB2 servers. Now find the checkbox and enable it. Since everything that I use is based on Microsoft technology, I am of course using Hyper-V as the platform for my virtual machines here in the lab. Within Hyper-V, if I right-click on my WEB1 server and head into the VM's settings, I can then click on my network adapter to see the various pieces that are changeable on WEB1's virtual NIC. And there it is, my **Enable spoofing of MAC addresses** checkbox. Simply click on that to enable, and you're all set.

If **Enable spoofing of MAC addresses** is grayed out, remember that the virtual machine must be completely shut down before the option appears. Shut it down, then open up the **Settings** and take another look. The option should now be available to choose.

Configuring NLB

Let's summarize where we are at this point. I have two web servers, WEB1 and WEB2, and they each currently have a single IP address. Each server has IIS installed which is hosting a single website. I have enabled MAC address spoofing on each, and I just finished installing the Network Load Balancing feature onto each web server. We now have all of the parts and pieces in place to be able to configure NLB and get that web traffic split between both servers.

Redundancy in Windows Server 2016

I will be working from WEB1 for the actual configuration of Network Load Balancing. Log in to this, and you will now notice that we have a new tool in the list of **Tools** that are available inside Server Manager, called **Network Load Balancing Manager**. Go ahead and open up that console. Once you have the NLB Manager open, right-click on **Network Load Balancing Clusters**, and choose **New Cluster**:

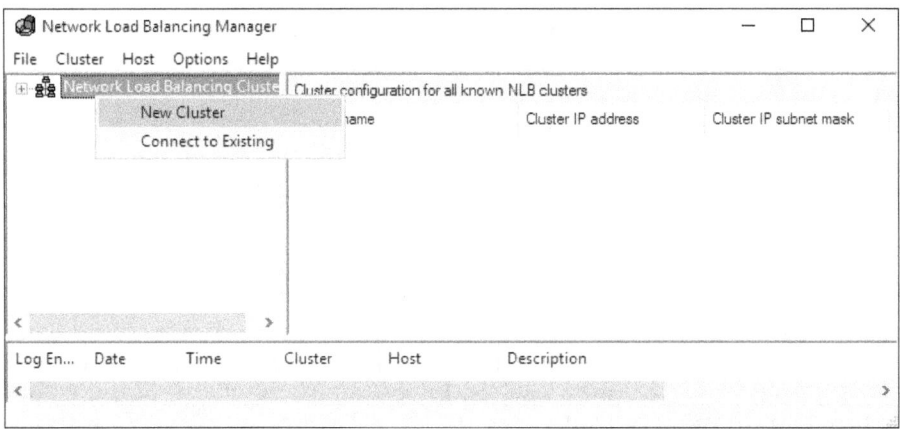

When you create a new cluster, it is important to note that currently there are zero machines in this cluster. Even the server where we are running this console is not automatically added to the cluster, and we must remember to manually place it into this screen. So first I am going to type in the name of my WEB1 server and click on **Connect**. After doing that, the NLB Manager will query WEB1 for NICs and will give me a list of available NICs upon which I could potentially set up NLB:

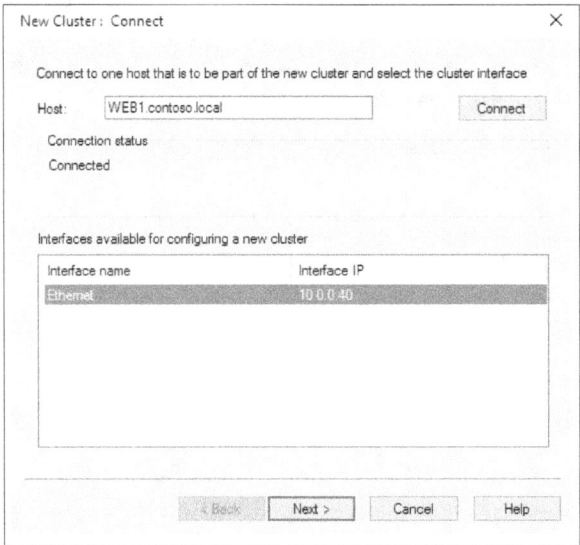

Chapter 9

Since I only have one NIC on this server, I simply leave it selected and click on **Next**. The following screen gives you the opportunity to input additional IP addresses on WEB1, but since we are only running one IP address I will leave this screen as is, and click on **Next** again.

Now we have moved on to a window asking us to input Cluster IP addresses. These are the Virtual IP Addresses (VIPs) that we intend to use to communicate with this NLB cluster. As stated earlier, my VIP for this website is going to be 10.0.0.42, so I click on the **Add...** button and input that IPv4 address along with its corresponding subnet mask:

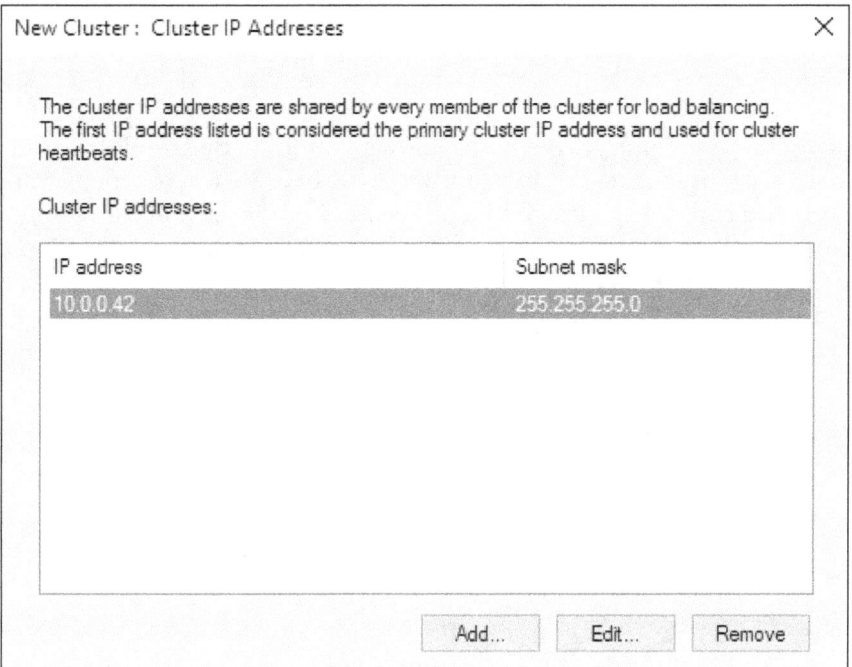

One more click of the **Next** button, and we can now see our option for which **Cluster operation mode** we want to run. Depending on your network configuration, choose accordingly between **Unicast**, **Multicast**, and **IGMP multicast**:

The following screen of our NLB wizard allows you to configure **Port Rules**. By default, there is a single rule that tells NLB to load balance any traffic coming in on any port, but you can change this if you so desire. I don't see a lot of people in the field specifying rules here to distribute specific ports to specific destinations, but one neat feature in this screen is the ability to disable certain ranges of ports. That piece could be very useful if you want to block unnecessary traffic at the NLB layer.

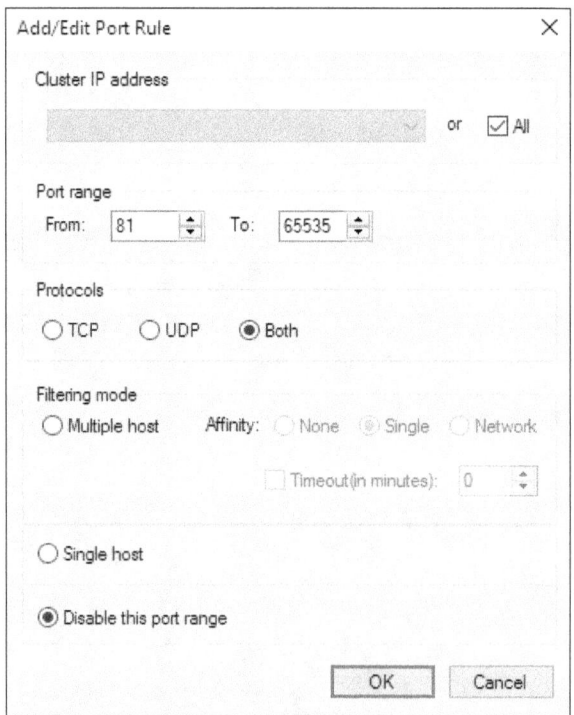

Chapter 9

Finish up that wizard, and you have now created an NLB cluster! However, at this point in time we have only specified information about the VIP, and about the WEB1 server. We have not established anything at all about WEB2. Go ahead and right-click on the new cluster, and select **Add Host To Cluster**:

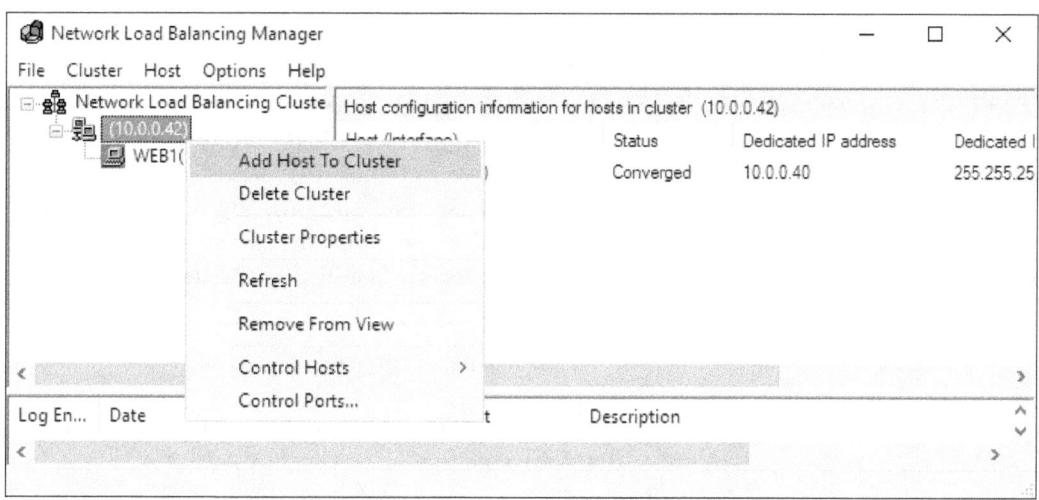

Input the name of our WEB2 server, click on **Connect**, and walk through the wizard in order to add the secondary NLB node of WEB2 into the cluster. Once both nodes are added to the cluster, our Network Load Balancing array, or cluster, is online and ready to use. If you take a look inside the NIC properties of our web servers, and click on the **Advanced** button inside TCP/IPv4 properties, you can see that our new cluster IP address of 10.0.0.42 has been added to the NICs:

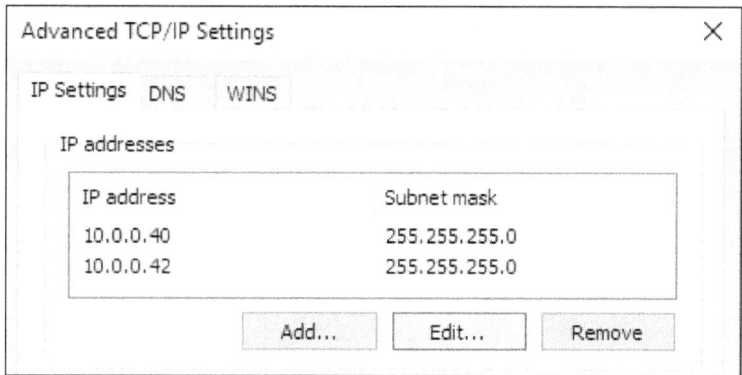

[279]

The traffic that is destined for the 10.0.0.42 IP address is now starting to be split between the two nodes, but right now the websites that are running on the WEB1 and WEB2 servers are configured to only be running on the dedicated 10.0.0.40 and 10.0.0.41 IP addresses, so we need to make sure and adjust that next.

Configuring IIS and DNS

Just a quick step within IIS on each of our web servers should get the website responding on the appropriate IP address. Now that the NLB configuration has been established and we confirmed that the new 10.0.0.42 VIP address has been added to the NICs, we can use that IP address as a website binding. Open up the IIS management console, and expand the **Sites** folder so that you can see the properties of your website. Right-click on the site name, and choose **Edit Bindings...**.

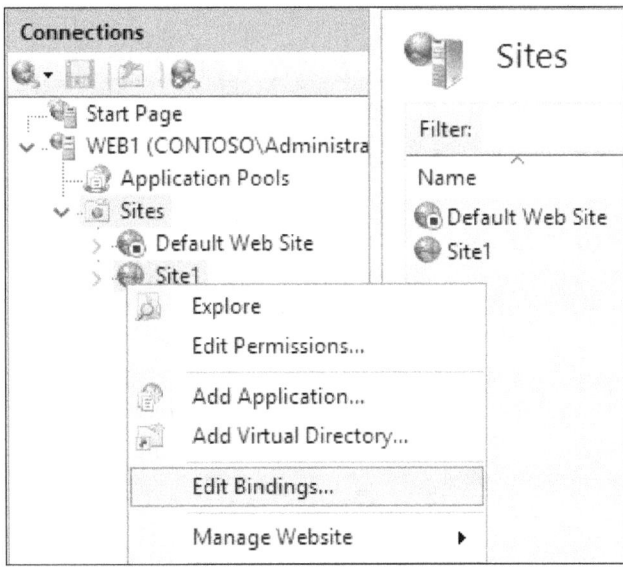

Chapter 9

Once inside **Site Bindings**, choose the binding that you want to manipulate, and click on the **Edit…** button. This intranet website is just a simple HTTP site, so I am going to choose my HTTP binding for this change. The binding is currently set to 10.0.0.40 on WEB1, and 10.0.0.41 on WEB2. This means that the website is only responding to traffic that comes in on these IP addresses. All I have to do is change that **IP address** dropdown to the new VIP, which is `10.0.0.42`. After making this change and clicking on **OK**, the website is immediately responding to traffic coming in from the 10.0.0.42 IP address.

Now we come to the last piece of the puzzle—DNS. Remember, we want the users to have the ability to simply enter `http://intranet` into their web browsers in order to browse this new NLB website, so we need to configure a DNS Host (A) record accordingly. That process is exactly the same as any other DNS Host record, simply create one and point `intranet.contoso.local` to `10.0.0.42`:

Test it out

NLB configured?—Check.

IIS bindings changed over?—Check.

DNS record created?—Check.

We are ready to test this thing out. If I open up an Internet browser on a client computer and browse to `http://intranet`, I can see the website!

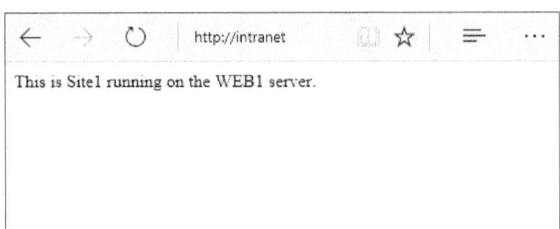

But how can we determine that load balancing is really working? If I continue refreshing the page, or browse from another client, I continue accessing `http://intranet`, and eventually the NLB mechanism will decide that a new request should be sent over to WEB2, instead of WEB1. When this happens, I am then presented with this page instead:

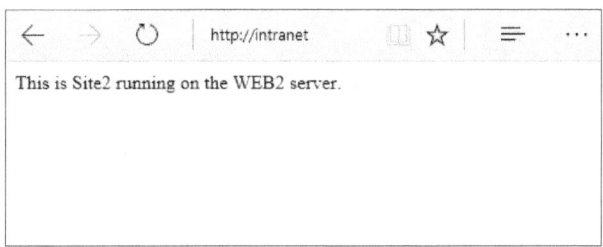

As you can see, I modified the content between WEB1 and WEB2 so that I could distinguish between the different nodes, just for the purposes of this test. If this were a real production intranet website, I would want to make sure that the content of both sites was exactly the same, so that users were completely unaware of the NLB even happening—all they need to know is that the website is going to be available and working, all of the time.

Flushing the ARP cache

Earlier we had a little discussion about how switches keep a cache of ARP information, which lessens the time those switches need to take when deciding where packets should flow. When you assign an NIC an IP address, the MAC address of that NIC gets associated with the IP address inside the ARP table of certain pieces of networking equipment. Switches, routers, firewalls—these tools commonly have what we refer to as an ARP table, and therefore they have a set of data in that table that is known as ARP cache.

When configuring NLB, particularly unicast, the NIC's MAC address gets replaced with a new, virtual MAC address. Sometimes the switches and networking equipment are very quick to catch on to this change, and they associate the new MAC address with the new IP address, and everything works just fine. However, I find that when configuring NLB the following is generally true: *The smarter and more expensive your networking equipment is, the dumber it gets when configuring NLB*. What I mean by that is, your networking equipment might continue to hold on to the old MAC address information that is stored in its ARP table, and doesn't get updated to reflect the new MAC addressing.

What does this look like in real life? Network traffic will stop flowing to or from those NICs. Sometimes when you establish NLB and it turns itself on, all network traffic will suddenly stop cold to or from those network interfaces. What do you need to do to fix this situation? Sometimes you can wait it out, within a few minutes, hours, or sometimes a few days the switches will drop the old ARP info and allow the new MACs to register themselves in there. What can you do to speed up this process? **Flush the ARP cache**.

The procedure for doing this will be different depending on what kind of networking equipment you are working on—whether it is a switch or router, what brand it is, what model it is, and so on. But each of these guys should have this capability, and it should be named something along the lines of *flushing the ARP cache*. When you run this function on your equipment, it cleans out that ARP table, getting rid of the old information that is causing you problems and allowing the new MAC addresses to register themselves appropriately into the fresh table.

I only wanted to point this out in the event that you configure NLB, only to see traffic flow cease on your server. More than likely you are dealing with ARP cache being stuck on one or more pieces of network equipment that is trying to shuttle the traffic to and from your server.

Failover clustering

We have established that Network Load Balancing is a great solution for stateless applications, with a prime example being websites that you want to make highly available. What about other server roles or functions that you want to make redundant? Well, the opposite of stateless is stateful, so how about giving high availability to stateful pieces of technology? **Failover clustering** provides this level of capability, and can be used in cases where the nodes within the cluster are accessing shared data. This is a key factor to the way failover clustering is designed, the storage used by the cluster nodes must be shared and accessible by each node that needs it.

There are many different roles and services that can take advantage of failover clustering, but there are a solid four specific technologies that seem to make up the majority of clusters running in datacenters today—Hyper-V, file services, Exchange, and SQL. If you are working with any of these technologies, and chances are that you work with all of them, you need to look into the high availability capabilities that can be provided for your infrastructure by use of failover clustering.

While failover clustering provided by Windows Server is Microsoft built and has the capacity to work very well out of the box with many Microsoft roles and services, it is important to note that you can establish failover clustering for non-Microsoft applications as well. Third-party applications that run on Windows Servers in your environment, or even home-grown applications that have been built in-house can also take advantage of failover clustering. As long as that application uses shared storage and you can specify the tasks that it needs to be able to perform against those applications for the clustering administration tools—how to start the service, how to stop the service, how to monitor the service health, and so on—you can interface these custom services and applications with failover clustering and provide some major redundancy for just about any type of application.

Clustering Hyper-V hosts

One of the most powerful examples of failover clustering is displayed when combining clustering with Hyper-V. It is possible to build out two or more Hyper-V servers, cluster them together, and give them the capability to each host all of the virtual machines that are stored in that virtual environment. By giving all of the Hyper-V host servers access to the same shared storage where the virtual hard disks are stored, and configuring failover clustering between the nodes, you can create an incredibly powerful and redundant virtualization solution for your company. When a Hyper-V server goes down, the VMs that were running on that Hyper-V host will fail over to another Hyper-V host server and spin themselves up there instead. After minimal service interruption while the VMs spin up, everything is back online automatically, without any administrative input. Even better, how about when you need to patch or otherwise take a Hyper-V host server offline for maintenance? You can easily force the VMs to run on a different member server in the cluster, they are live migrated over to that server so there is zero downtime, and then you are free to remove the node for maintenance and finish working on it at leisure before reintroducing it to the cluster. We use virtual machines and servers for all kinds of workloads, wouldn't it be great if you could rid yourself of any single points of failure within that virtualization environment? That is exactly what failover clustering can provide.

Scale-Out File Server

Clustering for file servers has been available for quite a while, but was originally only useful for document and traditional file utilization, in other words, information that remained static and unchanged for much of its life. With the onset of virtual machines, and now that we can make use of clustering to enhance our Hyper-V infrastructure, what is the best way to store those shared virtual hard disk files? It makes sense that you could also take advantage of failover clustering on your file servers in order to enable this highly available, shared network storage that all of the Hyper-V hosts could access, and you would be right.

While the original version of file server failover clustering was not comprehensive enough to handle files that were continuously open or being changed, like virtual hard disk files, **Scale-Out File Server (SOFS)** is designed to do exactly that. If you plan to host virtual machines using Hyper-V, you will definitely want to check out the failover clustering capabilities that are available to use with Hyper-V services. Furthermore, if you intend to use clustered Hyper-V hosts, then you will definitely want to check out Scale-Out File Server as an infrastructure technology to support that highly available Hyper-V environment. Scale-Out File Server helps support failover clustering by providing file servers with the capability to have multiple nodes online that remain persistent between each other constantly—this way if one storage server goes down, the others are immediately available to pick up the slack, without a cutover process that involves downtime. This is important when looking at the difference between storing static data such as documents, and storing virtual hard disk files being accessed by VMs. The VMs are able to stay online during a file server outage with Scale-Out File Server, which is pretty incredible!

Make sure to check out the end of this chapter where we discuss some of the brand new capabilities in Windows Server 2016 that are related to the idea of Software-Defined Storage. As Server 2016 starts rolling around datacenters, I expect that we will start to hear more and more about a couple of new items called **Storage Spaces Direct** and **Storage Replica**. More details coming in just a few pages!

Clustering tiers

An overhead concept to failover clustering that is important to understand is the different tiers at which clustering can benefit you. There are two different levels upon which you can use clustering. You can take an either/or approach and use just one of these levels of failover clustering, or you can combine both to really impress your HA friends.

Application layer clustering

Clustering at the application level typically involves installing failover clustering onto virtual machines. Using VMs is not a hard requirement, but is the most common installation path. You can mix and match virtual machines with physical servers in a clustering environment, as long as each server meets the installation criteria. This application mode of clustering is useful when you have a particular service or role running within the operating system that you want to make redundant. Think of this as more of a microclustering capability, where you are really digging in and making one specific component of the operating system redundant with another server node that is capable of picking up the slack in the event that your primary server goes down.

Host layer clustering

If application clustering is micro, then clustering at the host layer is more macro. The best example I can give of this is the one that gets most admins started with failover clustering in the first place, Hyper-V. Let's say you have two physical servers that are both hosting virtual machines in your environment. You want to cluster these servers together, so that all of the VMs being hosted upon these Hyper-V servers are able to be redundant between the two physical servers. If a whole Hyper-V server goes down, the second one is able to spin up the VMs that had been running on the primary node, and after a minimal interruption of service, your VMs which are hosting the actual services are back up and running, available for users and their applications to tap into.

A combination of both

These two modes of using failover clustering mentioned earlier can certainly be combined together for an even better and more comprehensive high availability story. Let's let this example speak for itself. You have two Hyper-V servers, each one prepared to run a series of virtual machines. You are using host clustering between these servers, so if one physical box goes down, the other picks up the slack. That in itself is great, but you use SQL a lot, and you want to make sure that SQL itself is also highly available. You can run two virtual machines, each one a SQL server, and configure application layer failover clustering between those two VMs for the SQL services specifically. This way if something happens to a single virtual machine, you don't have to failover to the backup Hyper-V server, rather your issue can be resolved by the second SQL node itself taking over. There was no need for a full-scale Hyper-V takeover by the second physical server, yet you utilized failover clustering in order to make sure that SQL was always online. This is a prime example of clustering on top of clustering, and in thinking along those lines you can start to get pretty creative with all of the different ways that you can make use of clustering in your network.

How does failover work?

Once you have configured failover clustering, the multiple nodes remain in constant communication with each other. This way when one goes down, they are immediately aware and can flip services over to another node to bring them back online. Failover clustering uses the registry to keep track of many per node settings. These identifiers are kept synced across the nodes, and then when one goes down, those necessary settings are blasted around to the other servers and the next node in the cluster is told to spin up whatever applications, VMs, or workloads were being hosted on the primary box that went offline. There can be a slight delay in services as the components spin up on the new node, but this process is all automated and hands-off, keeping downtime to an absolute minimum.

When you need to cut services from one node to another as a planned event, such as for patching or maintenance, there is an even better story here. Through a process known as **Live Migration**, you are able to flip responsibilities over to a secondary node with zero downtime. This way you can take nodes out of the cluster for maintenance or security patching or whatever reason, without affecting the users or system uptime in any way. Live Migration is particularly useful for Hyper-V clusters, where you will often have the need to manually decide which node your VMs are being hosted on, in order to accomplish work on the other node or nodes.

Setting up a failover cluster

We are going to take a few minutes and set up a small cluster of servers, so that you can see the management tools and the places that have to be touched in order to accomplish this. I have now backed out all of the NLB config on my WEB1 and WEB2 servers that we set up earlier, so that they are just simple web servers at the moment, once again with no redundancy between them. Let's set up our first failover cluster and add both of these servers into that cluster.

Building the servers

We have two servers already running with Windows Server 2016 installed. Nothing special has been configured on these servers, but I have added the **File and Storage Services** role to both of them, because eventually down the road I intend to utilize these as a cluster of file servers. The key point here is that you should have the servers as nearly identical as possible, with the roles already installed that you intend to make use of within the cluster.

One other note during the building phase, if possible it is a general best practice with clustering for member servers belonging to the same cluster to reside within the same OU in Active Directory. The reason for this is twofold. First, it ensures that the same GPOs are being applied to the set of servers, in an effort to make their configurations as identical as possible. Second, during the cluster creation some new objects will be autogenerated and created in AD, and when the member servers reside in the same OU, these new objects will be created in that OU as well. It is very common with a running cluster to see all of the relevant objects in AD be part of the same OU, and for that OU to be dedicated to this cluster:

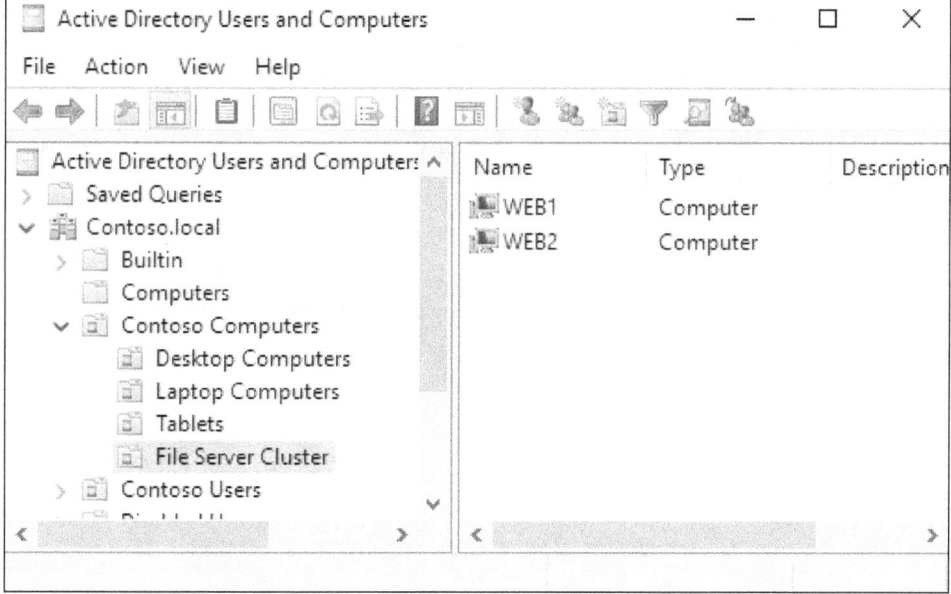

Installing the feature

Now that our servers are online and running, we want to go ahead and install the clustering capabilities on each of them. **Failover Clustering** is a feature inside Windows Server, so open up the **Add roles and features** wizard and add it to all of your cluster nodes:

Running the Failover Cluster Manager

As is the case with most roles or features that can be installed into Windows Server 2016, once implemented you will find a management console for it inside the **Tools** menu of Server Manager. Looking inside there on WEB1 now, I can see that a new listing for **Failover Cluster Manager** is available for me to click on. I am going to open that tool, and start working on the configuration of my first cluster from this management interface:

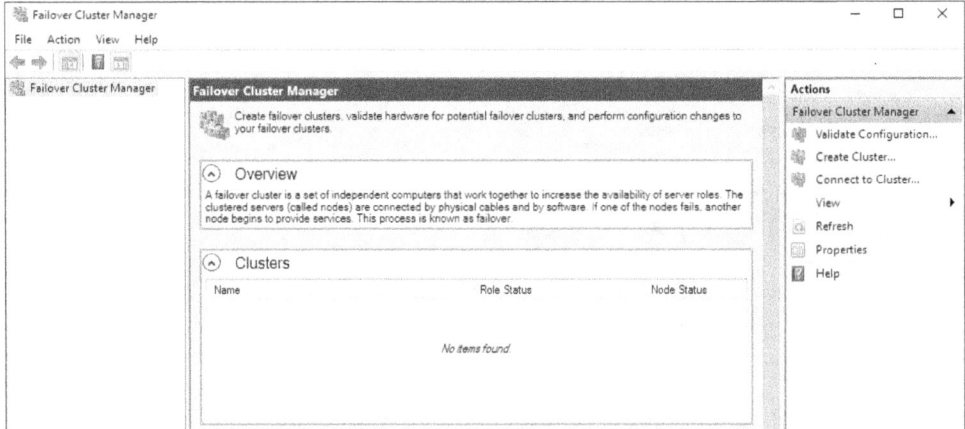

Running cluster validation

Now that we are inside the **Failover Cluster Manager**, you will notice a list of tasks available to launch under the **Management** section of the console, near the middle of your screen:

> **Management**
> To begin to use failover clustering, first validate your hardware configuration, and then create a cluster. After these steps are complete, you can manage the cluster. Managing a cluster can include copying roles to it from a cluster running Windows Server 2016
>
> Validate Configuration...
> Create Cluster...
> Connect to Cluster...

Before we can configure the cluster itself or add any server nodes to it, we must first validate our hardware configuration. Failover clustering is a pretty complex set of technology, and there are many places where misconfigurations or inconsistencies could set the whole cluster askew. Your intentions behind setting up a cluster are obviously for reliable redundancy, but even a simple mistake in the configuration of your member servers could cause problems large enough that a node failure would not result in automated recovery, which defeats the purpose of the cluster in the first place. In order to make sure that all of our "T's" are crossed and "I's" dotted, there are some very comprehensive validation checks built into the Failover Cluster Manager. Sort of like a built-in best practices analyzer. These checks can be run at any time, before the cluster is built or after it has been running in production for years. In fact, if you ever have to open a support case with Microsoft, it is likely that the first thing they will ask you to do is run the **Validate Configurations** tools and allow them to look over the output.

In order to start our validation process, go ahead and click on the link called **Validate Configuration...**. We are now launched into a wizard that allows us to select which pieces of the cluster technology we would like to validate. Once again we must put on our Microsoft "centralized management theology" thinking caps, and realize that this wizard doesn't know or care that it is running on one of the member servers which I intend to be part of the cluster.

Redundancy in Windows Server 2016

We must identify each of the server nodes that we want to scan for validation checks, so in my case I am going to tell it that I want to validate the WEB1 and WEB2 servers:

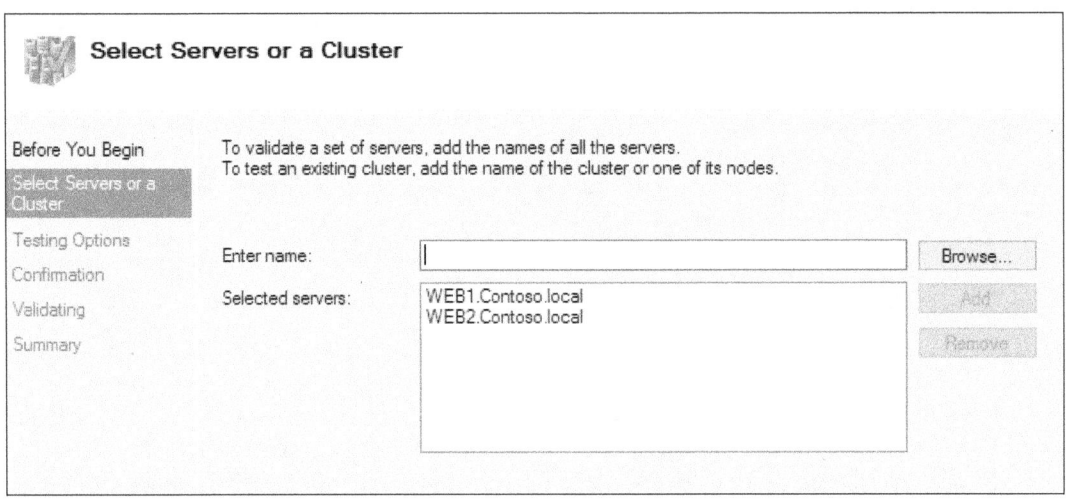

The **Testing Options** screen allows you to choose the **Run only tests I select** radio button and you will then be able to run only particular validation tests if you so choose. Generally when setting up a new cluster, you want to run all of the tests so that you can ensure everything measures up correctly. On a production system, however, you may choose to limit the number of tests that run. This is particularly so with respect to tests against **Storage**, as those can actually take the cluster offline temporarily while the tests are being run, and you wouldn't want to interfere with your online production services if you are not working within a planned maintenance window.

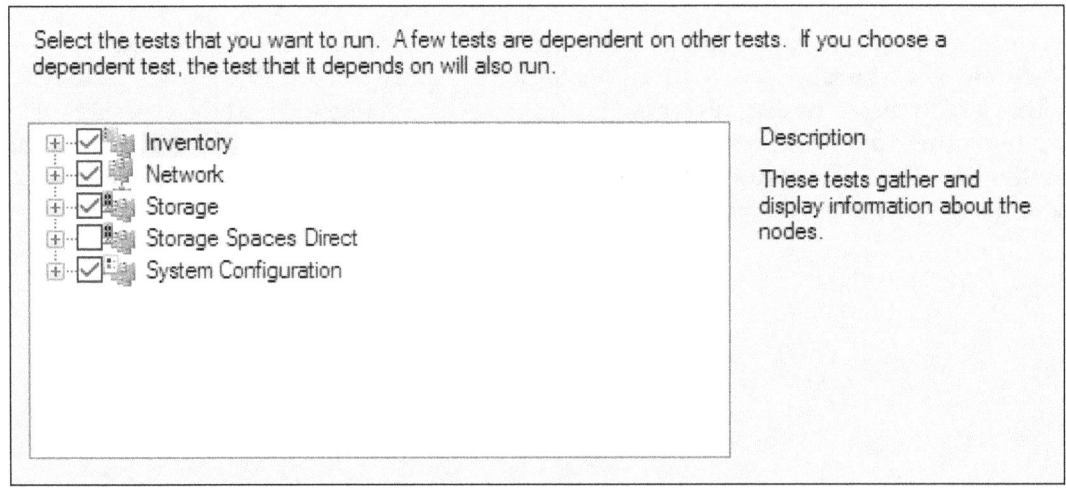

Since I am setting up a brand new cluster, I am going to let all of the tests run. So I will leave the recommended option selected for **Run all tests**, and continue.

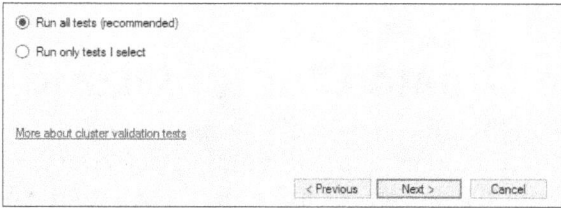

Once the tests have completed, you will see a summary output of their results. You can click on the **View Report...** button in order to see a lot of detail on everything that was run. Keep in mind that there are three tiers of pass/fail. Green is *good* and red is *bad*, but yellow is more like *it'll work but you're not running best practices*. For example, I only have one NIC in each of my servers, and the wizard recognizes that to be truly redundant in all aspects, I should have at least two. It'll let this slide and continue to work, but it is warning me that I could make it even better by adding a second NIC to each of my nodes.

By the way, if you happen to be logged in as the administrator like I am, you will be unable to open the validation report because the Edge browser isn't allowed to launch under the admin account. This is a great security check built into Windows Server 2016, and shame on me for doing anything inside the administrator account, but hey—this is a test lab. If you find yourself in a position where you cannot view the report for similar reasons, you can find that report stored inside `C:\Windows\Cluster\Reports`—copy it over to your local workstation, and open it up from there.

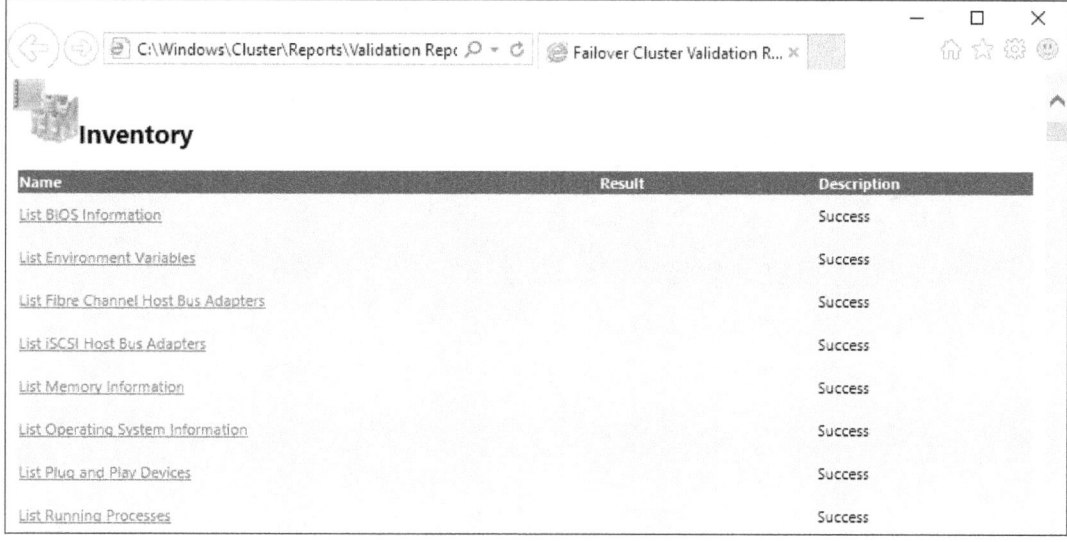

Remember, you can rerun the validation processes at any time to test your configuration using the **Validate Configuration...** task inside the Failover Cluster Manager.

Running the Create Cluster wizard

The validation phase might take a while, if you have multiple results that need fixing before you can proceed. But once your validation check comes back clean, you are finally ready to build out the cluster itself. For this, click on the next action that we have available in our Failover Cluster Manager console—**Create Cluster...**

Once again we must first specify which servers we want to be part of this new cluster, so I am going to again input my WEB1 and WEB2 servers. After this we don't have a whole lot of information to input about setting up the cluster, but one very key piece of information comes in the **Access Point for Administering the Cluster** screen. This is where you identify the unique name that will be used by the cluster, and shared among the member servers. This is known as a **Cluster Name Object (CNO)**, and after completing your cluster configuration you will see this name show up as an object inside Active Directory.

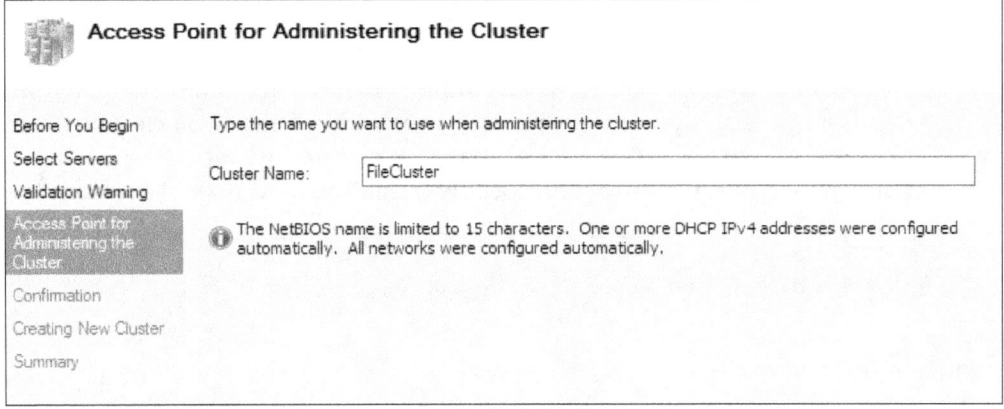

After finishing out the wizard, you can now see the new cluster inside the Failover Cluster Manager interface, and are able to drill down into more particular functions within that cluster. There are additional actions for things such as **Configure Role...** that will be important for setting up the actual function that this cluster is going to perform, and **Add Node...** which is your spot to include even more member servers into this cluster down the road.

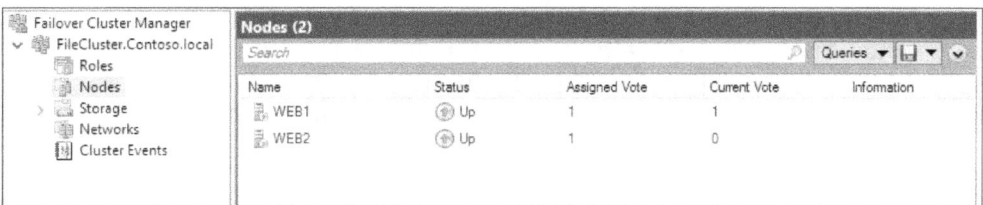

Clustering improvements in Windows Server 2016

Now that we understand what clustering is and have gotten our hands dirty by walking through the process of building our initial cluster, let's review some of the parts and pieces working with clustering that are brand new or improved in the Windows Server 2016 operating system.

Multi-Site clustering

Can I configure failover clustering across subnets? In other words, if I have a primary datacenter, and I also rent space from a CoLo down the road, or I have another datacenter across the country—are there options for me to set up clustering between nodes that are physically separate? There's a quick, easy answer here. Yes, failover clustering doesn't care! Just as easily as if those server nodes were sitting right next to each other, clustering can take advantage of multiple sites each hosting their own clustered nodes, and move services back and forth across these sites. Even better is that new in Windows Server 2016 is an organizational tool for managing multiple sites, giving you the ability to group cluster members together based on where they physically reside. This allows you to configure preferred sites, rather than allowing the clustering mechanism to decide for itself.

Cross-domain or workgroup clustering

Historically we have only been able to establish failover clustering between nodes that were joined to the same domain. Windows Server 2016 brings the ability to move outside of this limitation, and we can even build a cluster without Active Directory being in the mix whatsoever. In Server 2016 you can, of course, still create clusters where all nodes are joined to the same domain, and we expect this will still be true for the majority of installations out there. However, if you have servers that are joined to different domains, you can now establish clustering between those nodes. Furthermore, member servers in a cluster can now be members of a workgroup, and don't even need to be joined to a domain at all.

While this expands the available capabilities of failover clustering, it also comes with a couple of limitations. When using multidomain or workgroup clusters, you will be limited to only PowerShell as your cluster management interface. If you are used to interacting with your clusters from one of the GUI tools, you will need to adjust your thinking cap on this. You will also need to create a local user account that can be used by clustering and provision it to each of the cluster nodes, and this user account needs to have administrative rights on those servers.

Cluster Operating System Rolling Upgrade

This new capability given to us in 2016 has a bit of a strange name, but is a really cool feature. It's something designed to help those who have been using failover clustering for a while to be able to improve their environment. If you are running a cluster currently, and that cluster is Windows Server 2012 R2, this is definitely something to look into. **Cluster Operating System Rolling Upgrade** enables you to upgrade the operating systems of your cluster nodes from Server 2012 R2 up to Server 2016 **without downtime**. No need to stop any of the services on your Hyper-V or Scale-Out File Server workloads that are using clustering, you simply utilize this rolling upgrade process and in the end all of your cluster nodes are running the new Windows Server 2016, their cluster is still active, and nobody knows that it even happened. Except you, of course.

This is vastly different to the previous upgrade process, where in order to bring your cluster up to Server 2012 R2 it required taking the cluster offline, introducing new server nodes running 2012 R2, and then re-establishing the cluster. There was plenty of downtime, and plenty of headache in making sure that it all went as smoothly as possible.

The trick that makes this seamless upgrade possible is that the cluster itself remains running at the 2012 R2 functional level, until you issue a command to flip it over to the Server 2016 functional level. Until you issue that command, clustering runs on the older FL, even on the new nodes that you introduce which are running the Server 2016 operating system. As you upgrade your nodes one at a time, the other nodes that are still active in the cluster remain online and continue servicing the users and applications, so all systems are running like normal from a workload perspective. As you introduce new Server 2016 boxes into the cluster, they start servicing workloads like the 2012 R2 servers, but doing so at a 2012 R2 functional level. This is referred to as mixed mode. This enables you to take down even that very last 2012 R2 box, change it over to 2016, and reintroduce it, all without anybody knowing. Then once all of the OS upgrades are complete, issue the PowerShell command `Update-ClusterFunctionalLevel` to flip over the functional level, and you have a Windows Server 2016 cluster that has been seamlessly upgraded with zero downtime.

Virtual Machine Resiliency

As you can successfully imply from the name, **Virtual Machine Resiliency** is an improvement in clustering that specifically benefits Hyper-V server clusters. In the clustering days of Server 2012 R2, it wasn't uncommon to have some intra-array, or intracluster, communication problems. This sometimes represented itself in a transient failure, meaning that the cluster thought a node was going offline when it actually wasn't, and would set into motion a failover that sometimes caused more downtime than if the recognition patterns for a real failure would have simply been a little bit better. While for the most part clustering and failover of cluster nodes did work successfully, there is always room for improvement. That is what Virtual Machine Resiliency is all about. You can now configure options for resiliency, giving you the ability to more specifically define what behavior your nodes will take during cluster node failures. You can define things such as **Resiliency Level**, which tells the cluster how to handle failures. You also set your own **Resiliency Period**, the amount of time that VMs are allowed to run in an isolated state.

Another change is that unhealthy cluster nodes are now placed into a quarantine for an admin-defined amount of time. They are not allowed to join back into the cluster until they have been identified as healthy and have waited out their time period, preventing situations such as a node that was stuck in a reboot cycle from inadvertently joining back into the cluster and causing continuous problems as it cycles up and down.

Storage Replica

Storage Replica (SR) is a new way to synchronize data between servers. It is a data replication technology that provides the ability for block-level data replication between servers, even across different physical sites. Storage Replica itself is a new form of redundancy in Windows Server 2016 that we haven't seen before in the Microsoft world, we had to rely on third-party tools for this kind of capability in the past. Storage Replica is also important to discuss right on the heels of failover clustering, because SR is the secret sauce that enables Multi-Site failover clustering to happen. When you want to host cluster nodes in multiple physical locations, you need a way to make sure that the data used by those cluster nodes is synced continuously, so that a failover is actually possible. This data flow is provided by Storage Replica.

There are three different ways that you can accomplish Storage Replica, here is a summary of each so that you can decide what works best in your environment.

Stretch Cluster

The Storage Replica Stretch Cluster is just like the name implies, stretching a single cluster across multiple sites. The best real-world use case of this that I can think of is a Hyper-V cluster. Think about your Hyper-V environment being replicated to a disaster recovery site, always staying instantly up to date and being immediately available in the event that your main site disappears. Stretch Cluster features auto failover capabilities, and asynchronous replication.

Cluster to Cluster

Here we have a slightly different take for a different use case, cluster to cluster. This is the scenario where you would have a cluster in your main datacenter that is being replicated to another cluster that exists in your DR site.

Server to Server

Even if you aren't a cluster administrator, this one should peak your interest. The server to server mode of Storage Replica can be used as a powerful tool for data replication, think of it as your new file backup solution. You can have two separate servers running in two sites, and Storage Replica will keep their data identically replicated at all times. It is important to note that server to server mode involves a manual failover in the event that a site goes down, but it is still a very capable data backup tool. You even have the option to do "server to self" synchronization for small use cases. Perhaps a small business has a single file server and doesn't yet have the budget to implement another server, but wants to keep a backup copy of their data on the same server where it is being hosted from.

One of the neat data points about Storage Replica is that it finally allows a single-vendor solution, that vendor being Microsoft of course, to provide the end-to-end technology and software for storage and clustering. It is also hardware agnostic, giving you the ability to utilize your own preference for the storage media.

Additionally, since the storage is block level it doesn't matter what type of file system you are running, and it doesn't matter whether or not the files are currently in use, they will all be replicated as exact matches. Microsoft is touting "Zero RPO replication", guaranteeing that you will not lose data!

Storage Replica is meant to be tightly integrated and one of the supporting technologies of a solid failover clustering environment. In fact, the graphical management interface for Storage Replica is located inside the Failover Cluster Manager software—but is of course also configurable via PowerShell—so make sure that you take a look into failover clustering and Storage Replica as a "better together" story for your environment.

Storage Spaces Direct

There is another new offering inside Windows Server 2016 related to storage and clustering, and this one will be very important to anyone with large data storage needs. We have had the ability to do scale-out-file-servers for a few years now, but providing a Windows Server frontend that taps into a large disk space backend has typically required some vendor participation with regards to the backend. We most commonly set up some kind of shared SAS backend, typically involving an expensive SAN controller and some kind of JBOD enclosure that stores all of our SAS disks. Well, you can now take everything that you know and have spent the last number of years learning about how to make this SAN/SAS system work like you want it, and throw it all out the window!

Storage Spaces Direct is a technology running right inside Windows Server 2016 that takes the idea of Storage Spaces on a single server, and expands that mentality across multiple servers. Let's say you have two servers – or three, or four, and so on – and each of those servers has multiple hard drives inside it. This drives can be anything. They could be high performance SAS disks, or they could be simple SATA drives that you had laying around. Using either PowerShell or System Center, you can cluster these servers together, configure Storage Spaces Direct, and then create pools of data that shares space among all of the hard drives that are plugged into all of the servers. Storage Spaces Direct is really the flagship of Microsoft's new Software-Defined-Storage mentality, and they expect it to be used heavily in the years to come.

To me, one of the neatest parts of Storage Spaces Direct is down the road, after you have been using it for a while and suddenly realize that you are running out of space and need to add some additional storage. What to do? Simply create a new server, throw some drives in it, and run a simple PowerShell command to add that new server into the cluster. The existing cluster is extended to include the new server, and the storage pool and volumes you have created start expanding automatically!

Summary

Redundancy is a critical component to the way that we plan infrastructure and build servers in today's world. Windows Server 2016 has some powerful capabilities built right into it that you can utilize in your own environments, starting today! I hope that by gleaning a little more information about both Network Load Balancing, and about failover clustering, that you will be able to expand the capabilities of your organization by employing these techniques and stretching the limits of your service uptime. In my opinion, if there is any one avenue out of this chapter for you to pursue, it is the utilization of failover clustering in order to make your virtual machines redundant among multiple Hyper-V servers. This is such a powerful enhancement to a virtual server infrastructure, it will literally change the way that you work and give you some peace of mind that you didn't think was possible in a world aiming for 99.999% uptime.

10
Learning PowerShell 5.0

Let's be honest, the majority of us are still using Command Prompt on a daily basis. I shouldn't speak for you as a reader, if you have cut over and are using the newer PowerShell prompt as a total replacement for Command Prompt, I definitely applaud you! I, however, do still tend to open up cmd.exe as a matter of habit, though with the release of Windows 10 and Windows Server 2016, I am definitely making a more conscious effort to use the newer, "blue-er", prettier, and more powerful interface that is PowerShell 5.0. In this chapter, we are going to explore some of the reasons that you should do the same. Other than the fact that Microsoft seems to have shrunk the default text size in Command Prompt to deter us from using it, which I find pretty funny, we are going to take a look at some of the technical reasons that PowerShell is far and away more useful and powerful than Command Prompt could ever dream to be.

- Why move to PowerShell?
- Working within PowerShell
- PowerShell Integrated Scripting Environment
- Remotely managing a server
- Desired State Configuration

Why move to PowerShell?

I don't think there is any question in people's minds that PowerShell is indeed the evolution of Command Prompt, but the reason that many of us still default to the old interface is that it still has all of the capability to accomplish what we need to do on our servers. Rather, what Command Prompt really contains is the ability to do the same things that we have always done from Command Prompt, and nothing else. Without realizing it, there are a lot of functions that you use the GUI to accomplish that cannot be done well from within a Command Prompt window. The limitations within Command Prompt that force you into using your mouse to interface with the GUI do not exist with PowerShell. It is fully comprehensive, and capable of modifying almost any aspect of the Windows operating system. How did PowerShell come to be so much more powerful than Command Prompt? It differs from any classic I/O shell in that it is built on top of .NET, and runs much more like a programming language than simple in and out commands.

Cmdlets

Most of the functionality that a traditional server admin will use comes in the form of cmdlets (pronounced *command-lets*). These are commands that you run from within the PowerShell prompt, but you can think of them as tools rather than simple commands. Cmdlets can be used to both get information from a server, and to set information and parameters onto a server. Many cmdlets have intuitive names that begin with `get` or `set`, and similar to the way that most command-line interfaces work, each cmdlet has various switches or variables that can be configured and flagged at the end of the cmdlet, in order to make it do special things. It is helpful to understand that cmdlets are always built in a verb-noun syntax. You specify the action you are wanting to accomplish, such as `get` or `set`, and then your noun is the piece inside Windows that you are trying to manipulate. Here are a few simple examples of cmdlets in PowerShell to give you an idea of what they look like, and how they are named in a fairly simple way:

- `Get-NetIPAddress`: With this cmdlet, we can see the IP addresses on our system
- `Set-NetIPAddress`: We can use this guy to modify an existing IP address
- `New-NetIPAddress`: This cmdlet allows us to create a new IP address on the computer
- `Rename-Computer`: As we utilized earlier in the book, `Rename-Computer` is a quick and easy way to set the computer hostname of a system

Chapter 10

If you're ever struggling to come up with the name or syntax of a particular command, TechNet has a full page of information dedicated to each cmdlet inside PowerShell. That can be incredibly useful, but sometimes you don't want to take the time to pop over onto the Internet just to find the name of a command that you are simply failing to remember at the moment. One of the most useful cmdlets in PowerShell shows you a list of all the available cmdlets. Make sure to check out Get-Command.

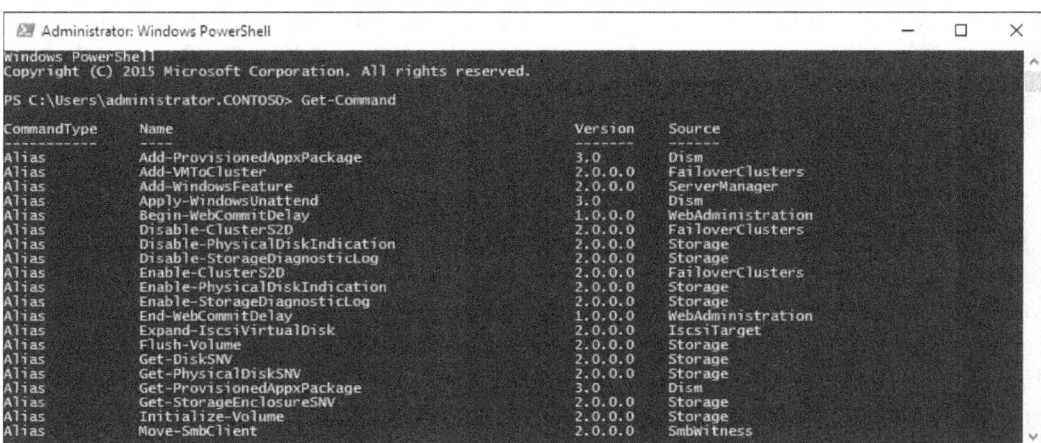

Whoa, there are pages and pages of cmdlets! Rather than scrolling through the entire list in order to find the one that you are looking for, it is easy to filter this list based on any criteria that you would like. If we were interested in seeing only the commands that deal with IP addressing, we could give this a try:

`Get-Command -Name *IPAddress*`

[303]

PowerShell is the backbone

As you will discover through this chapter, interfacing with PowerShell puts all kinds of power at your fingertips. What I sometimes find though is that admins don't fully trust PowerShell, because they are used to taking these actions and making these changes from a graphical interface. After running a single PowerShell cmdlet to set a configuration that would have otherwise taken you a dozen different mouse clicks in order to accomplish the same thing, it is easy to think that it must not have actually done anything. That was too easy, and it processed my command way too fast, right? I'd better go into that graphical interface anyway, just to double-check that PowerShell actually did the job.

When I started using PowerShell, I was tempted to do exactly that, all the time. But the more I used it and the more I started digging into those graphical interfaces themselves, the more I realized that I'm not the only one using PowerShell. A lot of the Administrative Tool GUIs use PowerShell too! Without even realizing it, you use PowerShell for quite a bit of tasks inside the Windows Server operating system. When you open up that management console for whatever you happen to be changing on the server, make your configurations, and then click on the Go or Finish button, how does that console put your configuration into place? PowerShell. Under the hood, in the background, the console is taking the information that you input, plugging that information into PowerShell cmdlets, and running them in order to do the actual configuration work.

So if you're hesitant to start using PowerShell because it just feels different, or you don't trust the process to be uniform to the way that it would have worked in the GUI itself, forget all of that. Because many times when you are using mouse clicks to change settings on your server, you are actually using PowerShell cmdlets anyway.

Scripting

The more you use PowerShell, the more powerful it becomes. In addition to running ad hoc, single commands and cmdlets, you have the ability to build extensive scripts that can accomplish all sorts of different things. I mentioned that PowerShell has similarities to a regular programming language, and scripting is where we start to navigate into that territory. PowerShell provides the ability to create script files, we will do that for ourselves coming up shortly, to be able to save them for easy running of those same scripts time and time again. Variables can also be used, like in other forms of coding, so that you can provide variable inputs and objects that can be used by the scripts, in order to make them more flexible and squeeze even more functionality out of them.

Server Core and Nano Server

If there was any one area where I think we as server admins could do a better job of using the technology at our disposal, it is using PowerShell to fulfill the Microsoft model of centralized management. When we have a task that needs to be accomplished on a server, it is our default tendency to log in to that server, then start doing the work. Logging in to the server is becoming more and more unnecessary, and we could save a lot of time by using the central management tools that we have available to us. PowerShell is one of these tools. Rather than RDPing into that server, simply use the PowerShell prompt on your local machine in order to reach out and change that setting on the remote server.

This kind of remote management becomes not only efficient, but necessary as we start dealing more with headless servers. Rolling out Server Core and Nano Server instances is something that I hope to see in all organizations over the next few years, and interacting with these servers is going to take a shift in your administrative mindset. By becoming familiar with accomplishing daily tasks from inside PowerShell now, you will better equip yourself for future administration of these headless machines that are going to require you to interface with them in this way.

Working within PowerShell

The first step to doing real work with PowerShell is getting comfortable interfacing with the platform, and becoming familiar with the daily routines of working from this command line, rather than relying on your mouse pointer. Here we will explore some of the most common ways that I have seen server administrators make use of PowerShell in order to enhance their daily workload.

Launching PowerShell

Pretty simple, the first thing we need to do is get PowerShell opened up to start using it. The PowerShell console is installed by default in Windows Server 2016, so you can run it from the Start menu, pin it to the desktop, or access it in any way that you normally open any application. Since I tend to prefer using my keyboard for everything, the way that I normally open PowerShell is to hold down the WinKey and press *R* in order to open a **Run** prompt, type the word `powershell`, and press *Enter*:

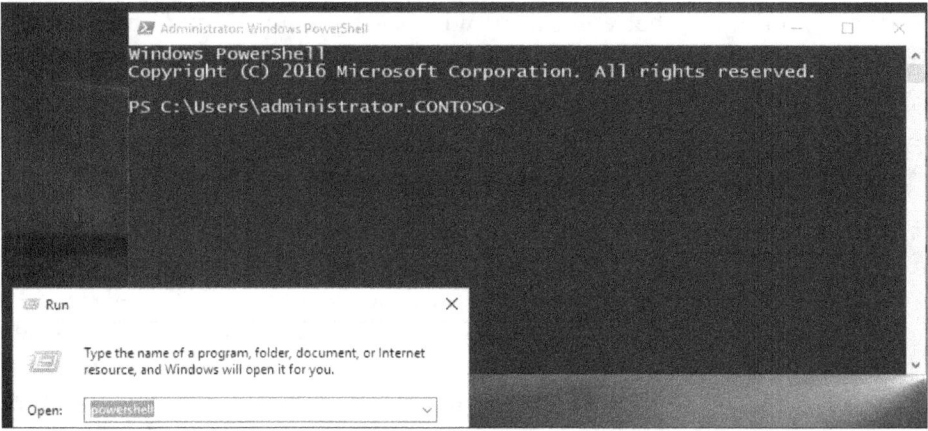

As you can see in the preceding screenshot, since I am logged in as a local administrator on my server, my PowerShell prompt has been opened with elevated permissions. It is important to note that, just like Command Prompt, you can open a PowerShell prompt with either regular user permissions, or elevated—Administrator—privileges. It is generally safer to work from within a regular PowerShell session that does not have elevated rights, unless the task that you are trying to accomplish requires those extra permissions.

You also have the option of entering into a PowerShell prompt from inside an existing Command Prompt window. Normally, when you are working from Command Prompt, you cannot make use of any PowerShell cmdlets. Let's go ahead and give this a shot. Open a regular Command Prompt window, then type `powershell` and press *Enter*. Instead of opening a separate PowerShell window, your prompt changes but the application window itself remains the same. You have now entered the PowerShell shell, from inside the black Command Prompt window, and you can start utilizing cmdlets as you wish. You can move from PowerShell mode back to regular Command Prompt mode by typing `exit`.

```
Administrator: Command Prompt - powershell                              —    □    ×
Microsoft Windows [Version 10.0.10586]
(c) 2016 Microsoft Corporation. All rights reserved.

C:\Users\administrator.CONTOSO>Get-NetIPAddress
'Get-NetIPAddress' is not recognized as an internal or external command,
operable program or batch file.

C:\Users\administrator.CONTOSO>powershell
Windows PowerShell
Copyright (C) 2015 Microsoft Corporation. All rights reserved.

PS C:\Users\administrator.CONTOSO> Get-NetIPAddress


IPAddress          : fe80::ed56:e062:48f3:3ac3%2
InterfaceIndex     : 2
InterfaceAlias     : Local Area Connection* 2
AddressFamily      : IPv6
```

Default Execution Policy

When you are working with the PowerShell command-line interface directly, you can simply open up PowerShell, start typing cmdlets, and start getting work done. However, one of the big advantages to using PowerShell comes when you start playing around with creating, saving, and running scripts. If you open up PowerShell, create a script, and then try to run it, you will sometimes find that it fails with a big messy error message, such as this one:

```
PS C:\scripts> .\script1.ps1
.\script1.ps1 : File C:\scripts\script1.ps1 cannot be loaded because running scripts is disabled
on this system. For more information, see about_Execution_Policies at
http://go.microsoft.com/fwlink/?LinkID=135170.
At line:1 char:1
+ .\script1.ps1
+ ~~~~~~~~~~~~~
    + CategoryInfo          : SecurityError: (:) [], PSSecurityException
    + FullyQualifiedErrorId : UnauthorizedAccess
PS C:\scripts>
```

This shouldn't happen on a fresh instance of Windows Server 2016, but could if you have any GPOs being applied to your new server or if you are using a different operating system and are trying to run some PowerShell scripts, you might find yourself stuck at one of these error messages right out of the gate. While the nature of some versions of Windows to block the running of scripts by default is a security enhancement, it can be a nuisance to work around when you are trying to get something done. Thankfully, if you do encounter this problem, the resolution to this issue is easy. You simply need to adjust the **Default Execution Policy** (DEP) inside PowerShell, so that it allows the execution of scripts to happen properly.

This is not a simple ON/OFF switch. There are five different levels within the Default Execution Policy, and it is important to understand each one so that you can set your DEP accordingly, based on the security that you want in place on your servers. Here are descriptions of each level, in order of most to least secure.

Restricted

The Restricted policy allows commands and cmdlets to be run, but stops the running of scripts altogether.

AllSigned

This requires that any script being run needs to be signed by a trusted publisher. When set to AllSigned, even scripts that you write yourself will have to be put through that validation process and signed before they will be allowed to run.

RemoteSigned

RemoteSigned is the default policy in Windows Server 2016. For scripts that have been downloaded from the Internet, it requires that these scripts are to be signed with a digital signature from a publisher that you trust. However, if you choose to create your own scripts, it will allow these local scripts to run without requiring that digital signature.

Unrestricted

Scripts are allowed to run, signed or unsigned. You do still receive a warning prompt when running scripts that have been downloaded from the Internet.

Bypass

In Bypass mode, nothing is blocked and no warnings are given when you run scripts. In other words, you're on your own.

Sometimes a single execution policy doesn't meet all of the needs, depending on how you utilize PowerShell scripts. DEPs can be further enhanced by setting an **Execution Policy Scope** that allows you to set different execution policies to different aspects of the system. For example, the three scopes that you can manipulate are **Process**, **CurrentUser**, and **LocalMachine**. By default, the DEP affects LocalMachine so that any scripts running adhere to the DEP. But if you need to modify this behavior so that different DEPs are set for the CurrentUser or even an individual process, you have the ability to do that.

If you are unsure about the current status of your DEP, or suspect that someone may have changed it, you can easily view the currently assigned execution policy with a simple cmdlet called `Get-ExecutionPolicy`. As you can see in the following screenshot, mine is set to Restricted, which explains my error message when I tried running the script:

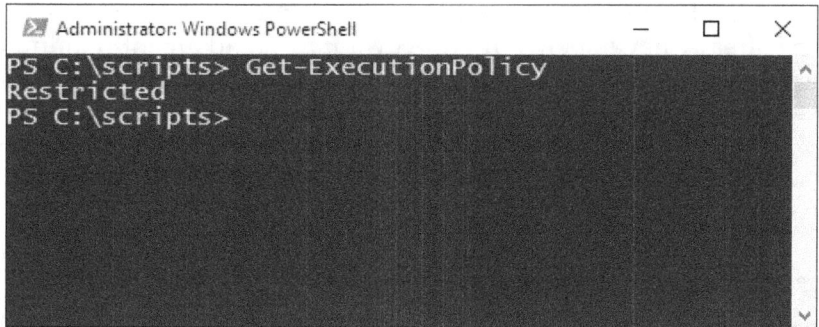

Once you have decided on the level of DEP that you want on your server or workstation, you can set it accordingly with a quick cmdlet as well. For example, since this is a test lab and I want scripts to be able to run, and I am not really concerned about security since I am isolated, I am going to change mine to Unrestricted. Here is my command for doing just that:

`Set-ExecutionPolicy Unrestricted`

Using the Tab key

Before we get started navigating around inside PowerShell, there is one more important note I wanted to point out. Get used to pressing that *Tab* key when you are inside the PowerShell prompt! If you type the first few letters of any command or cmdlet, and then press *Tab*, the remainder of the cmdlet name will be automatically populated on the screen.

If I type get-co and then press *Tab*, my prompt automatically populates the full Get-Command cmdlet. Since there are multiple cmdlets that started with get-co, if you press *Tab* numerous times you can see that it cycles through all of the available cmdlets that start with those letters.

Tab also works with file and folder names. For example, I downloaded a hotfix that needs to be installed onto a server. I want to launch this hotfix using the PowerShell prompt that I already have open, but I don't want to spend an entire minute or more trying to type out the huge filename of this hotfix. I have already navigated to the folder where my hotfix resides, and now if I simply type the first few letters of the filename and press the *Tab* key, PowerShell will populate the remainder of the filename. From there, all I need to do is press *Enter* to launch that installer:

```
PS C:\> cd .\Hotfixes\
PS C:\Hotfixes> .\abcdefghijklmnopqrstuvwxyz123456789.msi
```

Useful cmdlets for daily tasks

When I started incorporating PowerShell into my daily workflow, I found it useful to keep a list of commonly used commands and cmdlets nearby. Until you get to the point where they become memorized and second nature, if you don't have a quick and easy way to recall those commands, chances are that you aren't going to use them and will revert to the old methods of configuring your servers. Here is a list of some of the items I use regularly when I'm building servers. Some are traditional commands that would also work from a Command Prompt, and some are cmdlets, but they are all useful when working inside a PowerShell window.

Get-Command

We already discussed this one in a little bit of detail; it is useful for finding additional commands or cmdlets that you may want to run or research.

Get-Command -Name *example*

Enhance the usefulness of Get-Command by adding the -Name switch to the end of it, so that you can filter results to whatever types of cmdlet you are searching for.

GCM

This is simply a short alias for `Get-Command`. I only wanted to point this one out because some of the PowerShell cmdlets have aliases like gcm, which allow you to launch these commonly used cmdlets with fewer keystrokes.

Get-Alias

Since we just mentioned the GCM alias for `Get-Command`, you may be wondering what other aliases are available inside PowerShell. To see a complete list, simply plug in the `Get-Alias` cmdlet.

Rename-Computer

This allows you to set a new hostname for the server.

Add-Computer

Use the `Add-Computer` cmdlet to join servers to a domain.

Hostname

This displays the name of the system you are currently working on. I use hostname all the time to make sure that I really am working on the server that I think I am. Have you ever rebooted the wrong server? I have. By running a quick `hostname` command you can give some peace of mind that the function you are about to perform is really happening on the right system.

$env:computername

This one also presents you with the hostname of the system you are working on, but I call this one out to show that PowerShell can easily tap into your environment variables in order to pull out information. The more simple `hostname` command is useful when you are logged in to a local system and are simply trying to verify its name, but the ability to pull information like this from a variable like `$env:computername` will be much more useful when creating scripts or trying to perform a function against a remote system.

Logoff

The name is self-explanatory, `Logoff` just logs you out of the system. Rather than trying to find the **Sign out** function by clicking around in the user interface of your server, you can throw a quick `Logoff` command into either a Command Prompt or a PowerShell window, and it will immediately log you off that session. I use this one all the time when closing out RDP connections.

Learning PowerShell 5.0

`Shutdown` or `Restart-Computer`

Both of these functions are useful for shutting down or restarting a server. On my own computer, these commands are most commonly preceded by the `hostname` command. When rebooting a server, you want to take special care that you restart the correct machine, so I find it most reliable to open a PowerShell prompt, do a quick `hostname` check, and then run a restart command from that same prompt. This ensures that I am restarting the server, which was returned in the hostname output.

`Shutdown /r /t 0`

If you run a simple `shutdown` command, the system will shut down in one minute. I'm not sure why this is the default, as I have never found any IT administrator who actually wanted to wait that extra minute before shutting down their system. Instead, it is more efficient to set a time limit before that shutdown commences. In this command, I have told the `shutdown` command that I want to restart instead of shutting down, that is `/r`, and I have also told it to wait zero seconds before performing this restart. This way it happens immediately; I don't have to sit around and wait for that default 60 seconds.

`Query user` or `Quser`

Often most useful in RDS environments, the `query user` command will display all of the users that are currently logged in to a server.

`Quser /computer:WEB1`

Using `quser` in combination with the `/computer` switch allows you to see the currently logged in users on a remote system. This way you can remain logged in to a single server in your RDS farm, but check on the user sessions for all of your systems without having to log in to them. You could even write a script that runs this command against each of your session host servers, and outputs the data to a file.

`Install-WindowsFeature`

As we have already discussed, use PowerShell to simplify the installation of roles and features onto your servers.

`New-NetIPAddress -InterfaceIndex 12 -IPAddress 10.0.0.100 -PrefixLength 24 -DefaultGateway 10.0.0.1`

Use `New-NetIPAddress` in order to assign IP addresses to your NICs. Keep in mind that the information in the preceding cmdlet is clearly example data, and needs to be replaced with your own information.

`Set-DnsClientServerAddress -InterfaceIndex 12 -ServerAddresses 10.0.0.2,10.0.0.3`

Often used in combination with `New-NetIPAddress`, use this one to set the DNS server addresses in your NIC properties.

Using Get-Help

How many hundreds of times have you used the /? switch in Command Prompt to pull some extra information about a command that you want to run? The extra information provided by this help function can sometimes mean the difference between a command being useful, or completely useless. PowerShell cmdlets have a similar function, but you cannot simply /? at the end of a PowerShell cmdlet because a space following a cmdlet in PowerShell indicates that you are about to specify a parameter to be used with that cmdlet. For example, if we try to use /? with the `Restart-Computer` cmdlet in order to find more information about how to use `Restart-Computer`, it will fail to recognize the question mark as a valid parameter, and our output is as follows:

Instead, there is an even more powerful help function inside PowerShell. `Get-Help` is a cmdlet itself, and like any cmdlet we need to use information following the cmdlet in order to specify and pull the information that we are looking for. So instead of using `Get-Help` at the end of a command like we used to do with the question mark, we use it as its own entity.

Running a `Get-Help` by itself only gives us more information about the `Get-Help` command, which may be useful to look over, but right now we are more interested in finding out how we can use `Get-Help` to give us additional information for a cmdlet we want to run, such as the `Restart-Computer` function. What we need to do is use `Get-Help` as a cmdlet, and then specify the other cmdlet as a parameter to pass to `Get-Help`, by placing a space between them:

`Get-Help Restart-Computer`

```
PS C:\> Get-Help Restart-Computer
NAME
    Restart-Computer

SYNTAX
    Restart-Computer [[-ComputerName] <string[]>] [[-Credential]
    <pscredential>] [-DcomAuthentication <AuthenticationLevel>
    {Default | None | Connect | Call | Packet | PacketIntegrity |
    PacketPrivacy | Unchanged}] [-Impersonation
    <ImpersonationLevel> {Default | Anonymous | Identify |
    Impersonate | Delegate}] [-WsmanAuthentication <string>
    {Default | Basic | Negotiate | CredSSP | Digest | Kerberos}]
```

The information provided by `Get-Help` is very comprehensive, in some cases it has all of the same information that you can find on TechNet. Make sure to start utilizing `Get-Help` to further your knowledge of any cmdlet in PowerShell!

Formatting the output

When searching for information in PowerShell, I often encounter the case where so much information is provided to me that it's difficult to sort through. Are you trying to find useful cmdlets from `Get-Command`, or maybe track down a particular alias with `Get-Alias`? The output from these cmdlets can be staggeringly long. While we have discussed some parameters you can use to whittle down this output, like specifying particular `-Name` parameters, there are a couple of formatting parameters that can also be appended to cmdlets, in order to modify the data output.

Format-Table

The purpose of `Format-Table` is pretty simple, it takes the data output from a command and puts it into table format. This generally makes the information much easier to read and work with. Let's look at an example. We have used `Get-NetIPAddress` a couple of times, but, let's be honest, its output is a little messy. Running the cmdlet by itself on my virtual server, which only has a single NIC assigned to it, results in six pages of data inside my PowerShell window:

```
PS C:\> Get-NetIPAddress

IPAddress          : fe80::ed56:e062:48f3:3ac3%2
InterfaceIndex     : 2
InterfaceAlias     : Local Area Connection* 2
AddressFamily      : IPv6
Type               : Unicast
PrefixLength       : 64
PrefixOrigin       : WellKnown
SuffixOrigin       : Link
AddressState       : Preferred
ValidLifetime      : Infinite ([TimeSpan]::MaxValue)
PreferredLifetime  : Infinite ([TimeSpan]::MaxValue)
SkipAsSource       : False
PolicyStore        : ActiveStore

IPAddress          : fe80::5efe:169.254.2.83%7
InterfaceIndex     : 7
InterfaceAlias     : isatap.{5ABD7C74-B57E-4019-9A37-7630036FFB87}
AddressFamily      : IPv6
```

If I simply add Format-Table to my Get-NetIPAddress cmdlet, the generated data is much easier on the eyes, while still giving me the important information that I am really looking for—the IP addresses being used on the system:

```
Get-NetIPAddress | Format-Table
```

```
PS C:\> Get-NetIPAddress | Format-Table

ifIndex IPAddress                              PrefixLength PrefixOrigin
------- ---------                              ------------ ------------
2       fe80::ed56:e062:48f3:3ac3%2                      64 WellKnown
7       fe80::5efe:169.254.2.83%7                       128 WellKnown
4       fe80::109d:c682:bca4:282d%4                      64 WellKnown
5       fe80::5efe:10.0.0.40%5                          128 WellKnown
1       ::1                                             128 WellKnown
2       169.254.2.83                                     16 Manual
4       10.0.0.40                                        24 Manual
1       127.0.0.1                                         8 WellKnown

PS C:\>
```

Some of you may be familiar with a cmdlet called Select-Object, which can perform the same functions as Format-Table. While Select-Object seems to be the more widely known cmdlet, in my experience it is actually less powerful than Format-Table, and so I suggest you spend some time playing around with the one we have discussed here today.

Format-List

Similar to the way that Format-Table works, you can utilize Format-List in order to display command output as a list of properties. Let's give it a quick try. We already know that Get-Command gives us the available cmdlets within PowerShell, and by default it gives them to us in a table format. If we wanted to view that output in a list instead, with more information being provided about each cmdlet, we could tell Get-Command to output its data in a list format instead:

`Get-Command | Format-List`

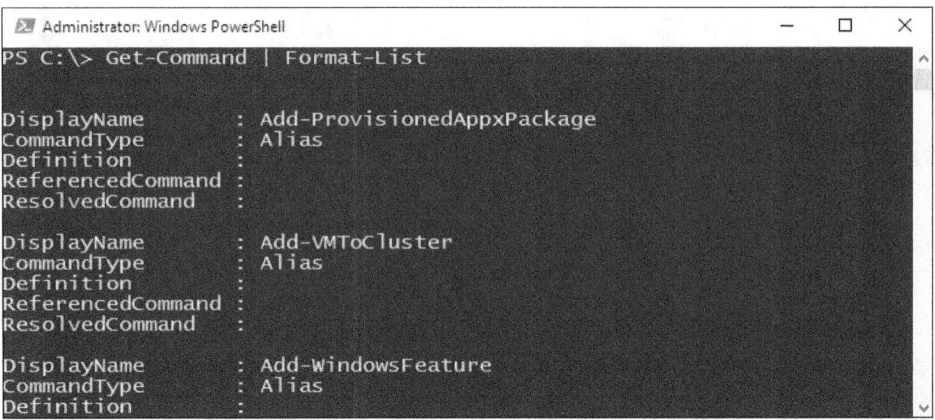

And we can hone that down even further, by telling PowerShell we would like to see a list of all the cmdlets, including the word "Restart", and see them in list format:

`Get-Command -Name *Restart* | Format-List`

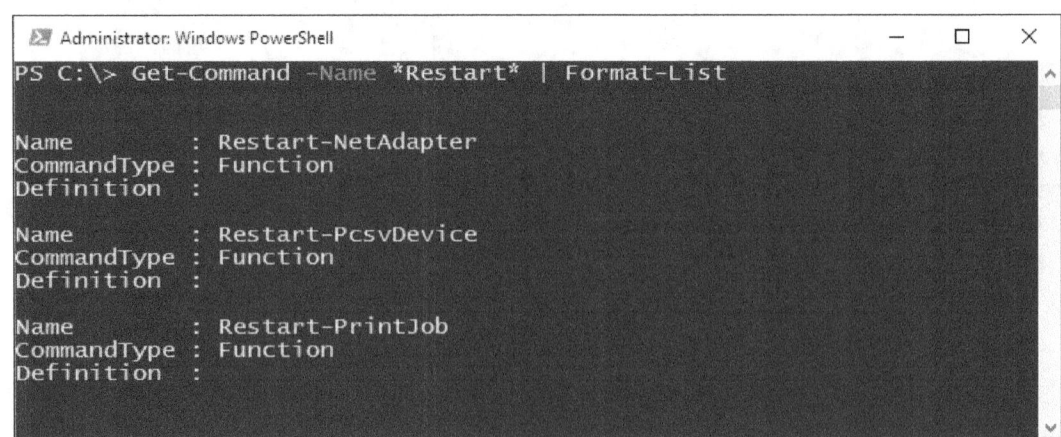

Chapter 10

PowerShell Integrated Scripting Environment

Most server administrators are familiar with the concept of creating batch files for use in the Command Prompt world. Have a series of commands that you want to run in sequence? Need to run this sequence of commands multiple times across different servers or over and over again in the future? Throwing multiple commands inside a text document and then saving it with the file extension .BAT will result in a batch file that can be run on any Windows computer, issuing those commands in sequence, which saves you the time and effort of having to plunk out these commands over and over inside the command-line interface.

Scripting in PowerShell is the same idea, but more powerful. Commands in Command Prompt are useful, but limited, while PowerShell cmdlets have the ability to manipulate anything within the operating system. With PowerShell we also have the ability to reference items from inside environment variables or the registry, we can easily issue commands to remote systems, and we can even utilize variables inside a PowerShell script, just like you would do with any full programming language.

Let's explore a couple of different ways that can be used to start creating your first PowerShell scripts.

PS1 file

Creating a .PS1 file—a PowerShell script file—is almost exactly the same idea as creating a .BAT file. All you have to do is open up a text document using your favorite editor, throw in a series of commands or cmdlets, and then save the file as FILENAME.PS1. As long as your PowerShell environment allows the running of scripts—see earlier in the chapter about the Default Execution Policy—you now have the ability to double-click on that .PS1 file, or launch it from any PowerShell prompt, to run the series of cmdlets inside that script. Let's give it a try and prove that we can get a simple script up and operational.

Since you are only going to create scripts that serve a purpose, let's think of a real-world example. I work with terminal servers quite a bit—pardon me, RDS servers—and a common request from customers is a log of what users logged in to which servers. A simple way to gather this information is to create a logon script that records information about the user session to a file as they are logging in. In order to do this, I need to create a script that I can configure to run during the logon process. To make the script a little bit more interesting and flexible down the road, I am going to utilize some variables for my username, the current date and time, and record the name of the RDS server being logged in to. That way I can look at the collective set of logs down the road, and easily sort between which users were on which servers.

I am going to use Notepad for creating this script. I have opened up a new instance of Notepad, entered in the following commands, and am now saving this as `C:\Scripts\UserReporting.ps1`:

```
$User = $env:username
$RDSH = $env:computername
$Date = Get-Date
echo $User,$Date,$RDSH | Out-File C:\Scripts\Reporting.txt -append
```

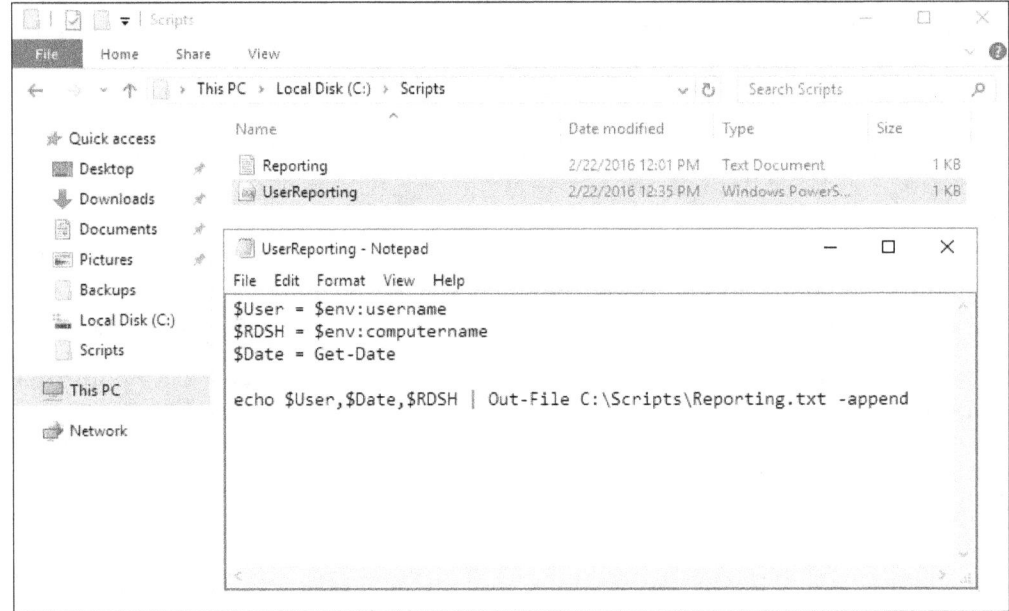

If I run this script a few times, I can open up my `Reporting.txt` file and see that it is logging the information that I specified each time I run the script.

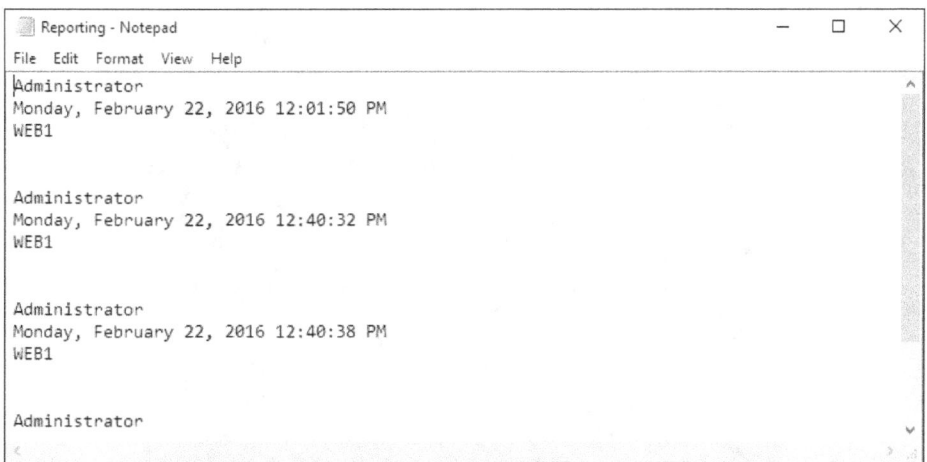

Integrated Scripting Environment

If I'm being honest, putting together that simple little script we just ran took a few tries. I didn't have a copy of it readily available to copy from, and I needed to test a couple of the lines individually in PowerShell before I was confident they would work in my script. I also first tried to pull the username without using the environment variable, and it didn't work. Why did I have so much trouble in putting together just those few simple lines of code? Because as I type those lines in Notepad, I have absolutely no idea whether or not they are going to work when I save and try to run that script. All of the text is just black with a white background, and I am fully trusting my own knowledge and scripting abilities in order to put together something that actually works.

Learning PowerShell 5.0

Thankfully, we have access to the **PowerShell Integrated Scripting Environment** (**ISE**). This is a program that is installed by default in Windows Server 2016, it is a scripting shell that allows you to write PowerShell scripts, and helps you along the way. Let's go ahead and open it up. If you right-click on the PowerShell icon itself, you will find an option to launch **Windows PowerShell ISE** right from that menu:

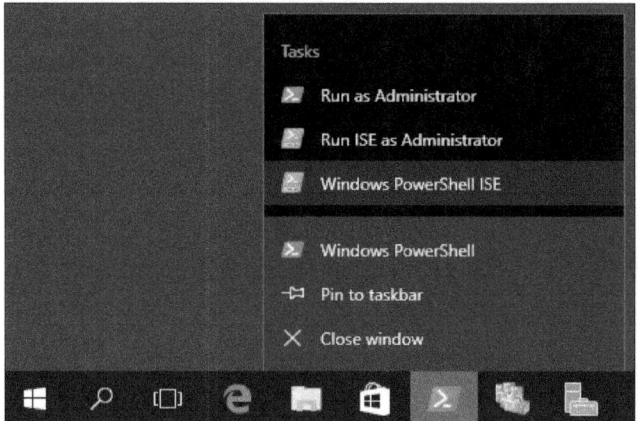

Now if we go ahead and start typing in the same script information that I used in Notepad a few minutes ago, you can see that even as we type we get pop-ups and prompts that help us decide which cmdlets or variables we want to utilize. Similar to the way that our autoprompt keyboards on our smart phones work, ISE will give suggestions about what it is you are starting to type, so that you don't necessarily have to remember what the cmdlets or parameters are called, you can take an educated guess on what letter it starts with and then choose one from the list that is presented.

There is also a list off to the right of all the commands available, and it is searchable! That is a great feature that really helps to get these scripts rolling.

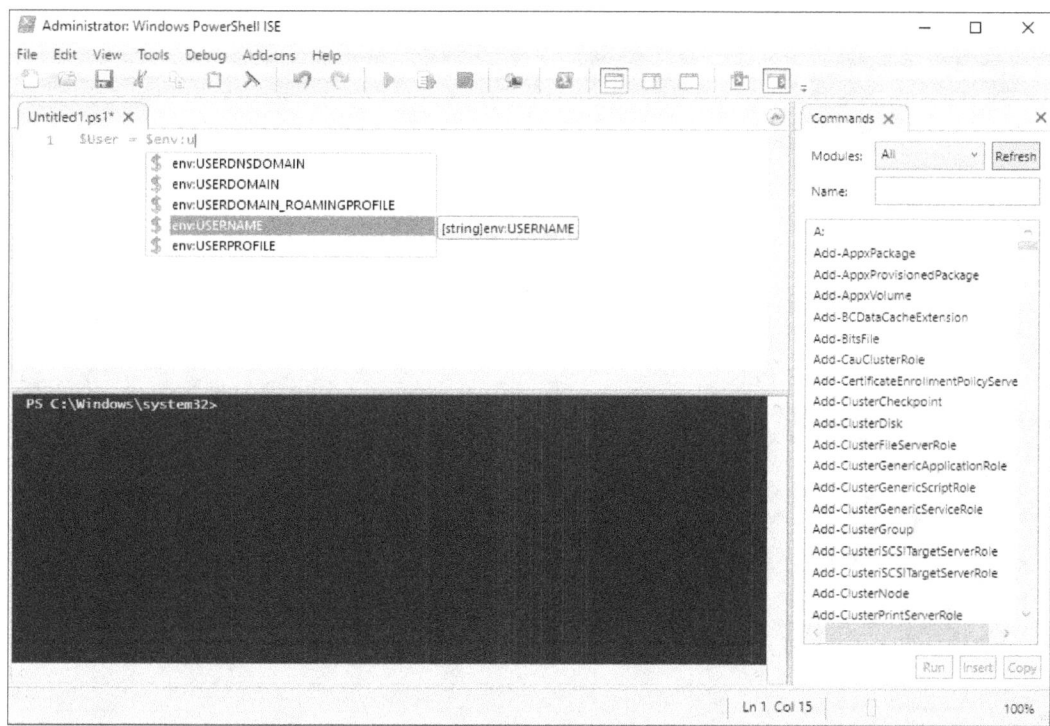

Also useful is the blue PowerShell mini screen that consumes the bottom half of the development window inside ISE. Basically, what happens is that you type in some commands in the above space, ISE helps you to make sure they are all going to work by color coding the cmdlets and parameters for easy identification, and then you can click on the green arrow button in the above taskbar that is labeled **Run Script**. Even if you haven't saved your script anywhere yet, ISE launches through your commands and presents the output in the below PowerShell prompt window.

Learning PowerShell 5.0

This allows you to test your script, or test changes that you are making to an existing script, without having to save the file and then launch it separately from an actual PowerShell window:

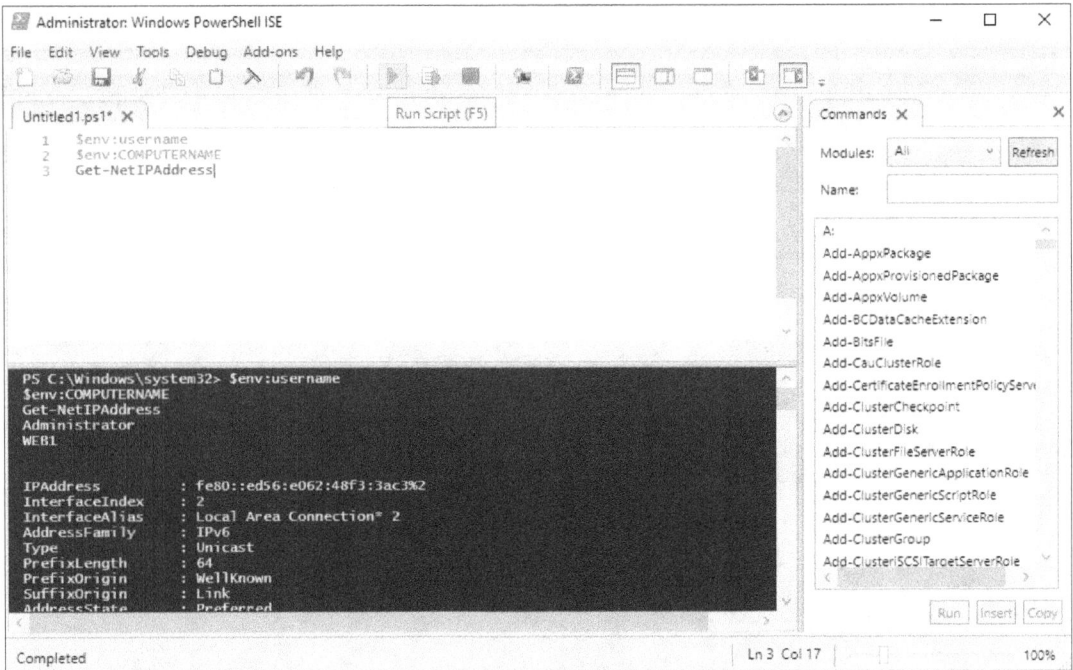

Remotely managing a server

Now that we have worked a little bit in the local instance of PowerShell, and have explored a couple of methods that can be used to start creating scripts, it is time to take a closer look at how PowerShell fits into your centralized administration needs. If you start using PowerShell for server administration, but are still RDPing into the servers and then opening PowerShell from there, you're doing it wrong. We already know that you can tap remote servers into Server Manager so that they can be managed centrally, and we also know that the tools inside Server Manager are, for the most part, just issuing a series of PowerShell cmdlets when you click on the buttons. Combine those two pieces of information, and you can surmise that PowerShell commands and cmdlets can be easily run against remote systems, ones that you are not currently logged in to.

Taking this idea and running with it, we are going to look over the criteria that are necessary to make this happen in your own environment. We are going to make sure that one of our servers is ready to accept remote PowerShell connections, and then use a PowerShell prompt on a different machine in order to pull information and make changes on that remote server.

Preparing the remote server

There are just a couple of items that need to be running and enabled on your remote servers in order for you to tap PowerShell into them from a different machine. If all of your servers are Windows Server 2016, in fact if they are all Windows Server 2012 or higher, then PowerShell remoting is enabled by default, and you may be able to skip the next couple of sections here. However, if you try to use PowerShell remoting and it's not working for you, it is important that you understand how it works under the hood. This way you can troubleshoot it and manually establish remote capabilities in the event that you run into problems, or are running some older operating systems where these steps may be necessary.

WinRM service

One piece of the remote management puzzle is the WinRM service. Simply make sure that this service is running. If you have stopped it as some sort of hardening or security benefit, you will need to reverse that change and get the service back up and running in order to use PowerShell remoting.

You can check the status of the WinRM service from `services.msc`, of course, or since we are using PowerShell in this chapter, you could check it with the following command:

```
Get-Service WinRM
```

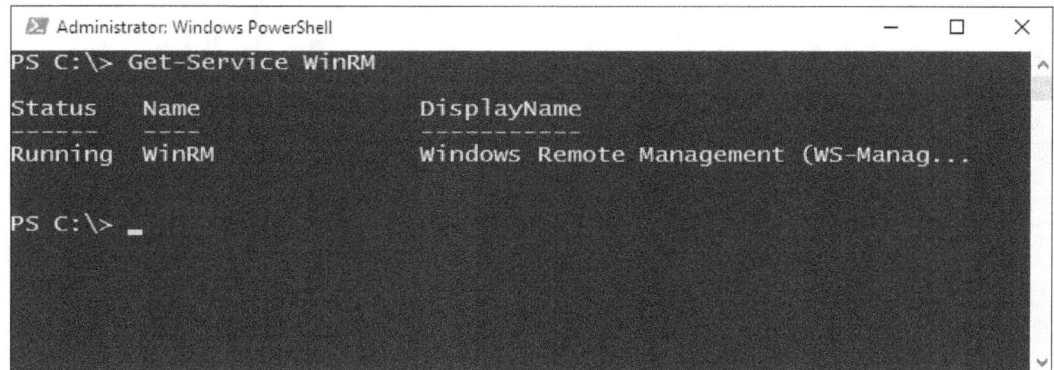

Enable-PSRemoting

Typically, the only other thing that needs to be accomplished on your remote server is to run a single, simple cmdlet. Well, it needs to have network access, of course, or you won't be able to see it on the network at all. But other than making sure network connectivity and flow are working directly from the console of your new server, you are then ready to issue the PowerShell command that enables this server to be able to accept incoming, remote PowerShell connections.

`Enable-PSRemoting -Force`

Using `-Force` at the end of the `Enable-PSRemoting` command causes the command to roll without asking you for confirmations. There are a few different things that `Enable-PSRemoting` is doing in the background here. It is attempting to start the WinRM service—then why did I already specify that you should check it manually? Because if you have it disabled as part of a lockdown strategy, you will interfere with this process. Checking WinRM before using `Enable-PSRemoting` increases your chances of success when running the `Enable-PSRemoting` cmdlet. There are two other things that this command is also doing: starting the listener for remote connections and creating a firewall rule on the system to allow this traffic to pass successfully.

If you intend to use PowerShell remoting on a large scale, it is a daunting thing to think about logging in to every single server and running this command. Thankfully, you don't have to! As with most functions in the Windows world, we can use Group Policy to make this change for us automatically. Create a new GPO, link and filter it appropriately so that it only applies to those servers which you want to be centrally managed, and then configure this settings: **Computer Configuration** | **Policies** | **Administrative Templates** | **Windows Components** | **Windows Remote Management (WinRM)** | **WinRM Service**.

Set **Allow remote server management through WinRM** to **Enabled**:

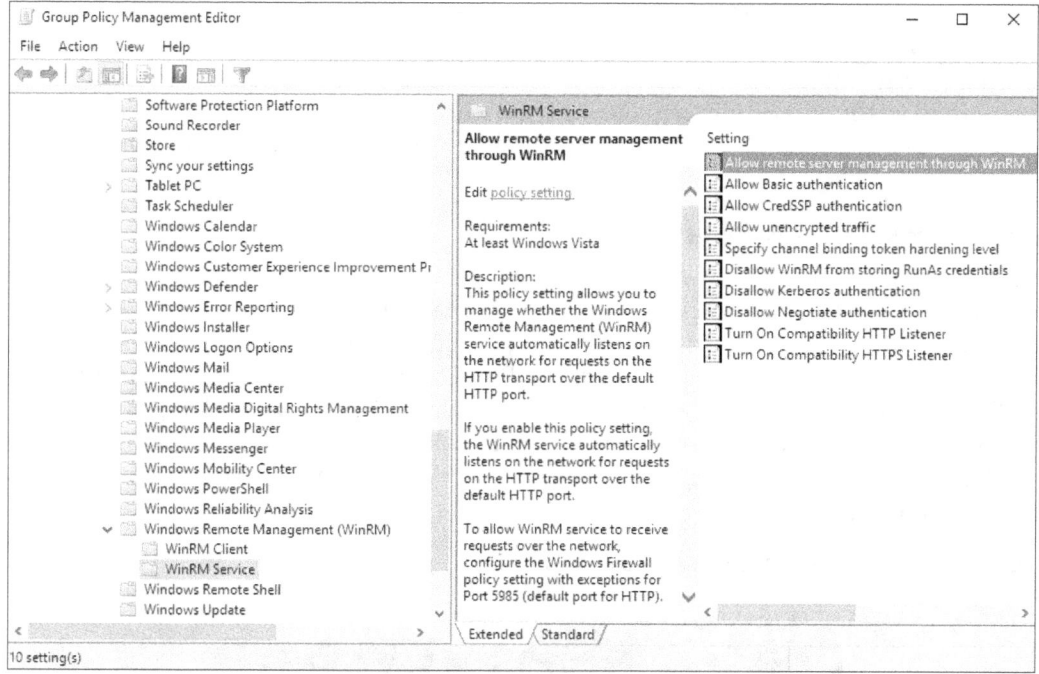

Allowing machines from other domains or workgroups

If you are working with servers that are all part of the same corporate domain, which will most often be the case, then authentication between machines is easy to accomplish. They automatically trust each other at this level. However, on the server you are prepping to accept remote connections, if you expect those computers will be members of a different domain that is not trusted—or even members of a workgroup—then you will have to issue a command to manually trust the individual computers that are going to be connecting in. For example, if I am planning to manage all of my servers from a client computer called Win10Client that is not trusted by the servers, then I would need to run the following command on these servers.

```
Set-Item wsman:\localhost\client\trustedhosts Win10Client
```

If you wanted to allow any machine to connect remotely, you could replace the individual computer name with a *, but in general this wouldn't be a good practice, as you may be inviting trouble by allowing any machine to connect to you in this way.

Learning PowerShell 5.0

Connecting to the remote server

I typically see administrators utilize remote PowerShelling in two different ways. You can perform some commands against remote systems on an ad hoc basis while your PowerShell prompt is still local, or you can launch into a full-blown remote PowerShell session in order to make your PowerShell prompt behave as if it is running directly on that remote system. Let's take a look at both the options.

Using –ComputerName

Many of the cmdlets available in PowerShell, particularly ones that begin with `Get-`, are able to be used with the `-ComputerName` parameter. This specifies that the command you are about to run needs to execute against the remote system that you specify in the `-ComputerName` section. For our remote PowerShell examples, I will be using a PowerShell prompt on my Windows 10 client computer to access information on some of my servers in the network. Here you can see that from my standard PowerShell prompt, I can query a service on my WEB1 server using the following command:

```
Get-Service WinRM -ComputerName WEB1
```

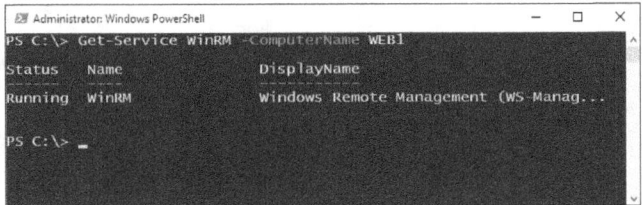

Alternatively, perhaps I want to see all of the roles currently installed on WEB1:

```
Get-WindowsFeature -ComputerName WEB1 | Where Installed
```

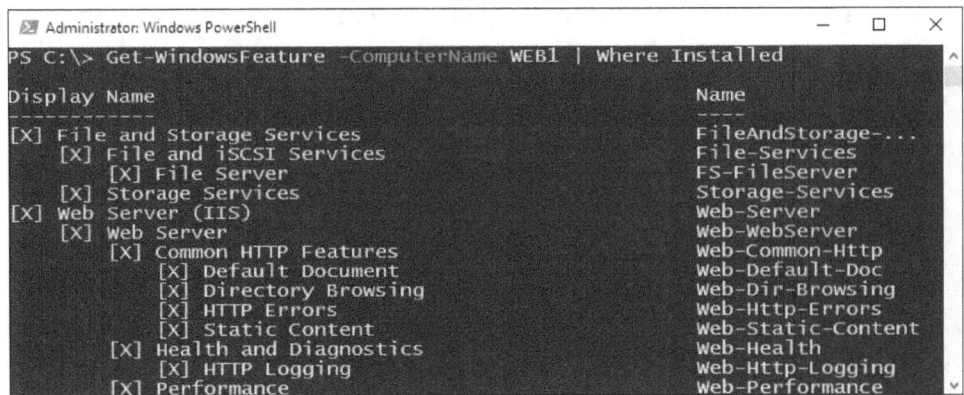

[326]

The `-ComputerName` parameter can even accept multiple server names at the same time. If I wanted to check the status of the WinRM service on a few of my servers, by using a single command, I could do something like this:

`Get-Service WinRM -ComputerName WEB1,WEB2,DC1`

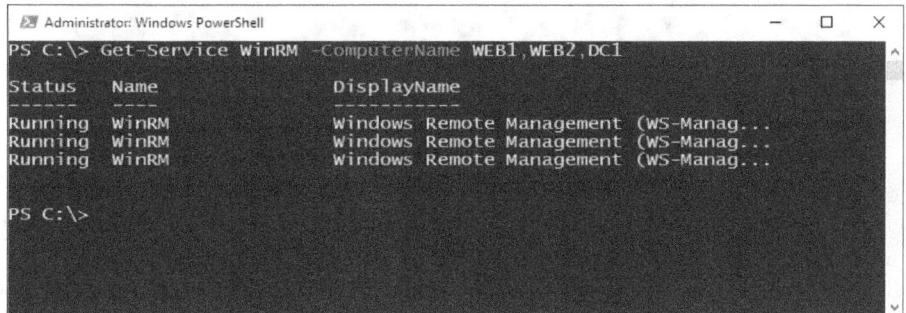

Using Enter-PSSession

On the other hand, sometimes you have many different cmdlets that you want to run against a particular server. In this case, it makes more sense to invoke the fully capable, fully remote PowerShell instance to that remote server. If you open up PowerShell on your local system, and utilize the `Enter-PSSession` cmdlet, your PowerShell prompt will be a full remote representation of PowerShell on that remote server. You are then able to issue commands in that prompt, and they will execute as if you were sitting at a PowerShell prompt from the console of that server. Once again, I am logged in to my Windows 10 client computer, and have opened up PowerShell. I then use the following command to remotely connect to my WEB1 server:

`Enter-PSSession -ComputerName WEB1`

You will see the prompt change, indicating that I am now working in the context of the WEB1 server.

 If your user account does not have access to the server, you can specify alternate credentials to be used when creating this remote connection. Simply append your `Enter-PSSession` cmdlet with `-Credential USERNAME` in order to specify a different user account.

[327]

Commands that I issue from this point forward will be executed against WEB1. Let's verify this. If I check a simple `$env:computername`, you can see that it presents me with the WEB1 hostname:

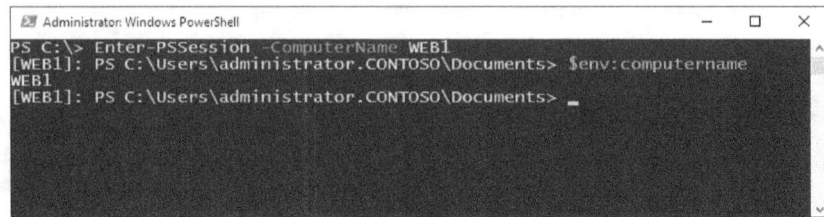

And to further verify this, if I check the installed Windows roles and features, you can see that I have the Web Server role installed, as well as Failover Clustering from earlier in the book. These are clearly items that are not installed on my Windows 10 machine, PowerShell is pulling this data from the WEB1 server:

`Get-WindowsFeature | Where Installed`

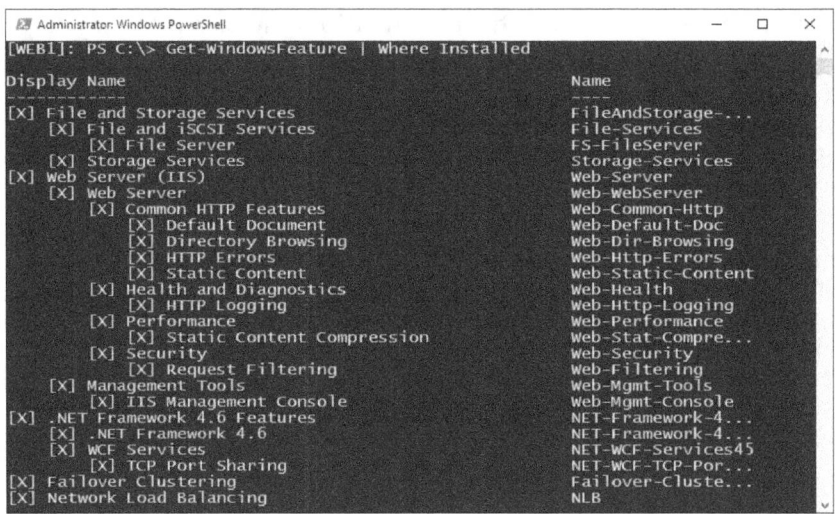

This is pretty powerful stuff. We are sitting at our local desktop computer, have a remote PowerShell session running to the WEB1 server, and are now able to pull all kinds of information from WEB1 because it is as if we are working from PowerShell right on that server. Let's take it one step further, and try to make a configuration change on WEB1, just to verify that we can. Maybe we can install a new feature onto this server. I use Telnet Client quite a bit, but can see that it is currently not installed on WEB1:

`Get-WindowsFeature -Name *telnet*`

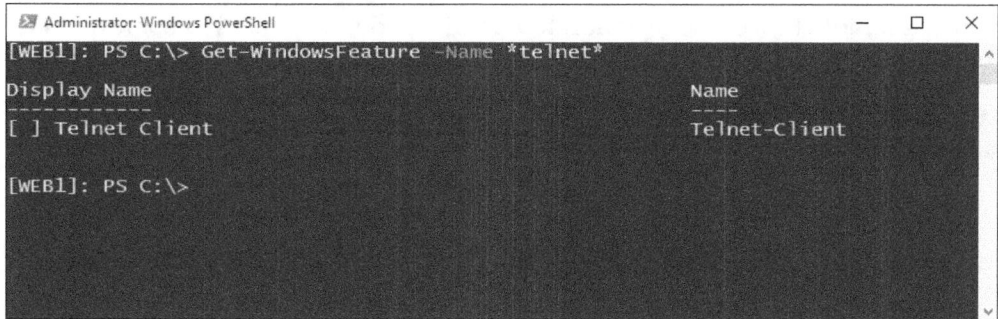

By using the `Add-WindowsFeature` cmdlet, I should be able to make quick work of installing that feature:

`Add-WindowsFeature Telnet-Client`

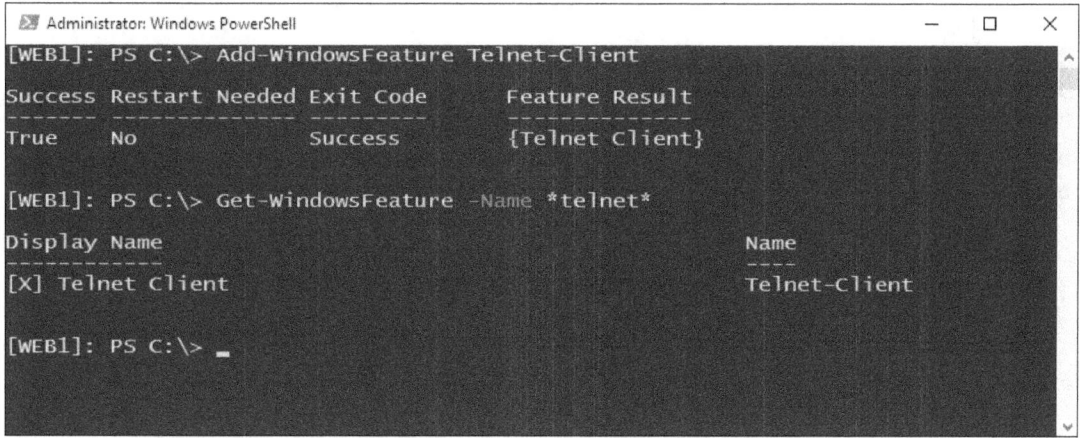

Learning PowerShell 5.0

Testing it with Server Core and Nano Server

So, this all works great when interacting with real servers that are running the full Desktop Experience operating system, as we have seen with the WEB1 server. But what about my server instances running Server Core or Nano Server? The process is exactly the same! PowerShell is integral to the way that Windows Server 2016 is built, and allows streamlined functionality and access across all instances of its platform. If my WEB1 server had been a Server Core or Nano Server, I would have been able to interface with it the same way I just did. We will run a quick test to verify this. I do have my CORE1 server up and running at the moment, so let's establish a remote PowerShell session to CORE1, and verify that it also outputs us with information from the CORE1 server:

`Enter-PSSession -ComputerName CORE1`

`$env:computername`

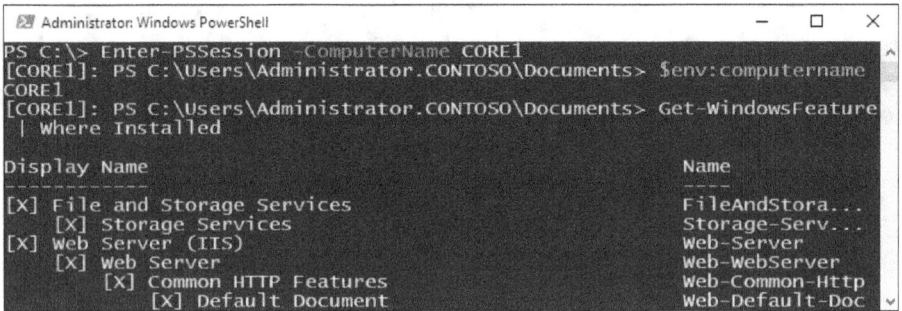

As you can see, we are now remoted into the PowerShell interface of the CORE1 server, and can manipulate that server in any way that we could with a full blown Desktop Experience server. PowerShell remoting will likely be the most common way that you interact with Server Core and Nano Server instances, so definitely make these tools part of your daily arsenal.

Desired State Configuration

There is some new and powerful functionality in PowerShell 5.0, provided by something called **Desired State Configuration** (**DSC**). DSC is a management platform plugged into PowerShell, which provides some new functions and cmdlets that you can take advantage of in your scripts to enable some really cool features. As the name implies, it allows you to build configurations inside PowerShell that will provided a *desired state*. What do I mean by that? Well, in a basic sense what DSC does is make sure that the PowerShell scripts you build will always work the same way, across all of the servers where you apply them.

It is quite easy to build a script in such a way that it will work correctly on the server you are currently working from, but if you try to roll that same script out to a different server that might reside in a different OU, or have different items installed on it to begin with, that the script could produce different results than what it was originally intended to. DSC was built to counteract these differences. In building your DSC configuration, you identify particular roles, settings, functions, accounts, variables, and so on—all of which you want to retain in your specific desired state. Once you identify and configure these variables, DSC will work to ensure they stay where you have them set, and that they remain uniform according to your DSC configuration policy, which means they are uniform against the other servers where you have run this script.

DSC also helps to prevent unwanted changes on servers. If your DSC-enabled script has identified that a particular service should be running all the time on your servers, and that service stops for some reason, DSC can be there to help spin it back up so that you don't experience an outage. Alternatively, perhaps you have a script that configures a server to a particular set of standards, and another person in the IT staff comes along and adjusts that configuration on the server itself—maybe they log in and stop the service purposefully for some reason. These are some of the situations where DSC can intervene and set the server back into the desired state in which you placed it originally. DSC is your scripting "nanny", so to speak. It helps to build configurations that will remain uniform across multiple platforms, and will then work to ensure these configurations are always true. You can then be confident that your servers are always running within the context of your specified desired state.

After building your configuration that identifies the items you want to be installed or monitored, something called the **Local Configuration Manager** (**LCM**) works to ensure the resources remain within the configuration specifications. LCM polls the system regularly watching for irregularities and changes, and takes action when needed to bring your servers back into the Desired State Configuration.

The ultimate goal of DSC is to keep everything constant and consistent across your servers and services. DSC's capabilities and access to reach into more and more places in the operating system grows constantly, as roles are rewritten to accept DSC parameters and monitoring. In the end, I believe that it will be Microsoft's goal that every server runs a DSC configuration script, ensuring that it is constantly working within your standards and helping to maintain your 99.999% uptime status.

There is very much that can be learned about DSC, and I encourage you to explore this topic some more once you are familiar with creating and using PowerShell scripts. Here are some great starting points for reading on the Desired State Configuration topic:

- `https://msdn.microsoft.com/en-us/powershell/dsc/overview`
- `https://mva.microsoft.com/en-US/training-courses/getting-started-with-powershell-desired-state-configuration-dsc--8672?l=ZwHuclG1_2504984382`

Summary

In Windows Server 2016, we see in multiple places that administration via PowerShell is the recommended path to interacting with our servers. The fact that the management GUIs are just shells running PowerShell scripts and that the default installation option for Windows Server is Server Core, we can assume the headless, command-line oriented servers are going to be our servers of the future. Even though PowerShell really has been at the core of our operating system functionality since Server 2012, until this point I believe that PowerShell has been viewed by most admins as simply an alternative way of managing servers. Yeah, I know it exists and that I should start using it, and the scripting looks pretty cool, but I can still do anything I want to with the old Command Prompt or my mouse button. That old mentality is quickly changing.

Now that we are experiencing the onset of new technologies such as DSC, we can see that PowerShell is starting to develop functionality that simply does not exist anywhere else in the operating system. This combined with the remote management accessibility provided by the standardized PowerShell platform that can be used across all of your current Windows devices means that we will definitely be seeing more and more PowerShell in subsequent Microsoft operating systems and services.

11
Application Containers and Docker

Many of the new technologies included in Windows Server 2016 are designed to reflect capabilities provided by cloud computing, bringing your private clouds to life and granting the ability to produce within your own physical infrastructure the same solutions given to you by public cloud providers. The last few iterations of the server operating system have also revolved much around virtualization, and the idea of application containers is something that taps into both of these mindsets. Application containers are going to make the deployment of applications more streamlined, more secure, and more efficient. Containers is a relatively new idea in the Microsoft world, and I haven't heard many IT admins talking about it yet, but that will soon change. This is something that has been enhancing Linux computing for a while now, and this newest Windows Server operating system brings it a little bit closer to home for us Microsoft-centric shops.

Application developers will be very interested in application containers provided by Windows Server 2016, and in truth they probably understand the concepts behind containers much better than a traditional server administrator. While the premise of this book is not focused on development opportunities, and is clearly not focused on Linux, we are going to discuss containers because the benefits provided are not only for developers. We as system operations will also benefit from using containers, and if nothing else it is going to be important for us to know and understand how to conceptualize, and how to spin up containers so that we can provide the infrastructure that our developers are going to require. Today we are going to cover some initial topics dealing with application containers, specifically the new capabilities that are available in Windows Server 2016 to bring this technology into our datacenters:

- Understanding application containers
- The differences between hypervisors and containers

- Windows Server Containers versus Hyper-V Containers
- Starting a container with PowerShell
- What is Docker?

Understanding application containers

What does it mean to contain an application? We have a pretty good concept these days of containing servers, by means of virtualization. Taking physical hardware and turning it into a virtualization host—like Hyper-V—and then running many virtual machines on top of it is a form of containment for those VMs. We are essentially tricking them into believing that they are their own entity, completely unaware that they are sharing resources and hardware with other VMs running on that host. At the same time that we are sharing hardware resources, we are also able to provide strong layers of isolation between VMs, because we need to make sure that access and permissions cannot bleed over across VMs. Particularly in a cloud provider scenario, as that would spell disaster.

Application containers are the same idea, at a different level. Rather than creating VMs, we create containers, which are much smaller. We then run applications inside those containers, and the applications are tricked into thinking that they are running on top of a dedicated instance of the operating system. Why is this important? Let's discuss a few answers to that question.

Sharing resources

Just like when we are talking about hardware being split up among VMs, application containers mean that we are taking physical chunks of hardware and dividing them up among containers. This allows us to run many containers from the same server—whether that be a physical or virtual server. However, in that alone, there is no benefit over VMs, because they simply share hardware as well. Where we really start to see benefits in using containers rather than separate VMs for all of our applications is that all of our containers can share the same base operating system image. Not only are they spun up from the same base set, which makes it extremely fast to bring new containers online, it also means that they are sharing the same kernel resources. Every instance of an operating system has its own set of user processes, and it is tricky business to run multiple applications together on servers because those applications traditionally have access to the same set of processes, and have the potential to be negatively affected by those processes. In other words, it's the reason that we tend to spin up so many servers these days, keeping each application on its own server, so that they can't hurt each other. Sometimes apps just don't like to mix. The kernel in Windows Server 2016 has been enhanced so that it can handle multiple copies of the user mode processes.

This means you not only have the ability to run instances of the same application over many different servers, but it also means that you can run many different applications—even if they don't typically like to co-exist—on the same server.

Isolation

One of the huge benefits of application containers is that developers can build their applications within a container on their own workstation. When built within this container sandbox, they will know that the application contains all of the parts, pieces, and dependencies that it needs in order to run properly, and that it runs in a way that doesn't require extra components from the underlying operating system. This means the developer can work on the application, make sure it works in their local environment, and then easily slide that application container over to the hosting servers where it will be spun up and ready for production use. That production server might even be a cloud provided resource, but the application doesn't care. The isolation of the container from the operating system helps to keep the application standardized in a way that it is easily mobile and movable, and saves the developer time and headaches since they don't have to accommodate for differences in underlying operating systems during the development process.

The other aspect of isolation is the security aspect. This is the same story as multiple virtual machines running on the same host, particularly in a cloud environment. You want security boundaries to exist between those machines, in fact most of the time you don't want them to be aware of each other in any way. You even want isolation and segregation between the virtual machines and the host operating system, because you sure don't want your public cloud service provider snooping around inside your VMs. The same idea applies with application containers. The processes running inside a container are not visible to the hosting operating system, even though you are consuming resources from that operating system. Containers maintain two different forms of isolation. There is namespace isolation, which means the containers are confined to their own filesystem and registry. Then there is also resource isolation, meaning that we can define what specific hardware resources are available to the different containers, and they are not able to steal from each other. Shortly, we will discuss two different categories of containers, Windows Server Containers and Hyper-V Containers. These two types of containers handle isolation in different ways, so stay tuned for more info on that topic.

We know that containers share resources and are spun up from the same base image, while still keeping their processes separated so that the underlying operating system can't negatively affect the application and also so that the application can't tank the operating system. But how is the isolation handled from a networking aspect? Well, application containers utilize technology from the Hyper-V virtual switch in order to keep everything straight on the networking side. In fact, as you start to use containers, you will quickly see that each container has a unique IP address assigned to it in order to maintain isolation at this level.

Scalability

The combination of spinning up from the same base image and the isolation of the container makes a very compelling scalability and growth story. Think about a web application that you host whose use might fluctuate greatly from day to day. Providing enough resources to sustain this application during the busy times weighed against too much expense for running the application during the lesser times is a difficult scale to balance. Cloud technologies are providing dynamic scaling for these kinds of applications today, but they are doing so many times by spinning up or down entire virtual machines. There are three common struggles today with dynamically scaling applications like this. First is the time that it takes to produce additional virtual machines; even if that process is automated, your application may be overwhelmed for a period of time while additional resources are brought online. Our second challenge is the struggle that the developer needs to go through in order to make that application so agnostic that it doesn't care if there are inconsistencies between the different machines upon which their application might be running. Third is cost. Not only hardware cost, as new VMs coming online will each be consuming an entire set of kernel resources, but monetary costs as well. Spinning virtual machines up and down in your cloud environment can get expensive in a hurry. These are all hurdles that do not exist when you utilize containers as your method for deploying applications.

Since application containers are using the same underlying kernel, and the same base image, their time to live is extremely fast. New containers can be spun up or spun down very quickly, and in batches, without having to wait for the boot and kernel mode processes to start. Also, since we have provided the developer this isolated container structure within which to build the application, we know that our application is going to be able to run successfully anywhere that we spin up one of these containers. No more worries about whether or not the new VM that is coming online is going to be standardized correctly, because containers for a particular application are always the same, and contain all of the important dependencies that the application needs, right inside that container.

The differences between hypervisors and containers

While the information given in the preceding paragraphs about containers shapes a viewpoint on what a container can do for you and how it can benefit your developers, I think that talking about differences between a hypervisor and a container helps to shape a picture of what a container really looks like. And more importantly, how you will start using it in the real world.

A hypervisor, such as Hyper-V or VMware, provides you with the ability to spin up many different virtual machines. As many VMs as your hardware can handle. Unfortunately, the number of VMs that you spin up can be seriously limited because each virtual machine is running an entire operating system. Everything from the boot kernel to the filesystem and processes are contained inside each and every virtual machine. This also means that each VM is vulnerable to operating system level attacks, and consumes even more resources when you start adding protectors onto it, like antivirus. It is very easy to spin up VMs when you need new servers, but if you start assigning each of your VMs 8GB of RAM, you'll overwhelm even the largest hypervisor servers in a hurry.

This is where containers swoop in and save the day. Since containers share the operating system boot kernel, there is no need to replicate it over and over again as you do with VMs. You can spin up container after container after container, and never have to install a new instance of the operating system. Yes, containers still have their own networking, filesystem, and processes, as they must in order to do their isolation job and keep both the applications and the operating system safe from bleeding over. However, I have heard that being able to share those core resources enables you to spin up four to six times the amount of containers on a particular server, when compared to the number of virtual machines that you would be able to run on that same server.

A lot of people think that containers are intended to replace virtual machines, but that is simply not true. VMs and Containers are completely different. So if you are a VM administrator, don't worry about containers taking over your day job. There will certainly still be need for full VMs to be running in our datacenters, I am almost sure they will still comprise of the majority of our infrastructure. However, containers do a great job of solving the impedance mismatch between developers and IT. Let's say a developer creates an application, and has it working flawlessly on their own laptop. They hand this perfect application with zero issues over to the IT guy to put on a server, and suddenly it doesn't work. This is a huge problem, and an enormous headache for the developer. Containers solve this problem, because the dev work environment is exactly the same as the environment upon which the application is going to live long-term. Both development and operations happen within a container!

If there is a downside to be had about containers when compared to VMs, it is flexibility. With a hypervisor server we can just as easily spin up a Linux server as we can a Windows server, and we can even spin them both up at the same time, on the same platform, without any problems between them. Containers on the other hand, since they are sharing the operating system kernel, can only function when they are all running on the same operating system. This can be a limiting factor, depending on what your applications look like and what you are hoping to accomplish with containers. Application developers will love the isolation and standardized compute environment provided by containers, and server administrators will love the stability and low resource utilization that containers can provide.

Another huge advantage to using containers is the unity that they bring between the development and operations teams. We hear the term DevOps all the time these days, which is a combination of development and operation processes in order to make the entire application rollout process more efficient. The utilization of containers is going to have a huge impact on the DevOps mentality, since developers can now do their job—develop applications—without needing to accommodate for the operations side of things. When the application is built, operations can take the container within which the application resides, and simply spin it up inside their container infrastructure, without any worries that the application is going to break servers or have compatibility problems.

I definitely foresee containers having an important role in our "cloud-focused" computing, but this will only happen if admins jump in and try it out for themselves. This is one of those things, especially because the documentation often references things like application development and Linux, that traditional server admins have a hard time adjusting to, and therefore have a hard time trusting. Hopefully, by the end of this chapter, you will have some comfort with the idea of containers, and some useful input on what they can do to help your day job, rather than make it more complicated.

Windows Server Containers versus Hyper-V Containers

When Microsoft had people start testing and using containers, what they found is that many places were deploying only one container per VM. Well, that's a little silly – sure they are getting the DevOps benefits out of using the container approach, but you aren't getting any benefits out of the resource sharing and small footprint of a container. After doing a little digging, they discovered that companies were doing this because containers natively share kernel. While this is imperative to the performance of containers, this is a problem for isolation, and organizations were reluctant to deploy multiple containers within a single VM. So, Microsoft created a compromise.

When spinning up your containers, it is important to know that there are now two categories of containers that you can run in Windows Server 2016. All aspects of application containers that we have been talking about so far apply to either Windows Server Containers or to Hyper-V Containers. Like Windows Server Containers, Hyper-V Containers can run the same code or images inside of them, while keeping their strong isolation guarantees to make sure the important stuff stays separated. The decision between using Windows Server Containers or Hyper-V Containers will likely boil down to what level of security you need your containers to maintain. Let's discuss the differences between the two so that you can better understand the choice you are facing. It is important to point out that the developers who are building applications inside your containers don't need to know or care about what kind of container the app is going to reside in. This is purely an IT decision, and has no bearing on how the application behaves within the container, or how it needs to be built.

Windows Server Containers

In the same way that Linux containers share the host operating system kernel files, Windows Server Containers make use of this sharing in order to make the containers efficient. What this means, however, is that while namespace, filesystem and network isolation is in place to keep the containers separate from each other, there is some potential for vulnerability between the different containers running on a server. For example, if you were to log in to the host operating system on your container server, you would be able to see the running processes of the container itself. The container is not able to see the host or other containers, and is still isolated from the host itself in various ways, but knowing that the host is able to view the processes within the container shows us that some interaction does exist with this level of sharing. Windows Server Containers are going to be most useful in circumstances where your container host server and the containers themselves are within the same *trust boundary*. In most cases, this means that Windows Server Containers are going to be most useful for servers which are company owned, and only run containers that are owned and trusted by the company. If you trust both your host server and your containers, and are okay with those entities trusting each other, then deploying regular Windows Server Containers is the most efficient use of your hardware resources.

Hyper-V Containers

If you're looking for an increased amount of isolation and stronger boundaries, that is where you will foray into Hyper-V Containers. Hyper-V Containers are more like a super-optimized version of a virtual machine. While kernel resources are still shared by Hyper-V Containers, so they are still much more performant than full virtual machines, each Hyper-V Container gets its own dedicated Windows shell within which a single container can run. This means you have isolation between Hyper-V Containers that is more on par with isolation between VMs, and yet are still able to spin up new containers at will and very quickly because the container infrastructure is still in place underneath. Hyper-V Containers are going to be more useful in multitenant infrastructures, where you want to make sure no code or activity is able to be leaked between the container and host, or between two different containers that might be owned by different entities. A minute ago we discussed how the host operating system can see into the processes running within a Windows Server Container, but this is not the case with Hyper-V Containers. The host operating system is completely unaware of and unable to tap into those services that are running within the Hyper-V Containers themselves. These processes are now invisible.

It is important to know that you can change regular Windows Server Containers to be Hyper-V Containers with a simple PowerShell command. This way if you are running a container and later realize that you created it incorrectly or simply decide that the other mode is better for your application's use, you simply stop the container and use PowerShell to convert it. In the very next section of this chapter, we will be using PowerShell in order to start up a new container, and we will also take a look at the `Set-Container` cmdlet to swing this container back and forth between a Windows Server Container and a Hyper-V Container.

The availability of Hyper-V Containers means that even if you have an application that must be strongly isolated, you no longer need to dedicate a full Hyper-V VM to this application. You can now spin up a Hyper-V Container, run the application in that container, and have full isolation for the application, while at the same time continuing to share resources and provide a better, more scalable experience for that application.

Starting a container with PowerShell

Any of you who have worked with containers already know that this section heading is misleading. I did that on purpose, as you will soon see that we can utilize PowerShell as our command line console to do the work, but that we aren't actually using PowerShell under the hood at all in order to accomplish our work with containers today. Let's take a look together and find out how easy it really is to start using containers inside Windows Server 2016. The first thing you need is, of course, your server. I have a fresh Windows Server 2016 running. There are a couple of things we need to accomplish on this server in order to prepare it for running containers.

I would like to note here that this process is still evolving, and may continue evolving throughout the infancy of Windows Server 2016. As of this writing, there is a quick-start process that we are going to use which makes the process of getting familiar with the commands and spinning up your first container pretty easy, but even this process may change in the future.

Preparing your container host server

To start using containers on your server, there is a simple feature that needs to be installed called **Containers**. Installing that feature installs the PowerShell cmdlets and functions needed in order to start and manage containers on your server. In addition to that, if you intend to utilize Hyper-V containers, then you also need to make sure that the Hyper-V role has been installed on your container host server. In taking this straightforward role installation approach, however, you will end up with no real way to start a container, because you won't have any base images from which you can start new containers. In order to make our server more robust and ready to actually start an image, we are also going to install something called Docker. If you aren't familiar with Docker, there is a section coming up later in this chapter that gives you a little detail on Docker itself. But for the purposes of spinning up your first container, you simply need to follow the directions which will install it for you.

Application Containers and Docker

Before we get started, I want to take a minute and chase down a rabbit trail. At this point, you may be wondering if my container host server needs to have the Hyper-V role installed, doesn't that mean it must be a physical server? You can't install the Hyper-V role onto a virtual machine, right? *Wrong*. Windows Server 2016 supports something called nested virtualization, which was added really for the purpose of containers. You see, requiring physical hardware is becoming a limiting factor for IT departments these days, as almost everything is done from virtual machines. It makes sense that companies would want to deploy containers, but that they would want their container servers to be VMs, with multiple containers being run within that VM. Therefore, nested virtualization was required to make this possible. If you are running a Windows Server 2016 physical hypervisor server, and a Windows Server 2016 virtual machine inside that server, you will now find that you are able to successfully install the Hyper-V role right onto that VM. I told you virtual machines were popular, so much so that they are now being used to run other virtual machines!

The main resource for Microsoft documentation on containers is `https://aka.ms/windowscontainers`. Make sure to check over this site in order to find the latest best practices and approved installation path for preparing your container host servers.

I have already installed the Hyper-V role onto my new server, now I am going to install the Containers feature by using the following PowerShell cmdlet:

`Install-WindowsFeature Containers`

After the installation of our new containers feature, make sure to reboot your server.

Now that containers is ready to go within Windows, giving us the core "under the hood" functionality, we need a special toolset called Docker to interact with these containers. The Docker files can be downloaded here:

`https://download.docker.com/components/engine/windows-server/cs-1.12/docker.zip`

Now, it is important to note there is not an actual installer that you have to run. Instead, unzip these files and place them somewhere on your system, such as inside `C:\Program Files\Docker`.

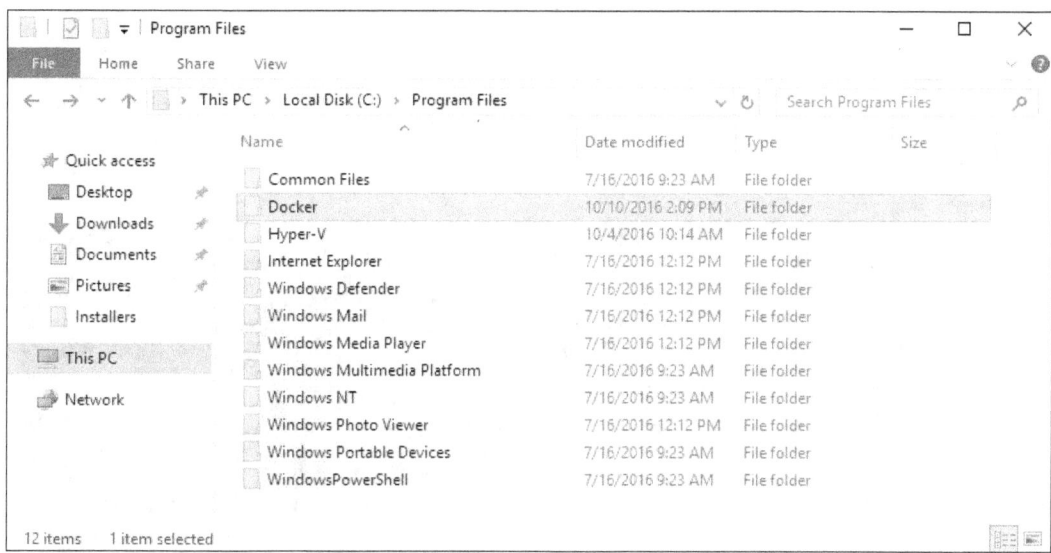

Next we have three commands to run from within PowerShell. These commands will add this new Docker directory to our system path so that we can run the commands within from any PowerShell prompt, and then our next commands will install Docker as a service, and start that service.

To set the path:

`[Environment]::SetEnvironmentVariable("Path", $env:Path + ";C:\Program Files\Docker", [EnvironmentVariableTarget]::Machine)`

To install the Docker service:

`Dockerd.exe -register-service`

Application Containers and Docker

To start the new service:

```
Start-Service docker
```

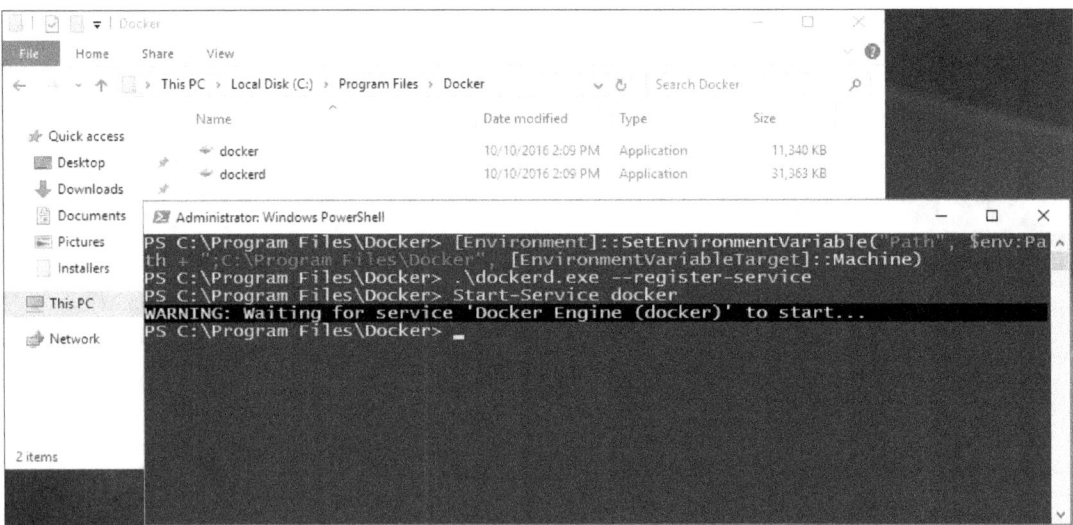

Starting a Windows Server Container

Now that our new Windows Server 2016 has been prepped to be able to run containers, let's jump right in and start one up. We will be doing this work from a PowerShell prompt. Before we can start a container we need to decide which base image we are going to use in order to build this container. You can use the command `docker images` in order to see currently available images on our system.

Well, that looks like a whole lot of nothing. We don't have any container base images on our system by default, so it looks like we need to reach out and get one. By using the integration with Docker that we have already installed, we have simple, easy-to-use commands that we can use to pull down sample base images from a repository that we will talk about at the end of this chapter, called Docker Hub. Microsoft has a repository on Docker Hub that allows us to pull down pre-created images that we can use to start up new containers. As an example, I am going to run the following command that will pull down a container image that is based on Server Core, and will have the IIS role installed:

```
Docker run -it -p 80:80 Microsoft/IIS cmd
```

```
PS C:\Program Files\Docker> .\docker.exe images
REPOSITORY            TAG                IMAGE ID            CREATED
    SIZE
PS C:\Program Files\Docker> .\docker.exe run -it -p 80:80 microsoft/iis cmd
Unable to find image 'microsoft/iis:latest' locally
latest: Pulling from microsoft/iis

9c7f9c7d9bc2: Downloading 4.866 MB/3.738 GB
081af1807c20: Downloading 4.865 MB/112.2 MB
552bd0bc6fa3: Download complete
0964ce0f4e6c: Download complete
```

Since I did not have this image on my system previously, it needs to take a few minutes and download it from the repository. Once complete, the container is automatically started, and IIS is up and running on this container. My server is not very powerful, and yet the process of starting up the container only took a few seconds to finish. That was a whole lot faster than spinning up a new virtual machine inside Hyper-V Manager!

Another way to get base images onto your Server 2016, without starting up containers automatically, is to issue a `docker pull` command which tells the machine to pull down Microsoft's base image of either Server Core or Nano Server. Here are those commands:

```
docker pull microsoft/windowsservercore
docker pull microsoft/nanoserver
```

After downloading those base images, you can use commands like the following to spin up new Windows Server Container instances:

```
docker run -it windowsservercore cmd
```

Application Containers and Docker

Or if you want to start a Hyper-V Container, you simply add one flag to the command:

```
docker run -it -isolation=hyperv nanoserver cmd
```

I have run some of these commands on my system, downloading the Server Core - IIS and the Nano Server base images, and now if I re-run `docker images`, I can see those base images on my system.

```
PS C:\Program Files\docker> docker pull microsoft/nanoserver
Using default tag: latest
latest: Pulling from microsoft/nanoserver

5496abde368a: Pull complete
Digest: sha256:1c514beb110052b91235fdfed4a9994d7bcadb15682d061be6a6aedc6dfdaae3
Status: Downloaded newer image for microsoft/nanoserver:latest
PS C:\Program Files\docker> docker images
REPOSITORY              TAG         IMAGE ID        CREATED
    SIZE
microsoft/iis           latest      6e30590a2139    10 days ago
    7.58 GB
microsoft/nanoserver    latest      853f9db844af    2 weeks ago
    652 MB
PS C:\Program Files\docker> docker ps
```

You may be wondering, why do we need to use this `docker` command to do everything? Where are the PowerShell cmdlets? This is a particularly confusing question at the moment because in earlier Technical Preview versions of Server 2016 there were PowerShell cmdlets available from which you could create containers, start containers, and interact with containers. But at some point in the process, Microsoft made the decision to re-visit this platform, and at the present time I am not able to find good information about whether or not PowerShell is going to be interfacing with containers in the future or not. All of the current documentation points at using Docker directly, so we are making the assumption at this point that the Docker controls will be your primary, and possibly only, way to interface with your containers.

What is Docker?

You're probably wondering why we waited to talk about Docker until now, when we have already installed it and have been using the commands in order to interact with containers. The reason I chose to jump right into using it first and explaining later is that many IT folks who would have started reading something about a toolset called Docker that is open source, works on Linux, and so on—would instantly glaze over and skip this section anyway. I know I would have. Since you can now clearly see that Docker is a control mechanism that we will need to get familiar with if we plan to work with containers, hopefully your interest is now peaked rather than being dissolved. So let's have just a few words on what Docker actually is.

Docker is an open source project—a tool set, really—that was originally designed to assist with the running of containers on Linux operating systems. Wait a minute, what? The words "Linux" and "open source" in a Microsoft book! What is this world coming to? You see, Microsoft thinks that containers are going to be a big deal, rightfully so. I still think they will end up putting cmdlets back into PowerShell that can be used to create, manage, and monitor containers, but I guess we'll have to wait and see. But there is an established following of people making heavy use of the Docker platform already in order to develop into containers, and Microsoft has made the decision with Windows Server 2016 to incorporate compatibility with the Docker engine right into the operating system. In the end, you may and probably will end up using a combination of PowerShell commands and the Docker tools, but if you are interested in looking closely into using application containers on your Windows Servers, make sure to install Docker and take a look at the extended capabilities provided here.

Developers have the ability to use Docker to create an environment on their local workstation that mirrors a live server environment, so that they can develop applications within containers and be assured that they will actually run once those applications are moved to the server. Docker is the platform that provides pack, ship, and run capabilities for your developers. Once finished with development, the container package can be handed over to the system administrator, who spins up the container(s) that will be running the application, and deploys it accordingly. The developer doesn't know or care about the container infrastructure, and the admin doesn't know or care about the development process or compatibility with his servers.

As I mentioned earlier, tools such as containers and Docker are part of the cloud-first vision. While the use of containers for most companies is going to start onsite, by using their own servers and infrastructure for the hosting of containers, this is a technology that is already capable of extending to the cloud. Because the containers themselves are so standardized and fluid, making them easy to expand and move around, sliding these containers into a cloud environment will be entirely possible.

Docker on Windows Server 2016

The real reason we are talking about Docker here is because it is a tool that has never been usable on a Microsoft operating system before, but all of this changes with Windows Server 2016. You can now install Docker right onto your Server 2016 container host server, and use it to create and interact with your containers running on that server, as we have already seen in the examples earlier. In fact, some folks may find that the Docker tools are comprehensive enough that you really don't need to utilize PowerShell in order to build new containers, and could work exclusively from the Docker world.

We have already run some commands to bring base images down onto our Server 2016 container server, but we didn't spin up a new container from one of those images. Let's use the Docker commands to do just that. First we can take a look at all of the container base images available to us with a command called `docker images`:

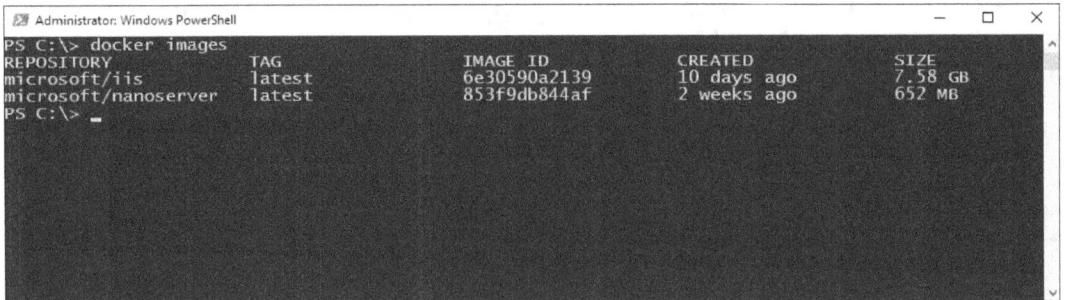

And we can create a new container named Cont6 by using the following Docker command:

```
docker run -name Cont6 -it nanoserver cmd
```

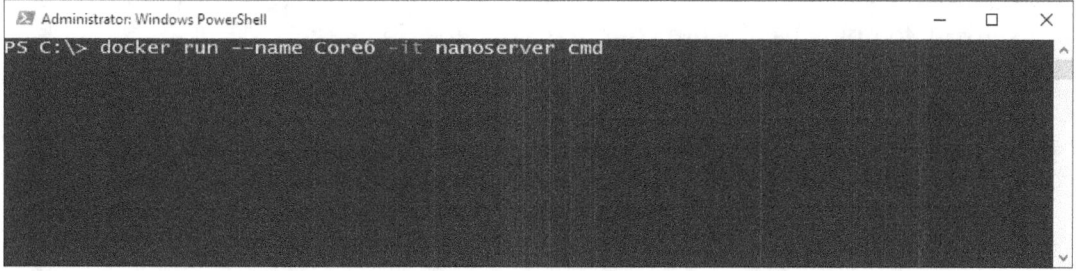

One important note to keep in mind as we start to blur the lines between Windows and Linux—the Docker daemon that runs in Windows Server 2016 isn't going to be able to run Linux containers! This is by design, as there isn't virtualization trickery happening here, Docker on Windows Server 2016 is re-using the host operating system kernel, just like what Docker does in the Linux world. This means that the operating systems between your container host server and the containers themselves need to match. You cannot run Windows containers on a Linux server, why would you be able to run Linux containers on top of a Windows server?

Docker Hub

When you work with containers, you are building container images that are usable on any server instance running the same host operating system—that is the essence of what containers enable you to do. When you spin up new instances of containers, you are just pulling new copies of that exact same image, which is all inclusive. This kind of standardized imaging mentality lends well to a shared community of images, a repository so to speak of images that people have built which might benefit others. Docker is open source, after all. Does such a sharing resource exist, that you can visit in order to grab container image files for testing, or even to upload your own images that you have created and share them with the world? Absolutely! And as part of the exercises in this chapter, you have already started using it, when we pulled down the base images from Microsoft. It is called **Docker Hub**, and is available at http://hub.docker.com.

Visit this site and create a login, and you immediately have access to thousands of container base images that the community has created and uploaded. This can be a quick way to get a lab up and running with containers, and many of these container images could even be used for production systems, running the applications that the folks here have pre-installed for you inside these container images. Or you can use Docker Hub to upload and store your own container images:

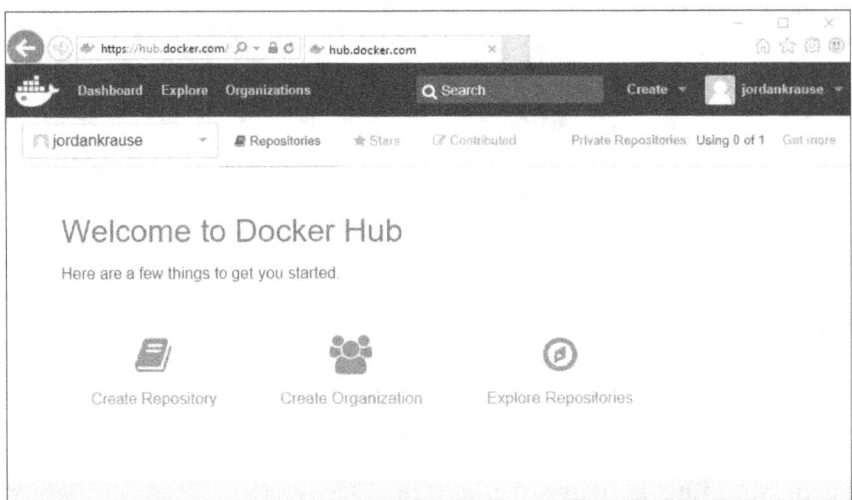

Docker Trusted Registry

If you're anything like me, you think the idea of Docker Hub is a great one, a neat place to store images and even to share them among the community. However, my next inclination is to look at this through an Enterprise spyglass, which quickly turns my perspective from *neat* to *insecure*. In other words, you may not be comfortable with placing images in this public repository. Certainly not images that contain anything sensitive to your organization, anyway.

Here is where **Docker Trusted Registry** may be something to look into. Docker Trusted Registry is a container image repository system, similar in idea to Docker Hub, but it's something that you can contain within your network, behind your own firewalls and security systems. This gives you a container image repository system without the risk of sharing sensitive information with the rest of the world.

Summary

Essentially two things are brought to the table with containers—the ability to run many more applications on your servers than you are doing today, and the ability to easily develop applications in a standardized way, a way that makes them ready for both scalability and cloud utilization. Usability of containers in the real world has been expanded greatly by the Docker project. The folks at Docker are clearly the front-runners in this space, enough so that Microsoft has decided to incorporate the use of Docker—an open source project developed by Linux guys!—straight into Windows Server 2016. We can now utilize both the Docker engine to run containers on our Windows servers, as well as the Docker toolset to manage and manipulate containers inside Windows in the same way we can work with containers in the Linux world.

Linux containers and Windows Server Containers have a lot in common, and function in basically the same way. If we were only looking at Windows Server Containers with the release of Windows Server 2016, I don't think that the hype surrounding this topic would be nearly as large as it is today. Microsoft's ingenious idea to create an additional scope of container, the Hyper-V Container, brings a solid answer to a lot of common security questions that present themselves when approaching the idea of containers in general. Everyone uses virtual machines heavily these days, I don't think anybody can disagree with that. Assuming the use of containers evolves into something that is easy to implement and administer, I think we could actually see Hyper-V Containers being used in a lot of places where we are currently using full Hyper-V virtual machines. This will save time, expense, and server space.

Speaking of Hyper-V, it has become such an integral part of so many of our corporate networks today, continue reading our final chapter in this book to learn more about this amazing virtualization technology.

12
Virtualizing Your Datacenter with Hyper-V

I've always been a country boy. Driving dirt roads, working on cars, and firearms tend to fill my free time. Traveling to cities, and particularly a recent trip to Hong Kong, always hits me with a bit of culture shock. All those skyscrapers and tall apartment buildings serve an important purpose though, and serve to fulfill my metaphor—if there isn't enough land to grow outward, then you have to build up. The vertical ascension of large cities is similar to what we have seen happening in our datacenters over the past five years. Cities need more and more places for people and businesses just like we need to house more and more servers every year. Rather than horizontal expansion, with enormous server rooms filled with racks and racks of hardware, we are embracing the skyscraper mentality, and virtualizing everything. We build considerably fewer servers, but make them incredibly powerful. Then on top of these super computers, we can run dozens, if not hundreds, of virtual servers. The technology that provides this hypervisor layer, the ability to run VMs, in Microsoft-centric shops is the Hyper-V role in Windows Server. This is one of the most critical roles to understand as a server administrator, because if your organization is not yet making use of server virtualization, trust me when I say that they will be soon. Virtualization is the way of the future. Here are some topics we are going to explore so that you can become familiar with the virtualization capabilities provided by Microsoft in Windows Server 2016:

- Designing and implementing your Hyper-V Server
- Using virtual switches
- Implementing a new virtual server
- Managing a virtual server
- Shielded VMs
- Hyper-V Server 2016

Designing and implementing your Hyper-V Server

Creating your own Hyper-V Server is usually pretty simple. Build a server, install the Hyper-V role, and you're ready to get started. In fact, you can even install the Hyper-V role onto a Windows 10 Pro or Enterprise computer, if you had a need to run some virtual machines from your own desktop. While most hardware that is being created these days fully supports the idea of being a hypervisor provider, some of you may try installing the Hyper-V role only to end up with the following error message:

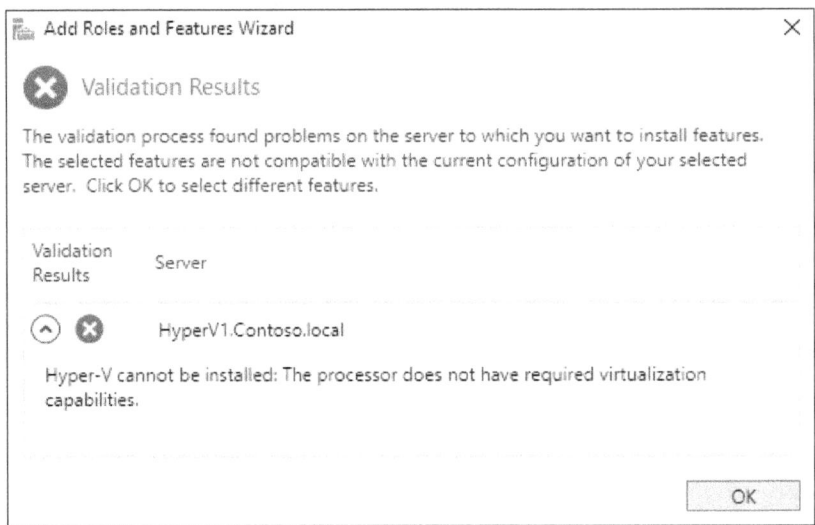

Uh oh, that's not good. This means one of two things—either my CPU really doesn't support virtualization, or I simply have some settings turned off inside BIOS on my server that are preventing this from working. There are three considerations you should check into on your server to make sure it is ready to run Hyper-V. First, you need to be running an x64-based processor. This is kind of a given, since Windows Server 2016 only comes in 64 bit anyway. If you don't have an x64 processor, you're not going to be able to install the operating system in the first place. Second, your CPUs need to be capable of hardware-assisted virtualization. This is typically called either Intel Virtualization Technology (Intel VT) or AMD Virtualization (AMD-V). And last but not least, you must have **Data Execution Prevention (DEP)** available and enabled on your system. If you have investigated the hardware itself and it seems to be virtualization capable, but it's still not working, then it is likely that you have DEP currently disabled inside the BIOS of that system. Boot into the BIOS settings and enable DEP.

Chapter 12

As long as your processors are happy to run virtual machines, you can turn just about any size of hardware into a hypervisor by installing the Hyper-V role. It is not important to think about minimum system requirements because you want your system hardware to be as large as possible in a Hyper-V Server. The more CPU cores, RAM, and hard drive space you can provide, the more virtual machines you will be able to run. Even the smallest Hyper-V Servers I have seen in production environments are running hardware like dual Xeon processors, 96 GB of RAM, and many terabytes of storage space. While 96 GB of RAM may seem like a lot—if your standard server build used to include 8 GB of RAM, which is a pretty low number, and you want to run a dozen servers on your Hyper-V Server—you are already past the capabilities of a Hyper-V Server with only 96 GB of RAM. Eight times twelve is 96, and you haven't left any memory for the host operating system to use! So the moral of the story? Go big or go home!

Installing the Hyper-V role

Hyper-V is just another role in Windows Server 2016, but during the installation of that role you will be asked a few questions and it is important to understand what they are asking, so that you can be sure your new Hyper-V Server is built to last and to work in an efficient manner. First of all, you will of course need to have Windows Server 2016 already installed, and use the **Add roles and features** function in order to install the role called **Hyper-V**:

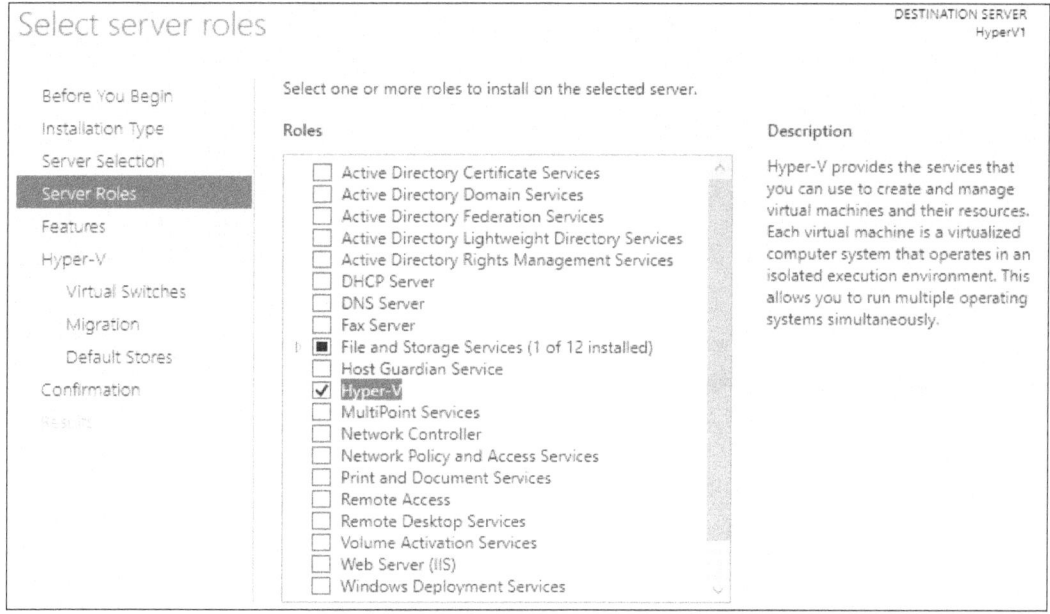

Virtualizing Your Datacenter with Hyper-V

As you continue walking through the wizard to install the role, you come across a screen labeled **Create Virtual Switches**. We will discuss networking within Hyper-V a little bit more in the next section of this chapter, but what is important here is that you get to define which of your server's physical NICs will be tied into Hyper-V, and available for your virtual machines to use. It is a good idea for each Hyper-V Server to have multiple NICs. You want one NIC dedicated to the host itself, which you would not select in this screen. Leave that one alone for the hypervisor's own communications. In addition to that NIC, you will want at least one network card that can bridge the VMs into the corporate network. This one you would select, as you can see in the upcoming screenshot. If you will be hosting many different VMs on this server, and they need to be connected to different physical networks, you might have to install many different NICs onto your Hyper-V Server:

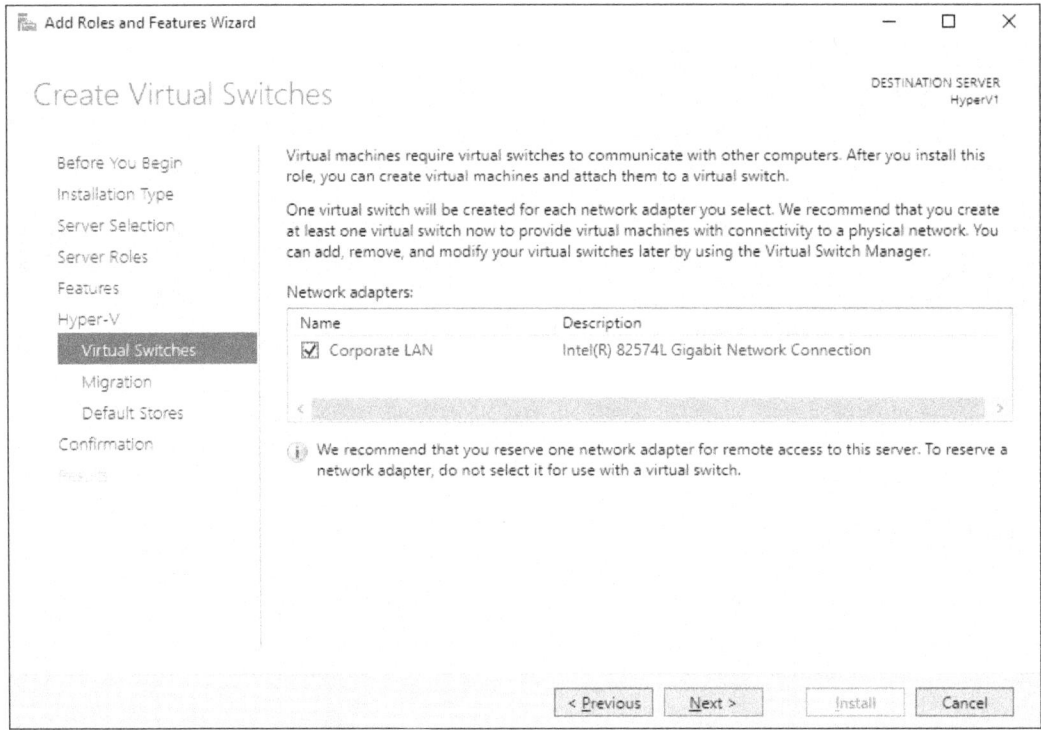

Chapter 12

After defining NICs, we get to decide whether or not this Hyper-V Server will be able to handle live migration of virtual machines. Live virtual machine migration is the ability to move a VM from one Hyper-V host to another, without any interruption of service on that VM. As you can see in the screenshot, there are a couple of different ways you can set up the server to prepare it for handling live migrations, and take note of the text at the bottom that is telling you to leave this option alone for now if you plan to make this Hyper-V Server part of a cluster. In clustered environments, these settings are handled at a different layer:

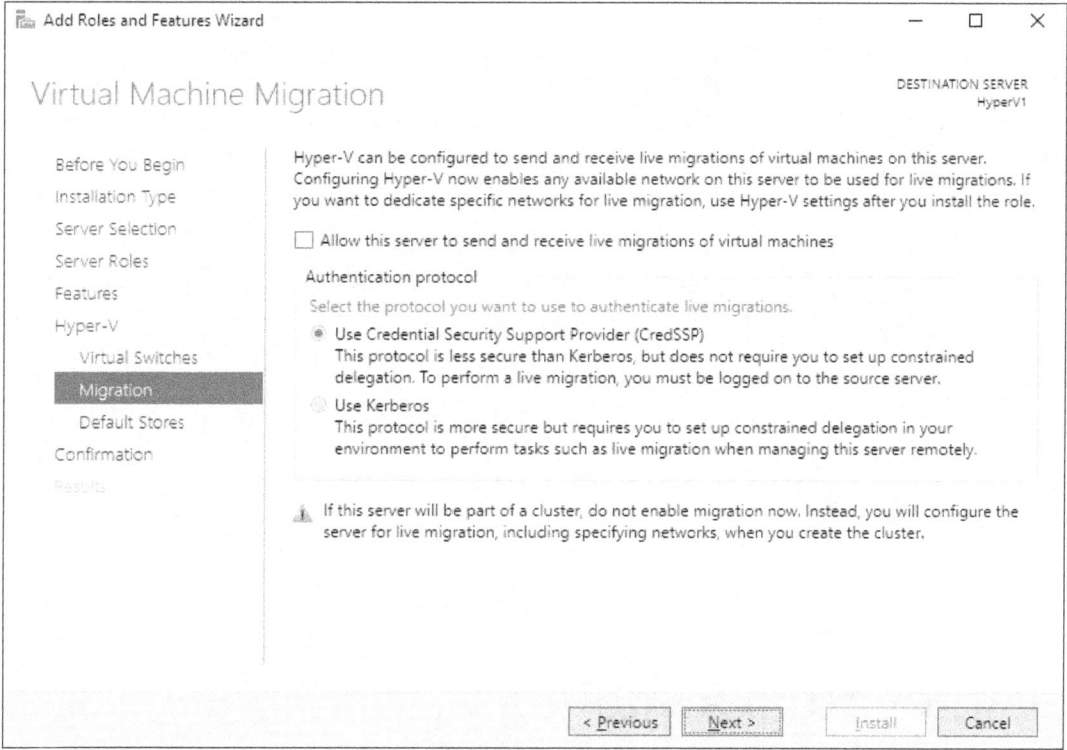

Virtualizing Your Datacenter with Hyper-V

The last screen that I wanted to point out is the definition of storage locations for your virtual machine data. After creating VMs and digging into what they look like at the hard disk level, in other words when you look to see what files are created per VM, you will see that there are two key aspects to a virtual machine. First is the virtual hard disk file—VHD or VHDX—and second is a folder containing configuration files for that VM. As you can see in the upcoming screenshot, the default locations for storing these items are something you would expect out of a client application you were installing onto a laptop, but you wouldn't expect something as heavy as Hyper-V to be storing its core files into `My Documents`. I suppose since Microsoft doesn't know the configuration of your server, they can't make any real guesses as to where you want to really store that data, and so they set the default to be something that would stand out as strange so that you will change it. Many Hyper-V Servers will have dedicated storage, even if only a separate hard disk, on which these files are planned to be stored. Make sure to take a minute on this screen and change the default storage locations of your VM files.

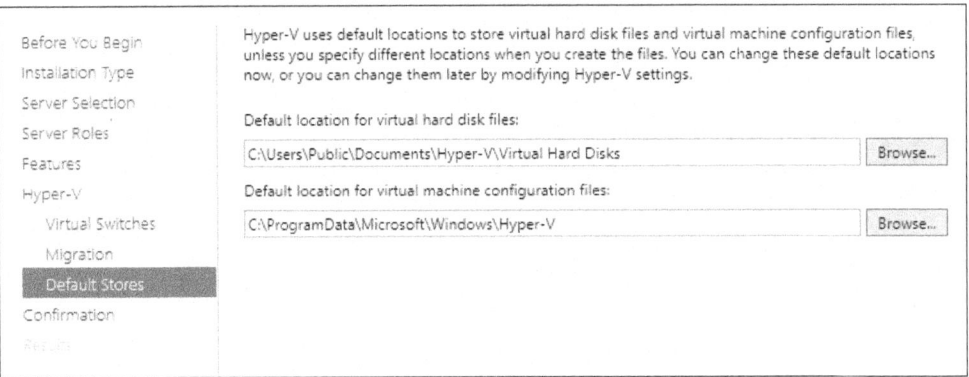

Using virtual switches

Upon completion of the Hyper-V role installation, your first inclination may be to jump right in and start creating VMs, but first you should really take a minute and make sure that the networking capabilities of your Hyper-V Server are adequate to meet your needs. During the role installation process, we selected the physical NICs which are to be passed through into Hyper-V, and that screen told us it was going to establish a virtual switch for each of these NICs. But what does that look like inside the console? And what options do we have for establishing networking between our virtual machines?

Chapter 12

In order to answer these questions, we need to open up the management interface for Hyper-V. As with any administrative tool of a Windows role, check inside the **Tools** menu of Server Manager, and now that the role has been installed, you will see a new listing for **Hyper-V Manager**. Launch that and we are now looking at the primary platform from which you will be managing and manipulating every aspect of your Hyper-V environment:

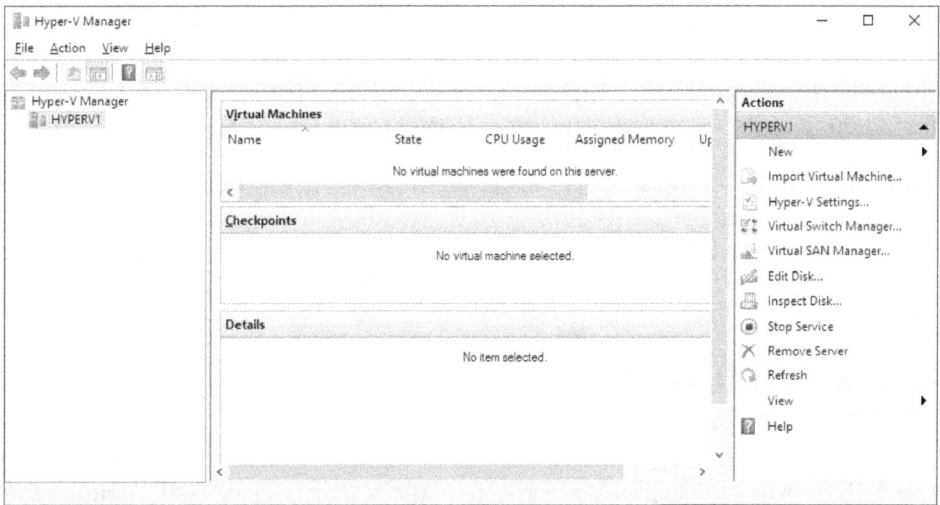

We currently have a lot of blank space in this console, because we don't have any VMs running yet. Over on the right side of **Hyper-V Manager**, you can see a link that says **Virtual Switch Manager...**. Go ahead and click on that link to be taken into the settings for our virtual switches and networking:

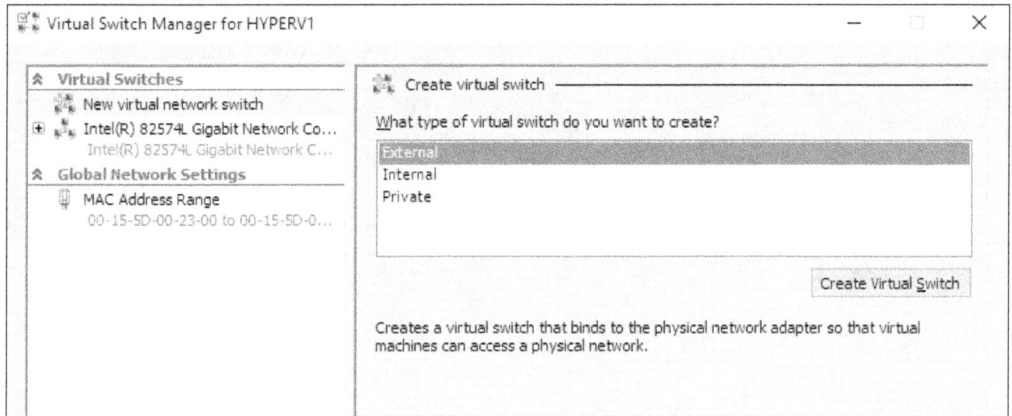

[359]

Toward the left you will see the current list of **Virtual Switches**. On my server there is only one switch listed there at the moment, which is named according to the physical NIC to which it is connected. This is that virtual switch which the role installation process created for us when we selected the NIC to be included with Hyper-V. If you selected multiple NICs during the role installation, you will have multiple virtual switches available here, each corresponding to a single physical NIC. Every VM that you create will have one or more virtual NICs, and you will see shortly that you have the ability to choose where each of those virtual NICs get connected. If there are five different physical networks that your VMs might have need to contact, you can use five physical NICs in the Hyper-V Server, plug each one into a different network, and have five virtual switches here in the console that your VM NICs can be plugged into.

As you can see in the previous screenshot, we have a button named **Create Virtual Switch**, which is self-explanatory. Obviously, this is where we go to create new switches, but there are three different types of switches that you can create. Let's take just a minute and discuss the differences between these three.

External virtual switch

The external virtual switch is the most common type to use for any VMs which need to contact a production network. Each external virtual switch binds to a physical NIC that is installed onto the Hyper-V Server. If you click on an external virtual switch, you can see that you have some options for configuring this switch, and that you can even change a switch type. In the following screenshot, I have renamed my external virtual switch so that it is easier to identify when I decide to add additional NICs to this server in the future:

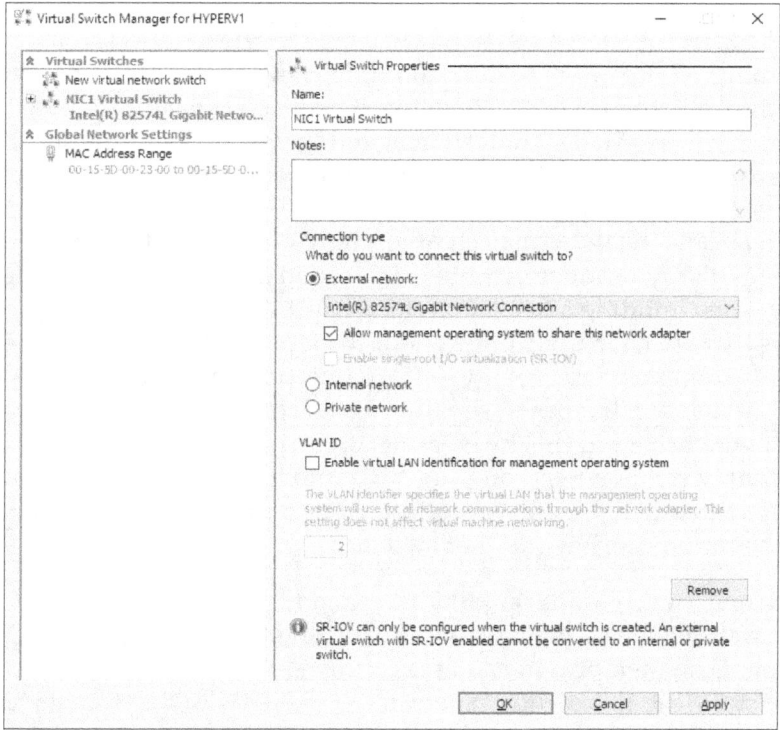

Internal virtual switch

Internal virtual switches are not bound to a physical NIC, and so if you create an internal virtual switch and connect a VM to it, that virtual machine will not be able to contact a physical network outside of the Hyper-V Server itself. Sort of a middleman between the other two types of switches, using an internal virtual switch is useful when you want the VM traffic to remain within the Hyper-V environment, but still provide network connectivity between the VMs and the host itself. In other words, VMs connected to an internal virtual switch will be able to talk to each other, and talk to the Hyper-V Server, but not beyond.

Private virtual switch

The private virtual switch is just what the name implies—private. VMs plugged into the same private virtual switch can communicate with each other, but not beyond. Even the Hyper-V host server does not have network connectivity to a private virtual switch. Test labs are a great example of a use case for private virtual switches, which we will discuss immediately following this text, when we create a new virtual switch of our own.

Creating a new virtual switch

Here is an example I use often. I am running this new Hyper-V Server, which is connected physically to my corporate network and so I can spin up new VMs, connect them to my external virtual switch, and have them communicate directly to the corp network. This allows me to domain join them, and interact with them like I would any server on my network. But maybe I have the need to create some VMs that I want to be able to talk with each other, but I do not want them to be able to communicate with my production network. A good example of this scenario in the real world is when building a test lab. In fact, I am taking this exact approach for all of the servers that we have used throughout this book. My physical Hyper-V Server is on my production network, yet my entire Contoso network and all of the VMs running within it are on their own separate network, which is completely segregated from my real network. I did this by creating a new private virtual switch. Remember from the description that when you plug VMs into this kind of switch, they can communicate with other VMs that are plugged into that same virtual switch, but they cannot communicate beyond that switch.

Inside the Virtual Switch Manager, all I have to do is choose the kind of virtual switch that I want to create, **private** in this case, and click on that **Create Virtual Switch** button. I can then provide a name for my new switch, and I am immediately able to connect VMs to this switch. You can see in the following screenshot that I have created two new private virtual switches, one to plug my test lab VM's internal NICs into, and another switch that will act as my test lab's DMZ network:

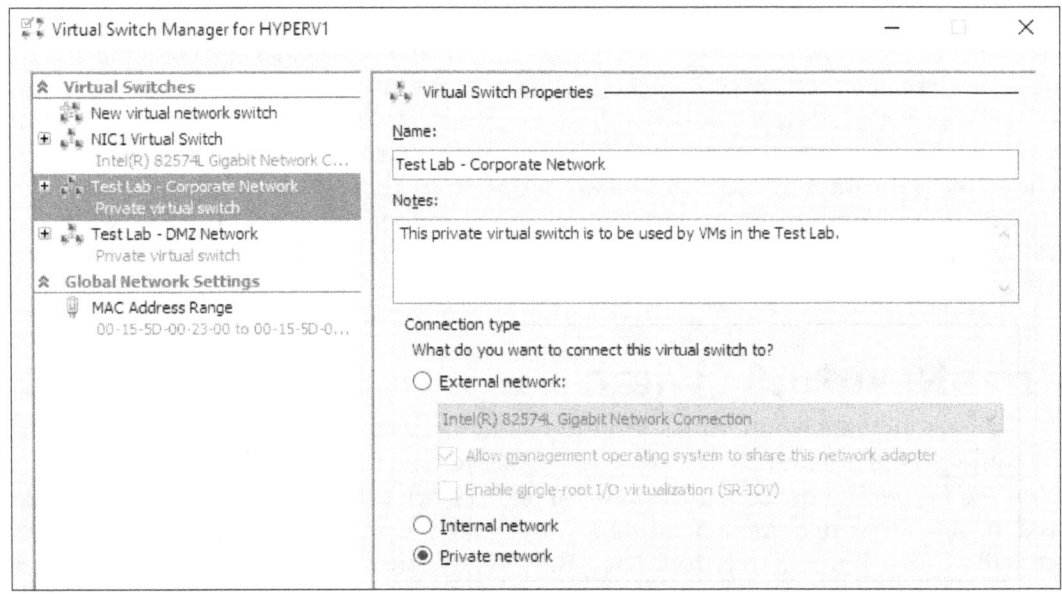

Implementing a new virtual server

Now we are ready to spin up our first virtual server! Similar to creating new virtual switches, the process for creating a new VM is fairly straightforward, but there are some steps along the way that might need some explanation if you haven't been through this process before. We start in the same management interface from which we do everything in the Hyper-V world. Open up **Hyper-V Manager**, and right-click on the name of your Hyper-V Server. Navigate to **New** | **Virtual Machine...** to launch the wizard:

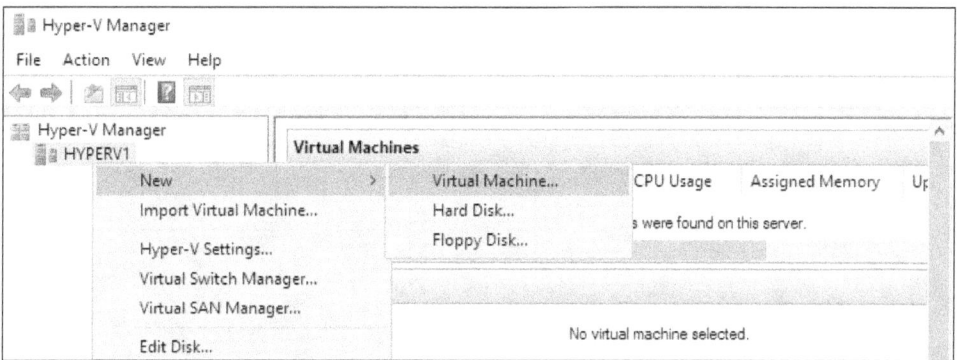

The first screen where we need to make some decisions is **Specify Name and Location**. Create a name for your new VM, that is easy enough. But then you also have the chance to store your VM in a new location. If you set a good default location for your virtual machines during Hyper-V role installation, chances are that you won't have to modify this field. But in my case, I chose the default options when I installed the role, and so it was going to place my VM somewhere in C:\Users, and I didn't like the look of that. So I selected this box, and chose a location that I like for my VM.

Virtualizing Your Datacenter with Hyper-V

You can see that I am using a dedicated disk for storing my virtual machines, which is a general good practice:

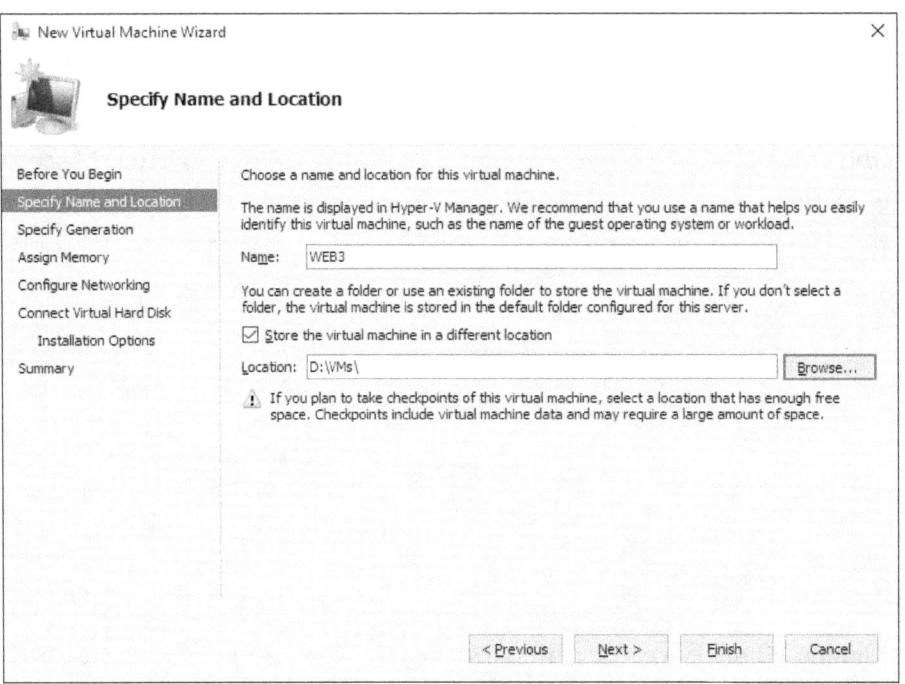

Next you have to decide whether you are creating a **Generation 1** or **Generation 2** virtual machine. We don't need to discuss this in very much detail, because explanations of the two are clearly stated on the page. If your VM is going to be running an older operating system, you should likely go with Gen 1 to ensure compatibility:

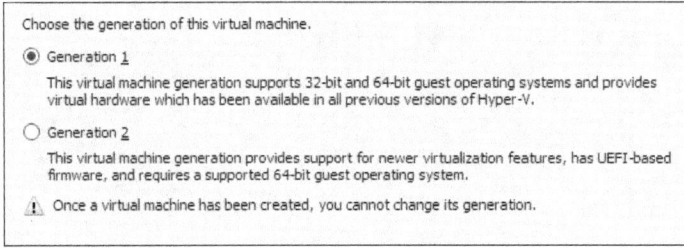

Now define how much memory you want to assign to this particular VM. Keep in mind that this is a setting that you can change in the future on this server, and so you don't have to plan too hard for this. The amount of RAM you dedicate to this virtual machine will depend upon how much RAM you have available in the Hyper-V host system, and upon how much memory is required to run whatever roles and services you plan to install on this VM. You can specify any amount of memory in this field. For example, if I wanted roughly 2 GB, I could type in around 2000 MB. However, what I find in the field is that most people still stick with the actual amount of MB, because that is what we have always done with hardware. So instead of rounding to 2000, I am going to set my 2 GB VM to an *actual* 2 GB—or 2048 MB.

Leaving the box unchecked for dynamic memory means that Hyper-V will dedicate an actual 2048 MB of RAM to this specific VM. Whether the VM is using 2048 MB or 256 MB at any given time, the full 2048 MB will be dedicated to the VM and will be unusable by the rest of the Hyper-V Server. If you select that box for **Use Dynamic Memory for this virtual machine**, then the VM only takes away from the Hyper-V host what it is actually using. If you set it to 2048 MB, but the VM is sitting idle and only consuming 256 MB, it will only be taxing Hyper-V with a 256 MB load:

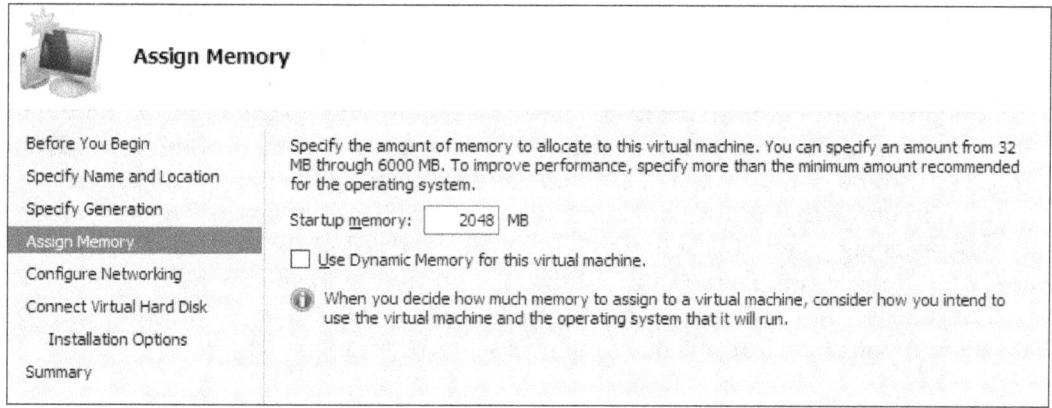

Virtualizing Your Datacenter with Hyper-V

Configure Networking is the next screen we are presented with, and here we are simply choosing which virtual switch our VM's NIC gets plugged into. We do have the ability to add additional NICs to this VM later, but for now we get a standard single NIC during the creation of our new VM, and we just need to choose where it needs to be connected. For the time being, this new web server I am building will be connected to my Test Lab's internal corporate network, so that I can build my web app and test it out, before introducing it into a real production network. If I dropdown the list of available connections here, you will see that my original external virtual switch, as well as the two new private virtual switches that I created, are available to choose from:

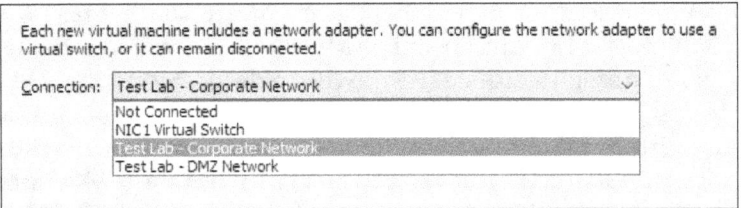

A few details are also needed so that this new virtual machine can have a hard drive. Most commonly, you will utilize the top option here so that the new VM gets a brand new hard drive. There are also options for using an existing virtual hard disk if you are booting from an existing file, or to attach a disk later if you aren't prepared yet to make this decision. We are going to allow the wizard to generate a brand new virtual hard disk, and the default size is 127 GB. I can set this to whatever I want, but it is important to know that it does not consume the full 127 GB of space. The disk size will only be as big as what is actually being used on the disk, so only a fraction of that 127 GB. I mention this to point out that the number you specify here is more of a *maximum* size, so make sure to plan your disks appropriately, specifying enough size that you and your applications have the necessary room to grow:

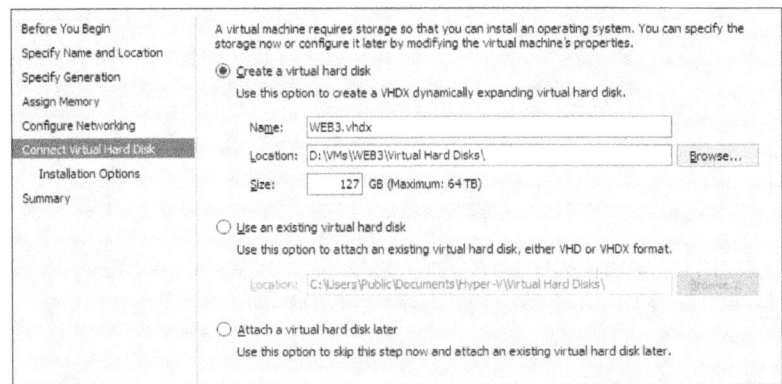

Our last screen of options in the wizard allows us to define specifics on what operating system our new VM is going to run. Or rather, where that operating system will be installed from. We are going to purposefully leave this set to **Install an operating system later**, because that is the default option, and it will give us the chance to see what happens when you do not specify any actual settings on this screen:

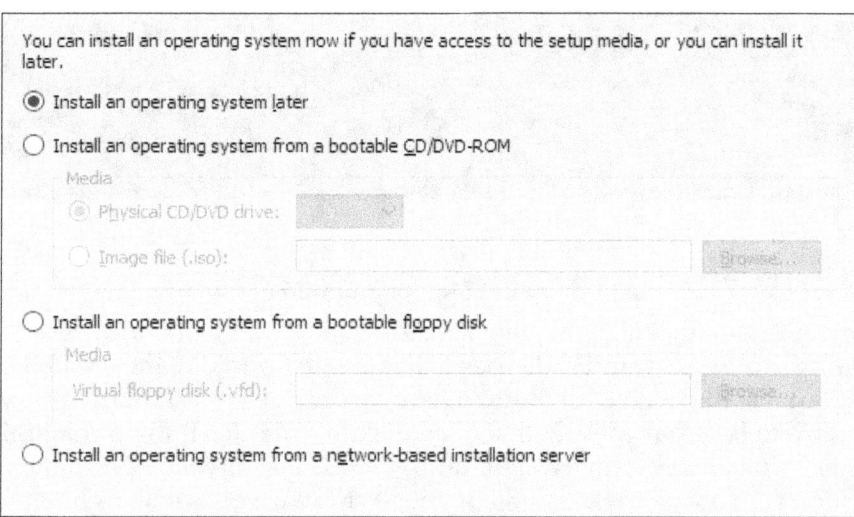

Starting and connecting to the VM

We have now created a virtual machine, which you can see inside the **Hyper-V Manager** console. Starting the VM is as simple as right-clicking on it, and then selecting **Start**. After selecting the option to start the VM, right-click on it again and click on **Connect...**. This will open a console window from which you can watch the boot process of your new server:

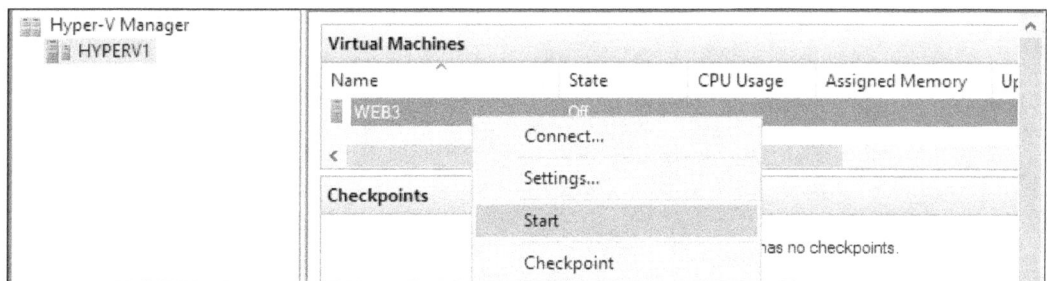

Now that our new VM has been started, what can we expect to see inside the console window? A boot failure error, of course!

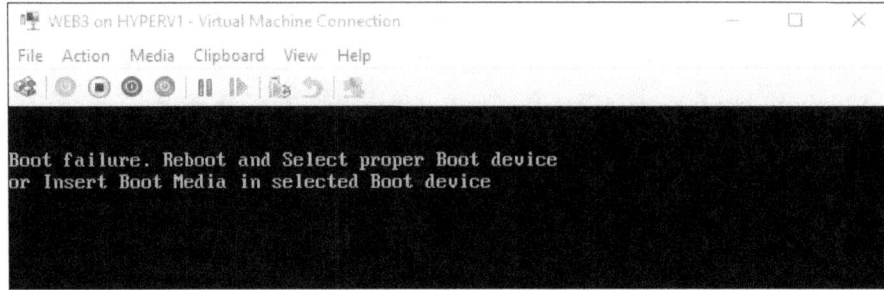

Installing the operating system

We get a boot failure message because we didn't specify any operating system media during our wizard, and so Hyper-V has created our VM and created our new hard disk, but just like when you build a new server out of fresh hardware, you need software to be installed onto that hard disk in order for it to do something. Luckily, installing an operating system onto a VM is just as easy as installing it onto a physical server. Heading back into the **Hyper-V Manager** console, right-click on the name of your new VM and go to **Settings...**

Inside settings, you will see that this VM has a **DVD Drive** automatically listed in **IDE Controller 1**. If you click on **DVD Drive**, you can easily tell it to mount any ISO to that drive. Copy the ISO file of the operating system installer you wish to run onto the hard drive of your Hyper-V Server—I typically place all of my ISOs inside a dedicated folder called ISOs, right alongside my VMs folder—and then **Browse...** to it from this screen. Connecting an ISO to your VM is the same as if you were plugging a physical installation DVD into a physical server:

Chapter 12

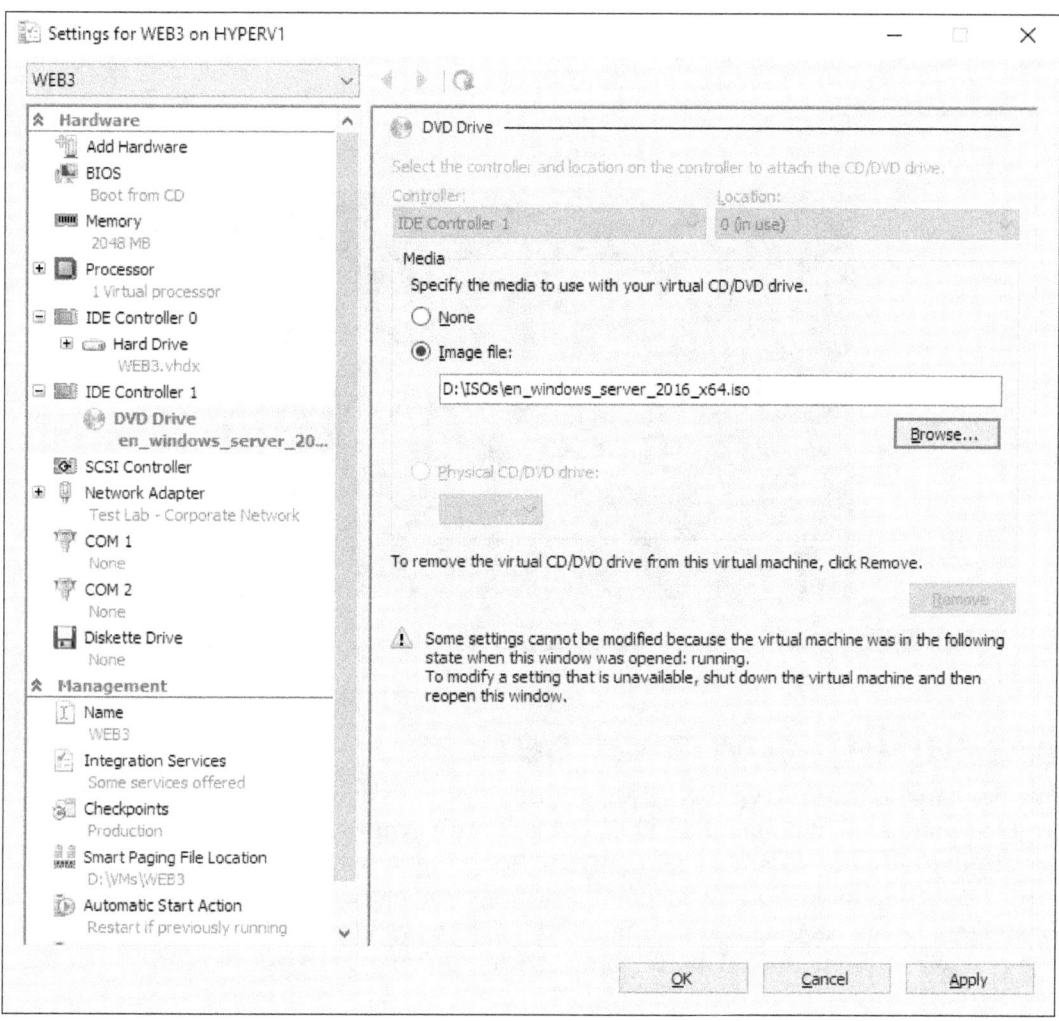

Virtualizing Your Datacenter with Hyper-V

After mounting the media, restart the VM and you will see that our operating system installer kicks off automatically:

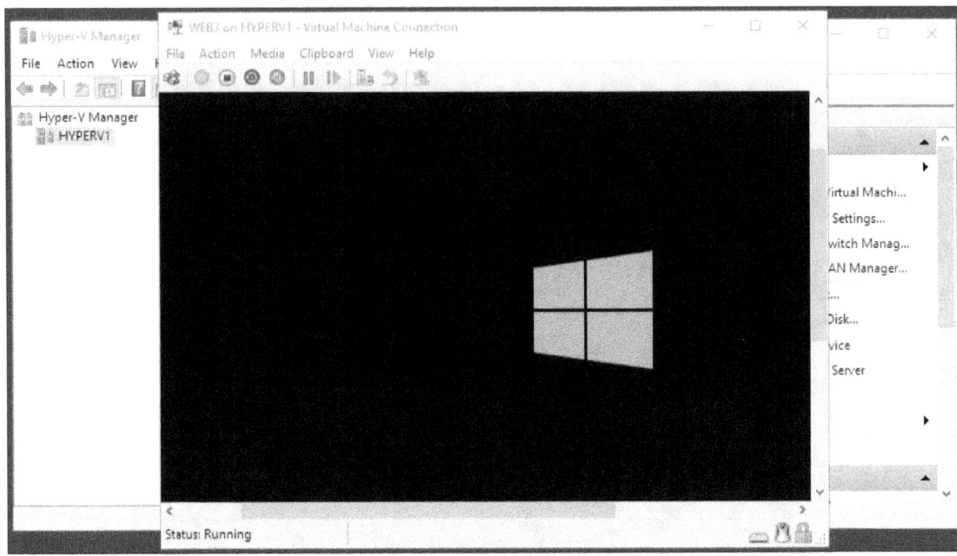

Managing a virtual server

We have made use of **Hyper-V Manager** in order to manage our virtual switches, and to create a virtual machine. This tool is all powerful when it comes to manipulating your VMs, and I find myself accessing it frequently in my daily job. Let's take a look at a few of the other things you can do from inside **Hyper-V Manager**, as well as discuss other methods that can be used in order to work with the new virtual machines that are being created on your Hyper-V Server.

Hyper-V Manager

As you know, Hyper-V Manager is the primary tool for managing a Hyper-V Server. It is a nice console that gives you a quick status on your virtual machines, and allows you to manage those VMs in a variety of ways. Something we did not cover, because I only have one Hyper-V Server running, is that you can manage multiple Hyper-V Servers from a single **Hyper-V Manager** console. Just like any MMC-style console in the Microsoft world, if you right-click on the words **Hyper-V Manager** near the top-left corner of the screen, you will have an option that says **Connect to Server....** By using this function, you can pull information from other Hyper-V Servers into this same pane of glass.

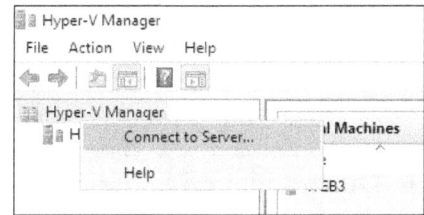

Furthermore, this enables you to run the **Hyper-V Manager** software on a client computer—you can install the Hyper-V role onto many Windows 10 machines, which will also install this console—and then use that local copy of Hyper-V Manager running on your desktop in order to manage your Hyper-V Servers, without needing to log in to those servers directly.

Some of the most useful actions inside **Hyper-V Manager** are listed along the right side of the console, things like **Virtual Switch Manager** and the ability to create a new VM. Once you have VMs up and running, you will find a lot of useful functions listed inside the context menu that appears when you right-click on a virtual machine, as you can see in the following screenshot:

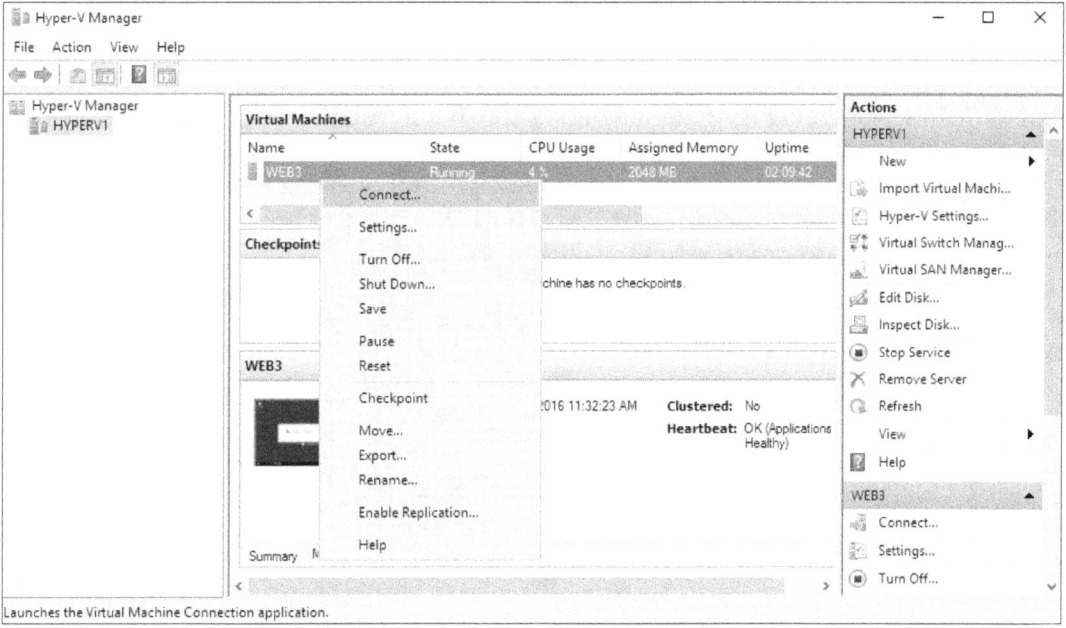

Some of these are self-explanatory, and some are worth playing around with. We have already used **Connect…** to connect to our VM's console. **Settings…** opens up a ton of possibilities, and we will take a look further inside the settings menu immediately following this text. One of the most common reasons I open up this right-click menu is for power functions on my VMs. You can see that you have the ability to **Turn Off…** or **Shut Down…** your VM. Turning it off is like pressing the power button on a server, it cuts off power immediately to that server and will cause Windows some grief when doing so. The shutdown function, on the other hand, initiates a clean shutdown, at least when you are using Microsoft operating systems on the VMs. Shutting down a server is no big deal, but the real power here comes from the fact that you can shut down multiple VMs at the same time. For example, if I was running a dozen different VMs all for my test lab, and I decided that my lab was taking up too many resources and causing problems on my Hyper-V Server, I could select all of my VMs, right-click and then click on **Shut Down…** just one time, and it would immediately kick off the shutdown process on all of the VMs that I had selected. Once a VM is shut down or turned off, then right-clicking on that VM will give you a **Start** function, and you can also select many different servers and start them all at once by using this right-click menu.

Settings menus

Making in-depth modifications to any of your VMs typically means right-clicking on that VM, and then navigating to **Settings…** for that particular VM. Inside settings, you can adjust any aspect of your virtual machine's hardware, which is the most common reason to visit this screen. Immediately upon opening the settings, you have the option to **Add Hardware** to your VM. This is the place you would go in order to add more hard drives or NICs to your virtual server.

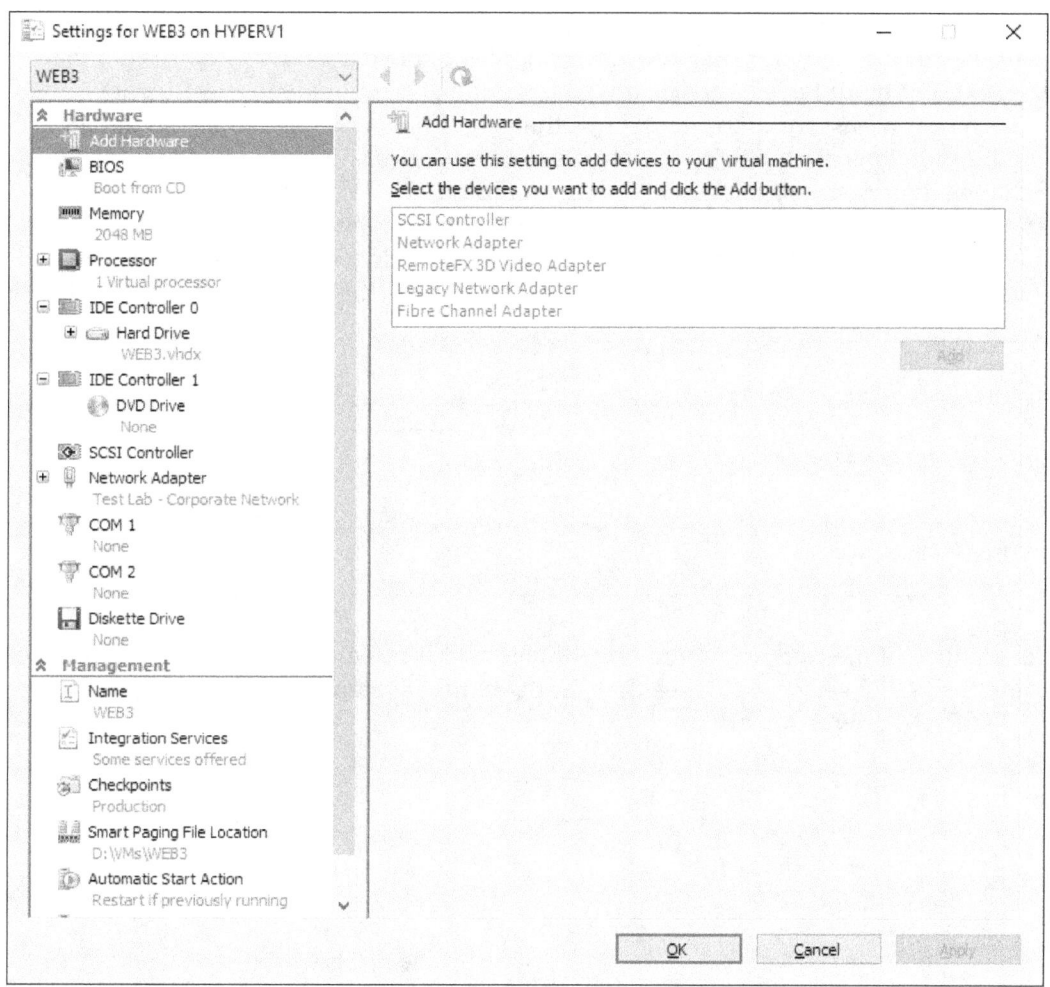

I don't know if you can tell from the preceding screenshot, but the **Add** button is currently grayed out. This is important to discuss. Many functions inside settings can be manipulated on the fly, while the virtual machine is running. Some functions cannot be accomplished unless the VM is turned off. Adding hardware is one of those functions. If you want to add a new hard drive or NIC to your VM, you will need to shut down that server before you are able to do it.

Virtualizing Your Datacenter with Hyper-V

Next we should talk about the **Memory** screen. This one is fairly simple, right? Just input the amount of RAM that you want this VM to have available. The reason that I want to point it out is that a major improvement has been made in this functionality. You can now adjust the amount of RAM that a VM has while it is running! In the previous versions of Hyper-V, you were required to shut down the VMs in order to change their memory allocation, but even though my WEB3 server is currently running and servicing users, I can pop in here and increase RAM at will. Let's say my 2 GB isn't keeping up with the task load, and I want to increase it to 4 GB. I leave the server running, open up **Hyper-V Manager** settings for the VM and adjust to 4096 MB.

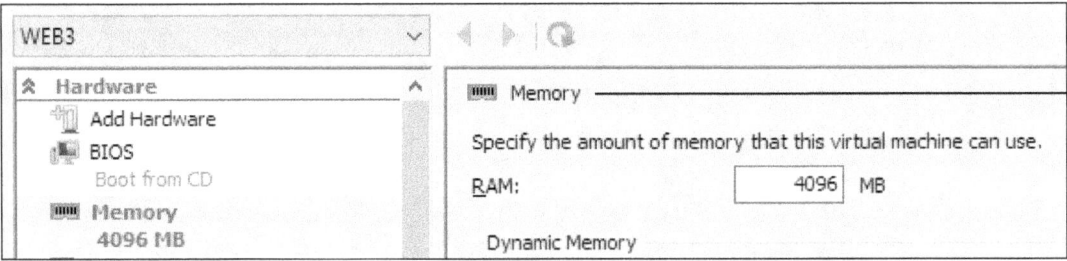

The amount of memory immediately adjusts, and if I open up system properties inside the WEB3 server, I can see that the operating system has updated to reflect 4 GB of RAM now installed:

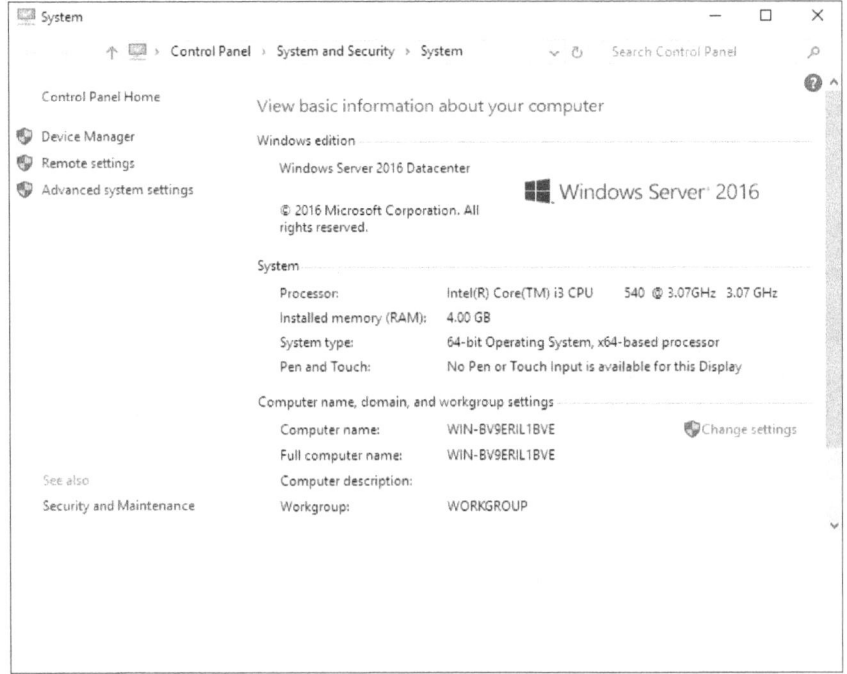

Chapter 12

The other useful settings screens are the **Processor** and **Network Adapter** sections. You have the ability to define the number of virtual processors currently assigned to the VM, and performance weights associated with these processors. In the **Network Adapter** screen, you can change which virtual switch your virtual NICs are plugged in to. I find myself accessing this section often as I move servers from one location to another.

Checkpoints

The last part of the settings menus that I want to discuss is called **Checkpoints**. These were formerly called snapshots, which I think makes a little more sense to most of us. Checkpoints is a function that you can invoke from **Hyper-V Manager** by right-clicking on one or more VMs. It essentially creates a *snapshot in time* for the VM. Another way to look at checkpoints is that they are creating rollback points for your servers. If you create a checkpoint on Tuesday, and on Wednesday somebody makes a config change on that server which causes problems, you can restore the checkpoint from Tuesday and bring the VM back to that day's status.

There are a couple of different ways that checkpoints can be run, and the settings menu is where we define those particulars:

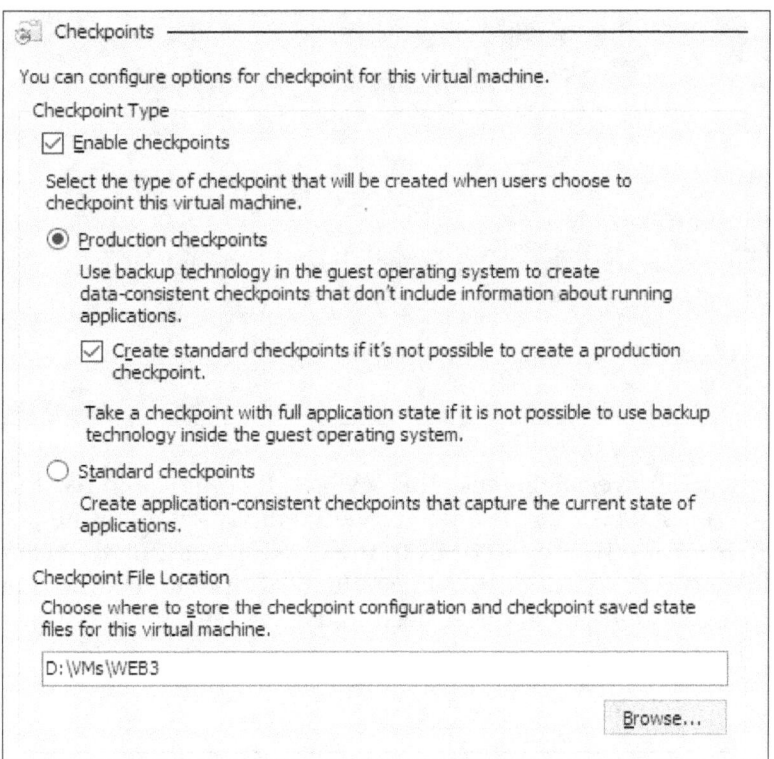

Hyper-V Console, RDP, and PowerShell

While hardware adjustments to VMs need to be made through the Hyper-V Manager, your daily interaction with these VMs running as servers in your environment does not necessarily mean you have to log in to your Hyper-V Server whatsoever. As you have seen, if you happen to be inside Hyper-V Manager anyway, then you can quickly and easily use that **Connect** function in order to interact with the console of your servers, through the use of the Hyper-V Console tool. Accessing your servers this way is beneficial if you need to see something in BIOS, or otherwise outside of the Windows operating system that is running on that VM, but it's not often that you require this level of console access.

When you have Windows Servers running as VMs, it is much more common to interact with these servers in the exact same ways that you would interact with physical servers on your network. While I have been accessing my WEB3 server through the Hyper-V Console so far throughout this chapter, now that I have Windows Server 2016 installed onto WEB3 and I have enabled the RDP capabilities on it, there is no reason I couldn't just pop open MSTSC and log in to WEB3 that way.

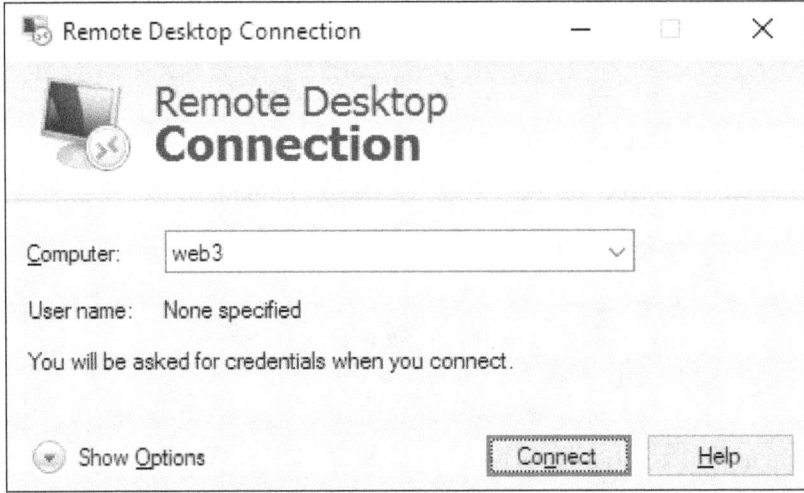

The same is true for PowerShell. Since this VM is fully online and has the server operating system installed, I can use PowerShell remoting to manipulate my WEB3 server as well, from another server or from my desktop computer. Once you are finished building out the hardware and installing the operating system on a VM, it becomes a rare event that you actually need to use the Hyper-V Console in order to interact with that server.

Shielded VMs

There is a new capability in Windows Server 2016 that is going to be very important as companies roll forward with the cloud mentality. In order to explain the benefits that shielded VMs bring to the table, we are going to look at an example of what happens when virtual machines are *not* shielded. Unless you have already taken the time to roll out all shielded VMs in your environment, what I am about to show you is currently possible on any of your existing virtual machines.

You already know that I am running a Hyper-V host server and on that host I have a virtual machine called WEB3. Now, let's pretend that I am a cloud hosting provider, and that WEB3 is a web server that belongs to one of my tenants. I have provided my tenant with a private virtual switch for networking, so that they can manage the networking of that server and I don't have access to that VM at the networking level. Also, it is a fact that this WEB3 server is joined to my tenant's domain and network, and I as the cloud hoster have absolutely no access to domain credentials, or any other means that I can utilize to actually log in to that server.

Sounds pretty good so far, right? You as a tenant certainly wouldn't want your cloud provider to be able to snoop around inside your virtual machines that are being hosted in that cloud. You also wouldn't want any other tenants who might have VMs running on the same cloud host to be able to see your servers in any way. This same mentality proves itself out in private clouds as well. If you are hosting a private cloud and are allowing various companies or divisions of a company to have segregated VMs running in the same fabric, you would want to ensure those divisions had real security between the VMs, and between the VMs and the hoster.

Now, let's have a little fun and turn villain. I am a rogue cloud hoster employee, and I decide that I'm going to do some damage before I walk out the door. It would be quite easy for me to kill off that WEB3 server completely, since I have access to the host administrative console. However, that would probably throw a flag somewhere and the tenant would just spin up a new web server, or restore from a backup. So even better than breaking the VM, I'm going to leave it running and then change the content of the website itself. Let's give this company's clients something to talk about!

To manipulate my tenant's website running on WEB3, I don't need any real access to the VM itself, because I have direct access to the virtual hard drive file. All I need to do is tap into that VHD file, modify the website, and I can make the website display whatever information I want.

Virtualizing Your Datacenter with Hyper-V

First I log in to the Hyper-V Server, and browse to the location of the VHD file which WEB3 is using. This is all on the backend, so I don't need any tenant credentials to get here. I simply right-click on that VHD and select **Mount**:

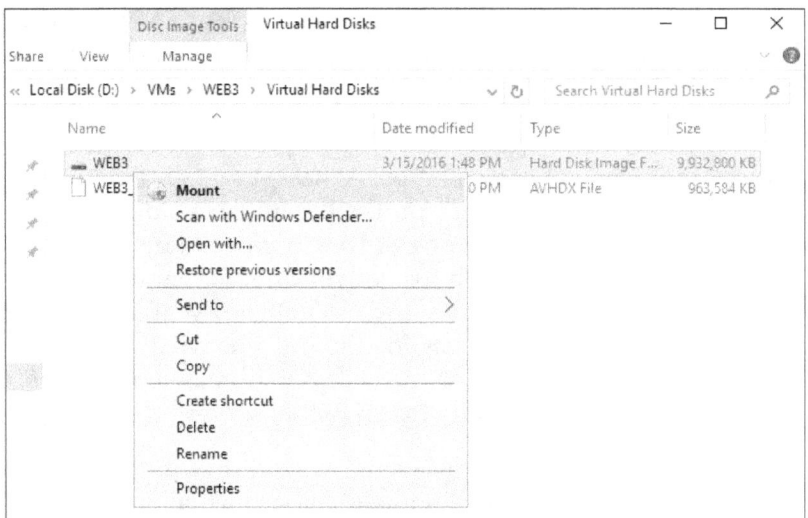

Now that the VHD has been mounted to the host server's operating system directly, I can browse that VM's hard drive as if it were one of my own drives. Navigate to the `wwwroot` folder in order to find the website files, and change the default page to display whatever you want:

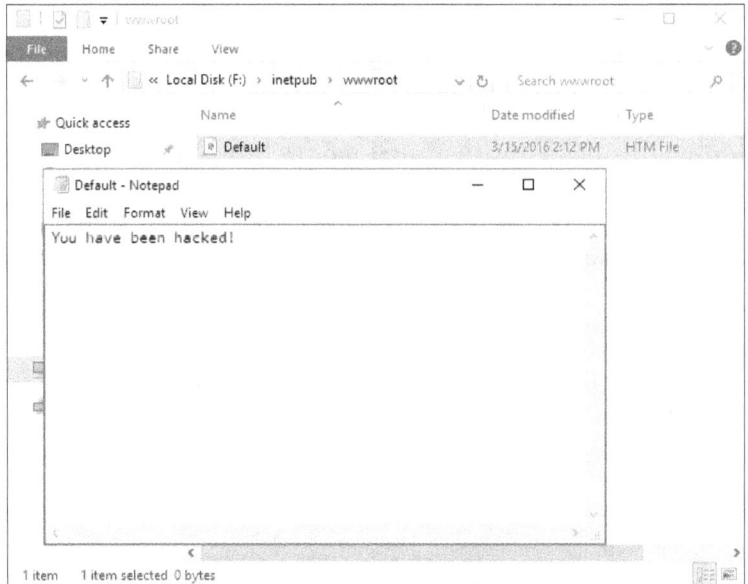

When I'm finished playing around with the website, I can open up **Disk Management**, right-click on that mounted disk, and select **Detach VHD** to cover my tracks:

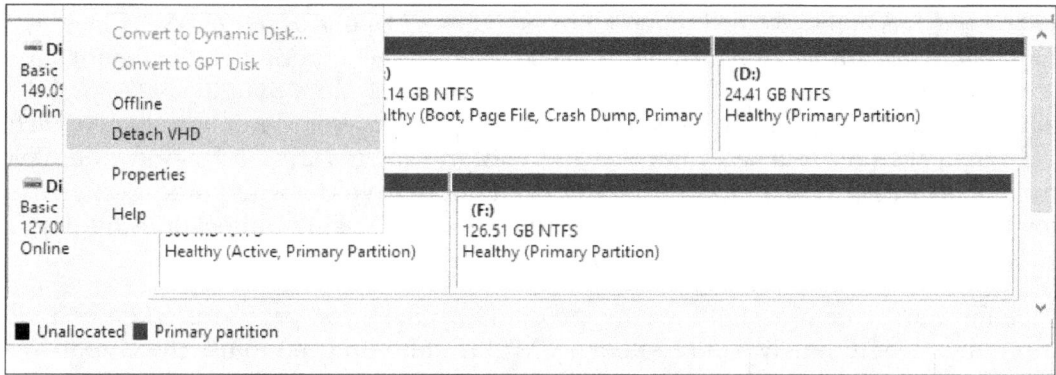

How do you feel about hosting virtual machines in the cloud now? This example cuts to the core of why so many companies are scared to take that initial step into cloud hosting—there is simply an unknown level of security for those environments. Thankfully, Microsoft has alleviated this security loophole with a new technology called **shielded VMs**.

Encrypting the VHDs

The idea behind shielded VMs is quite simple. Microsoft already has a great drive encryption technology, it's called BitLocker. Shielded VMs are Hyper-V virtual machines that have BitLocker drive encryption enabled. When your entire VHD file is protected and encrypted with BitLocker, nobody is going to be able to gain backdoor access to that drive. Attempting to mount the VHD like we just successfully accomplished would result in an error message, and nothing more:

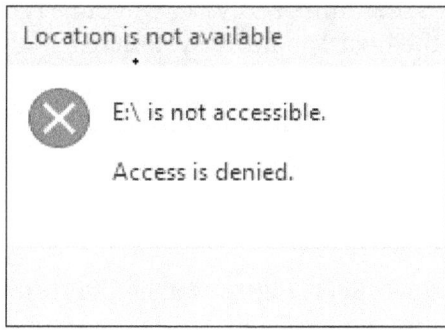

Even better is that when you set up your infrastructure to support shielded VMs, you also block Hyper-V Console access to the VMs which are shielded. While this in itself isn't as big of a deal as the drive encryption, it's still important enough to point out. If someone has access to the Hyper-V host server and opens up **Hyper-V Manager**, they would generally have the ability to use the **Connect** function on the tenant VMs in order to view whatever was currently on the console. More than likely this would leave them staring at a login screen that they, hopefully, would not be able to breach, but if that VM's console had somehow been left in a logged-in state, they would have immediate access to manipulate the VM, even if the drive was encrypted. So when you create a shielded VM, it not only encrypts the VHD using BitLocker technology, it also blocks all access to the VM from the Hyper-V Console.

Does this hard-core blocking have the potential to cause you problems when you are trying to legitimately troubleshoot a VM? What if you need to use the Hyper-V Console in order to figure out why a VM won't boot or something like that? Yes, that is a valid point, and one that you need to consider. Shielded VMs make security of your VMs much higher. So much so that you could, in fact, lock yourself out from being able to troubleshoot issues on that server. As is often the case with everything in the IT world, we are trading usability for security.

Hyper-V Server 2016

It's very easy to get excited about virtualization. Build some hardware, install Windows Server 2016, implement the Hyper-V role, and bam! You're ready to start rolling out hundreds and hundreds of VMs in your environment…right?

Not necessarily. We haven't talked at all about licensing yet, and too often our technological prowess is limited by licensing requirements. The same is true with Hyper-V. Every VM that you spin up needs to have its own operating system license, of course. That requirement makes sense. What isn't as obvious, however, is the fact that you can only run a certain number of VMs on your Hyper-V Server, depending on what SKU you use for the host operating system itself.

The biggest *gotcha* that catches people off guard is that using Windows Server 2016 Standard Edition as your Hyper-V Server will result in your ability to run two VMs. Two! That's it, no more. You will be able to launch a couple of virtual machines, and will then be restricted from running any more. Clearly, the Standard Edition SKU isn't designed to be used as a Hyper-V Server.

That leaves you with Windows Server 2016 Datacenter Edition. Fortunately, Datacenter allows you to run *unlimited* VMs! This is great news! Except for one thing—Datacenter Edition costs many thousands of dollars. This is a very limiting factor for deployments of Hyper-V Servers.

All of this talk about licensing and how messy or expensive it can be leads to one point—**Hyper-V Server 2016**. Isn't that just a Windows Server 2016 with the Hyper-V role installed? No, not at all.

Hyper-V Server 2016 is its own animal. It has its own installer, and a whole different user interface than a traditional server. Installing Hyper-V Server 2016 onto a piece of hardware will result in a server that can host an unlimited number of Hyper-V VMs, but nothing else. You cannot use this as a general-purpose server to host other roles or services.

The *huge* benefit of Hyper-V Server 2016—it's FREE. You are still responsible for licenses on each of the VMs themselves, of course, but to have a free host operating system that can run an unlimited number of VMs, now that is something my wallet can really agree with.

I have burned the ISO installer for Hyper-V Server 2016 onto a DVD, and just finished installing it onto my hardware. The installation of the operating system itself was completely familiar, all of the installation screens and options were the same as if I were installing the full version of Windows Server 2016. However, now that the installer has finished and I have booted into the actual operating system of my Hyper-V Server 2016, everything looks entirely different:

```
C:\Windows\System32\cmd.exe - C:\Windows\system32\sconfig.cmd
Microsoft (R) Windows Script Host Version 5.812
Copyright (C) Microsoft Corporation. All rights reserved.

Inspecting system...

============================================================
                     Server Configuration
============================================================

1) Domain/Workgroup:                    Workgroup:  WORKGROUP
2) Computer Name:                       WIN-DE6A8VTB5RV
3) Add Local Administrator
4) Configure Remote Management          Enabled

5) Windows Update Settings:             Automatic
6) Download and Install Updates
7) Remote Desktop:                      Disabled

8) Network Settings
9) Date and Time
10) Help improve the product with CEIP  Not participating

11) Log Off User
12) Restart Server
13) Shut Down Server
14) Exit to Command Line

Enter number to select an option:
```

We are presented with only a Command Prompt, and inside that prompt it has autolaunched a configuration utility. By using the keyboard here, I can do things like set the hostname of this server, join it to a domain, and change networking settings. Once you have finished using this CLI interface to set the core requirements on the server, we really don't need to access the console of this Hyper-V Server again, unless you need to backtrack and re-visit this configuration screen in order to change something. Instead, after configuring the Hyper-V Server, you simply utilize **Hyper-V Manager**, or PowerShell, on another server or desktop inside your network to tap remotely into the management of the virtual machines that are running on this Hyper-V Server. In the following screenshot, you can see that I have launched Hyper-V manager on my Windows Server 2016 that happens to have the Hyper-V role installed—but it is not an actual Hyper-V Server—and I have used that instance of **Hyper-V Manager** to connect remotely to my Hyper-V Server 2016 instance. I can now create new VMs on that Hyper-V Server, and modify them just as if they were running directly on this server:

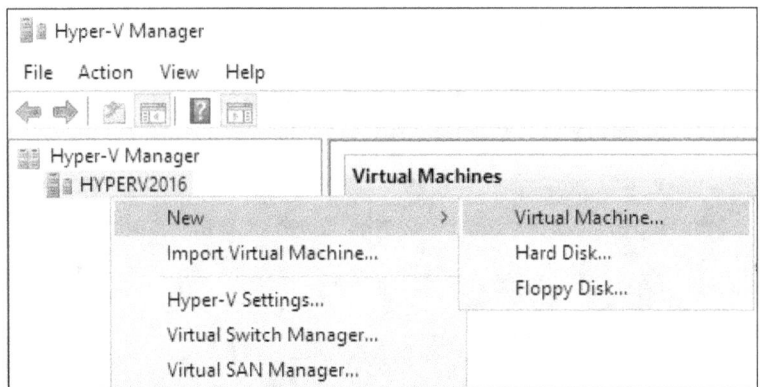

Similar to the way that most tasks performed on a Server Core or Nano Server are handled remotely, through the use of remote consoles or PowerShell, we make all ongoing maintenance and administration of this Hyper-V Server happen from the Hyper-V Manager console.

Hyper-V Server gives you the security benefits of a GUI-less interface, combined with the flexibility benefits of hosting an unlimited number of virtual machines, and a price point that nobody can argue with!

Summary

I don't have official numbers, but I would risk it to say that today there are already more virtual servers running than physical servers, keeping our world online. While the battle continues to rage between which hypervisor platform is the best—typically the argument is split between either Hyper-V or VMware—you cannot ignore the fact that virtualization is the way of the future. Microsoft puts great amounts of time and resources into making sure that Hyper-V is always staying on top of the game, and introducing more and more features with every release so that you can keep your virtualized infrastructure up and running perfectly, all the time. Is the capability of cloud virtualization even more powerful than on-premise Hyper-V Server? I would say yes, because the infrastructure that is in place at a cloud service provider is going to be the all-powerful Oz compared to what a single company can provide in their own datacenter. Does this mean you can forget about Hyper-V altogether and just use cloud-provided servers? Maybe someday, but that day will be a long time coming. The need for on-premise servers and services is still immense, and some industries are simply never going to permit their data and applications to be hosted by a third party. Understanding the capabilities in Hyper-V, and being able to build this infrastructure from the ground up, will give you a major advantage when looking for or accepting a technology job in a Microsoft-centric organization.

This brings us to the end of our story on the new Windows Server 2016. Many of the topics we discussed are comprehensive enough to fill entire books, and I hope that the ideas provided in this volume are enough to prompt you to dig further into those technologies which you plan to work with. Microsoft technology reigns as the king in most datacenters across the globe. The new and updated features inside Windows Server 2016 will ensure that this trend continues, long into the future.

Index

A

AAAA record 84
Access Control List (ACL) 171
Active Directory 62
Active Directory Administrative Center
  about 71, 72
  Dynamic Access Control (DAC) 73
Active Directory Certificate Services
  (AD CS) 113-115
Active Directory Domains and Trusts 69
Active Directory Domain Services (AD DS)
  about 62
  Active Directory Administrative
    Center 71, 72
  Active Directory Domains and Trusts 69
  Active Directory Sites and Services 70
  AD Users and Computers 64
  for organizing network 63
  Read-only domain controllers (RODC) 73
Active Directory Federation Services
  (AD FS) 200
Active Directory Migration Tool
  (ADMT) 69
Active Directory Users and Computers
  about 64
  computer accounts, prestaging 67, 68
  Security Groups 66
  user accounts 65
administrative consoles, Windows Firewall
  Windows Firewall settings 210
  Windows Firewall, with Advanced
    Security 210, 211
Advanced Threat Analytics (ATA) 229

alias record 85
application containers
  about 334
  isolation 335
  resources, sharing 334
  scalability 336
A record 84
autoenrollment policy
  creating 129-134

B

back up
  about 94
  regular backups, scheduling 94-96
best practices, general security
  about 231
  different computer, used for accomplishing
    administrative tasks 233
  distinct accounts, using for administrative
    access 232
  internet, not browsing from servers 233
  Just Enough Administration (JEA) 234, 235
  perpetual administrators, getting
    rid 231, 232
  Role Based Access Control (RBAC) 234
Bing 30
BitLocker 222, 379

C

centralized management and monitoring
  about 44
  RDP, using 51

Remote Desktop Connection Manager 51
Remote Server Management Tool (RSMT) 49
Server Manager 44-48
Certificate Revocation List (CRL) 110
certificates
 exporting 140
 exporting, from IIS 141
 exporting, from MMC 140, 141
 importing 140
 importing, onto second server 142
 issuing 119
 requesting from MMC 122-125
 requesting from web interface 126-129
 template, publishing 120, 121
Certificate Signing Request (CSR) 137
certificates, used with DirectAccess
 about 185
 machine certificates, on DA clients 187
 machine certificates, on DA server 187
 SSL certificate, on DirectAccess server 186
 SSL certificate, on NLS web server 186
certificate template
 creating 115-118
certificate types
 about 108
 computer certificates 109
 SSL certificates 109
 user certificates 108, 109
certification authority (CA) 108
Cloud
 about 3
 Private cloud 4
cluster 268
clustering improvements, in Windows Server 2016
 about 295
 cluster operating system rolling upgrade 296, 297
 cross-domain clustering 296
 multi-site clustering 295
 Storage Replica (SR) 298
 Virtual Machine Resiliency 297
 workgroup clustering 296
Cluster Name Object (CNO) 294

Cluster Operating System Rolling Upgrade 296
cmdlets
 about 302, 303-312
 Get-NetIPAddress 302
 New-NetIPAddress 302
 Rename-Computer 302
 Set-NetIPAddress 302
CNAME 85
Command Prompt
 route, adding 163, 164
ComputerName
 used, for connecting remote server 326, 327
container host server
 preparing 341-343
containers
 container host server, preparing 341-343
 reference link 342
 starting, with PowerShell 341
 versus hypervisors 337, 338
 Windows Server Container, starting 344-346
Control Panel
 Settings screen, using through 20

D

Dedicated IP Address (DIP) 270
Default Execution Policy (DEP)
 about 307, 308
 AllSigned policy 308
 Bypass policy 308, 309
 RemoteSigned policy 308
 Restricted policy 308
 Unrestricted policy 308
default gateway
 adding, to routing table 161, 162
Desired State Configuration (DSC)
 about 330, 331
 reference link 332
DirectAccess
 considerations 176-178
 prerequisites 178
 using 176
 versus VPN 196

DirectAccess, versus VPN
  about 196
  auto versus manual launch 197
  domain-joined, versus
      non-domain-joined 196
  login issues 198
  password issues 198
  software, versus built-in 197
DNS records
  about 83
  alias record 85, 87
  host record 84, 85
  ipconfig /flushdns 88, 89
  Mail Exchanger (MX) record 87
  Name Server (NS) record 88
Docker
  about 347
  on Windows Server 2016 348, 349
Docker Hub
  about 349
  URL 349
Docker Trusted Registry 350
Domain Controller (DC) 62, 63
Domain Name System (DNS)
  about 81, 82
  DNS records 83
Dynamic Host Configuration Protocol
      (DHCP)
  about 89
  reservations 91-93
  scope 90
  versus static addressing 89

E

Enable-PSRemoting 324
Encrypting File System (EFS) 224
encryption technologies
  about 222
  BitLocker 222, 223
  Encrypting File System (EFS) 224
  IPsec 224
  Shielded VMs 223
  Virtual TPM 222, 223
End-to-End IPsec Connection
  securing, reference link 229

enterprise CA 113
Enter-PSSession
  used, for connecting remote server 327, 329
Execution Policy Scope 308
external virtual switch 360

F

failover clustering
  about 284
  Hyper-V hosts, clustering 285
  Scale-Out File Server (SOFS) 286
Failover Cluster Manager 290
failover cluster, setting up
  about 288
  cluster validation, running 291-294
  Create Cluster wizard, running 294, 295
  Failover Cluster Manager, running 290
  feature, installing 290
  servers, building 289
feature
  installing 35, 36
  installing, with PowerShell 41-43
features, Windows Server
  about 3
  built-in malware protection 6
  Nano Server 6
  PowerShell 5.0 5
  Shielded Virtual Machines 7
  soft restart 6
  Software-Defined Networking (SDN) 5
  Web Application Proxy (WAP) 7
  Windows 10 5
flack 238
Flush the ARP cache process 284
forest 69
Format-List 316
Format-Table 314, 315

G

Generic Routing Encapsulation (GRE) 171
Get-Help
  using 313, 314
GPO Security Filtering 80

Group Policy
  about 74
  Default Domain Policy 75, 76
  GPO, creating 77-79
  GPO, linking 77-9
  GPOs, filtering to particular devices 80
Group Policy Objects (GPOs) 74

H

hops 151
host record 84
hybrid clouds 170
Hyper-V Console
  used, for managing virtual server 376
Hyper-V Container
  about 340
  versus Windows Server Containers 339
hypervisors
  versus containers 337, 338
Hyper-V Manager
  used, for managing virtual server 370-372
Hyper-V Network Virtualization
  about 168
  Generic Routing Encapsulation (GRE) 171
  hybrid clouds 170
  Microsoft Azure virtual network 172
  Network controller 171
  private clouds 168, 169
  System Center Virtual Machine
    Manager 171
  Windows Server Gateway 172
  working 170
Hyper-V Server
  designing 354, 355
  implementing 354, 355
  installing 355, 356, 357, 358
Hyper-V Server 2016 380-382

I

ICMP traffic 150
interface navigation
  about 7
  hidden Admin menu 9
  programs, pinning to taskbar 12

  right-click, using 13-15
  Search function, using 10, 11
  Start menu 8, 9
interfacing, with Server Core
  about 240, 241
  Command Prompt, closing
    accidently 251-253
  PowerShell, invoking 242
  Remote Server Administration Tools
    (RSAT), using 249-251
  Server Manager 248, 249
internal virtual switch 361
Internet Information Services (IIS) 134
ipconfig/flushdns 88
IPsec
  about 224, 225
  configuring 225
IPsec configuration
  about 225
  client policy 226
  secure server policy 226
  Security Policy snap-in 227
  server policy 226
  WFAS, using 228, 229
IPsec Security Policy snap-in 225
IPv6
  about 144-149
  considerations 176-178
IPv6 packets
  6to4 181
  external NIC, installing into Internet 182
  installing, behind NAT 183
  IP-HTTPS 182
  Teredo 182

J

Just Enough Administration (JEA) 234

L

Live Migration 288
load balanced website configuration
  about 273
  ARP cache, flushing 283
  DNS, configuring 280-282

IIS, configuring 280-282
NLB, configuring 275-279
NLB, enabling 274
testing 282, 283
Local Configuration Manager (LCM) 331

M

MAC address 92
Mail Exchanger (MX) record 87
Microsoft Azure 4
Microsoft Azure virtual network
  about 172
  URL 172
Microsoft Management Console
    (MMC) 102, 103
Microsoft System Preparation Tool 53
MSC shortcuts 103, 104
Multicast with Internet Group Membership
    Protocol (IGMP) 273
multihomed servers
  executing 161

N

Name Server (NS) record 88
Nano Server
  about 254, 305
  administering 261
  other management tools 265
  Recovery Console 261, 262
  Remote PowerShell 263-265
  remote server, testing 330
  setting up 257
  Windows Remote Management 265
Nano Server, setting up
  about 257
  VHD file, preparing 257-259
  Virtual Machine, creating 260
Nano Server, versus Server Core
  about 254
  accessibility 255
  capability 256
  installation 256
  maintenance numbers 255
  sizing 255

Netmon
  packet, tracing 159
  URL 159
Network controller 171
networking toolbox
  about 149
  packet tracing, with Netmon 159
  packet tracing, with Wireshark 159
  pathping 152, 153
  ping 149, 150
  TCPView 159
  Telnet 155, 157
  Test-Connection 153, 154
  tracert 151
Network Load Balancing Manager 276
Network Load Balancing (NLB)
  about 268
  dedicated IP addresses 270
  enabling 274
  MAC address spoofing, enabling
    on VMs 274
  modes 271
  round-robin DNS example 269
  using, by roles 269, 270
  virtual IP addresses 270
Network Load Balancing (NLB) modes
  about 271
  multicast 272
  multicast with Internet Group Membership
    Protocol (IGMP) 273
  unicast 271, 272
Network Virtualization Generic Routing
    Encapsulation (NVGRE) 172
NICs, DirectAccess servers
  Edge Mode 180
  multiple NICs 180
  single NIC Mode 179

O

offline root 114
One-Time-Password (OTP) 183
operating system
  installing, for virtual server 368, 370
Organizational Unit (OU) 64

output format, PowerShell
  Format-List 316
  Format-Table 314, 315

P

pathping 152, 153
ping 149, 150
PowerShell
  cmdlets 302-312
  cmdlets, used for managing IP
      addresses 243-245
  containers, starting 341
  Default Execution Policy (DEP) 307, 308
  domain, joining 246, 247
  Get-Help, using 313, 314
  graphical interface 304
  launching 306
  Nano Server 305
  need for 302
  output, formatting 314
  route, adding 166
  scripting 305
  Server Core 305
  server hostname, setting 245
  Tab key, using 309
  used, for feature installation 41-43
  used, for managing virtual server 376
  using 242, 243
  working with 305
PowerShell 5.0 5
**PowerShell Integrated Scripting
    Environment (ISE)**
  about 317-321
  PS1 file 317-319
prerequisites, DirectAccess
  certificates 185
  domain joined 178
  Getting Started Wizard!, avoiding 188, 189
  NAT 181
  Network Location Server (NLS) 184
  servers, with NICs 179
  supported client operating systems 179
private clouds 168, 169
private virtual switch 361

profiles, Windows Firewall
  domain profile 212
  private profile 212
  public profile 212
public authority SSL certificate
  certificate request, submitting 137, 138
  Certificate Signing Request (CSR),
      creating 135-137
  downloading 138, 139
  installing 138, 139
  obtaining 134
Public Key Infrastructure (PKI)
  about 108
  CA role, installing onto domain
      controller 115
  enterprise, versus standalone 113, 114
  planning 113
  root, versus subordinate 114

R

Read-Only Domain Controller (RODC) 63
Remote Access Management Console
  about 190
  configuration 191
  dashboard 192
  Operations Status page 193
  Remote Client Status screen 194
  reporting 194
  Tasks bar 195
Remote Desktop Connection Manager
  about 51
  download link 51
Remote Desktop Protocol (RDP)
  about 44
  used, for managing virtual server 376
Remote Desktop Services (RDS) 37
remote server
  connecting 326
  connecting, with ComputerName 326, 327
  connecting, with Enter-PSSession 327-329
  Enable-PSRemoting 324
  machines, authenticating 325
  managing 322
  preparing 323

testing, with Nano Server 330
testing, with Server Core 330
WinRM service 323
Remote Server Administration Tools (RSAT) 249
Remote Server Management Tool (RSMT)
  about 49
  download link 49
Resiliency Level 297
Resiliency Period 297
restore
  about 94
  restoring, from disc 98-102
  restoring, from Windows 97, 98
role
  installing 35, 36
  installing, with wizard 36-40
  in Server Core 253
root CA 114
route
  adding, with Command Prompt 163, 164
  adding, with PowerShell 166
  building 163
  deleting 165
routing table
  building 160
  default gateway, adding 161, 162
  multihomed servers, executing 161
  route, building 163

S

same server 139
Scale-Out File Server (SOFS) 286
scenarios, running on Nano Server
  Cloud Application Server 256
  DNS Server 256
  File Server 256
  Hyper-V 256
  Web Server 256
server 2016 improvements, to WAP
  about 201
  client IP addresses, forwarded to applications 202
  HTTP to HTTPS redirection 201
  improved administrative console 203
  preauthentication, for HTTP Basic 201
  Remote Desktop Gateway, publishing 202
Server Core
  about 238, 239, 305
  remote server, testing 330
  roles 253
  server, changing 239, 240
  used, for interfacing 240, 241
  versus Nano Server 254
Server Manager 36, 44
Settings menu
  Settings screen, using through 21, 22
Settings screen
  about 16-19
  navigating 20
  new user, creating through Control Panel 20
  new user, creating through Settings menu 21, 22
shielded VMs
  about 377-379
  VHD file, encrypting 379, 380
soft restart 6
Software-Defined Networking (SDN)
  about 167
  Hyper-V Network Virtualization 168
SSL certificates
  about 109-111
  single-name certificate 111
  Subject Alternative Name (SAN) certificates 112
  wildcard certificate 112
standalone CA 113
star (*) 112
Storage Replica (SR) 298
subordinate CA 114
sysprep tool
  about 53-55
  customizations, configuring onto new server 54
  master image of drive, creating 57, 58
  new servers, building with master image copies 58, 59

running, for master server
    preparation 55-57
running, for shutdown of server 55-57
updates, configuring onto new server 54
used, for quick server rollouts 52, 53
Windows Server 2016, installing onto new
    server 54
**System Center Operations Manager
    (SCOM) 265**
**System Center Virtual Machine
    Manager 171**

T

Tab key
  using 309
taskbar
  programs, pinning to 12
Task Manager 22-25
Task View 26, 27
TCPView
  about 159
  URL 160
Telnet 155-157
Test-Connection 153, 154
tiers clustering
  about 286
  application layer clustering 287
  failover clustering, working 288
  host layer and application layer clustering
      combination 287
  host layer clustering 287
tracert 151

U

Unified Access Gateway (UAG) 199

V

VHD file
  encrypting, via shielded VMs 379, 380
**Virtual Extensible Local Area Network
    (VXLAN) 172**
Virtual IP Address (VIP) 270

Virtual Machine Manager (VMM)
  about 171, 265
  reference link 171
Virtual Machine Resiliency 297
Virtual Private Networking (VPN) 175
virtual server
  connecting 367
  implementing 363-366
  managing 370
  managing, with Hyper-V Console 376
  managing, with Hyper-V Manager 370-372
  managing, with PowerShell 376
  managing, with RDP 376
  operating system, installing 368-370
  settings menus 372-375
  starting 367
virtual switches
  creating 362
  external virtual switch 360
  internal virtual switch 361
  private virtual switch 361
  using 358, 359, 360
Virtual TPM 223

W

WAP
  about 199
  requirements 200
  server 2016 improvements 201
Wide Area Network (WAN) 70
Windows Defender
  about 206
  disabling 208
  installing 206
  user interface, exploring 207, 208
Windows Firewall
  about 208, 209
  administrative consoles 209
  new Inbound rule 213-215
  profiles 212, 213
  rule, building for ICMP 216-218
  WFAS, managing with Group
      Policy 218-221

Windows Firewall with Advanced Security
    (WFAS) 209, 225
Windows Management Instrumentation
    (WMI) 265
Windows Server 2016
  clustering improvements 295
  Docker 348, 349
  features, overview 5
  installing 29
  interface navigation 7
  purpose 2, 3
  Settings screen 16
Windows Server 2016 installation
  about 29, 30
  installer, running 31-34
  ISO, building 30
Windows Server Container
  about 339
  starting 344-346
  versus Hyper-V Containers 338
Windows Server Desktop Experience 254
Windows Server Gateway 172
WinRM service 323
Wireshark
  packet, tracing 159
  URL 159

www.ingramcontent.com/pod-product-compliance
Lightning Source LLC
LaVergne TN
LVHW080310260326
834688LV00038B/1038